OUT and PROUD in CHICAGO

An Overview of the City's Gay Community   EDITED BY **TRACY BAIM**

SENIOR EDITORS

William B. Kelley
Jorjet Harper

CONTRIBUTORS

Tracy Baim
John D'Emilio
Ron Dorfman
Lucinda Fleeson
Jorjet Harper
Chad Heap
Jonathan Ned Katz
Owen Keehnen
Marie J. Kuda
John D. Poling
Tim Samuelson

ADDITIONAL CONTRIBUTIONS BY

Jonathan Abarbanel	Ron Ehemann	Richard Pfeiffer
Jeff Berry	Patrick K. Finnessy, Ph.D.	John "Jack" Ryan
William Burks	Ross Forman	Cathy Seabaugh
John Cepek	William Greaves	Mark Sherkow
Richard Cooke	Lola Lai Jong	Mel Wilson
Andrew Davis	Richard Knight, Jr.	Amy Wooten
Suzanne Deveney	Dr. Judith Markowitz	Yvonne Zipter

A companion to www.ChicagoGayHistory.org and the WTTW11 documentary Out and Proud in Chicago, 2008

S

SURREY BOOKS

CHICAGO

Printed in China.

ISBN-10: 1-57284-100-1

ISBN-13: 978-1-57284-100-0

10 9 8 7 6 5 4 3 2 1

Surrey Books is an imprint of Agate Publishing, Inc.

Archival photos and images are credited individually inside this book.

Materials provided by:
Chicago History Museum, The Newberry Library, and The University of Chicago Library Special Collections Research Center.

Additional materials provided by:
Chicago Gay and Lesbian Hall of Fame, Gay Games VII/Chicago 2006, Inc., Gay Chicago Magazine, GayLife newspaper, M. Kuda Archives, Leather Archives & Museum and Chuck Renslow, and Outlines and Windy City Times newspapers.

All photographs copyrighted by the individual photographers or publications listed. Images provided by:
Hal Baim, Tracy Baim, Steve Becker, Caryn Berman, John Faier, Kat Fitzgerald, William Greaves, Athen Grey, Vern Hester, Lisa Howe-Ebright, Nancy J. Katz, Amy Moseley, Genyphyr Novak, Mary Patten, Rich Pfeiffer, Otis Richardson, Tim Samuelson, Mark Sherkow, Bonnie Tunick, and Mark Wojcik.

Marie J. Kuda articles are all © 2008 Marie J. Kuda.

John D'Emilio articles are all © 2008 John D'Emilio.

Chad Heap's gay history essay revised from the original entry in the Encyclopedia of Chicago.
The Electronic Encyclopedia of Chicago © 2005 Chicago Historical Society and The Encyclopedia of Chicago © 2004 The Newberry Library.
All rights reserved. Used with permission.

Jonathan Ned Katz's Henry Gerber essay © 1976, 1992 Jonathan Ned Katz. Used with permission.
Originally printed in Gay American History: Lesbians and Gay Men in the U.S.A., by Jonathan Ned Katz.

John D. Poling's essay on Mattachine Midwest originally appeared in the spring 2005 issue of Chicago History, the Chicago History Museum's magazine, © 2005, and is used with permission of both Poling and the Chicago History Museum.

Lucinda Fleeson's article, The Gay '30s, from the November 2005 issue of Chicago magazine, © 2005, is reprinted with permission of both Fleeson and Chicago magazine.

COVER PHOTOS: *Top row* — Pearl M. Hart, photo courtesy of M. Kuda Archives. A rainbow pylon on North Halsted Street, photo by Tracy Baim. Makoto Hioki and Samson Chan of Asians and Friends–Chicago in 1994, photo by Tracy Baim. 1990 ACT UP Chicago protest, by Lisa Howe-Ebright. *Middle* — The gay contingent in the 1994 Bud Billiken Parade on the city's South Side, by Tracy Baim. Jim Darby on board a U.S. Navy ship in the 1950s, photo courtesy of Jim Darby. The Gay Games VII Opening Ceremony at Soldier Field on July 15, 2006, photo by John Faier, courtesy of Chicago 2006, Inc. *Bottom* — An ACT UP Chicago arrest at the American Medical Association, 1990, by Lisa Howe-Ebright. Queer Nation Chicago's 1992 presidential candidate Joan Jett Blakk in 1991, photo by Genyphyr Novak. Henry Gerber, who started the first known U.S. gay-rights organization, in the 1920s in Chicago, photo courtesy of M. Kuda Archives, Oak Park, Ill.

The appearance of a name, image or photo of a person or group in this book or its companion Web site does not indicate the sexual orientation of such individual or group.

Prairie Avenue Productions: info@chicagogayhistory.org, www.ChicagoGayHistory.org.

Surrey and Agate books are available in bulk at discount prices. For more information, go to agatepublishing.com.

"Nothing could be worse than the fear that one had given up too soon, and left one unexpended effort that might have saved the world." – **JANE ADDAMS**

THIS BOOK IS DEDICATED TO

Marie J. Kuda, Jean Albright, Renee Hanover, Toni Armstrong Jr., Jorjet Harper, Kathy Munzer, William B. Kelley, Michael Leppen, and Chuck Renslow

And to all the pioneers whose lives have been lost to AIDS, cancer, violence, suicide, accidents—and time.

"There is a way to look at the past. Don't hide from it. It will not catch you—if you don't repeat it." – **PEARL BAILEY**

THANK YOU There is a word, "crabbing," that refers to the tendency of crabs to pull each other down in a tank rather than work together to find a way out. We are often too busy fighting one another, instead of the larger enemies in society. Despite the infighting, however, Chicago's gay community has accomplished much in a short window of time. In 2007, I wanted to begin the process of a deeper documentation of our community—more than the weekly newspaper work I have done for nearly a quarter of a century. I was assisted in this by dozens of supporters. Wendy Jo Carlton and her team shot video as I interviewed more than 250 people on camera. Marie J. Kuda allowed me to scan hundreds of her documents. Lola Lai Jong, Robb Olsen, Diane Mareci and others transcribed interviews. My dad, Hal Baim, took photos of the subjects. Dozens of others assisted in some way.

And then, in February 2008, WTTW–Channel 11, which had been working on a gay documentary, approached Agate Publishing about doing a book as a companion volume to the video. I had been volunteering with WTTW to provide ideas for the film, and WTTW realized it could not pull together a book in six weeks. In the tradition of Life Cereal's "Let's get Mikey to eat it" commercial, WTTW suggested I could tackle this. We had six weeks to produce a 224-page history of gay Chicago. Could what normally would take five or more years be done in six weeks? Only with a solid team, and only if existing scholarship could be used.

Almost every person who was asked to assist did so, including mainstream institutions. Chicago History Museum (Russell Lewis, Rob Medina and Debbie Vaughan), The University of Chicago Library Special Collections Research Center, The Newberry Library and others provided materials. Jonathan Ned Katz, John Poling, Chad Heap and Lucinda Fleeson (for her Chicago magazine piece) allowed reprints of their work. Kuda, John D'Emilio, Tim Samuelson, Ron Dorfman, Jorjet Harper, Judith Markowitz, William Burks and Owen Keehnen wrote new pieces. Dozens of other writers joined me in writing the rest of the book.

William B. Kelley and Jorjet Harper have been amazing senior editors. Additional editing was provided by Kelli Martin and Perrin Davis.

Photographers were also generous. We have included many images from the newspapers I have published, Windy City Times and Outlines, but other media, including Gay Chicago and GayLife, also donated photos. Rich Pfeiffer of PrideChicago donated photos and newspapers, as did Nancy J. Katz, Otis Richardson and Caryn Berman, among others. The Leather Archives & Museum donated posters, and dozens of individual photographers, including Lisa Howe-Ebright and Genyphyr Novak, offered their work for use. The Chicago Gay and Lesbian Hall of Fame and William Greaves shared materials. We had many people scanning old photos and newspapers, including Mary Schultz, Jean Albright, Vern Hester and Brad Kohnert. The Web site is being created by Materville Studios. Jerry Glover provided legal support. Kirk Williamson assisted on graphics. The Windy City Media Group staff helped in various ways.

Since I started work in gay media in 1984, I have met many mentors in the community who made me strive for excellence. This short six-week journey to a book was informed by 24 years of working with amazing people. Some are mentioned here, but there are hundreds more. Thank you to Nan Schaffer, the late Mary York, Fred Eychaner, Modesto "Tico" Valle, Mona Noriega, Evette Cardona, Dick Uyvari and Joe La Pat, and those listed above. To my friends and family (Jean, Marcy, Anthony, Clark, Eden, Hal, Kathy, Kelli, Deb, Diane, and more), who have been patient as I keep committing to major projects: You all make the impossible possible. And last, to my late parents—my mother, Joy Darrow, and stepfather, Steve Pratt—thank you for allowing me to dream.

The approach of this book is obviously more journalistic than academic. Many books could be written about the Chicago gay movement, and I hope to write more in the future. Out and Proud serves as an overview, especially focused on the years pre-1980, so I thank the community in advance for not "crabbing" about this book. Not everyone could be included, but the www.ChicagoGayHistory.org Web site will feature thousands of people, starting in June 2008. Enjoy—and be inspired to write down your own histories. ▼ —*Tracy Baim*

TABLE OF CONTENTS

1990s: TAKING CHARGE

2000s: PROSPECTS FOR THE FUTURE

Activists celebrate with Mayor Eugene Sawyer after the passage of gay-inclusive human rights legislation in the Chicago City Council in 1988. See pages 166–167. From left: Vince Samar, Charlotte Newfeld, Steve Jones, Linda Henderson, Chris Cothran, Bill Williams, Mayor Sawyer, Vern Huls, Rick Garcia, Rick Dean, Laurie Dittman, Jon-Henri Damski (hidden), Kit Duffy, an unidentified woman, Art Johnston (partially hidden) and Jon Simmons. Front: Phyllis Doering and Rene Luna. Courtesy Outlines/Windy City Times archives.

At a late-1980s ACT UP "die-in" in downtown Chicago. Front is Ortez Alderson, a prominent AIDS activist who helped organize a major People of Color AIDS Conference. He died in 1990 from AIDS complications. See pages 148–157. Photo by Lisa Howe-Ebright.

INTRODUCTION by TRACY BAIM

IF AN ACTIVIST STANDS ON THE CORNER WITH A SIGN AND NOBODY TAKES A picture, did it really happen?

The "tree falls in the forest" metaphor may not be a perfect fit, but the work of thousands of gay activists has been lost to history because it was never documented. As generations of our community die, our history dies with them.

A few brave people did try to document our community, either as major events were happening or through groundbreaking historical research. These writers, journalists, photographers, filmmakers, academics and historians have tried to find many needles in the haystack, through interviews with pioneers, digging into old university and museum archives, and reading the often-biased coverage of the mainstream media. In some cases, finding out if there was a "there" there meant reading between the lines and piecing together what it was to be "gay" 100 years ago, when letters and photos may have been destroyed. People usually did not "come out" in any political sense, and families tried to hide any trace of "immoral" behavior once their famous relatives passed on.

Unfortunately, this still happens today. I began covering the Chicago gay community in 1984, just as AIDS was starting its devastation. As people died, their families often shunned partners and friends and threw away archival materials. This happened time and again, as older gays died in nursing homes, lesbians died of cancer and many young activists were struck down in their prime by violence, accidents or suicide. A few managed to leave a lasting, documented legacy, foremost among them Greg Sprague, who started a history project in the 1970s and was a force behind the founding of our city's main gay and lesbian library and archives. His materials are now stored at the Chicago History Museum.

There are many others who have contributed to documenting our community. Although national gay and lesbian historians have tried to include Chicago in their works, their efforts can only go so deep into any one city. Because Chicago lost some of our earlier historical pioneers, and perhaps because this is such a "working" town with activists intensely focused on building community, there have been few efforts to put our gay history down on paper or in other forms in a comprehensive way.

This is beginning to change. Several history projects (books, films, Web sites) are in the works, and as our community ages, more people are interested in making sure we learn from the past, and honor those who came before us. Why now? Maybe it is not just because individuals are aging, but also because our community as a whole is approaching 40 years past some of our own major events. From the Trip raid and Democratic National Convention riots in 1968, to our first Pride parade in 1970, and the Anita Bryant protests in 1977, we are at a point in time where we can reflect back. From those early events, the community came into the 2000s stronger than ever, hosting Gay Games VII in 2006 and witnessing the opening of the Center on Halsted in 2007.

As a working journalist writing articles and taking photos, I have tens of thousands of photos and articles of my own to help retrace the footsteps of our movement. In early 2007, I realized that much of this work, especially what was done prior to the Internet, would be lost for the next generations, who mostly get their information online, rather than from libraries and museums. I do believe they want to learn about the past, just as I was hungry for such information when I was a young adult. We must follow the path to the future and digitize our archives before they become irrelevant, or before the materials deteriorate.

This is not to dismiss the role of physical institutions. They are critical parts of our community, and especially important to researchers. But there has to be more, an effort to get these materials onto the Internet so we can reach and teach even more people in our community. It is also a way for those just coming out to safely learn about their history, during a time when they may be afraid to pick up a gay newspaper or ask a librarian for a gay research text.

So, in early 2007, I launched the Chicago Gay History Project. I deliberately chose the word "gay" as all-encompassing because the word has historical significance. "Queer" is too modern, and including gay, lesbian, bisexual, trans, queer/questioning, intersex and allies (GLBTQIA), etc., is difficult to explain in a mainstream context. We were once "gay," and that included men, women, transgender, bisexuals and more. We are now GLBTQIA, and we are still a community. "Gay" simplifies, but it does not deny the reality of our diversity. I am a lesbian, but I am also "gay" and "queer" and "dyke" and whatever other words someone chooses to use to define me when they love me or hate me, fire me or hire me, attack me or honor me. We have also alternately used LGBT and GLBT throughout the book, because there is no one standard used by the community.

The first stage of the History Project was collecting information and interviews. In May 2007 my first video interview was with Ferd Eggan, who passed away a few weeks later. Attorney Mary York died just four months after her interview. There were 10 people on my list who died before I was able to interview them. As every death occurred, it further validated the reasons for collecting these stories. More than 250 people were interviewed on video, and hundreds more completed written surveys. Ultimately, thousands of people will be included in the History Project. The main qualification is to have had an impact in Chicago, whether short- or

An early Chicago Pride march. Photo courtesy the Chicago History Museum.

long-term. This could be in politics, culture, sports, academia, history, the law or other areas.

I also began the process of scanning old photos; I received donations from many photographers, as well as publications such as GayLife and Gay Chicago Magazine. I also dived deep into the archives of the publications I have produced, including Windy City Times, Outlines, BLACKlines and others. Our team also scanned complete copies of old Chicago gay and feminist media. The most important person in this process has been Marie J. Kuda, Chicago's treasured historian and writer, who has tens of thousands of her own documents, many of which she has shared for the first time for this project.

The ultimate goal is a Web site with hundreds of thousands of images, interviews, articles, publications

and more. The Web site will formally launch in the summer of 2008, and it will continue the task of digitally archiving our community and its oral histories.

While I was working on the Web site, www.ChicagoGayHistory.org, Chicago's public television station WTTW created a documentary about Chicago's gay movement to air in June 2008. It seemed a natural fit that the materials I was collecting could also be used by WTTW. Expanding on that, we worked with Agate Publishing to create a book as a companion to both the Web site and the WTTW film, Out and Proud in Chicago, which was co-produced by Daniel Andries and Alexandra Silets. That is why this book carries the same title as the documentary—to make it clear that all three of these projects are companion pieces.

There is no way that one book, or one film, can fully document the history of the Chicago gay community. We especially wanted to emphasize pre-1980 events, as that is more "historical." There are hundreds of people and groups that have played key roles in our community whose stories could not be included here because of space limitations. The Web site will be an important supplement to these projects, and it will grow for years to come. As you read this book, know that this is truly the tip of the Chicago gay iceberg. We are so much more than can fit in between these covers, and we hope to include additional companion books in the coming years.

Enjoy this visual overview of our community. If you have your own stories to tell or photos to share, visit the Web site, www.ChicagoGayHistory. org. ▼

GAYS AND LESBIANS IN CHICAGO: AN OVERVIEW
by CHAD HEAP

AS ONE OF THE BUSIEST INDUSTRIAL CENTERS AND TRANSPORTATION HUBS IN the United States, Chicago at the beginning of the 20th century attracted thousands of single women and men with new employment opportunities and nonfamilial living arrangements in the lodging-house districts of the Near North and Near South sides. The anonymous and transient character of these neighborhoods permitted the development of Chicago's lesbian and gay subculture.

During the early years of the century, much of this subculture was centered in the Levee, a working-class entertainment and vice district. Here, several saloons and dance halls catered to gay men and featured female impersonation acts. By 1911, the Vice Commission of Chicago noted the presence of "whole groups and colonies of these men who are sex perverts," many of them working as department-store clerks in the Loop. The lesbian presence in the city was less visible during these years, in part because many working-class lesbians "passed" as men in order to gain access to better-paying jobs; Chicago newspapers carried occasional sensationalized stories about local "men," many of them "married," who had been unmasked as women.

By the 1920s, a visible lesbian and gay enclave was well established in the Near North Side bohemian neighborhood known as Towertown. In the tearooms and speak-easies of this district, lesbians and gay men from throughout the city and the Midwest met and socialized with local artists and with heterosexuals bent on obtaining a glimpse of gay life. The Dill Pickle Club on Tooker Alley hosted group discussions and debates on homosexuality and lesbianism, while the Bally Hoo Cafe on North

The main dining room of the Palmer House Hotel, late 1800s. The Palmer House was among the more popular hotels for men to meet one another, including after World War II. Image courtesy of the Chicago History Museum.

Halsted Street featured male and female impersonation acts, as well as a contest for cross-dressed patrons. In 1930, *Variety* estimated that there were 35 such venues on the city's Near North Side. Gay men also gathered along Michigan Avenue and on Oak Street Beach and mingled with lesbians, hobos, and political radicals in Bughouse Square.

Yet while these public spaces played an important role in the construction of Chicago's lesbian and gay community, private parties and personal networks remained the foundation of gay culture. One such network, headed by Henry Gerber, who was a postal clerk and Bavarian immigrant to Chicago, founded the nation's earliest documented gay rights organization in 1924; the Society for Human Rights published two pamphlets before its members were arrested and the group disbanded.

With the arrival of southern Black migrants during the Great Migration, a lesbian and gay enclave also developed on the city's South Side. African-American lesbians and gay men became regular fixtures, as both patrons and entertainers, in Prohibition-era cabarets, including the Plantation Cafe on East 35th Street and the Pleasure Inn on East 31st. In 1935 a Black gay street hustler and nightclub doorman, Alfred Finnie, launched a series of drag balls on the South Side. Building on the success of the interracial drag balls that had been held at the Coliseum Annex on the Near South Side since the 1920s, the Finnie's Ball became a celebrated Halloween event, drawing thousands of gay and lesbian participants and heterosexual onlookers to the South Side well into the 1960s.

After the repeal of Prohibition in 1933, the first bars catering exclusively to lesbians and gay men opened in Chicago. Among the best-known were Waldman's, a gay male bar run by a married Jewish couple on North Michigan Avenue near East Randolph Street, and the Rose-El-Inn, a lesbian bar on North Clark Street near West Division Street. During the 1930s and 1940s, the Loop became an increasingly important meeting place for gay men; the theaters, restaurants and bars of this district sup-

plemented the Near North Side venues as gathering spots for both gay men and the soldiers and sailors who swarmed the city during World War II. Lesbian bars on both the Near North and Near South Sides, especially those run by the lesbian entrepreneur Billie Le Roy, drew sizable crowds, as did the South Side's Cabin Inn, which featured a chorus line of cross-dressed Black men. The residential and social concentration of gay men in the Rush Street area

The 1911 Vice Commission Report.

drew the attention of Alfred C. Kinsey in 1939 and provided a significant sample pool for his landmark 1948 study, *Sexual Behavior in the Human Male*.

During the 1950s and 1960s, the Near North Side and Near South Side remained important lesbian and gay neighborhoods, and new enclaves

formed in Old Town, Hyde Park and in the Lake View neighborhood near the intersection of North Clark Street and West Diversey Parkway. The gay leather community also coalesced during this period—first, around Omar's Grill in the Loop, and in the early 1960s at the Gold Coast, Chicago's first gay leather bar.

As Chicago's lesbian and gay population grew larger and more visible, municipal authorities launched vigorous campaigns to suppress it. Raids on lesbian and gay bars became more frequent, and thousands of women and men were arrested, both in the bars and on the streets, for being inmates of disorderly houses (a label the authorities applied to lesbian and gay bars) or for violating the municipal ordinance against cross-dressing. Although Illinois became the first state in the nation to legalize private, consensual, homosexual relations in 1961, the authorities remained intent on eliminating public expressions of homosexuality; the local media assisted in this endeavor by publishing the names and addresses of those arrested in raids.

Lesbians and gay men began to organize in response to police tactics. Earlier local chapters of the Mattachine Society and the Daughters of Bilitis, two national homophile organizations, had been short-lived and largely social, but in 1965 a more politically active Mattachine Midwest was founded. Under the leadership of Jim Bradford (a pseudonym) for most of the late 1960s, this group organized a 24-hour telephone information and referral line, published and distributed a monthly newsletter to local bars informing patrons of recent police crackdowns and, with the help of lesbian attorney Pearl Hart and others, aided in the defense of gay men and lesbians who had been entrapped on morals charges or arrested in bar raids.

Following the June 1969 Stonewall riots in New York City, a more militant gay liberation organization formed at the University of Chicago. This group sponsored a citywide dance at the Coliseum Annex in 1970, the first public lesbian and gay dance (aside from the annual Halloween drag balls)

At a late-1980s ACT UP downtown Chicago protest. Ferd Eggan, an ACT UP leader, is pictured far left. He passed away in 2007. Photo by Lisa Howe-Ebright.

Future alderman Tom Tunney with Mayor Harold Washington in the mid-1980s.

Windy City Times/Outlines archives.

held in Chicago. Shortly thereafter, the university group merged with the newly founded Chicago Gay Liberation and led a successful picketing campaign to force the Normandy on North Rush Street to become the first gay bar in Chicago to obtain a dance license and to permit same-sex dancing. A Women's Caucus and a Black Caucus formed within CGL to address the specific concerns of lesbians and Black gay men, later breaking away to become Chicago Lesbian Liberation and the Third World Gay Revolution, respectively.

These groups and others organized Chicago's first annual Gay Pride Parade in June 1970. Later that year, moderate members of CGL established the Chicago Gay Alliance, which operated a short-lived community center on West Elm Street and lobbied for the passage of a local gay-rights ordinance forbidding discrimination in housing and employment. (A bill was first introduced in 1973 but did not pass until 1988.)

Throughout the 1970s and early 1980s lesbian and gay bars, dance clubs and bathhouses multiplied. A community library and archives (now Gerber/Hart Library and Archives), a film festival, a bookstore and numerous political organizations, publications, choruses and athletic and religious groups were also founded during this period. By the early 1980s, a new gay and lesbian commercial and residential center had emerged along North Halsted Street in Lake View, and in August 1982 area merchants launched the Northalsted Market Days, an annual neighborhood street fair that soon rivaled June's Gay Pride festivities.

During the 1980s the gay community was devastated by acquired immune deficiency syndrome (AIDS). Thousands of local gay men succumbed to this disease, which also fueled a new wave of discrimination and hate crimes against gay men and lesbians. Inadequate public funding to fight AIDS led the Howard Brown Memorial Clinic (now Howard Brown Health Center), founded in 1974 as a venereal disease clinic associated with Gay Horizons (now Center on Halsted), to redirect its services toward AIDS prevention and treatment.

As community organizations distributed safer-sex pamphlets and condoms in bars, Dykes and Gay Men Against Repression/Racism/Reagan (DAGMAR) began a campaign of militant AIDS activism in early 1987. Merging with the activist group Chicago for Our Rights (C-FOR) in 1988, they formed C-FAR (Chicago for AIDS Rights, or Coalition for AIDS Rights). This new group, in turn, became the Chicago chapter of the AIDS Coalition to Unleash Power (ACT UP/Chicago) and launched a series of demonstrations to pressure pharmaceutical companies and local, state and federal governmental agencies to provide quicker access to AIDS treatments and increased funding for research and education. In the 1990s other activist organizations, such as Queer Nation and the Lesbian Avengers, led protests against anti-gay violence and against continued police harassment, organized "queer nights" at popular heterosexual nightclubs, and campaigned to raise awareness of lesbian health concerns, including breast cancer.

By the late 1980s, lesbians and gay men had begun to make inroads into traditional Chicago politics. Mayor Harold Washington appointed the Mayor's Committee on Gay and Lesbian Issues in 1985 and eventually hired a full-time liaison to the lesbian and gay community. When Mayor Richard M. Daley took office in 1989, he reconfigured the mayor's committee into an advisory council of the Commission on Human Relations. In 1991 this new Advisory Council on Gay and Lesbian Issues (now the Advisory Council on Lesbian, Gay, Bisexual and Transgender Issues) founded the nation's first city-supported Gay and Lesbian Hall of Fame, which has honored the lives and work of community activists and organizations annually ever since. Building on the passage of Chicago's human rights ordinance in 1988, a Cook County ordinance protecting lesbians, gay men and bisexuals from discrimination was passed in 1993, and the city voted to provide domestic-partnership benefits to municipal employees in 1997. Five years later, transgender activists secured the passage of an amendment to the city's human rights ordinance that extended the law's protections against discrimination to cover gender identity. This development not only brought Chicago's law in line with that of neighboring Evanston, which had provided such protection to transgender individuals since 1997, but also reflected the community's growing awareness of its own diversity and the various forms of prejudice that its members faced.

The 1990s witnessed the first significant electoral victories of Chicago's lesbian and gay community. With his 1994 win in the Cook County Circuit Court race, Thomas R. Chiola became the first openly gay elected official in the city. Shortly thereafter, Joanne Trapani won a seat on the Oak Park village board, becoming the state's first openly lesbian elected official; she was elected board president (also referred to as mayor) in 2001. Nancy J. Katz became Chicago's first openly lesbian official upon her 1999 appointment and subsequent election to the same court as Chiola, and gay restaurateur Thomas M. Tunney was elected as the city's first openly gay alderman in 2003. At the state level, Larry McKeon, a former mayoral liaison to Chicago's lesbian and gay community, became Illinois' first openly gay state legislator in 1996, when he was elected to represent a district including Andersonville, the city's second largest lesbian and gay enclave. Deborah Mell, who ran unopposed in the 2008 Democratic primary, faces no general-election opponent and is, therefore, poised to become Illinois' first openly lesbian state legislator. ▼

This article has been revised from the original entry in the Encyclopedia of Chicago. The Electronic Encyclopedia of Chicago © 2005 Chicago Historical Society and The Encyclopedia of Chicago © 2004 The Newberry Library. All rights reserved. Used with permission.

Chad Heap is associate professor of American studies at The George Washington University in Washington, D.C. He received his doctorate in history from the University of Chicago, where he curated an exhibition and wrote an exhibition catalog titled Homosexuality in the City: A Century of Research at the University of Chicago. He is also the author of Slumming: Sexual and Racial Encounters in American Nightlife, 1885–1940, which will be published by the University of Chicago Press in the summer of 2008.

SELECTED BIBLIOGRAPHY

Bruce, Earle W. Comparison of Traits of the Homosexual from Tests and Life-History Materials. M.A. thesis, University of Chicago, 1942.

Drexel, Allen. "Before Paris Burned: Race, Class, and Male Homosexuality on the Chicago South Side, 1935–1960." In: Creating a Place for Ourselves: Lesbian, Gay, and Bisexual Community Histories, ed. Brett Beemyn, 119–44. New York: Routledge, 1997.

Gould, Deborah B. "Sex, Death, and the Politics of Anger: Emotions and Reason in ACT UP's Fight Against AIDS." Ph.D. diss., University of Chicago, 2000.

Heap, Chad. Slumming: Sexual and Racial Encounters in American Nightlife, 1885–1940. Chicago: University of Chicago Press, 2008.

Johnson, David K. "The Kids of Fairytown: Gay Male Culture on Chicago's Near North Side in the 1930s." In: Creating a Place for Ourselves: Lesbian, Gay, and Bisexual Community Histories, ed. Brett Beemyn, 97–118. New York: Routledge, 1997.

Jones, James H. Alfred Kinsey: A Public/Private Life. New York: W.W. Norton & Co., 1997.

Katz, Jonathan Ned. Gay American History: Lesbians and Gay Men in the U.S.A. rev. ed. New York: Meridian, 1992.

Oral histories, Chicago Gay and Lesbian History Project. Gregory A. Sprague Papers. Chicago History Museum, Chicago, Ill.

"Pansy Parlors, Tough Chicago Has Epidemic of Male Butterflies." Variety, Dec. 10, 1930.

Sprague, Gregory. "Chicago's Past: A Rich Gay History." Advocate, Aug. 18, 1983.

Unpublished field notes and student research papers. Ernest W. Burgess Papers. Special Collections Research Center, University of Chicago Library.

Vice Commission of Chicago. The Social Evil in Chicago: A Study of Existing Conditions with Recommendations by the Vice Commission of Chicago. Chicago: Gunthorp-Warren Printing Co., 1911.

Zorbaugh, Harvey Warren. The Gold Coast and the Slum: A Sociological Study of Chicago's Near North Side. Chicago: University of Chicago Press, 1929.

FROM PRAIRIE SETTLEMENT TO 1949

The Transformation of Denial Into Hope

G ENERATIONS OF CHICAGO GAYS AND LESBIANS HAVE GROWN UP deprived of their evidence in history and denied role models and reinforcement of a positive self-image. Unfortunately, much of our early history has been buried in police reports, medical logs or sensational newspaper accounts of previous generations. Anthropologists, explorers and missionaries have left some records, but these are filtered through their personal prejudices and racial and sexual biases. A few of our kind have left behind diaries or letters, an occasional photograph, preserved moments in fiction, or rare autobiographies.

Particularly difficult to uncover is information about the pre-1950 years, because most of the people are gone, and the evidence is buried with them.

Someday, perhaps, students at the Von Steuben and Cather schools will be told about the sexual orientation of their school namesakes and how that affected their contribution to our common culture. There is no way to assess the positive effects on African-American students when poems or plays by Langston Hughes or Chicagoan Lorraine Hansberry were first presented to them as by Black writers in their classrooms. Today, they, like James Baldwin and Audre Lorde, are often part of literary history curricula. Why would it not be an equally positive experience to note that these gifted writers also loved members of their own sex, and to examine how that translated into their creative efforts?

Gregory A. Sprague, who in the 1970s initiated the Gay and Lesbian History Project and what would later become the Gerber/Hart Library and Archives, also wrote articles on Chicago gay male history for GayLife and The Advocate. His research archives and several of his slide shows are on deposit at the Chicago History Museum, as are many of the papers

Langston Hughes. Drawing by Otis Richardson.

Opposite: Black-and-tan clubs often featured African-American performers and a mixed audience. Some would view the clubs as exploitative of women and/or people of color. See page 29. Photo courtesy the Chicago History Museum.

of attorney Pearl Hart and Thing 'zine founder Robert Ford. Jonathan Ned Katz preserved documents from many sources in his monumental resource guides Gay American History: Lesbians and Gay Men in the U.S.A.: A Documentary (Crowell, 1976) and Gay/Lesbian Almanac: A New Documentary (Harper, 1983). Without the guideposts these volumes offered, research would have been much more difficult.

The wider culture has grounded "gay" and "lesbian" in a sexual/genital definition that, while valid for a certain element, fails to consider love. Documentary reports and brief biographies can only show a sliver of the community, but they do give evidence of our existence and hint at the ordinary men and women in Chicago who chose to love their own kind and lead quiet and unremarkable lives. Until such time as the history of all our people can be told without the exclusion of any group for reason of race, gender, religion or sexual orientation, it falls to gays and lesbians in Chicago to preserve and disseminate our own record.

Parts of this chapter have been adapted and updated from a 1994 article by Marie J. Kuda in Outlines newspaper. Kuda and others explore a few of the key players, news and events of this period in Chicago, from the Civil War and the 1893 World's Fair to the Vice Commission and World War II. Jonathan Ned Katz's investigation into the work of Henry Gerber is an astonishing look at the first known gay organization in the United States. Lucinda Fleeson takes us back to the "pansy craze" of the 1930s in Chicago.

While the pre-1950 years were difficult, the next decade in Chicago would not be easy—McCarthyism was on the horizon, and machine politics were more firmly entrenched than ever. Roaring '20s mobsters were replaced by a more subtle underground that controlled gay clubs, bars and bathhouses. For most of us, World War II ended on a note of hope. We may have been different, but now we knew we were not alone. ▼

Above left: Sailors dancing. Above right: Many Chicago lesbians were among those fighting for women's right to vote in the United States, which finally happened with the 19th Amendment in 1920. The battle was echoed in the 1970s when the Equal Rights Amendment was working its way through the states. Despite strong activism from lesbians and gay men and a very committed women's movement, the state's conservatives, including Phyllis Schlafly, a longtime anti-gay and anti-feminist activist, prevailed. She had said the ERA would lead to, among other things, gay marriage. Ironically, years later, Schlafly's son John would be outed as gay. Photo of suffragist Mabel Vernon in Chicago, June 16, 1916. Below: The Chicago Fire of 1871 had a devastating—and renewing—impact on the city. Images courtesy of the Chicago History Museum.

EARLY CONTACTS: NATIVE AMERICANS TO CIVIL WAR   *by MARIE J. KUDA*

EARLY FRENCH AND SPANISH EXPLORERS and missionaries, including Marquette, wrote no fewer than six reports documenting the practices of cross-dressing and same-sex relations among Native American people living on the western bank of what is now Lake Michigan between 1673 and 1724.

Writers commented on men dressing as women and doing "women's work." Some reports assumed the practice was involved with religious functions; others used a tone of moral censure and claimed that young boys were "bred for this purpose." Still others commented that persons engaging in such behavior were "persons of consequence" among their peers.

The tribes mentioned were the Miami and the Illinois. It's not clear if the Illinois were the Illini group that included the Peoria, Moingwena, Kaskaskia and others joined by the Algonquian languages or were a separate people like the Sauk, Fox, Winnebago and others who moved through what is now the state of Illinois ahead of encroaching settlement.

There is considerable evidence to support the fact that cross-dressing women fought in early American wars. Deborah Sampson fought alongside men in the Revolutionary War. Like Dr. Mary Walker in the Civil War, she cross-dressed, but unlike Walker, she attempted to hide her sex. Walker, a surgeon, was awarded the Congressional Medal of Honor as its only woman recipient, but it was later revoked along with some 900 others that had not been awarded for "actual combat with an enemy." She continued to wear male clothing after the war and agitated for a woman's right to dress as she chose. Decades after her death, her medal was restored under President Jimmy Carter, on appeal from women's liberation groups.

Other women concealed their sex and continued to pass as men in their civilian lives—even marrying and successfully passing in all ways until accident or death revealed their secrets.

Of the 150-or-so recorded instances of "passing women" from the Civil War, one made the headlines in Chicago papers after the turn of the century. Jennie Hodgers, an Irish immigrant, had served honorably as Albert D. J. Cashier. When Cashier applied for a military pension, "he" was able to present a "bulging" file containing testimony from fellow comrades-in-arms. A 1910 accident eventually unmasked the former soldier's sex and led to the headline "A Woman in an Old Soldiers Home!" Hodgers/Cashier, who served in an Illinois regiment, left behind a daguerreotype, which has been reprinted in several sources.

Another Chicago enlistee was Frank Miller (Frances Hook), who successfully masqueraded until wounded and captured by the Confederates. Hook's story was reported by the Chicago Tribune in 1909. And there is the case preserved for us by the historian Jonathan Ned Katz, of Nicholas de Raylan, who served as secretary to the Russian consul in Chicago. Twice married, he served as a soldier during the Spanish-American War, and was divorced by his first wife of 10 years for "misconduct with chorus girls." His untimely death at 33 in 1906 revealed Nicholas to be a woman. In a will, "Nicholas" had made elaborate provisions to prevent detection. Neither wife would believe the truth, insisting "Nicholas" was a man. The reports say de Raylan wore "a very elaborately constructed artificial penis." ▼

VICE: NO BIG DEAL

There is hardly a clearer statement of bluenose frustration with life as it is lived than the lament of the 1911 Chicago Vice Commission, apportioning blame among officials and institutions for the prevalence of "the social evil": "[T]he greatest criticism is due the citizens of Chicago, first, for the constant evasion of the problem, second, for their ignorance and indifference to the situation, and third, for their lack of united effort in demanding a change in the intolerable conditions as they now exist."

The commission was especially vexed at the form of vice it called "sex perversion." Estimates of its extent "seemed incredible before an investigator was put in the field" who found "whole groups and colonies" of perverts openly thumbing their powdered noses at social convention and being neither arrested by the police nor afflicted with deadly diseases. The commission urged enforcement of the law as it had stood in Illinois since 1845, providing severe penalties for "sodomy, or other crime against nature."

It would take another 50 years, but the law came into sync with people's indifference in 1961 with the adoption of the Illinois Criminal Code, eliminating the crime of sodomy. The fact that Illinois was the first state to wipe sodomy laws off the books was an enormous progressive step forward for gay rights, yet it was of so little consequence to the general public that the Chicago Tribune failed to even mention it in contemporary recaps reporting changes in the law. Local ordinances such as those prohibiting same-sex dancing and wearing gender-discordant clothing in public fell away as proper homosexuals transformed themselves into GLBT militants in the 1970s and savvy political infighters in the '80s and '90s. Ninety-four years after the Vice Commission, the Illinois legislature made it unlawful to discriminate against gay people, and straight guys were seeking the approbation of queer eyes—on national television. Out of the closet, indeed.   **— Ron Dorfman**

A GAY PRESIDENT? *by MARIE J. KUDA*

THIRTY-SOME YEARS AGO, THE APRIL 1976 issue of The Chicago Gay Crusader ran an article titled "Lincoln's Other Love." The author, Dennis Doty, drew his suggestion that Abraham Lincoln might be gay from several sources going all the way back to a newspaper story by New Salem resident John Hill that appeared 27 years after Lincoln's assassination. Doty bolstered his argument with excerpts from Lincoln's letters quoted in the eight-volume Collected Works of Abraham Lincoln (1953–55).

Doty wasn't the first gay scholar to make the claim. In 1971, iconic archivist Jim Kepner recorded his gleanings from Illinois' good gray poet Carl Sandburg's multi-volume 1926 biography of the president. In The Prairie Years, Sandburg noted the "streak of lavender" and "spots soft as May violets" that ran through Lincoln and Joshua Fry Speed, who slept together nightly for four years in a bed above the Springfield store where Lincoln clerked. Lest the misguided think Sandburg was merely waxing ecstatic over prairie flowers, I refer them to the chapter "They Said It With Violets in 1926" in Kaier Curtin's history of gays on the American stage. The imagery of violets and lavender was well known to most literate Americans in the early 20th century and was commonplace when Sandburg's book was published.

By the 1980s the first wave of amateur and tenured gay historians were hastily "outing" every queer they could, adding them to the growing pantheon of fellow travelers who accomplished much but had their sexuality hidden from history. Unfortunately, many blindly followed their predecessors' published findings without digging deeper into shallow scholarly graves. Kepner eventually published his thoughts on Lincoln in his privately printed From the Closet of History (1984), mistakenly citing a 1956 edition of the Sandburg work as his source. In fact, as notes in C.A. Tripp's posthumously published The Intimate World of Abraham Lincoln (2005) suggest, Sandburg's publisher had purged the suggestive homoerotic 1926 references from later editions; therefore, lazy copiers of Kepner give themselves away by citing an edition that does not carry the material.

Jonathan Ned Katz, whose scrupulous accretion of documents filled his early books, notes in Love Stories: Sex Between Men Before Homosexuality (2001) that the Doty article was the first he read suggesting Lincoln's possible homosexuality. In a chapter headed "No Two Men Were Ever More Intimate" (a quote from Speed on his relationship with Lincoln), Katz begins his exploration of the 19th-century conception and labeling of homoeroticism.

In his study, Tripp introduced a handful of other men whom he suggests were intimate with Lincoln and were among the subjects of what Sandburg called the "invisible companionships that surprised me," mentioned in his research of "stacks and bundles of fact and legend": William "Billy" Greene, with whom Lincoln shared a bed in New Salem so narrow that when one turned, the other had to turn also; Army Capt. (later Maj.) David V. Derickson, who frequently shared the president's bed when Mary was absent; Col. Ephraim Elmer Ellsworth, with whom Lincoln had a "knight and squire" relationship and who was killed in the Civil War; Abner Y. Ellis, who came to Springfield and took quite a "fancy" to Lincoln and ended up in his bed; and others. Tripp tries to answer the question everyone seems obsessed with, echoing a London reviewer of The Life of Lorena Hickok, E.R.'s Friend (1980): "Were orifices penetrated?"

The crux of the matter is the rhetorical question, Why do so many try so hard to discredit even minor evidence suggesting homosexuality in beloved or renowned public figures? ▼

Lincoln, circa 1860. Courtesy the Chicago History Museum.

OSCAR WILDE IN CHICAGO, 1882

by TIM SAMUELSON

ON JANUARY 3, 1882, BRITISH AUTHOR AND CRITIC Oscar Wilde arrived in New York to begin an ambitious yearlong lecture tour across North America. "I am here to lecture and see your country," he told assembled reporters, ending with the vow: "I have come here to get acquainted with the big-hearted American people, and I shan't return to Europe until I do." His experiences included two stops to lecture in Chicago.

Oscar Wilde's first Chicago lecture was anticipated with great interest and curiosity, fueled by the extensive press coverage of his previous lectures in other cities as well as detailed accounts of his personal activities, appearance and manner of dress. To accommodate the expected crowds in Chicago, Wilde was booked to appear in the Central Music Hall, a 2,000-seat auditorium at State and Randolph streets. On Feb. 13, 1882, the hall was filled to standing-room capacity.

The audience listened politely and attentively as Wilde advocated truth and honesty in art and architecture. To make his point relevant to the Chicago audience, Wilde questioned why the city's Water Tower was clad with Gothic-styled stonework of another time and place, instead of expressing the simple dignity of the iron standpipe within. To the amusement of the crowd, Wilde dismissed the much-loved survivor of Chicago's Great Fire of 1871 as a "castellated monstrosity with pepperboxes stuck all over it."

Although Wilde's mention of the Water Tower was only a small and relatively minor part of his overall lecture theme, the comment gained considerable attention in the local newspapers. When a reporter asked the following day about wounding the pride of the local citizenry with his remarks, Wilde was decidedly unrepentant: "I can't help that. It's really too absurd. If you build a water tower, why don't you build it for water and make a simple structure of it, instead of building it like a castle, where one expects to see mailed knights peering out of every part. It seems like a shame to me that the citizens of Chicago have spent so much money on buildings with such an unsatisfactory result from an architectural point of view. Your city looks positively too dreary to me."

Wilde returned to Chicago March 12 to deliver a lecture on the subject of interior and exterior house decoration, but the presentation did not achieve the same degree of success and notoriety as his earlier appearance. ▼

Caricature by Edward Jump in Chicago, circa 1880-95. Photo and caricature courtesy the Chicago History Museum.

THE 1893 WORLD'S FAIR   *by MARIE J. KUDA*

CHICAGO, INCORPORATED AS A TOWN IN 1833 and a city in 1837, grew at an incredible pace. By the 1860s the population surpassed 100,000, with 58 passenger trains arriving daily and half again as many freight trains. After the 1871 fire, the city rebuilt at twice the speed and by 1890 had a population of more than 1 million.

People flocked to Chicago for two reasons: business and pleasure. The Armours and the stockyards, the McCormick Reaper factory, and the great dry-goods houses founded by Palmer, Field and others supplied the business. The opera at Crosby's Opera House, the Auditorium or, later, the Civic Opera House, the theater and music halls, the Art Institute and, later, Orchestra Hall provided the pleasure. As always, there were ventures that hoped to combine both and relieve immigrants, weary workers or the nouveau riche of their money.

Society lived on the South Side, with the big money along Prairie Avenue. The Tenderloin districts were Custom House Place at what would now be the south end of the Loop, and the infamous Levee district, home of swank brothels such as the parlor house owned by the Everleigh sisters, at 2131 S. Dearborn St.

In 1892 Chicago leapt at the chance to show the world it had spectacularly recovered from the fire and was a world-class city. The World's Columbian Exhibition, popularly known as the World's Fair of 1893, was the vehicle chosen to display this triumph. The fabulous "White City," with myriad plaster buildings designed to stand only a few years, was sprawled on landfill and artificial lagoons along the lakefront to what is now Jackson Park.

Oak Park native Katharine Coman and her partner Katharine Lee Bates, both teachers at Wellesley College in Massachusetts, were three years into their 25-year relationship when they returned to Chicago for the World's Columbian Exhibition. Bates continued alone to a summer teaching job in Colorado Springs, Colo. Her train trip across the wheat fields of the Great Plains and trek up Pikes Peak were wedded to her impressions of the fair in a poem later set to music as "America the Beautiful," popular runner-up for our national anthem. Pikes Peak allowed a view of "the purple mountain majesties above the fruited plain"; the "amber waves of grain" were seen from her railroad car window in Iowa, Kansas and Nebraska; and "Thine alabaster cities gleam" came from the impression, viewed with her lover, of that magnificent creation on the bank of Lake Michigan replete with Mrs. Potter Palmer's triumph, the Woman's Building, splendid in the midst of the world's fair's man-made "White City."

Mrs. Palmer was elated at her hard-won success in securing a Woman's Building for the fair, but some women in the suffrage movement saw it as segregation. Prominent women submitted works with the proviso that they not be shown with displays of quilts and kitchenware.

Sculptor Harriet Hosmer, then working in Paris, steadfastly refused to allow her commissioned statue of Queen Isabella (in the act of handing her jewels to Columbus to finance the discovery of the New World) to be exhibited in the Woman's Building. It was displayed eventually in a courtyard of the California Building. Hosmer had a relationship with American stage actress Charlotte Cushman, who seems to have had a thing for sculptors, also numbering Emma Stebbins (as well as Emma Crow) among her conquests.

Mrs. Palmer also worked long and hard to obtain "the most famous painting in the world by a woman" for her building. But lesbian artist Rosa Bonheur's masterpiece The Horse Fair had been snapped up by the Metropolitan Museum. Bonheur did exhibit, as did American Anna Klumpke, who became Bonheur's second "wife." Nathalie Micas, Bonheur's first partner until her death, was represented in the Hall of Science by a railway brake she had patented.

Chicago sculptor Lorado Taft had numerous women working under him to complete monumental commissions for the fair. These became known as his "White Rabbits." Taft has sculpted himself and the Italian workman with whom he was intimate holding hands at the back of his monumental Fountain of Time. This became a sort of rendezvous for lovers on the Midway Plaisance in Hyde Park (near the University of Chicago).

Most of the women's art and the Woman's Building itself, designed by 22-year-old architect Sophia Hayden, were lost after the fair. Among works that survived were Enid Yandell's magnificent caryatids, the figures of women supporting the roof of the Museum of Science and Industry in Jackson Park. Yandell became the prototype of "the bachelor maid" when portrayed in a fair memoir, Three Girls in a Flat. ▼

Lorado Taft's Fountain of Time.
Courtesy the Chicago History Museum.

EARLY 1900s: A WOMAN'S PLACE *by MARIE J. KUDA*

IN THE EARLY 1900s, A BAR CALLED THE SAPPHO, RUN BY AMY Leslie at 2159 S. Dearborn St., next door to the Everleigh Club, may have been a lesbian establishment or may only have furnished "shows" for brothel customers. You could get anything in the Levee district. Circus clubs occasionally featured "acts" with prostitutes and animals. A club in the 2100 block of Armour Avenue (today's South Federal Street) had window shades printed "Why Not?" Called a "vicious resort," it may have been, among other things, the first S&M club in Chicago. A "resort" designated a bar, a brothel or semidetached cribs, usually with a dance hall or crude entertainment. Gay bars continued using names such as "Paradise" and "The Why Not Club" into the 1970s and '80s.

Girls working in factories would be lucky to make $1 a day. Prostitutes could make many times that amount, and strong-arm women (those who "protected" the prostitutes), who generally worked in pairs or gangs (sometimes of mixed races), could bring in cash in the mid-five-figure range annually. Reformers had their work cut out for them.

In 1895, Pulitzer Prize-winning lesbian author Willa Cather (1873–1947) made the first of many train journeys across the plains to attend opera performances in Chicago, a city she would feature in two novels, Lucy Gayheart and The Song of the Lark. The latter title was drawn from a painting of that name that she saw at the Art Institute. The book's heroine, Thea Kronborg, is patterned after Wagnerian soprano Olive Fremsted, whom Cather first heard in a Chicago performance. Fremsted and Emma Calvé, whose tour de force was Bizet's Carmen, were quite fond of the ladies and numbered prominent lesbians on two continents among their admiring coteries.

Mary Gourley Porter, born in Chicago in 1884, was raised in Evanston and inherited a considerable amount of money through a great-uncle whose business, the Deering Harvester Company, merged with the McCormick Harvesting Machine Company to form the International Harvester Company. Her career in social work led her to cross paths with Mary Williams Dewson in 1909. In 1912 Polly Porter and Molly Dewson, 10 years her senior, entered into a 52-year "partnership" detailed by biographer Susan Ware in Partner and I: Molly Dewson, Feminism and New Deal Politics. The women would become great friends and political mentors to Eleanor Roosevelt. Dewson became absorbed into the Roosevelt political organization in 1928 and was an active participant in the New Deal through the 1940 Democratic National Convention in Chicago, which nominated FDR for his third term. As director of the Women's Division of the Democratic National Committee, she worked to obtain positions for women in government and to effect social changes to benefit women and children. Ware notes that the important career decisions made by Dewson were "based upon the impact they would have on her relationship with Polly Porter." She even relinquished positions that required their separation for any period of time.

Loïe Fuller, later dubbed "the electric fairy," was born in Fullersburg, Ill. (where Oak Brook and Hinsdale are today), in 1862. After an unremarkable career as a

Loïe Fuller, "the electric fairy." Courtesy M. Kuda Archives, Oak Park, Ill.

fledgling dancer, she created a Serpentine Dance using colored silks and electric lights that would take her to the capitals of Europe and make her the darling of artists and royalty. Fuller, whose dancing career preceded Isadora Duncan's, premiered her creation at the Auditorium Theatre in 1894. Many tried to capture her swirling silks and electric gyrations. In a commemorative exhibit at the California Palace of the Legion of Honor in San Francisco in the late 1970s, contemporary interpretations of her dances were staged near a hall filled with representations of her in sculpture, art-deco lithographs, paintings and photographs. Her diary was on display, turned to a page about her intimate friend, Queen Marie of Romania. Fuller lived in Paris with her lover, Gabrielle Bloch, returning to the U.S. on several occasions, once to organize an exhibition of Rodin's—his first one-man show in America—and later with Alma de Bretteville Spreckels to found the California Palace of the Legion of Honor as a museum for Rodin in America.

Havelock Ellis' Studies in the Psychology of Sex is a gold mine of data on Chicago gays and lesbians. Unfortunately, his case histories are not cross-referenced by city, but the search is made simpler when you check the author index in all the volumes for contributions submitted by Drs. J.G. Kiernan and G. Frank Lydston, who practiced in Chicago and wrote copiously for various medical journals around the turn of the century. Ellis' wife, Edith Lees, was a lesbian. In 1915 she lectured to a packed house at the Auditorium Theatre on "Sex and Eugenics." The historian Jonathan Ned Katz records Margaret Anderson's response to this speech as "the earliest defense of homosexuality by a lesbian documented in the United States." ▼

JANE ADDAMS: THE NEEDS OF IMMIGRANTS

RESPONDING TO THE NEEDS OF THE INFLUX of immigrants was at the heart of the founding of Hull House, which would become a prototype for settlement houses around the country. Jane Addams (romantically linked for 40 years to Mary Rozet Smith) and her friend Ellen Gates Starr opened their center in 1889 and found themselves at the hub of a social services reform movement.

Female support networks and bonding among women united in a common cause have been extensively studied by feminist scholars in recent years (notably, Blanche Wiesen Cook). By creatively expanding the definition of lesbian to put such relationships in the context of their times, many writers now conclude that Addams and some other women who shared her efforts were lesbian. Certainly the author Edith Hamilton, who was the doyenne of ancient mythology and sister of Dr. Alice Hamilton, who served at Hull House, was in satisfactory long-standing love relationships known to her biographers.

On Dec. 8, 2007, the Chicago History Museum hosted a lecture, play and film on Addams (1860–1935), founder of what has become known as the Chicago School of Social Work. Chicago has previously honored Addams with a hunk of expressway and a lakefront park, the latter dedicated on Women's Equality Day in 1996 with a poem composed and read by laureate Gwendolyn Brooks.

Addams received many honors in her lifetime. In 1931 she became the first American woman to receive the Nobel Peace Prize. She had been a pacifist well before World War I. Addams would go on to found the Women's Peace Party, which morphed into the Women's International League for Peace and Freedom.

Addams was deeply concerned with the welfare of women and children in Chicago and with securing legislation for their protection. She was involved in private clubs and public committees agitating for social change. She publicly supported the candidacy of attorney Pearl Hart, long active in juvenile and women's court cases, when Hart ran for associate judge of the Chicago Municipal Court in 1928. Hart would later become a well-known civil rights attorney in the McCarthy era and supporter of gay rights.

Jane Addams in her early years, and reading in Chicago, 1915. Photos courtesy of the Chicago History Museum.

Addams and Ellen Gates Starr founded Hull House together, with much of its early financial support coming from Addams' intimate friend Smith, one of the richest women in America at the time. Mary and Jane traveled together frequently; a letter preserves their demand of a hotel for a double bed to be shared, instead of two singles. Smith maintained a summer home they shared in Bar Harbor, Maine. Addams destroyed most of Smith's letters to her, but one popularly quoted letter exchange between Addams and Smith does indicate their passion. Addams: "I miss you dreadfully and am yours 'til death." Smith: "You can never know what it is to me to have had you and to have you. ... I feel quite a rush of emotion when I think of you."

Their "loving partnership" ended with Smith's death in 1933. Addams died in 1935, just days after attending a celebratory dinner hosted by another woman-loving woman, the future first lady and U.N. delegate Eleanor Roosevelt. ▼

This essay is in part compiled from the writings of Marie J. Kuda for Outlines and Windy City Times newspapers.

TORMENTED ARCHITECT: LOUIS SULLIVAN

by MARIE J. KUDA

CHICAGO OWES MUCH OF ITS EARLY REPUTATION FOR architecture to the designs and ornamentation of Louis H. Sullivan (1856–1924). Still standing and on every architectural tour are the magnificent Auditorium Building (1886–90) at South Michigan Avenue and East Congress Parkway; the former Schlesinger and Mayer department store (1898–99 and 1902–04, later Carson Pirie Scott & Co.), at South State and East Madison streets; and the tiny Krause Music Store (1922), whose facade survives at 4611 N. Lincoln Ave. Remnants of the 1893–94 Chicago Stock Exchange Building at 30 N. LaSalle St. (where attorney Pearl M. Hart had her office until the building's destruction in 1972) are displayed in the Art Institute of Chicago. A few tombs of early movers and shakers and dozens of other projects survive. Sullivan also is known for his writings and his pre-eminent student, Frank Lloyd Wright.

Sullivan's biographer, Robert Twombly, documents his position that "there is a good deal of evidence—some personal, some architectural—to suggest that Louis Sullivan may have been homosexual." The point in exploring his sexuality (as is the case for author Henry Blake Fuller, other 19th-century Chicago figures, or even Ernest Hemingway) is how their sexuality affected their work. While Twombly may seem to go a bit overboard in noting Sullivan's "ejaculatory imagery" with geometric male forms exploding into female decoration, most critics yield that his ornamentation is "female." Some even note a "lack of manliness" in his work. Sullivan moved to Chicago in 1873, joined all-male athletic clubs, enjoyed Greco-Roman wrestling, "lovingly drew men's bodies" and moved in circles of all-male friends. He studied architecture in France for two years and returned to Chicago in 1879 during the post-Fire building boom.

In 1899 he married at age 43. The marriage lasted 10 years (no children), and it is generally assumed that his wife was having an extramarital affair for at least the last five years. About the time he married, Sullivan resumed boxing (à la Hemingway), no doubt to exude an air of machismo.

In a phrase reminiscent of Harriet Monroe's eulogy for her friend Henry Blake Fuller, Twombly notes that Sullivan "did not let people get too close," that he refused to "reveal himself or let others know who he was inside." ▼

Source: Louis Sullivan: His Life and Work, by Robert Twombly, University of Chicago Press (1986).

Portrait of Louis H. Sullivan, oil painting, by Frank A. Werner.
Courtesy the Chicago History Museum.

DANCING FOR THE STARS: MARK TURBYFILL   by MARIE J. KUDA

MARK TURBYFILL (1896–1991), POET, DANCER AND ARTIST, WAS truly a Renaissance man. Judged by many as "unsung and unappreciated," he is past due for rediscovery. Born in Indian Territory in what is now Oklahoma, he moved to Chicago with his family as a teenager. His father was an architect who traced his family back to a liegeman of William the Conqueror at the Battle of Hastings. Turbyfill was handsome, with the grace of a dancer, always welcome in "polite society" as an "extra" man, the stereotypical lifelong bachelor.

While a student at Lake View High School, Turbyfill approached Margaret Anderson of The Little Review with one of his poems. She would eventually publish some of his poetry in her magazine, and she and her partner, Jane Heap, would become his lifelong friends. Later, for the first and only time, Harriet Monroe would devote an entire issue of Poetry: A Magazine of Verse to one poem,

Mark Turbyfill wearing a quasi-Russian smock designed by the late Quill Monroe. Courtesy Ann Barzel Dance Research Collection, The Newberry Library, Chicago.

Turbyfill's magnum opus (five years in the making), "A Marriage with Space" (May 1926). His poems appeared in nearly a dozen issues.

It was at Poetry that he met Chicago novelist Henry Blake Fuller, who described himself as "an old satyr" and would be Turbyfill's mentor and friend until Fuller's death in 1929. Pascal Covici published A Marriage with Space, and Other Poems, in Chicago in 1927. A new edition was published here in 1974.

Turbyfill's first book of poetry, The Living Frieze (1921), was published in Evanston in a limited edition by Monroe Wheeler (later of the Museum of Modern Art in New York and lover, in a long-standing ménage à trois, of writer Glenway Wescott and photographer George Platt Lynes). Wheeler and Wescott had met as students in Chicago in 1919 and would remain Turbyfill's lifelong friends.

Turbyfill was co-author of Evaporation: A Symposium (1923) with his good friend, journalist and author Samuel Putnam. In 1924, while Putnam was working as a reporter for the Chicago Herald and Examiner, he managed to get Turbyfill (posing as a cub reporter) into the Leopold and Loeb trial; they were seated directly behind defense attorney Clarence Darrow and the two boys. Putnam heeded the advice of Henry Blake Fuller and moved to Paris, where he edited The New Review and This Quarter (Turbyfill contributed to both) and wrote Paris Was Our Mistress: Memoirs of a Lost & Found Generation (1947).

Turbyfill had a second passion, the ballet. He studied under partners Andreas Pavley and Serge Oukrainsky, and he danced in the Chicago Grand Opera Company corps de ballet on opening night when Mary Garden sang in Pierre Louÿs' Aphrodite at the Auditorium Theatre. He studied in New York with Michel Fokine and later, 1924–26, became premier danseur with Chicago Allied Arts (under former Diaghilev star Adolph Bolm), the first full-fledged ballet company in the United States. According to dance critic and historian Ann Barzel (who also studied with Bolm), Turbyfill was often paired with Chicago legend Ruth Page in avant-garde productions such as Chicago composer John Alden Carpenter's The Birthday of the Infanta, based on a story by Oscar Wilde.

In 1929, Turbyfill was introduced to the "dashingly beautiful" Katherine Dunham, "an ambitious Negro girl, who had never had a lesson in her life in the art, but who wanted to become a ballet dancer." He took her on as a student, opening a small studio of his own for Dunham and other Black students in one of the tiny East 57th Street buildings left over from the 1893 World's Fair (his friend Margaret Anderson and other Chicago literati met in another). He put together an advisory board for a proposed Ballet Nègre, commissioned a score, and began work on the choreography. Some of the people (such as Robert S. Abbott, later of the Chicago Defender) whom he approached showed little interest in supporting a Black ballet company. Dunham eventually debuted in a production choreographed by Ruth Page with an all-Black supporting cast, at the 1933 Century of Progress Exposition. She went on to become a legend on stage, in film and as a choreographer, teacher and doyenne of West Indian and Afro-American dance.

Through the influence of his friend Mark Tobey, Turbyfill worked at becoming an artist. His poetry found its way into his abstract expressionist oil paintings. Critics dubbed one series of watercolors using a calligraphic white-writing technique on black backgrounds as "Turbyfiligrees." He had modest success from his first solo exhibition in 1948 throughout the 1960s.

In his mature years Turbyfill would return to dance, using the spoken word to

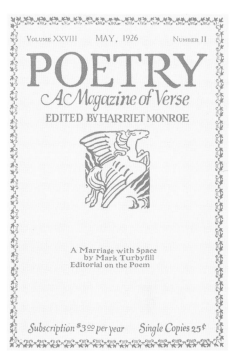

Authors of Evaporation, Mark Turbyfill (left) and Samuel Putnam. Right: An entire issue of Poetry Magazine was dedicated to Turbyfill's poetry. Photo by Jun Fujita in 1923. Images courtesy M. Kuda Archives, Oak Park, Ill.

replace music as an accompaniment for dance. His book The Words Beneath Us: Balletic Poems (1951) has a few photographs of the experimental performance interwoven with his poems, ending with commentary by critics Claudia Cassidy and Ann Barzel.

Turbyfill had been living in western Rogers Park and attending Metropolitan Community Church services since the 1970s. He confirmed that he was gay and that he had lovers among his male dance students. The only woman he had had relations with was Georgette Leblanc Maeterlinck (Margaret Anderson's partner after Jane Heap) because, he said, that was as close as he could get to his idol, Maurice Maeterlinck. His Chicago neighborhood became too much of a chal-

lenge, and a young gay friend from MCC, Ken Frank, helped him pack and move.

In the late 1960s, Turbyfill placed 242 letters from 126 correspondents (1906–66) with the Gotham Book Mart in New York. Southern Illinois University purchased that correspondence, and it now rests in the Special Collections Research Center at Carbondale. Most of his other papers, including books inscribed by authors and a few copies of his unpublished autobiographical memoir, Whistling in the Windy City, went to the Newberry Library in 1988. The David and Alfred Smart Museum of Art at the University of Chicago holds approximately 100 of his paintings and watercolors, most recently exhibited in 2006. ▼

BEAUTY ON SKID ROW: NOVELIST WILLARD MOTLEY

In his novel Knock on Any Door (1947), set on Chicago's old Skid Row, mixed-race author Willard Motley created Nicky Romano, a beautiful young thug who "mooched, jackrolled and played the queen for money," often beating his male tricks senseless after sex. Halfway through the novel, when at his lowest, Nicky is befriended by Owen, a gay man who cares for him in a brotherly manner until Nick kills a cop and subsequently turns on him. Owen was lost in the film version, which starred John Derek as Nick, who uttered the iconic line: "Live fast, die young, and leave a good-looking corpse."

Motley again used the West Side setting in his sequel, Let No Man Write My Epitaph (1958). The film version starred James Darren as Nicky's son. Motley's second novel, We Fished All Night (1951), told the stories of three white soldiers returning to Chicago after World War II.

Motley was raised as a younger brother to his cousin, the artist Archibald J. Motley Jr. His last novel was set in Mexico, where he lived with his adopted lover. Some recent African-American critics fault him for writing white characters. — *Marie J. Kuda*

MAN ABOUT TOWN: HENRY BLAKE FULLER   *by MARIE J. KUDA*

HENRY BLAKE FULLER (1857–1929), AUTHOR, editor, poet, critic and composer, has been praised by three generations of literary critics and is mentioned in every significant work on Chicago history, yet he remains virtually unknown. His significance to Chicago is his contribution to our unique literary heritage in his novels and short-story collections set

Henry Blake Fuller. Courtesy M. Kuda Archives, Oak Park, Ill.

in this city—The Cliff-Dwellers (1893), With the Procession (1895), Under the Skylights (1901), and On the Stairs (1918).

Fuller's play At Saint Judas's from his collection, The Puppet-Booth: Twelve Plays (1896), is

effectively the first play on a homosexual theme published in America. The one-act play is set in a church sacristy. The Bridegroom and the Best Man, both in uniform and wearing swords, are embroiled in a revealing conversation in front of a surrealistic tableau vivant of stained-glass windows representing the seven deadly sins and the fall of Lucifer. The exposition reveals homoerotic love and jealousy that end in a fatal sword fight. The difficulty of staging the moving windows prohibited its performance in its day. At Saint Judas's was reprinted in Lovesick: Modernist Plays of Same-Sex Love, 1894–1925, compiled by Laurence Senelick (1999). Senelick is a drama professor and former Chicagoan who earned his undergraduate degree at Northwestern University. In his introduction to the play, he decries the neglect of Fuller and ranks him as a figure equal to Henry James or E.M. Forster in the pantheon of gay writers of the period. The play received its first performance of record, staged by local impresario David Zak, at Bailiwick Repertory's first annual Trailblazer Awards in 2000.

Fuller was 62 when he courageously published a philosophic novel centered on homosexual characters, Bertram Cope's Year (1919). Young college English teacher Bertram is pursued by an older man and a woman with marriageable females in tow. He partners-up for a time with a rather nellie young thing who does drag in a Blackfriars-like production at a thinly veiled Chicago university. While

described by later critics as "Fuller's best work" and as "full of dynamite scrupulously packed," it was ill-received and largely ignored in his lifetime. His disillusionment over its reception drove Fuller to destroy the manuscript and kept him from writing another novel for 10 years. Turtle Point Press issued a reprint of the novel in 1998; the publisher had been alerted to the work by Bruce Kellner, a professor of English and executor of the estate of Carl Van Vechten (1880–1964), a novelist, critic and photographer best known for his association with the Harlem Renaissance. Van Vechten had been unrestrained in his praise of the novel and of Fuller's stature in literary history. In an afterword, Andrew Solomon suggests that the book does a great service by portraying the "normative homosexuality" of the era.

Fuller was "an old settler," a third-generation Chicagoan and the last male in a family descended from Mayflower Pilgrims. His grandfather was a successful merchant, and his father organized the city's first trolley car system. His grandfather's cousin Margaret Fuller, who published Around the Lakes, a book about her travels in our area in the 1800s, also wrote: "I believe that a man can love a man and a woman can love a woman."

Fuller had a love-hate relationship with Chicago and its crass commercialism, stockyards, and dirt-spewing industries. He was prescient in his vision of a city with "rushing streams of commerce" channeled into the man-made cliffs towering along the lakefront, leaving behind a decimated prairie. He wrote that Chicago was "the only great city in the world to which all its citizens have come for the one common, avowed object of making money." He was an outspoken critic of America's imperialistic tendencies and racism. Unlike other writers who left town after making a name for themselves, Fuller stayed and "tried to break the chains which enslaved Chicago to New York, America to Europe, and the present to the past."

Fuller is an enigmatic figure. He was the first Chicago author to gain positive critical attention from the Eastern literary establishment, but today is little known outside academia and those interested in that period of literary history known as the Chicago Renaissance. He has been the subject of four biographies, a dozen or more chapters in books of literary criticism, and innumerable references in local biographies and works on Chicago history. In writings since 1970 it was generally assumed that Fuller was gay; Kenneth Scambray clinched it in his definitive A Varied Harvest: The Life and Works of Henry Blake Fuller (1987).

In his best-known Chicago novel, With the Procession (1895, reprinted in 1965 by the University of Chicago Press), his brother-and-sister characters, Jane and David Truesdale, can be viewed as both sides of Fuller's nature. He tells the city's story from the Prairie Avenue perspective, handling the machinations of the marriage market, the entrenched old guard, and the newly rich merchant class as adroitly as Jane Austen.

An experimental author, Fuller wrote novels about Americans in Europe (novels compared favorably to those by Edith Wharton and Henry James), was said to be the "Father of American Realism" for his novels set in Chicago, and was something of a muckraker in his diatribes against American imperialism in Cuba, Mexico, the Philippines and Panama. He was a sharp critic of the Chicago merchant-class social scene and an early environmentalist as he watched the increasingly polluted city eating up the prairie.

On the personal side, Fuller was a social plus, a witty raconteur. He entertained at the piano and was always welcome in stately homes. His friends described him as a gentleman of taste, cultivation and great personal charm. Fuller was at the center of Chicago's first "arts" club, The Little Room, and was associated with Maurice Browne and Ellen Van Volkenburg's Little Theatre. He wrote satire, reviews, editorials and criticism for local and national journals. He also wrote short stories and poetry, serving for a number of years as editor of Harriet Monroe's legendary Poetry: A Magazine of Verse. He liked to visit the studio of his friend, sculptor Lorado Taft, and meet the new students at the long luncheon table. He was a fixture at the Indiana Dunes summer home

of University of Chicago friends, always overflowing with young people. Sometimes he would meet young men on the sandy beaches such as William Emery Shepherd, 40 years his junior, who accompanied him on his last trip to Europe. He would cultivate young men of talent and breeding such as Mark Turbyfill (see related article).

Among his papers at the Newberry Library are a handful of letters from a young Canadian friend who was apparently having trouble finding suitable men. Fuller had advised him to hold out for "commercial travelers," perhaps a class of men he met in his own circumspect life. His protégés Turbyfill and Shepherd were among the 70-plus contributors to a memorial volume published by drama pioneer Anna Morgan as a tribute to her friend. Other contributors included Carl Van Vechten, Thornton Wilder, Arthur Meeker, Lorado Taft and Jane Addams. Fuller had volunteered at Hull House and had partnered with Addams as a peace activist.

The significance of noting Fuller's sexual orientation lies in its effect on his work. The disapprobation of homosexuality led to self-censorship, coding, alternative expression and sometimes self-destruction. There was a consensus among some who knew Fuller well, and among recent critics, that his seemingly natural reticence was exacerbated by his homosexuality. The most telling contribution to his memorial volume came from his old Poetry magazine friend Harriet Monroe, who wrote: "Henry Fuller found it impossible to tell his whole story. He could not give himself away, and therefore it may be that the greatest book of which his genius was capable was never written." ▼

At the foot of Top-o-Dune, Tamarack, Indiana Dunes, 1920. From left: Pianist Winifred Middleton, novelist Henry Blake Fuller, poet/dancer Mark Turbyfill. Courtesy M. Kuda Archives, Oak Park, Ill.

CRUISING WITH NED ROREM

Gay teenagers in the late 1940s and '50s came out cruising. Composer Ned Rorem (1923–) walked the lakefront parks with a suggestive book in hand; Michael Shimandle (1945–2004) was told by guys who picked him up to put on a suit and tie to look older (he would later own gay bars, such as Bushes); Guy Warner, former Mattachine Midwest president and Parents and Friends of Lesbians and Gays/Chicago founder, made his connections at Far South Side movie theaters. Letters tell of meeting partners at downtown theaters and ushers at Orchestra Hall. In the '60s the tacky Clark Theatre at 11 N. Clark St. and Monroe Theatre at 57 W. Monroe St. were popular rendezvous, along with a few others in the Loop, on the Near North Side and in outlying neighborhoods.

LEGAL PIONEER: PEARL M. HART, 1890–1975 *by MARIE J. KUDA*

IN 1987 JOURNALIST KATHLEEN O'MALLEY, writing about the Gerber/Hart Library in Windy City Times, bemoaned the lack of information about Pearl M. Hart and wondered why the library bore her name. The then-recent deaths of founder Greg Sprague and librarian Joe Gregg because of complications from HIV/AIDS surely contributed to that ignorance. But in large part, Pearl Hart's own reticence about her sexuality and personal affairs may have kept the average gay person in the dark. Her reputation as a pioneer woman lawyer, civil libertarian and social activist was well known in other communities.

Hart was born in Michigan April 7, 1890, as Pearl Minnie Harchovsky, first American-born and youngest of five daughters of Russian immigrant parents. Four years later her rabbi father moved his family to Chicago. Pearl graduated from high school, worked in a law office to help support the family and "read" law at night. She changed her name to "Hart," graduated from John Marshall Law

School and passed the Illinois bar in 1914. She worked with Jane Addams of Hull House and was considered one of the foremost authorities on juvenile law in the United States; she drafted Illinois children's adoption laws and related statutes. She began teaching commercial law in the early 1920s.

According to lesbian novelist Valerie Taylor, Hart's first experience with lesbians came while defending "ladies of the evening" in Chicago's Morals Court (later Women's Court). Hart served as the first public defender appointed to Women's Court. A 1971 Chicago Tribune article noted that at one time Hart was the only woman lawyer in Chicago specializing in criminal law. In the interview, Hart remarked: "When I went into that court none of the women had defense attorneys and 90 percent of the accused were found guilty. When I left four years later, the statistics were reversed and 90 percent went free."

Later, with the support of Addams, Hart ran but was defeated for Municipal Court judge. In 1937

Hart was a founding member of the National Lawyers Guild, a leftist alternative to the American Bar Association. She ran again in 1948 as a Progressive Party candidate for judge, besides running on the party's ticket for a Chicago City Council seat in 1947 and 1951.

In the 1920s Hart met Blossom Churan, an attractive actress some years her junior. Hart would live with Churan in a fluctuating relationship (kept secret from her family) for more than 40 years.

In the 1940s Churan took as a lover a prominent Chicago physician, Bertha Isaacs. Rather than let Churan go, Hart took the new lover into their home on North Pine Grove Avenue, and, according to Taylor, the three lived "a rather gothic existence" until Churan's death in 1969. Taylor wrote: "Neighbors saw three aging women, two with successful careers, one who stayed at home. Out-of-town relatives or friends stayed in nearby hotels. They kept their lives compartmentalized." As Churan became more

Opposite left: Pearl M. Hart. Courtesy M. Kuda Archives, Oak Park, Ill.

Opposite right: Decades before Chicago had its first gay alderman, Pearl Hart ran for office in that same ward—the 44th. Image courtesy the Chicago History Museum.

frail, she was less interested in sex and "leaned on Pearl as she had in the beginning."

At the 1992 National Lawyers Guild annual convention in Chicago, the Women's Luncheon was held as a tribute to Hart. Among those eulogizing her, in addition to a lesbian speaker, were the children of immigrants she had defended in deportation and denaturalization cases arising out of cases involving the House Un-American Activities Committee, the McCarran-Walter Act, the Smith Act and the McCarthy witch-hunts of the 1950s.

Hart was probably the first lesbian to appear before the U.S. Supreme Court, in her appeal connected with the deportation case of Chicago printer George Witkovich, decided April 29, 1957. Her advice to her client—to refuse to answer questions, not on Fifth Amendment (self-incrimination) but on First Amendment (right-to-privacy) grounds—was upheld by the court when it held that the questions fell outside the scope of immigration authorities' statutory power to seek information relevant to determining an alien's continued availability for deportation. Justice Felix Frankfurter wrote the court's opinion (353 U.S. 194), which also acknowledged that construing the statute to permit broader immigration questioning might implicate the constitutional issues Hart raised. A strict constitutionalist, she was also one of the attorneys in the Smith Act case of an Illinois Communist Party leader, Claude Lightfoot.

Hart was president of the Women's Bar Association of Illinois. In 1960 she became a founding board member of the Midwest Committee for Protection of Foreign Born.

In the early 1960s, Valerie Taylor was a guest speaker at a public meeting of the Mattachine Society, the second incarnation of a failed Chicago chapter of the West Coast gay rights organization. She met Hart, who would become "the love of my life."

She took an apartment on West Surf Street, around the corner from Hart, accepting the "neurotic situation" at the Pine Grove house. Taylor was about 50 and Hart was 73. Taylor later became a charter member of a wholly new corporation, Mattachine Midwest, founded in 1965 with Hart's assistance.

Hart taught at John Marshall Law School for years until just weeks before her death. In 1971, Hart joined her protégé, the attorney Renee Hanover, in formation of a Women's Law Center after they had to surrender separate offices in Louis Sullivan's Stock Exchange Building at 30 N. LaSalle St. prior to its destruction.

During her lifetime, Hart was lionized by those she served across Chicago's various persecuted communities. Major events honored her 60th and 80th birthdays; dozens whom she had defended spoke; recordings and memorial booklets testify to her legal prowess and compassion. John Marshall Law School awarded her an honorary doctorate, noting her as a "pioneer and exemplar ... an imperturbable trial advocate and a scholar of ingenuity as well as intellect" for half a century.

Taylor was refused entry to Hart's hospital room during Hart's final days. Hospital policy, she was told, permitted family members only. Hanover, acting on her behalf, finally obtained permission. By then, Hart was in a coma. She died March 22, 1975.

In 1991 Pearl Hart was among the first inductees inaugurated into the city of Chicago's Gay and Lesbian Hall of Fame. The city Department of Cultural Affairs also erected a memorial sign to honor Hart at 2821 N. Pine Grove Ave., one of 20 houses so marked for Chicago movers and shakers who made "an important positive contribution" to the city. There is a major entry on Hart in *Women Building Chicago 1790–1990: A Biographical Dictionary* (2001), and most of Hart's papers are in the Chicago History Museum. ▼

KADDISH

The following is the last poem Val Taylor wrote for Pearl Hart.

March 22
I light yahrzeit candles,
dust your photograph
that watches over my bed
and remember your touch.

You are an institution now,
a library,
a scholarship for women lawyers.

As long as I breathe
you are a living woman
moving through my mind.

—*Valerie Taylor (1991)*

PEARL M. HART
70TH BIRTHDAY CELEBRATION
SATURDAY, APRIL 2 · BALLROOM · MIDLAND HOTEL

The invitation for Pearl M. Hart's 70th birthday celebration. Courtesy M. Kuda Archives, Oak Park, Ill.

THE LITTLE REVIEW

VOL. VI.   AUGUST, 1919   No. 4

CONTENTS

Poems	Jessie Dismorr
Interim (Chapter Three)	Dorothy Richardson
A Sentimental Scheme	Emanuel Carnevali
Advice to a Butter-Cup	Maxwell Bodenheim
God Bless the Bottle	John Rodker
Poems	Mark Turbyfill

Discussion:

Aldington's Images of Desire	Mary Butts
A Maker	William Carlos Williams
Notes	John Rodker
Pastoral	Louis Gilmore
Ulysses (Episode XI)	James Joyce

Subscription price, payable in advance, in the United States and Territories, $2.50 per year; Canada, $2.75; Foreign, $3.00. Published monthly, and copyrighted, 1919, by Margaret C. Anderson.
Manuscripts must be submitted at author's risk, with return postage.
Entered as second class matter March 16, 1917, at the Post Office at New York, N. Y., under the act of March 3, 1879.

MARGARET C. ANDERSON, Publisher

24 West Sixteenth Street, New York, N. Y.

Foreign Office: 43 Belsize Park, Gardens, London N. W. 3.

The August 1919 issue of The Little Review featured poems by gay dancer Mark Turbyfill. Courtesy M. Kuda Archives, Oak Park, Ill.

AN EARLY STONE WALL; NELLA LARSEN

In 1930, Chicago's Eyncourt Press published a pseudonymous autobiography by Mary Casal titled The Stone Wall, which detailed in a matter-of-fact way her life as a lesbian from the 1860s to 1930—from thinking she was the only one in the world who had feelings such as hers to the search for and discovery of Juno, her soul mate. Some activists have said that her book may have been the namesake of the Stonewall, the dyke dive in Greenwich Village that later became a bar for young transvestites and flamed into gay history with the 1969 Stonewall Riots.

Nella Larsen (1891–1964), a biracial woman born and raised in Chicago, became prominent in the Harlem Renaissance. Her novel Quicksand (1928), with early chapters set in Chicago, was widely praised. Margaret Busby, editor of the literary anthology Daughters of Africa (1992), hails her as a pioneer in writing about Black female sexuality, noting that Larsen's second novel, Passing (1929), not only dealt with "Blacks who 'pass' for white, but also [was] about sexual desire between women." The two women of the story are both from Chicago.

CHICAGO'S LITERARY RENAISSANCE   *by MARIE J. KUDA*

THE SO-CALLED CHICAGO LITERARY RENAISSANCE IS GENERALLY thought of as the years 1885–1920, when literary lions like Theodore Dreiser, Frank Norris and Upton Sinclair wrote realistic, gritty city novels. Architecture and journalism flourished, and little theaters and little magazines had sprung up everywhere.

A literary men's club patterned after The Players in New York was founded by Hamlin Garland and called The Cliff Dwellers because of its location on top of Orchestra Hall. Homosexual author Henry Blake Fuller had written a book titled The Cliff-Dwellers that referred to skyscraper living and was unrelated to the club. He preferred The Little Room, a mixed-gender literary club that met in the Fine Arts Building and included such members as author George Ade, sculptor Lorado Taft, sculptor and dancer Lou Wall Moore, social reformer Jane Addams and Poetry magazine's Harriet Monroe. Fuller's last novel, With the Procession, had a coded homosexual theme.

Another informal club of sorts formed in the bohemian area around the East 57th Street art colony that had once housed shops for the World's Fair. During 1905–06, creative lights who espoused sexual freedom met and partied there. Twenty-year-old Margaret Anderson (later founder of The Little Review), writer Floyd Dell, poet Vachel Lindsay, poet (later war correspondent) Eunice Tietjens and others were regularly on the roster.

Margaret Anderson is a unique presence in Chicago's literary history. She was vivacious and equally appealing to men and women, and her primary goal in life was never to be bored. In 1914 she founded The Little Review as a revolt against "culture" and its standards. Anderson saw her magazine as a crusade for "art that makes no compromise with public taste." When the magazine began to publish from Room 917 in the Fine Arts Building downtown, the response in the artistic community was immediate. Frank Lloyd Wright donated $100. Eunice Tietjens gave Anderson a diamond ring to sell and use for expenses. She couldn't retain advertisers because of the magazine's anarchist associations, so she took a cheaper studio downstairs, "room 834 on the Renaissance court where the fountains and the pianos tinkled all day."

In 1916 she met Jane Heap, a graduate of the School of the Art Institute: "Jane and I began talking. We talked for days, months, years." Heap joined the magazine and moved with it and Anderson to California, New York, and eventually Paris. They published Djuna Barnes, Gertrude Stein, Ernest Hemingway, and Ezra Pound; smuggled in sections of James Joyce's Ulysses; and had their magazine impounded and were tried for circulating obscene materials through the mails. When they found nothing suitably stimulating to grace their pages, they published a blank issue and hoped their subscribers would understand. The first of Anderson's three volumes of autobiography, My Thirty Years' War, deals in part with her Chicago years.

Memoirs of almost any man of the Chicago Literary Renaissance period, from journalist and playwright Ben Hecht to novelist Sherwood Anderson, have words of praise and fascination for this gutsy lesbian whose later lovers included soprano and author Georgette Leblanc and Enrico Caruso's widow, Dorothy. ▼

DRAG BALLS AND TEAROOMS

THE GAY AND LESBIAN COUNTERCULTURE thrived throughout the 1930s and up to the war years. Drag balls at the Coliseum had begun as far back as the days of the legendary 1st Ward Balls of the scandalous aldermen "Bathhouse" John Coughlin and Michael "Hinky Dink" Kenna. Levee district madams and all their charges stomped and sweated at command performances. By the 1930s there were two established gay balls, at New Year's and Halloween.

A report on a dance held by "The Goblins" at the Coliseum Annex on Oct. 30, 1932, noted 1,000 people in attendance, about 100 in feminine costume. The writer noted that 600 or 700 did not dance, 25 lesbians were present as were "15 colored, 10 [in] drag costume, one in Turkish," and most participants were over the age of 25. When Chicago gay liberation groups held their post-Stonewall celebration dance at the Coliseum in 1970, many didn't realize the 2,000 participants were merely following a long-established tradition.

A University of Chicago observer reported on a visit to the Bally Hoo Cafe at 1942 N. Halsted St. on Sept. 24, 1933. He noted "100 queer people in the cafe." Again 25 is given as the number of lesbians present—whether that included the "hostess dressed in masculine attire" who, with the emcee, was billed as "Mack and Marge," the writer didn't say. Along with laughter and falsetto voices, there was dancing and lots of drinking: "Beer was served at 15 cents the glass, no cover charge." The lesbians at the next table apparently were a little more flush as they "had a large bottle of gin."

One lesbian told him "queer people dislike jam people." Studs Terkel, who had a gay roommate at one time, was called "jam"; he explained that this meant "straight," but did not necessarily have a negative connotation.

Other reports of the period note that Henrici's Restaurant attracted "high-class-type" queers and a few musicians, but all types could be found at La Masque at East Delaware Place and North Rush Street. The poorer classes hung around Bughouse Square (officially, Washington Square Park, adjacent to the Newberry Library). Jack's Turkish Baths, at 829 N. Dearborn St., and the Oak Street Beach along the Gold Coast were good for cruising. The tearoom trade were said to frequent restrooms at Berghoff's Grill, the LaSalle Street Station and the Illinois Central stations at East Randolph and at East Van Buren streets. Sally's Shoppe was another popular bar for "high-class queers." One odd entry is Madam Black's Spiritualist, at 5519 S. Drexel Blvd.: "A place for queer[s] to go and carry on quite gay."

Two excellent essays on the early years of Chicago's gay movement can be found in *Creating a Place for Ourselves: Lesbian, Gay, and Bisexual Community Histories* (Routledge, 1997), edited by Brett Beemyn. David K. Johnson writes about "The Kids of Fairytown" in his chapter about gay male culture on Chicago's Near North Side in the 1930s. In "Before Paris Burned," Allen Drexel writes about race, class, and male homosexuality on the South Side from 1936 to 1960.

"It is unclear precisely when the first drag balls took place in Chicago or who sponsored them," Drexel writes. "But like those in New York and other major cities, the balls in Chicago by 1930 had begun attracting considerable public attention and crowds of several hundred attendees. ... The first Chicago balls, like those in subsequent years, were racially integrated. ... Chicago's balls during the thirties and forties generally took place in rented rooms or halls adjoining taverns or clubs on the city's predominantly black, poor South Side, or at the Coliseum Annex, a large convention hall located in a commercial district on the Near South Side. ... The first Finnie's Ball, staged in 1935 by a black gay street hustler and gambler named Alfred Finnie, was held in the basement of a tavern on the corner of 38th Street and Michigan Avenue. ... Until 1943—the year that Finnie was killed in a gambling brawl—the ball was held up to five times annually at a number of different venues. ... [N]ews accounts of Finnie's Balls typically drew attention to the most 'extravagant' aspects of the events.

In the 1920s and '30s, white gays were welcome at some of Bronzeville's "Black-and-tan" clubs. Prohibition and the influx of jazz musicians tossed Black and white gays together in the speak-easies, jazz clubs and ballrooms. Ma Rainey and Bix Beiderbecke were gay artists. A fictional film version of Beiderbecke's life, Young Man With a Horn, portrayed his love interest (Lauren Bacall) as a lesbian. Photo courtesy of the Chicago History Museum.

Ebony's story on the 1953 ball, for example, reported that 'More than 1,500 spectators milled around outside Chicago's Pershing Ballroom to get a glimpse of the bejeweled impersonators who arrived in limousines, taxis, Fords, and even by streetcar.' ... In The Chicago Defender's extensive coverage of the 1955 ball, for example, John Earl Lewis, the honorary 'Mayor of Bronzeville,' was depicted on stage flanked by 'the finery bedecked winners' of that year's extravaganza," Drexel writes. ▼

TONY JACKSON: MUSIC LEGEND

by TIM SAMUELSON

DURING HIS BRIEF LIFETIME OF 44 YEARS, Tony Jackson (1876–1921) was a musical bridge between the multicultural sounds of his native New Orleans and the emerging syncopated music of his adopted Chicago home—both important precursors of modern jazz. Jackson was widely respected in both cities as an engaging performer, a prolific composer and a mentor to emerging younger musicians. Although no recordings were ever made to document Jackson's unique style of singing and piano playing, his most enduring musical legacy was creating the familiar chorus of the 1916 hit song "Pretty Baby."

Born in New Orleans in 1876, Tony Jackson gained much of his musical education by observing the entertainers at the saloons, gambling houses and brothels in the city's notorious Storyville district. He began playing piano in honky-tonks while in his early teens and was considered one of the top entertainers of New Orleans by the time he was 18. With an outgoing personality, an animated way of singing and a mastery of New Orleans-style piano, Jackson had the ability to perform instantly any song or type of music requested by the customers—from ragtime to the classics.

Despite his growing popularity as a musician and entertainer, Jackson found life as a gay male in New Orleans to be a challenging experience. Seeking a more receptive home for his music and sexuality, he relocated to Chicago in about 1908. Here he gained steady employment in the theaters and cafes of the South Side's African-American entertainment district centered along South State Street—popularly known as "The Stroll." In Chicago as well as New Orleans, younger musicians gravitated to Jackson's performance style and musicianship. Among those he inspired and mentored were jazz pioneers Ferdinand

Left: Tony Jackson at the piano. From the William Russell Jazz Collection, courtesy of the Historic New Orleans Collection, accession no. 92-48-L, mss 520.

Top: Tony Jackson (standing, left) and a friend. From the William Russell Jazz Collection, courtesy of the Historic New Orleans Collection, accession no. 92-48-L, mss 520. Center: Tony Jackson's song "Pretty Baby."

"Jelly Roll" Morton and prolific composer and bandleader Clarence Williams.

New Orleans jazz historian Al Rose claimed that the familiar imagery of early-1900s saloon pianists (flashily dressed with arm garters, checkered vests and pearl-gray derbies) was directly inspired by the way Tony Jackson dressed when performing. While many musicians were frustrated that they couldn't match Jackson's performance talents, they did their best to imitate his style of clothing—which has since become the stereotypical manner of dress for depicting saloon pianists in movies, plays and popular culture.

Tony Jackson left a small legacy of published songs but retained the majority of his personal compositions for his own performances, and they are now lost. According to popular legend, the original lyrics for Jackson's 1916 hit song "Pretty Baby" were written for a gay companion, but no evidence of this early version is known to survive. The words and musical verse of "Pretty Baby" as commercially published were reworked by songwriters Gus Kahn and Egbert Van Alstyne, but the signature chorus remained true to Jackson's original melody. Tragically, Jackson sold his rights to this popular hit for a reported sum of $45. ▼

VALENTINO VISITS

Rudolph Valentino, smoldering sex god of the silent screen and early talkies, created the image of the virile "sheik" who carried swooning women off to his desert tent. A personal appearance in Chicago in 1926, however, prompted a scathing editorial in the Chicago Tribune laying the blame for the effeminization of a generation of young men on Valentino's pomaded hair, masculine cosmetics and slave bracelets. The writer alluded to Chicago's "powder puffs." Kenneth Anger in Hollywood Babylon reports that "Rudy hardly thought it sporting he should be blamed for the mannerisms of a bunch of young Clark Street faggots, and furiously challenged the Tribune hatchet man to a duel."

Valentino also had the dubious distinction of being married to two lesbians at once (the divorce from the first was not finalized before he married the second). His marriages to both Jean Acker and Natacha Rambova were said to have been stage-managed by legendary actress-writer-director Alla Nazimova, whose all-gay adaptation of Salomé seems to have been forgotten.

A further Chicago connection: Valentino gave actor Ramon Novarro (star of the silent version of Ben-Hur) an art-deco lead phallus, said to be a model of Rudy's own. Some have claimed that when Novarro was murdered in Hollywood in 1968 by two hustler brothers from Chicago, Paul and Tom Ferguson, that dildo was jammed down his throat. — *Marie J. Kuda*

HENRY GERBER: GAY PIONEER   *by JONATHAN NED KATZ*

From Jonathan Ned Katz's Gay American History: Lesbians and Gay Men in the U.S.A.: A Documentary History, revised edition, 1992.
Copyright © 1992 Jonathan Ned Katz. Reprinted with permission.

The Chicago Society for Human Rights:
"To combat the public prejudices"

On December 10, 1924, the state of Illinois issued a charter to a nonprofit corporation named the Society for Human Rights, located in Chicago. This society is the earliest documented homosexual emancipation organization in the United States, as is evidenced by the group's charter, unearthed in the research for this article.

According to this charter, the object of the society's formation is

to promote and to protect the interests of people who by reasons of mental and physical abnormalities are abused and hindered in the legal pursuit of happiness which is guaranteed them by the Declaration of Independence, and to combat the public prejudices against them by dissemination of facts according to modern science among intellectuals of mature age. The Society stands only for law and order; it is in harmony with any and all general laws insofar as they protect the rights of others, and does in no manner recommend any acts in violation of present laws nor advocate any matter inimical to the public welfare.

The management of the society is vested in a board of seven, listed in the charter as:

Rev. John T. Graves, President
Al Meininger, Vice-President
Henry Gerber, Secretary
Ellsworth Booher, Treasurer
Fred Panngburn, Trustee
John Sather, Trustee
Henry Teacutter, Trustee

The charter is signed by Rev. John T. Graves, Al Meininger, and Henry Gerber.[1]

In 1953, twenty-nine years after the society's founding, a short, anonymous letter from Henry Gerber, published in ONE, the then new homosexual emancipation monthly magazine, briefly described the fate of the early organization.[2]

In 1962, ONE published a more detailed account of the historic Chicago society, written by Henry Gerber, this time under his own name:

Just 37 years ago, in 1925, a few of my friends and myself were dragged off to jail in Chicago causing our own efforts to ameliorate the plight of homosexuals to come to an early end.

From 1920 to 1923, I had served with the Army of Occupation in Germany after World War I. In Coblenz on the Rhine I had subscribed to German homophile magazines and made several trips to Berlin. ... I had always bitterly felt the injustice with which my own American society accused the homosexual of "immoral acts." I hated this society which allowed the majority, frequently corrupt itself, to persecute those who deviated from the established norms in sexual matters.

What could be done about it, I thought. Unlike Germany, where the homosexual was partially organized and where sex legislation was uniform for the whole country, the United States was in a condition of chaos and misunderstanding concerning its sex laws, and no one was trying to unravel the tangle and bring relief to the abused. ...

I realized at once that homosexuals themselves needed nearly as much attention as the laws pertaining to their acts. How could one go about such a difficult task [that of homosexual emancipation]? The prospect of going to jail did not bother me. I had a vague idea that I wanted to help solve the problem. I had not yet read the opinion of Clarence Darrow that "no other offence has ever been visited with such severe penalties as seeking to help the oppressed." All my friends to whom I spoke about my plans advised against my doing anything so rash and futile. I thought to myself that if I succeeded I might become known to history as deliverer of the downtrodden, even as Lincoln. But I am not sure my thoughts were entirely upon fame. If I succeeded in freeing the homosexual, I too would benefit.

What was needed was a Society, I concluded. My boss, whom I had pleased by translating a work of philosophy from the German, helped me write a Declaration of Purpose for our new Society for Human Rights, the same name used by the homosexuals of Germany for their work.[3] The first difficulty was in rounding up enough members and contributors so the work could go forward. The average homosexual, I found, was ignorant concerning himself. Others were fearful. Still others were frantic or depraved. Some were blasé.

Many homosexuals told me that their search for forbidden fruit was the real spice of life. With this argument they rejected our aims. We wondered how we could accomplish anything with such resistance from our own people.

The outline of our plan was as follows:

1. We would cause the homosexuals to join our Society and gradually reach as large a number as possible.

2. We would engage in a series of lectures pointing out the attitude of

Opposite: Henry Gerber. Courtesy M. Kuda Archives, Oak Park, Ill.

33

society in relation to their own behavior and especially urging against the seduction of adolescents.

3. Through a publication named Friendship and Freedom we would keep the homophile world in touch with the progress of our efforts. The publication was to refrain from advocating sexual acts and would serve merely as a forum for discussion.[4]

4. Through self-discipline, homophiles would win the confidence and assistance of legal authorities and legislators in understanding the problem; that these authorities should be educated on the futility and folly of long prison terms for those committing homosexual acts, etc.

The beginning of all movements is necessarily small. I was able to gather together a half dozen of my friends and the Society for Human Rights became an actuality. Through a lawyer our program was submitted to the Secretary of State at Springfield, and we were furnished with a State Charter. No one seemed to have bothered to investigate our purpose.

As secretary of the new organization I wrote to many prominent persons soliciting their support. Most of them failed to understand our purpose. The big, fatal, fearful obstacle seemed always to be the almost willful misunderstanding and ignorance on the part of the general public concerning the nature of homosexuality. What people generally thought about when I mentioned the word had nothing to do with reality. …

Nevertheless, we made a good start, even though at my own expense, and the first step was under way. The State Charter had only cost $10.00. I then set about putting out the first issue of Friendship and Freedom and worked hard on the second issue. It soon became apparent that my friends were illiterate and penniless. I had to both write and finance. Two issues, alas, were all we could publish. The most difficult task was to get men of good reputation to back up the Society. I needed noted medical authorities to endorse us. But they usually refused to endanger their reputations.

The only support I got was from poor people: John, a preacher who earned his room and board by preaching brotherly love to small groups of Negroes; Al, an indigent laundry queen; and Ralph, whose job with the railroad was in jeopardy when his nature became known. These were the national officers of the Society for Human Rights, Inc. I realized this start was dead wrong, but after all, movements always start

A copy of Friendship and Freedom, the "paper" published by the Chicago Society for Human Rights, appears prominently in this photo of a collection of early, mostly German, homosexual emancipation periodicals, verifying both the existence of the American periodical and suggesting the authenticity of Gerber's account. No copies of Friendship and Freedom are now known to be extant.[6]

small and only by organizing first and correcting mistakes later could we expect to go on at all. The Society was bound to become a success, we felt, considering the modest but honest plan of operation. It would probably take long years to develop into anything worth while. Yet I was will[ing] to slave and suffer and risk losing my job and savings and even my liberty for the ideal.

One of our greatest handicaps was the knowledge that homosexuals don't organize. Being thoroughly cowed, they seldom get together. Most feel that as long as some homosexual sex acts are against the law, they should not let their names be on any homosexual organization's mailing list any more than notorious bandits would join a thieves' union. Today [1962] there are at least a half dozen homophile organizations working openly for the group, but still the number of dues-paying members is very small when we know that there are several million homosexuals in the U.S.

The Society, says Gerber, "decided to concentrate our efforts on the State of Illinois," and to focus on reform of those laws criminalizing homosexual acts.

We had agreed to make our organization a purely homophile Society, and we had argued and decided to exclude the much larger circle of bisexuals for the time being. Neither I nor John, our elected president, had been conscious of the fact that our vice-president, Al, was that type. In fact, we later found out that he had a wife and two small children. …

One Sunday morning about 2 a.m., I returned from a visit downtown. After I had gone to my room, someone knocked at the door. Thinking it might be the landlady, I opened up. Two men entered the room. They identified themselves as a city detective and a newspaper reporter from the Examiner. The detective asked me where the boy was. What boy? He told me he had orders from his precinct captain to bring me to the police station. He took my typewriter, my notary public diploma, and all the literature of the Society and also personal diaries as well as my bookkeeping accounts. At no time did he show a warrant for my arrest. At the police station I was locked up in a cell but no charges were made against me. In the morning I was given permission to call my boss who, for my work's sake, fixed my status as "absent on leave."

With a few other persons, unknown to me, I was taken to the Chicago Avenue Police Court where I also found John the preacher and Al the laundry queen and a young man who happened to be in Al's room at the time of arrest. No one knew what had happened. A friendly cop at the station showed me a copy of the Examiner. There right on the front page I found this incredible story:

STRANGE SEX CULT EXPOSED[5]

The article mentioned Al who had brought his male friends home and had, in full view of his wife and children, practiced "strange sex acts" with them. Al's wife had at last called a social worker who reported these "strange doings" to the police. A raid of the flat, the report continued, had turned up John, a preacher, and Henry, a postal employee, and all were put under arrest. Among the effects in Al's flat they found a pamphlet of this "strange sex cult" which "urged men to leave their wives and children."

What an outright untruth; what a perversion of facts! John was alone in his room when arrested, and I was too. We were not with Al; nor did we know of his being married and having children.

There had been no warrants obtained for our arrests. The police, I suppose, had hoped or expected to find us in bed. They could not imagine homosexuals in any other way. My property was taken without excuse. This, in the United States *anno domini* 1925 with the Constitution to protect the people from unreasonable arrest and search. Shades of the Holy Inquisition.

So, that was it! Al had confessed his sins but assured us that the reports of the detective and reporter were distorted. On Monday, the day after our arrest, in the Chicago Avenue Police Court, the detective triumphantly produced a powder puff which he claimed he found in my room. That was the sole evidence of my crime. It was admitted as evidence of my effeminacy. I have never in my life used rouge or powder. The young social worker, a hatchet-faced female, read from my diary, out of context: "I love Karl." The detective and the judge shuddered over

such depravity. To the already prejudiced court we were obviously guilty. We were guilty just by being homosexual. This was the court's conception of our "strange cult."

The judge spoke little to us and adjourned court with the remark he thought ours was a violation of the Federal law against sending obscene matter through the mails. Nothing in our first issue of Friendship and Freedom could be considered "obscene" of course.

At this first trial the court dismissed us to the Cook County Jail. Our second trial was to be on Thursday. They separated John from Al and me. In our cell Al broke out crying and felt deeply crushed for having gotten us into the mess. George, who had been arrested with Al, did not lose any time while a guest of the Chicago police. Among the prisoners was a young Jew who asked me if I wanted a lawyer. He recommended a friend of his, a "shyster" lawyer who practiced around criminal courts. I made a request to see him and he appeared the next morning. He seemed to be a smart fellow who probably knew how to fix the State Attorney and judges. He had the reputation of making a good living taking doubtful cases. He also handled the bail bond racket and probably made additional money each month from this shady practice.

The lawyer told me at once that our situation looked serious. But he said he could get me out on bail. He would charge $200.00 for each trial. I accepted his services, although I know that it would have been cheaper to merely accept the maximum fine of $200.00.

We were in a tough spot. … The following Thursday the four of us were taken before the same judge. This time two post office inspectors were also present. Before the judge appeared in court, one of the inspectors promised that he would see to it that we got heavy prison sentences for infecting God's own country.

As the trial began, our attorney demanded that we be set free since no stitch of evidence existed to hold us. The judge became angry and ordered our attorney to shut up or be cited for contempt. The post office inspectors said that the federal commis-

sioner would take the case under advisement from the obscenity angle. The second trial was then adjourned until Monday. The lawyer made one last request that we be released on bail. The judge hemmed and hawed but set bail at $1,000.00 for each of us. The lawyer made all the arrangements and collected his fees.

Being a free man once more, I went down to the post office to report for work. But I was told that I had been suspended—more of the dirty work of the post office inspectors. Next I called upon the managing editor of the Examiner. I confronted him with the article in the paper. He told me he would look into the matter and make corrections, but nothing was ever done. I had no means to sue the paper, and that was the end of that.

Meanwhile a friend of mine succeeded in getting me a better lawyer—the one who had made our request for a charter. He agreed to take my case, also for $200.00 a trial. Calling the shyster, I told him of my inability to pay for another trial. …

… I knew before hand that our case would be dismissed since my new lawyer advised me that everything had been "arranged" satisfactorily.

The day of the third trial we met a new judge. The detective who had made the arrests was there, the prosecuting attorney, the two post office inspectors, and even my first lawyer who found he had become interested in the case. The judge, who had reviewed our earlier trials, immediately reprimanded the prosecution. He said "It is an outrage to arrest persons without a warrant. I order the case dismissed." Al who had pleaded guilty to disorderly conduct received a fine of $10.00 and costs. The social worker was not present at this trial. Our lawyer told the judge in the presence of the baffled post office inspectors that he knew for sure that the Commissioner would take no action as far as the alleged obscenity of mailed literature was concerned. The judge also ordered the detective to return my property to me. I got my typewriter, but my diaries had been turned over to the postal inspectors and I never saw them again. I had never put down in my diaries anything that could be used against me, fortunately. …

… The experience generally convinced me that

we were up against a solid wall of ignorance, hypocrisy, meanness and corruption. The wall had won. The parting jibe of the detective had been, "What was the idea of the Society for Human Rights anyway? Was it to give you birds the legal right to rape every boy on the street?"…

The lawyer advised me he could get my post office job back. But I had no more money for fees and took no action. After a few weeks a letter from Washington arrived advising me that I had been officially dismissed from the Post Office Department for "conduct unbecoming a postal worker." That definitely meant the end of the Society for Human Rights.[7]

In June 1932, a periodical titled The Modern Thinker published an essay, "In Defense of Homosexuality," by "Parisex," a pen name of Henry Gerber. An introduction to the essay explains that it "is one of the numerous replies" attacking "The Riddle of Homosexuality" by W. Beran Wolfe, M.D., which had appeared in the April issue.[8]

In his rejoinder, Gerber congratulates Dr. Wolfe for urging that laws against homosexuality be struck down, but notes that oppression by church and state are historical antecedents to the more insidious persecution by modern psychoanalysts. He charges psychoanalysts with constructing a new set of myths and taboos which rival the Sodom legend in their pernicious effects on homosexuals. He challenges the categorization of homosexuality as a neurotic symptom, and the popular notion of a "cure." Gerber rejects Wolfe's attribution of insecurity, antisocial behavior, and criminal tendencies to homosexuals. He argues that those homosexuals who are disturbed have been made so by societal oppression.

Wolfe is attacked for relying upon the concepts of Freud, Jung, and Adler; in rebuttal, Gerber approvingly cites Havelock Ellis and Magnus Hirschfeld. This leads Gerber to discuss the "nature versus nurture" debate on the origins of homosexuality. Gerber refuses to align himself with either position, conceding that both inborn and social reasons may influence sexual object choice.

Gerber further objects to Wolfe's single-minded focus upon sexual acts, and suggests that psychology should deal equally with purely affectional ties between members of the same gender. He argues that the institution of marriage, and even monogamy, is disintegrating under the impact of modern conditions, and, citing Edward Carpenter, Gerber envisions a future society which will fully accept the unique contributions of its homosexual members.

Gerber concludes:

After all, it is highly futile for Dr. Wolfe to worry about neurotic homosexuals when the world itself, led and ruled by the strong heterosexual "normal" men is in such chaotic condition, and knows not where to turn.

It is quite possible that if called upon, the homosexuals of this country would put up the money to send Dr. Wolfe to Washington to examine these great big "normal" men, who guide the destinies of millions, to find their "neurosis" and to cure it.[9]

In 1934, Gerber is listed as circulation manager of a mimeographed literary magazine entitled Chanticleer, and twelve articles by him are included under his own name. Three are devoted entirely to homosexuality, the others contain passing references.[10]

The February 1934 issue of Chanticleer includes Gerber's review of "Recent Homosexual Literature," and his critical comments on the novels The Well of Loneliness, Twilight Men, and Strange Brother as "anti-homosexual propaganda." Gerber's introduction accuses a coalition of capitalists, clerics, and politicians of defending monogamy and suppressing sexual freedom of all kinds:

The 100% patriots are vociferously proclaiming that this is a Free Country; however, when asked if Love is free, or if they are for Free Love, they conveniently avoid the issue by retreating with sundry maledictions and such epithets as "Bolshevic, Libertine, Swine." In my last article, in the initial

issue of "Chanticleer", I pointed out that politicians and priests clamor for bigger and better morons. They are in fact responsible for sex suppression in America. Capitalism, loyally supported by the churches, has established a Public Policy that the Sacred Institution of Monogamy must be enforced; and such a fiat is the deathknell to all sexual freedom. Monogamy is the ideal of this state and all deviations from this ideal are strictly suppressed, including free love in all of its forms, birth control, and homosexuality. For these forms of sexual freedom, if free to practice, would defeat the sacred institution of monogamy. In Russia, where the government is no longer capitalistic and is not bound to religious sex superstitions, sex is free. One may gratify one's sexual appetite as one may see fit, just as one may choose what to eat for supper. Sex only becomes a social concern there when children are born, in which case both parents are held mutually responsible.

Homosexuality has until recently been strictly taboo and no "decent" author or publisher considered it fit to mention in print. However, in the last decade, several medical works have appeared about homosexuality and recently a few books of homosexual fiction have dared to show themselves among the flood of heterosexual books.

Gerber disposes of The Well Of Loneliness (he is quoted in the following history), and then goes on:

TWILIGHT MEN, by Andre Tellier, deals with a young Frenchman, who comes to America, is introduced into homosexual society in New York, becomes a drug addict for no obvious reason, finally kills his father and commits suicide. It is again excellent anti-homosexual propaganda, although the plot is too silly to convince anyone who has known homosexual people at all.

STRANGE BROTHER, by Blair Niles, is the story of a sensitive young man. The author causes him to go through as many mental sufferings as she can, then puts a pistol in his hand and lets him shoot himself and end the book. Again an ideal anti-homosexual propaganda, but no more logical than the book mentioned before.[11]

The September 1934 Chanticleer contains Gerber's comments on "Hitlerism and Homosexuality," in which he discusses the reaction to the then-recent murders by Hitler of Ernst Roehm, SA chief, and other SA officers, June 29 to July 1, 1934. In this essay, Gerber mistakenly credits Roehm with leading a group in opposition to Hitler's tyranny.

Gerber writes, in part:

A few weeks ago Herr Adolf Hitler in part justified the bloody murder of his intimate friends with the accusation that his Chief of Staff of Nazi storm troops and his clique had been guilty of the most revolting (to normal healthy people) sexual aberrations. It seems strange that Hitler should have found that out so late. After having been intimately associated with Roehm all his life, he must have been well acquainted with Roehm's inclinations. But such a little slip of memory does not bother the great corporal.

A short time ago an American journalist pointed out in the liberal "Nation" that the whole Hitler movement was based on the homosexual Greek attachments of men for each other, and the same Jewish author stated that it was another of the Hitler contradictions that the "Leader" should have acquiesced in the burning of the books of Dr. Magnus Hirschfeld, who had dedicated his life to the liberation of the enslaved homosexuals in all lands. Thus we get a glimpse of the insanity of the whole movement: A Jewish doctor working for the interests of homosexuals is persecuted by a heterosexual mob, led by homosexuals.

Of course, our American journalists who reap large profits from the publication of all the filthy details of heterosexual and homosexual perverts, especially among the "Pillars of Society" in Hollywood and New York alike, managed to get one of their reporters into the bedroom of Herr Roehm just before Hitler arrived to call his erstwhile bosom friend to face the muzzle of his own gun, and even

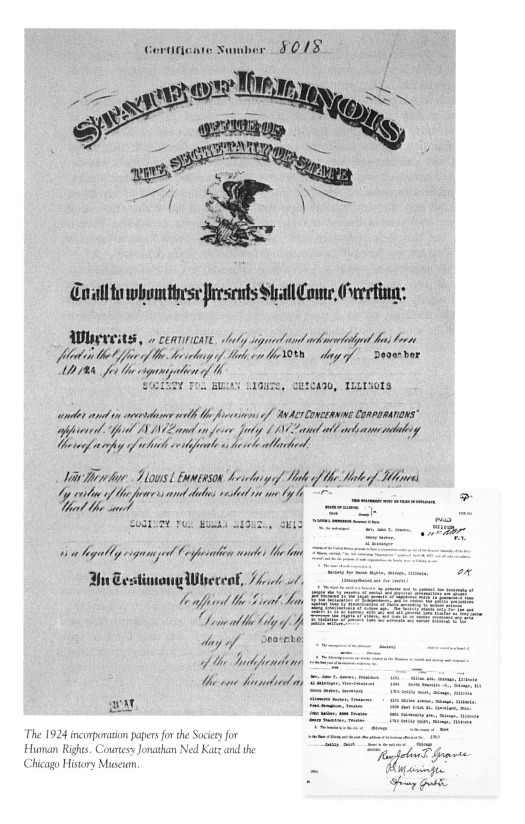

The 1924 incorporation papers for the Society for Human Rights. Courtesy Jonathan Ned Katz and the Chicago History Museum.

such a conservative and "decent" paper as the New York Times (I was told) reported that while no evidence could be found in Roehm's boudoir, his chief of police was found in bed with a fair young man. The newspapers of America were strangely compromised by this Hitler story. Should they praise the murderer Hitler for suppressing homosexuals, or should they give credit to Roehm and his homosexual camorra [society] for being the only men in Germany virile enough to attempt to wipe out the unspeakable Hitler? The newspapers condemned both and saved their faces.

Changing the subject, Gerber discusses the legal oppression of homosexuals.

Have you ever honestly asked yourself why homosexuals should be persecuted or punished by law? Of course, you know that in France, Spain, Belgium, Russia, Czecho-Slovakia, Mexico, South America, and even in our own Philippine Islands, homosexuals are not persecuted or punished unless they commit anti-social acts. …

… Wonder no one thought of blaming our depression on homosexuality. If Hoover had only thought of it, he would have been reelected, for when it comes to persecute homosexuals, no lies and defamations are too stupid not to be believed. …

No one has yet brought forth a plausible reason why homosexuals should be wiped out, except the age-old reasoning which is also applied to atheism and communism, that it is contrary to the welfare of the state (the profit and exploitation system of the capitalists). That is the real and only reason, and the churches have conveniently joined the chorus and labeled homosexuals "unnatural," "abnormal," and what not. With the waning of capitalism and organized religion, the opposition of the govern-

ments to homosexuals will also wane, as has been seen by the example of Russia and Czecho-Slovakia. You cannot, therefore blame homosexuals, if they throw in their support with the communists and atheists.

As a matter of fact, when the German Reichstag Committee, chosen to revise the German Penal Code, voted, the socialists and communists outvoted

Gerber's 1710 N. Crilly Ct. address, which the city of Chicago has recognized with a plaque. Photo courtesy the Chicago History Museum.

the nationalist and clerical party, and brought about the repeal of the notorious paragraph 175 which punished homosexuals for their acts (but not female homosexuals), in 1927 [1929 is correct].

Roehm and his valiant men have been defeated, but the homosexuals will go on fighting to rid the world of tyranny.[12]

The December 1934 Chanticleer includes Gerber's "More Nonsense About Homosexuals," a review of the book Strange Loves by La Forest Potter, M.D.

… I think the history of psychology is … damning evidence of man's credulity and outright stupidity. The volume under review by Dr. La Forest Potter, who boasts of being a "late member of the New York County Medical Society, Massachusetts Medical Society," etc, etc. … proves to me two significant facts: 1) that the medical authorities in America, of which Dr. Potter is a shining example, are about 100 years behind the times, and 2) that most psychologists in this country are mere yesmen who blindly and obediently follow the current authorized moral code without any regard to common sense or the results of modern scientific research. …

While the title of the book would indicate that the author had in view all phenomena of sex which seem strange to him and to the ignorant public alike, Dr. Potter deals mainly with homosexuality. … such a title is a profitable device for the sale of books, for the morons are always looking for something new and "strange" in sex matters. In other words, the book of Dr. Potter is just another instance of the morbid sex racket, a lurid description of sex abnormalities under the moral guise of condemnation of the queer sinners dealing in such "strange" loves in order to get the filthy details by the post office censors of "obscene" literature. Krafft-Ebing was perhaps the first author to start this racket and the volume in review is evidence of the sad fact that the end of it is not yet.

In the accepted fashion of Krafft-Ebing's potboiler, Dr. Potter goes through the various artificial classification of homosexuals. He has Chapters on the Riddle of Homosexuality, … a chapter on the history of … the various unsuccessful attempts of "scientists" to solve the "riddle," … special chapters on Lesbians (female homosexuals), in which the author makes the sensational statement that "there isn't a man on earth who has a Chinaman's chance against a Lesbian, once she has thoroughly seduced a woman to her wiles" (any doctor having knowledge of gynecology ought to know the reason to be due to the fact that males are very deficient in the fine art of satisfying a woman's sexual needs), [etc.]. ...

... Dr. Potter views the psychoanalytical method of dealing with homosexuals and cites cases in which homosexuals have been "cured" by psychoanalysts. ...

But the author does evidently not think so much of this "cure" of homosexuals, for he cautiously warns that homosexuals can be cured only if they want to be cured. The only way to cure a [male] homosexual of his foible is to make him love women, a very simple process indeed, but Dr. Potter does not seem to realize that heterosexual men can be cured exactly in the same fashion from their love for women, by getting them to like men. By the same method, Pop-eye the sailor cures children who do not like spinach by making them believe that spinach is really good for them and that every normal citizen must eat it.[13] ▼

FOOTNOTES, AS LABELED.

1. Society for Human Rights, Inc., Chicago, charter signed Dec. 10, 1924; certificate no. 8018, State of Illinois, Office of the Secretary of State, Commercial Department, Springfield, Ill. I wish to thank Jim Kepner for information which led to the discovery of this document, for identifying Gerber as the author of the following letter, and for providing other information about Gerber from the Gerber letters and documents in his possession.

2. [Henry Gerber,] letter signed G.S., Washington D.C., ONE (Los Angeles), vol. 1, no. 7 (July 1953), p. 22.

3. The group to which Gerber refers was the Bund für Menschenrecht (The Society for Human Rights), founded in 1919 by Hans Kahnert. The Bund was the largest of the Gay groups in Germany during the 1920s, one that aimed at being a "mass" organization, and it criticized Hirschfeld's scientistic approach. The Bund seems to be the particular homosexual emancipation group with which Gerber identified. Three recently discovered articles, bylined "Henry

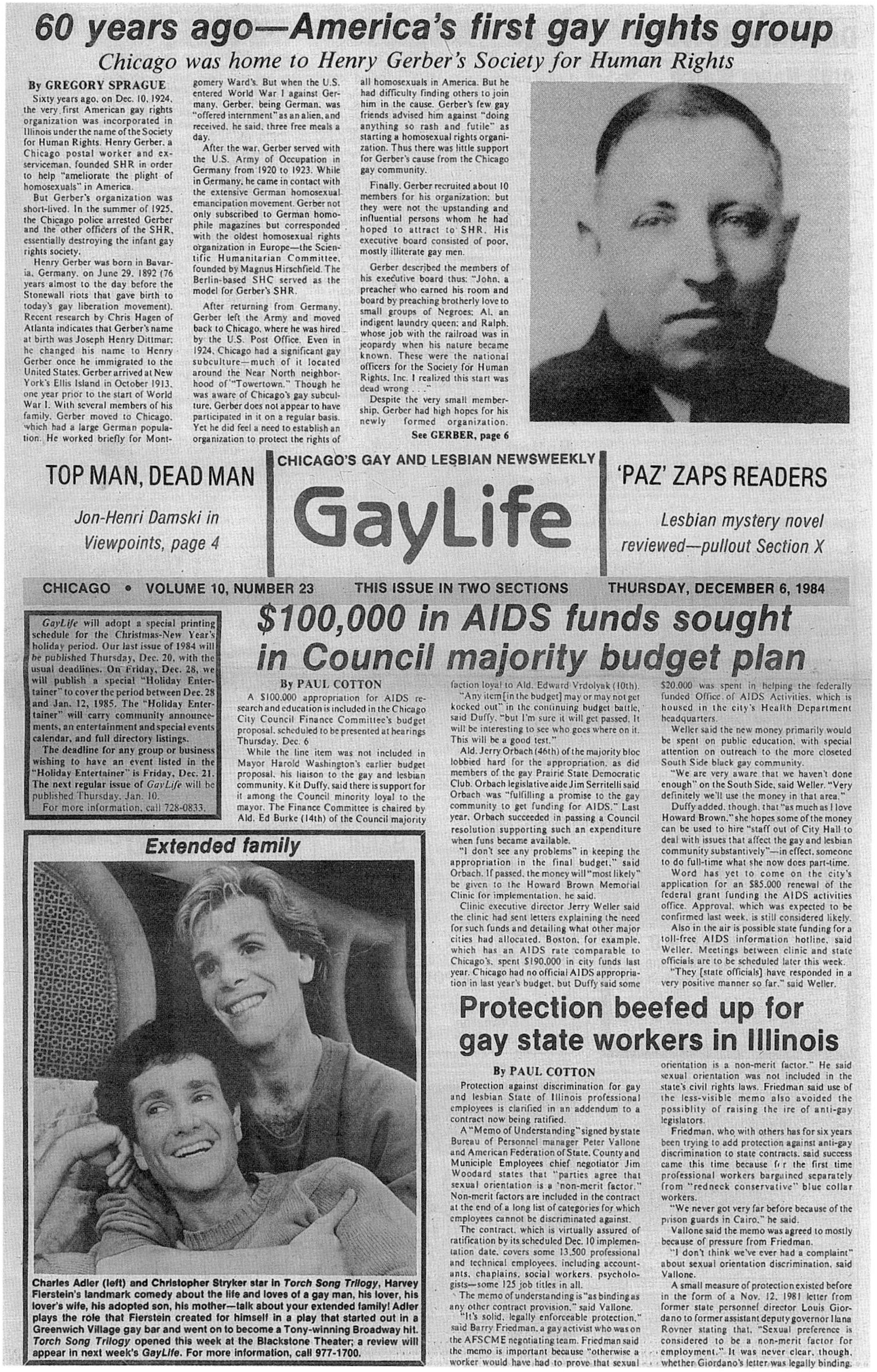

60 years ago—America's first gay rights group

Chicago was home to Henry Gerber's Society for Human Rights

By GREGORY SPRAGUE

Sixty years ago, on Dec. 10, 1924, the very first American gay rights organization was incorporated in Illinois under the name of the Society for Human Rights. Henry Gerber, a Chicago postal worker and ex-serviceman, founded SHR in order to help "ameliorate the plight of homosexuals" in America.

But Gerber's organization was short-lived. In the summer of 1925, the Chicago police arrested Gerber and the other officers of the SHR, essentially destroying the infant gay rights society.

Henry Gerber was born in Bavaria, Germany, on June 29, 1892 (76 years almost to the day before the Stonewall riots that gave birth to today's gay liberation movement). Recent research by Chris Hagen of Atlanta indicates that Gerber's name at birth was Joseph Henry Dittmar; he changed his name to Henry Gerber once he immigrated to the United States. Gerber arrived at New York's Ellis Island in October 1913, one year prior to the start of World War I. With several members of his family, Gerber moved to Chicago, which had a large German population. He worked briefly for Montgomery Ward's. But when the U.S. entered World War I against Germany, Gerber, being German, was "offered internment" as an alien, and received, he said, three free meals a day.

After the war, Gerber served with the U.S. Army of Occupation in Germany from 1920 to 1923. While in Germany, he came in contact with the extensive German homosexual emancipation movement. Gerber not only subscribed to German homophile magazines but corresponded with the oldest homosexual rights organization in Europe—the Scientific Humanitarian Committee, founded by Magnus Hirschfield. The Berlin-based SHC served as the model for Gerber's SHR.

After returning from Germany, Gerber left the Army and moved back to Chicago, where he was hired by the U.S. Post Office. Even in 1924, Chicago had a significant gay subculture—much of it located around the Near North neighborhood of "Towertown." Though he was aware of Chicago's gay subculture, Gerber does not appear to have participated in it on a regular basis. Yet he did feel a need to establish an organization to protect the rights of all homosexuals in America. But he had difficulty finding others to join him in the cause. Gerber's few gay friends advised him against "doing anything so rash and futile" as starting a homosexual rights organization. Thus there was little support for Gerber's cause from the Chicago gay community.

Finally, Gerber recruited about 10 members for his organization; but they were not the upstanding and influential persons whom he had hoped to attract to SHR. His executive board consisted of poor, mostly illiterate gay men.

Gerber described the members of his executive board thus: "John, a preacher who earned his room and board by preaching brotherly love to small groups of Negroes; Al, an indigent laundry queen; and Ralph, whose job with the railroad was in jeopardy when his nature became known. These were the national officers for the Society for Human Rights, Inc. I realized this start was dead wrong . . ."

Despite the very small membership, Gerber had high hopes for his newly formed organization.

See GERBER, page 6

TOP MAN, DEAD MAN

Jon-Henri Damski in Viewpoints, page 4

CHICAGO'S GAY AND LESBIAN NEWSWEEKLY

GayLife

'PAZ' ZAPS READERS

Lesbian mystery novel reviewed—pullout Section X

CHICAGO • VOLUME 10, NUMBER 23 THIS ISSUE IN TWO SECTIONS THURSDAY, DECEMBER 6, 1984

GayLife will adopt a special printing schedule for the Christmas-New Year's holiday period. Our last issue of 1984 will be published Thursday, Dec. 20, with the usual deadlines. On Friday, Dec. 28, we will publish a special "Holiday Entertainer" to cover the period between Dec. 28 and Jan. 12, 1985. The "Holiday Entertainer" will carry community announcements, an entertainment and special events calendar, and full directory listings.

The deadline for any group or business wishing to have an event listed in the "Holiday Entertainer" is Friday, Dec. 21. The next regular issue of *GayLife* will be published Thursday, Jan. 10.

For more information, call 728-0833.

$100,000 in AIDS funds sought in Council majority budget plan

By PAUL COTTON

A $100,000 appropriation for AIDS research and education is included in the Chicago City Council Finance Committee's budget proposal, scheduled to be presented at hearings Thursday, Dec. 6

While the line item was not included in Mayor Harold Washington's earlier budget proposal, his liaison to the gay and lesbian community, Kit Duffy, said there is support for it among the Council minority loyal to the mayor. The Finance Committee is chaired by Ald. Ed Burke (14th) of the Council majority faction loyal to Ald. Edward Vrdolyak (10th).

"Any item [in the budget] may or may not get kocked out" in the continuing budget battle, said Duffy, "but I'm sure it will get passed. It will be interesting to see who goes where on it. This will be a good test."

Ald. Jerry Orbach (46th) of the majority bloc lobbied hard for the appropriation, as did members of the gay Prairie State Democratic Club. Orbach legislative aide Jim Serritelli said Orbach was "fulfilling a promise to the gay community to get funding for AIDS." Last year, Orbach succeeded in passing a Council resolution supporting such an expenditure when funs became available.

"I don't see any problems" in keeping the appropriation in the final budget," said Orbach. If passed, the money will "most likely" be given to the Howard Brown Memorial Clinic for implementation, he said.

Clinic executive director Jerry Weller said the clinic had sent letters explaining the need for such funds and detailing what other major cities had allocated. Boston, for example, which has an AIDS rate comparable to Chicago's, spent $190,000 in city funds last year. Chicago had no official AIDS appropriation in last year's budget, but Duffy said some $20,000 was spent in helping the federally funded Office of AIDS Activities, which is housed in the city's Health Department headquarters.

Weller said the new money primarily would be spent on public education, with special attention on outreach to the more closeted South Side black gay community.

"We are very aware that we haven't done enough" on the South Side, said Weller. "Very definitely we'll use the money in that area."

Duffy added, though, that "as much as I love Howard Brown," she hopes some of the money can be used to hire "staff out of City Hall to deal with issues that affect the gay and lesbian community substantively"—in effect, someone to do full-time what she now does part-time.

Word has yet to come on the city's application for an $85,000 renewal of the federal grant funding the AIDS activities office. Approval, which was expected to be confirmed last week, is still considered likely.

Also in the air is possible state funding for a toll-free AIDS information hotline, said Weller. Meetings between clinic and state officials are to be scheduled later this week.

"They [state officials] have responded in a very positive manner so far," said Weller.

Extended family

Charles Adler (left) and Christopher Stryker star in *Torch Song Trilogy*, Harvey Fierstein's landmark comedy about the life and loves of a gay man, his lover, his lover's wife, his adopted son, his mother—talk about your extended family! Adler plays the role that Fierstein created for himself in a play that started out in a Greenwich Village gay bar and went on to become a Tony-winning Broadway hit. *Torch Song Trilogy* opened this week at the Blackstone Theater; a review will appear in next week's *GayLife*. For more information, call 977-1700.

Protection beefed up for gay state workers in Illinois

By PAUL COTTON

Protection against discrimination for gay and lesbian State of Illinois professional employees is clarified in an addendum to a contract now being ratified.

A "Memo of Understanding" signed by state Bureau of Personnel manager Peter Vallone and American Federation of State, County and Municiple Employees chief negotiator Jim Woodard states that "parties agree that sexual orientation is a 'non-merit factor.'" Non-merit factors are included in the contract at the end of a long list of categories for which employees cannot be discriminated against.

The contract, which is virtually assured of ratification by its scheduled Dec. 10 implementation date, covers some 13,500 professional and technical employees, including accountants, chaplains, social workers, psychologists—some 125 job titles in all.

The memo of understanding is "as binding as any other contract provision," said Vallone.

"It's solid, legally enforceable protection," said Barry Friedman, a gay activist who was on the AFSCME negotiating team. Friedman said the memo is important because "otherwise a worker would have had to prove that sexual orientation is a non-merit factor." He said sexual orientation was not included in the state's civil rights laws. Friedman said use of the less-visible memo also avoided the possiblity of raising the ire of anti-gay legislators.

Friedman, who with others has for six years been trying to add protection against anti-gay discrimination to state contracts, said success came this time because for the first time professional workers bargained separately from "redneck conservative" blue collar workers.

"We never got very far before because of the prison guards in Cairo," he said.

Vallone said the memo was agreed to mostly because of pressure from Friedman.

"I don't think we've ever had a complaint" about sexual orientation discrimination, said Vallone.

A small measure of protection existed before in the form of a Nov. 12, 1981 letter from former state personnel director Louis Giordano to former assistant deputy governor Ilana Rovner stating that, "Sexual preference is considered to be a non-merit factor for employment." It was never clear, though, whether Giordano's letter was legally binding.

Gregory Sprague writes about Gerber in GayLife newspaper, 1984.

Gerber, New York," appear in German homosexual emancipation journals edited by Friedrich Radzuweit, chairman of the Bund. Gerber's articles are: "Englische Heuchelei" [English Hypocrisy], Blätter für Menschenrecht ["Journal of Human Rights"] (Berlin), vol. 6, no.15 (Oct. 1928), p. 4–5 (the subject is the prosecution in England of Radclyffe Hall's The Well of Loneliness); "Die Strafbestimmungen in den 48 Staaten Amerikas und den amerikanischen Territorien für gewisse Geschlechtsakte" ["The Penalties in the 48 American States and the American Territories for Certain Sexual Acts"], Blätter für Menschenrecht, vol. 7, no. 8 (Aug. 1929), p. 5–11; "Zwei Dollars oder fünfzehn Jahre Zuchthaus" ["Two Dollars or Fifteen Years in Prison"], Das Freundschaftsblatt ["The Friendship Journal"] (Berlin), vol. 8, no. 41 (Oct. 9, 1930), p. 4. I wish to thank James Steakley for providing the information in this and the following note.

4. A German homosexual emancipation periodical entitled Freundschaft und Freiheit (Friendship and Freedom) was published from 1919 until at least 1926.

5. An unsuccessful attempt was made to locate the newspaper story which Gerber says was headed "Strange Sex Cult Exposed" and appeared in the Chicago Herald and Examiner, on the front page, probably on a Monday, probably in 1925. I am deeply grateful to Nick Patricca for voluntarily hiring a researcher who examined the front pages and skimmed the rest of (a microfilm of) this paper from Dec. 31, 1924 to Dec. 31, 1925. It is possible that the item appeared earlier in 1924, as the charter for the Society for Human Rights had been issued on Dec. 10 of that year.

6. This photo, including Friendship and Freedom among a selection of Gay periodicals, originally appeared in Magnus Hirschfeld's article "Die Homosexualität" in Leo Schidrowitz, ed., Sittengeschichte des Lasters (Vienna: Verlag für Kulturforschung, 1927), p. 301. It is reprinted in James D. Steakley's The Homosexual Emancipation Movement in Germany (N.Y.: Arno, 1975), opposite p. 78. I wish to thank James Steakley for providing a reproduction copy of this photo.

7. Henry Gerber, "The Society for Human Rights—1925," ONE Magazine (Los Angeles), vol. 10, no. 9 (Sept. 1962), p. 5–10.

After his trouble with the law in Chicago, in 1924 (1925?), Gerber went to New York where, from 1930-39, he published a mimeographed newsletter, Contacts, for persons seeking penpals. The last nine issues of this newsletter are in

the collection of Jim Kepner (Kepner to J.K., Jan. 2, 1974).

8. [Henry Gerber] Parisex, pseud., "In Defense of Homosexuality," The Modern Thinker, June 1932, p. 286–97; photo reprint in A Homosexual Emancipation Miscellany; c. 1835-1952 (N.Y.: Arno, 1975). Gerber's authorship of this "Defense" is identified in a letter of his to Manuel Boyfrank, Jan. 4, 1945 (p. 5), now in the collection of Jim Kepner (Kepner to J.K., May 11, 1974 [p. 4]). Dr. W. Beran Wolfe's "The Riddle of Homosexuality" appeared in The Modern Thinker, April 1932.

9. [Gerber,] Parisex, p. 297.

10. The index for vol. 1 (1934) of Chanticleer (in vol. 1, no. 12 [Dec. 1934]) lists twelve articles by Henry Gerber:

"Theism and Atheism reconciled," no. 1 (Jan.)

"Recent Homosexual Literature," no. 2 (Feb.)

"What is Atheism?," no. 3 (March)

"Sterilization," no. 4 (April)

"Escape from Reality," no. 5 (May) (This issue also includes: William Chiles, "A Heterosexual looks at Homosexuality")

"A New Deal for Sex," no. 6 (June)

"A Study in Pessimism," no. 7 (July)

"Tannhauser," no. 8 (Aug.)

"Hitlerism and Homosexuality," no. 9 (Sept.)

"Moral Warfare," no. 10 (Oct.)

"Rationalism or Dogma," no. 11 (Nov.)

"More Nonsense about Homosexuals," no. 12 (Dec.)

The editor is Jacob Hauser, the circulation manager is Henry Gerber; associate editors are H. P. Seguin, William Chiles, B. G. Hagglund. No place of publication is listed. Communications are to be addressed to a post office box in N.Y.C. A complete run of vol. 1 of Chanticleer is available at the Widener Library, Harvard University. I wish to thank Warren Johansson for help in locating this document.

11. Gerber, "Recent Homosexual Literature," Chanticleer, vol. 1, no. 2 (Feb. 1934), p. 4. In Dec. 1917, the Bolshevik government of the Soviet Union had done away with all laws against homosexual acts. Gerber had not yet heard of

the rebirth of anti-homosexual persecution in the U.S.S.R. In Jan. 1934, mass arrests of homosexuals occurred in major Soviet cities. In March 1934, as a result of Stalin's personal intervention, a law punishing homosexual acts with imprisonment up to eight years was introduced (John Lauritsen and David Thorstad, The Early Homosexual Rights Movement [1864-1935] [N.Y.: Times Change Press, 1974], p. 68–69).

12. Henry Gerber, "Hitlerism and Homosexuality," Chanticleer, vol. 1, no. 9 (Sept. 1934), p. 1-2.

13. Henry Gerber, "More Nonsense about Homosexuals," Chanticleer, vol. 1, no. 12 (Dec. 1934), p. 2-3.

A group of approximately two hundred letters exchanged between Gerber and Manuel Boyfrank (about 30 percent by Gerber, c. 1935–c. 1957) is in the collection of Jim Kepner (Kepner to J.K., March 11, 1974). This is no doubt one of the most valuable collections of original Gay American history manuscripts that will ever be found. The correspondence contains references to the 1924 Chicago organizing attempt, to articles Gerber published under pseudonyms, to four books written by Gerber, to plans for a new homosexual emancipation organization. These letters should be carefully edited, and published in a scholarly edition-a project for which a grant is badly needed.

Between 1927 and 1930, an American art connoisseur and ex-patriot, Edward Perry Warren, published in London, under the pseudonym Arthur Lyon Raile, his three-volume Defense of Uranian Love (London: Cayme Press, 1928, 1930), described by Timothy d'Arch Smith as "a sixty-thousand word apologia for an acceptance of the preeminence of the Hellenic paederastic philosophies." Warren, says Smith, was an anglophile, who lived almost his entire life in England, and who spoke "zealously for the revival of the Greek paederastic ideal which he found embodied in the classical art works he collected." Warren's Itamos: A Volume of Poems, first published in 1903, is said to present the Greek pederastic ideal with "great fervor," celebrating their author's "own very real friendships, loves, and quarrels." In 1884, at Oxford, Warren had met John Marshall, the "soulmate" with whom he lived until Marshall's death in 1928. Warren's novel of Oxford life, A Tale of Pausanian Love (London: Cayme, 1927), is said to present a "trenchant argument in favor of Uranian affection." (Timothy d'Arch Smith, Love in Earnest; Some Notes on the Lives and Writings of English 'Uranian' Poets from 1889 to 1930 [London: Routledge & Kegan Paul, 1970], p. 2, 114–17, 148, 253, 267–68).

THE LEGACY OF GERBER AND HART *by TRACY BAIM*

THIS CHAPTER OF OUT AND PROUD FEATURES HENRY
Gerber and Pearl M. Hart for their work as gay and lesbian pioneers in
Chicago. They had an impact here and across the country: Gerber for
founding the first-known U.S. gay group, and Hart for her legal and
civil-rights efforts on behalf of gay and non-gay clients.

Chicago's Gerber/Hart Library is named for them. Its founding was
due in large part to the work of historian Greg Sprague, who began his
Chicago Gay History Project in 1978. That project joined with the Gay
Academic Union–Chicago Chapter and Gay Horizons to launch the
Gerber/Hart Library in January 1981. By Nov. 20, 1981, it was a stand-
alone nonprofit agency.

The Chicago Gay and Lesbian Hall of Fame inducted Sprague in
1994. The library itself, Henry Gerber, and Pearl Hart are all also in the
Hall of Fame. When inducting Sprague, the Hall of Fame stated:
"Gregory A. Sprague lived in Chicago for ten years during which he
made an impact not only within the local gay and lesbian community
but also throughout scholastic and educational communities in which
gay and lesbian history was considered taboo and ignored as an area of
study. He was nationally known for his research in Chicago lesbian and
gay history. Sprague was co-founder of the Committee on Lesbian and
Gay History of the American Historical Association. He served for several years on the national board of directors of the Gay Academic Union
and was on the steering committee of the Chicago chapter."

The library was first located in the same building complex that Gay
Horizons (now known as Center on Halsted) occupied, at 3225 N.
Sheffield Ave. The library moved to various locations over the years,
including a large space at 3352 N. Paulina St., and then to its current
home, 1127 W. Granville Ave. on the city's Far North Side. While it has
more than 14,000 volumes, 800 periodicals and 100 archival collections,
it is primarily volunteer-run and has limited hours open to the public.

The library, like many Chicago gay groups, has also suffered losses
due to AIDS and other causes. Sprague died of AIDS complications in
February 1987. Joseph Gregg, a key archivist and librarian, died of AIDS
complications in November of that same year. Volunteers have also been
lost, including Kathleen O'Malley, who died of asthma in 1993, age 33.

Gerber/Hart is often billed as the Midwest's largest GLBT archives.
Its programming includes ongoing book groups, special exhibitions, lectures, and guest authors.

Sprague's archives are at the Chicago History Museum, which in recent years has begun extensive programming on Chicago gay and lesbian history through its Out at CHM series, held in conjunction with
Center on Halsted and the Elizabeth Morse Charitable Trust. ▼

*Top: Hanging at the library in the 1980s: Joseph Gregg
is seated up front, reading. Left: Gregory Sprague.
Below: Gerber/Hart in the May 24, 1984, GayLife news-
paper, after electing a new board, including, from left,
Joe Loundy, Karen Mix, co-director Joe Gregg, Gregory
Sprague, secretary Diane Weinerman, and co-director
Ruth Ketchum. Not pictured: board members Kathleen
Carney, acting president and treasurer David Goodwill,
archivist S. David Huntington and Marie Kuda. Photo
by Conrad M. Willy. Photo courtesy GayLife archives.*

Ernest W. Burgess. Courtesy of the Special Collections Research Center, University of Chicago Library.

THE GAY '30s

by *LUCINDA FLEESON*

For a brief but wild time in the 1920s and 1930s, an openly gay culture thrived in Chicago—a period historians call the "Pansy Craze." Nightclubs and cabarets drew crowds of homosexuals, lesbians and voyeurs—among them, sociologists who dutifully recorded the proceedings. Recently rediscovered recollections from that era have landed the city in the forefront of the small but popular field of gay historical research.

AS MIDNIGHT APPROACHED ON HALLOWEEN in 1932, men in vampy satin ball gowns and French-heeled slippers, with teased coiffures and rouged lips, crowded into the Chicago Coliseum. Over the years, the old building at South Wabash Avenue and East 15th Street had played host to political conventions and hockey games, but these men were there to dance the night away.

Lurking in the shadows that evening, a nondescript, bespectacled man in a plain suit and tie scrawled notes. A sociology professor at the University of Chicago, Ernest W. Burgess was carrying out the country's first extensive research project into homosexuality. "When the drags entered," he wrote at one point, "there was much laughing, particularly about one elderly man dressed in women's clothing, glasses, boyish bob and out-of-date costume, shaved but chin showing growth of a beard."

For a brief time in the late 1920s and early 1930s, similar scenes unfolded up and down the city, as a relatively open gay culture thrived in Chicago, with gay cabarets and nightclubs proliferating throughout the Near North and South sides. By 1930, Variety reported, there were 35 "pansy parlors" in Towertown, the neighborhood named for its proximity to the old Chicago Water Tower. A place called Diamond Lil's, at 909 N. Rush St., was packed so tight with partying gays that people were turned away.

The historian Chad Heap has noted that the flowering of gay life at that time covered much of the city's ethnic landscape: "African American drag entertainers performed for racially mixed audiences at some of the South Side's most famous 'black and tan' [cabarets]. Mexican 'queers' carved out a space for themselves along Ashland Avenue, and ethnic working-class 'queens' from the city's North, South and West Sides met at private parties and public drags throughout the city."

The nighttime entertainments did not attract just gays. High society and the middle class flocked to the cabarets to gawk or to experience the prurient thrill of dancing with one of the "homos." The so-called Bughouse Square in front of the Newberry Library was such a well-known pickup spot that the Chicago Gray Line sightseeing company included it on its Chicago-By-Night tour, advertising the promise of "the unusual, strange and different" in "gay night life."

With its wildly relaxed attitudes, Chicago's Pansy Craze, as the brief phenomenon has come to be known, emerged from Prohibition just as homosexuality first came to be recognized in this country as a distinct sexual orientation. The outburst lasted only until the mid-'30s, when the impact of the Depression and a series of sensationalized sex crimes led to a crackdown.

"The Pansy Craze was part of the same phenomenon that produced the Negro vogue in Harlem," says the Yale University history professor George Chauncey. "Massive waves of immigrants from Europe and the American South were arriving in American cities so that white middle-class urbanites became fascinated with exploring the new communities taking place in their midst, whether immigrant, bohemian, black, or gay."

The remarkable era might have dropped largely from history were it not for the pioneering efforts of Burgess, a founder of the "Chicago school" of urban sociology. He assigned dozens of his students to take notes at nightclubs, interview gay men and a few

women, and write term papers on the subject. The results are now contained in 107 linear feet of typewritten reports on fading paper, notebooks in longhand, photographs and other records, all meticulously cataloged and preserved as part of the Burgess papers in the Special Collections vaults at the University of Chicago's Regenstein Library.

Thanks in part to Burgess' studies—which anticipated Alfred Kinsey at Indiana University by a decade—Chicago has been in the forefront of research into gay history, once a tiny field but now increasingly popular. The country's two most prominent historians of gay life have worked here: Chauncey at UC and John D'Emilio at the University of Illinois at Chicago. Their universities host doctoral students researching gay topics, unheard-of as an approved academic endeavor only a decade or two ago. Burgess "encouraged things to be studied that weren't studied or even looked at by academia," says D'Emilio.

A lifelong bachelor, Burgess remains something of an enigma. Little is known about his personal life. He lived in Hyde Park near the Gothic university towers with his sister, Roberta, and vacationed at a summer home in Indiana.

He himself took part in the research. He attended at least two drag balls in 1932 and was so intent on his observations at a New Year's Eve "fairy ball" that he followed several of the drag queens into the bathrooms. "[They] put up their dresses to urinate," he recorded in his distinctive, slanting, bold script.

His students' reports are vivid. The party was just coming into full swing when one researcher arrived at the Ballyhoo Café, at 1942 N. Halsted St., at 11:30 p.m. on Sept. 24, 1933: "Seventy-five were queer fellows and 25 queer girls. The hostess dressed in masculine style was queer as well as the M.C." The girls—"mentes," as they were called—got drunk on gin. Probing all the while, the researcher asked one to dance. He reported that she talked about the "jam" people—code for "straight"—and confided that queer people despised them.

The student returned to the Ballyhoo two months later for more reporting: "Mack, the master of ceremonies and also a female impersonator, who is

about six foot three inches tall, and very slim in build, gave his number. Dressed in female costume, he impersonated a woman and walked gracefully about the room making wise cracks. Someone in the crowd called out for him to give the 'Alice in her little blue gown' number. As he sang the song, he made gestures toward his lower extremities:

Then in fashion it grew,
And I did, do doodle do."

For decades beginning as early as the 1880s, the Chicago physicians James G. Kiernan and G. Frank Lydston published reports on "sexual perverts" in "sexology" essays for their medical journal. "As shown by some recent arrests, certain cafes patronized by both Negroes and whites, are the seat of male solicitation," Kiernan wrote in 1916. "Chicago has not developed a euphemism yet for these male perverts. In New York they are known as 'fairies' and wear a red necktie. In Philadelphia they are known as 'Brownies.'" In its famous 1911 report on prostitution and other illicit activities, The Social Evil in Chicago, the Chicago Vice Commission described a homosexual subculture of "at least 20,000," which had developed its own cant and networks.

Of course, anti-sodomy laws and others modeled after British statutes banning "crimes against nature" had been in effect across America since Colonial days. (Most have been repealed only in recent years; in 2003, the U.S. Supreme Court ruled that a Texas law outlawing sodomy between consenting adults was unconstitutional.) Surprisingly to many, however, homosexuality was a visible and even accepted part of working-class street life in the first decades of the 20th century.

In his celebrated book Gay New York: Gender, Urban Culture, and the Making of the Gay Male World, 1890–1940, George Chauncey showed that until the 1930s, working-class men engaged in sex with other men without feeling that they were abnormal. There were rules about what had to take place for them to retain their identification as "normal"—they had to be receiving the sexual favors, for instance, not providing. In those days, most wives didn't engage in oral sex, and to get it, a man typically had to find a prostitute or a gay man.

Chauncey showed that popular sexual identities had shifted over the past century. Prior to the Pansy Craze, a man was perceived as manly if he exhibited the outward signs of his gender—masculine looks and behavior. But Chauncey posits that after the voyeuristic slumming during the Pansy Craze, the middle class constructed a view of homosexuals as different from themselves, as "the other."

By the Roaring '20s, Chicago had evolved into Sin City, offering an array of vices and entertainments, many dominated by gangsters. Those tumultuous years were marked by enormous social upheaval—women obtained the vote in 1920, bobbed their hair, and embraced emancipation, while post-World War I modernist European ideas poured into the caldron of Chicago's explosive growth. Throughout the Midwest, tales of Chicago's freedoms reached secreted gays. Burgess collected a May 1934 letter written by a Saginaw, Mich., man named Bill to a Chicago friend: "Yes, I did hear of your gay parks and beaches," Bill wrote. Back in Saginaw he had to lie low because "as for gay places there just aren't any in town. We generally go to Detroit."

Chicago's Democratic mayor, William Dever, began his term in 1923 with crackdowns on the city's illegal saloons, vowing to "drive hard against every vicious cabaret in every part of the city." But his actions were unpopular—even the Chicago Tribune opposed Prohibition. Gangsters were said to be grossing almost $13 million in beer sales, gambling and prostitution during the first two terms of Dever's predecessor, William Hale "Big Bill" Thompson. When Big Bill emerged from retirement to run again, in 1927, he promised, "We will not only reopen places these people have closed, but we'll open 10,000 new ones."

New York City was the other urban magnet for homosexuals in the 1920s and 1930s. As Chauncey documents in Gay New York, cabarets in Greenwich Village and Harlem headlined female impersonators and gay-oriented entertainments. One of Chauncey's graduate students, Chad Heap, now an associate professor of American studies at George Washington University, concentrated on the same period for his thesis, which documented how the Pansy Craze capti-

vated Chicago. (Heap's account, titled Slumming: Sexual and Racial Encounters in American Nightlife, 1890–1940, was published in book form by the University of Chicago Press in the spring of 2008.)

In Burgess' sociological examinations of urban Chicago, he studied all sorts of populations—African-Americans, the poor and prisoners, for example—with his most extensive work concentrated on the institution of marriage. He began investigating the homosexual community in the late 1920s, and no evidence suggests that anyone objected.

The term "gay" would not be in wide currency until the 1940s and 1950s, except as code to the cognoscenti. Homosexuals themselves used the words "faggot," "fairy" and "queer," or they sometimes called themselves "temperamental," but the sociologists were not quite sure what term to use. As a result, they threw around words such as "indeterminates" and "third sex," as well as the pejorative "degenerate."

One student, Conrad Bintzen, submitted his "Notes on the Homosexual in Chicago" for Burgess' Sociology 270 class. The report included Bintzen's field observation at one of the cabarets of mixed race—called "black and tans"—on the city's South Side. (Excerpts from his report, like the others cited in this article, are presented as written, edited only slightly for clarity.)

"Through the blue cigarette smoke you can make out the outlines of crowded tables," Bintzen wrote. "Before long, the orchestra strikes up a tune and the master of ceremonies appears on the stage. This person is a huge mulatto with wide shoulders and narrow hips. … It [sic] is a lascivious creature that strikes the normal as extremely repulsive. With a deep husky voice it begins to sing a wild song and as the tempo increases the stage rapidly fills with a remarkable collection of sexual indeterminates. Each is dressed in a long formal, and each has the same peculiar physical appearance."

Bintzen's paper continued: "After the floorshow the homos danced together … in all sorts of fantastic routines. They all act far more feminine than a normal girl, carrying filmy handkerchiefs which they draw out of their sleeves and flutter around. … They talk and joke about girdles and brassieres,

which seem to be the source of most of their humor.

"Quite a number have painted fingernails. Some of the customers are just there to watch and ridicule the homos. The management not only encourages the displays, but has arranged a complete line of cosmetics in the men's lavatory."

My own investigation into Chicago's gay history began in a roundabout way, when I started researching a book on Allerton Garden, a botanical masterpiece on the Hawaiian island of Kauai founded by a Chicagoan, Robert Allerton, and his lover, John Gregg Allerton. The son of the wealthy meatpacker Samuel Allerton, Robert was profiled in the Tribune as the city's "most eligible bachelor," but he preferred men. According to my research, to keep up the disguise, he adopted John Gregg as his son.

Robert and John had left Chicago in the late 1930s, and I wanted to find out what was going on in the city that drove these elegant, sophisticated men to move to what was essentially a sugar plantation island for the rest of their lives. I was not entirely surprised to find that Chicago had grown inhospitable to gays just about the time the Allertons left. But I was also transfixed by the startling, sometimes poignant first-person accounts contained in the Burgess papers. That feeling increased when I visited the Chicago Historical Society (now the Chicago History Museum) and started listening to audiotapes of old-timers describing early gay life for the historian Gregory Sprague. He collected material for a thesis on Chicago's gay history but died of AIDS in 1987 before it was finished.

A man named Galen Moon, for example, told Sprague he was 14 and fresh from an orphanage in New Orleans when he went to work in the Chicago Athletic Club kitchens in 1916. One day the chef told him to don a busboy's jacket and deliver room service to one of the residents, a Dr. S. "The Dr. was much more interested in who brought food than the food on the cart," Moon recounted to Sprague. They had sex, and the doctor introduced the young man to other wealthy residents for more of the same. One day the doctor asked Moon, "You need some money, don't you? I know of an opportunity where you could make $100 a night. … There would have to be a pair of you. There's a student at a hospital I know who would be glad to work with you."

Moon and his partner ended up at a place near Crystal Lake called the Officers' Club, a private lounge with food, a bar and a glass enclosure where Moon and his partner put on "demonstrations," as Moon termed it. "We went out there once a week for five weeks," he recounted. "Put money into [a] savings account. I had no trouble, whatever, going through with the thing. There was a bed covered with silk, and the whole atmosphere was enough to sort of help you out. The audience disturbed me at first, the first time, a little bit. All these guys watching, maybe 40 or 50 men. The doctor told me it was a club for military officers. I'm sure it was not approved by any services of the kind."

Some interview subjects, both with Sprague and with Burgess' students, revealed a longing for marriage, family and social acceptance and their torment over being homosexual. A 27-year-old man identified only as Mr. X told a student, "I seemed to know all my life that I was not like other boys." At 15, he began to engage in homosexual relations in earnest, but hid it from his mother. He went to a roller rink to meet partners and cruised the beaches at night, though he continued to teach Sunday school on the weekends. Then, he said, he met a man named Harold, with whom he dreamed of setting up housekeeping. "The only failure in gay life that I can figure," he told the interviewer, "is flitting from one to another and never having a thought of having and finding a mate that you can be happy with. Ending up being an old Aunty that isn't wanted by anyone."

Another Burgess subject, known as Case E, said, "I felt there was something wrong with me that I admired men. I thought it was the worst thing that could happen to anybody. I knew how people made fun of sissies. I always had a terrible feeling that I would be found out, and I felt inferior to men. … Homosexuals mean very little to me, because their life seems so futile; there is nothing to their lives, and that is why I do not associate with them."

Another unnamed interviewee, immediately after describing a homosexual encounter, segued into expressing his desire for marriage. His gay friends counseled against it. "One fellow said, do not get married until you are absolutely sure you are not that way—queer—because it is a terrible situation to be

in," the man recounted. "I told them I would get married some day and they would laugh. … Every man should marry and have children."

The Pansy Craze reached its height in 1933 as Chicago prepared for the Century of Progress world's fair. Organizers, criminals and social reformers geared

WORDPLAY

Chicago's shadowy homosexual world of the 1930s was so well developed that participants devised their own cant. Professor Ernest W. Burgess compiled a "Glossary of Homosexual Terms." Among them:

Auntie — Older queer, or one who acts old

Belle — Any homosexual person; one who is usually aware of his condition

Bitch — Term for homosexuals, usually among themselves

Blind — Homosexual traveling with a girl, or who marries to conceal his condition

Chorus moll — Type of young homosexual who is effeminate, uses rouge, lipstick, dresses foppishly

Dirt — Persons, often trade, who blackmail or rob homosexuals. Usually picked up in public places

French — Fellatio

Green — Homosexual who is ignorant of his condition; average person who is ignorant of homosexuality

Marjorie — Homosexual who is affected, flirty, very effeminate, "sweet and lovely"

Miss Lesbos — Term applied to lesbian girl

Party — Sexual act; usually involves fellatio

Tea room — Public toilet

Trade — One who will permit homosexuals to have sexual relations with him, usually for money

— *Lucinda Fleeson*

for an explosion of entertainment offerings, both licit and illicit. "Happy days will be here again when the world's fair opens next June," one brothel owner was quoted as telling a Juvenile Protection Agency investigator. Dozens of cabarets opened on the South Side, a boon to Chicago's Depression economy. The drag shows featured at the K-9 Club (advertised as "Chicago's oddest Nite Club"), at 105 E. Walton St., drew capacity crowds.

The fair closed down in the autumn of 1934, about 10 months after the repeal of Prohibition. But legalizing liquor didn't create a boom in nightclubs, bars and permissiveness. Rather, the opposite occurred. The crush of the Depression descended. The tourist trade evaporated. Even the prostitutes complained. A young New York hustler named Rodey who traveled to Chicago for the fair told one of Burgess' students that business turned bad after the fair closed: "The Depression has hurt hustling. I used to get $5.00 but now sometimes go down the alley to get $.50 or $1.00."

Still, reformers demanded that Mayor Edward J. Kelly clean up nightlife, and they campaigned against strippers and female impersonators. Early in 1935, police padlocked the K-9 Club and the Ballyhoo. Two lesbian cafes, the Twelve-Thirty Club, at 1230 N. Clybourn Ave., and the Roselle Inn, at 1251 N. Clark St., were shut. In October 1935, police raided two nightspots near 35th and South State streets, the Cabin Inn and the De Luxe Cafe. "Put on pants or go to jail," police ordered the drag queens. For a while black-and-tan cafes were allowed to continue their drag shows, but then they, too, were shut down. Police raided the Halloween balls at the Coliseum. By the end of 1935, Mayor Kelly had eliminated gay nightlife.

Soon Chicago and the rest of the country hurtled into a full-scale sex panic, driven by what came to be known as the "moron menace." Beginning in 1936, a series of crimes, petty and heinous, by peeping Toms, rapists, child molesters and murderers surged onto the front pages of the tabloids. Homosexuality began to be seen as a mental disease, and its practitioners were equated with psychopaths and child molesters, all of them called "sex morons" and "sex fiends."

There was legitimate concern—a higher-than-usual number of attacks on women and children were reported over two years in Chicago, but few by homosexuals. That didn't stop police from stepping up their surveillance of theaters and cruising spots, including a stretch of South State Street that had become popular, and routinely arresting gays seeking consensual sex.

And then, on Nov. 13, 1936, five-year-old Antoinette Tiritilli was lured from the McLaren schoolyard on West Flournoy Street by a man with the promise of candy. He slashed her throat. In her last words to rescuers, she described her attacker as a "fat man with a white face." When captured, Andrew Capoldi, 27, would be dubbed "the gorilla man" because of his hulking form and pockmarked features. The lurid Chicago American blared details across its front page in 2-inch type and pronounced Capoldi the most disgusting sexual degenerate in capable of bestial sex crimes … at large in Chicago!"

Nearly every day, the papers played up reports of sex crimes—no matter that they happened as far away as Buffalo or Tacoma, Wash. Fifty irate club-women in hats descended on the mayor's office calling for action. Fears rose so high that the City Council passed a law to require "moron alarms"—sirens or bells on fire escapes to warn of intruders. The reformers succeeded in pressuring the Illinois legislature to pass a sexual psychopath law in 1938, providing that anyone even suspected of deviance could be sent for an indeterminate time to the psychiatric division of the penitentiary at Menard or to the Illinois Security Hospital at Chester. (Michigan was the first state to pass such a law, followed by Illinois, then a spate of others. Since then, almost all these laws have been eliminated.)

Once the fad of slumming at gay nightspots disappeared in the late 1930s, its existence was soon nearly forgotten. Chauncey discovered it only by chance, in the 1980s, as he was researching New York City's early gay history for his Ph.D. thesis at Yale University. Scrolling through rolls and rolls of microfilmed archives of entertainment newspapers, such as Variety, he noticed the growing number of clubs in Times Square with gay performers, often described as "pansies." "Suddenly I saw so much material and realized that there was a pattern of something we didn't know existed before," he remembers.

Because many gays and lesbians died alone during periods when homosexuality was vilified, their personal papers were not saved, or their families destroyed embarrassing documents. Historians typically sift through vast amounts of material on gays to find smatterings of references or documentation. Only in the past 10 or 15 years have archivists recognized these documents as worth saving. There has been tremendous excitement among gay historians as they uncover and collect this material, and the thrill of discovery is part of the attraction of the field.

"It's what makes me love doing research," says D'Emilio. "You get to read things that weren't meant to be read. The best stuff is when you realize that this is really uncensored." By the time the Pansy Craze was over, "most people began thinking of themselves as either hetero- or homosexual, while a century ago people did not think of themselves or organize their emotional lives through those categories," says Heap.

Of course, suppression could not kill homosexuality, only drive it underground, and ironically the crackdown led to a dispersal of gay entertainments. When female impersonators were banned in Chicago and New York City, they went on the road, popping up in Milwaukee, Atlantic City and beyond. And another social upheaval was about to

BOHEMIAN LIFE

In Harvey Warren Zorbaugh's The Gold Coast and the Slum (1929) and from other sources, we get confirmation of the existence of a bohemian area similar to New York's Greenwich Village, extending from the foot of the Water Tower on North Michigan Avenue to North LaSalle Street. Alternately known as "the village" or "Towertown," the area was home to all kinds of sexual behavior and free-love advocates.

Women ran most of the art shops, bookstalls, and tearooms (real tea, not sex rooms). There were a number of artists' studios and students from the Art Institute; the Wobblies were there, and a few radical bookstores, as well as that fabled bastion of free speech, the Dill Pickle Club. Zorbaugh quotes references to "girls in the apartment across the well" and to parties attended by the "best-known fairies and lesbians in Chicago." A nurse observed of some of the girls "across the well" that they "would put on men's evening clothes, make love to the others, and eventually carry them off in their arms into the bedrooms."

He also makes reference to a male village leader and his retinue of "blue birds" who would promenade down toward the Drake Hotel. The area also held the Tent, the Paradise Club, and the old Chez Pierre. — *Marie J. Kuda*

Chicago history, "one of the most dangerous sexual morons who ever lived." He was convicted of murder and sent to a penitentiary for the "criminally insane" in Menard, Ill.

By December 1936, reformers were agitating for stronger laws and punishments. A bill to castrate sex criminals gained momentum in the legislature. The Chicago American trumpeted revelations that sex criminals had easily escaped in recent years: "Danger! One thousand escaped feeble-minded and insane persons … most of them occur, one that would blow open the closet with gale force. World War II and the military draft would bring together thousands of men, from rural prairie states and seaside cities. Concentrated in such large numbers, gay men inevitably gathered and began to talk and compare their experiences. Irrevocably, the stage for openness among homosexuals was set. ▼

This article is adapted from an article that first appeared in the November 2005 Chicago magazine. Copyright © 2005 Chicago magazine.

SAMUEL STEWARD: TATTOOS AND TEACHING   *by OWEN KEEHNEN*

SAMUEL M. STEWARD WAS BORN IN 1909 IN Woodsfield, Ohio, the only son of an auditor and a schoolteacher. In 1927 he moved to Columbus to earn multiple degrees at Ohio State University. It was here that Steward's life began to change in other ways as well. At Ohio State he began to explore his sexuality more fully.

During this time, Steward also began corresponding with Gertrude Stein and eventually met her and Alice B. Toklas in 1937, developing a friendship that lasted years. In a 1993 interview with this writer, he said of Stein: "I found her very warm and almost maternal towards me. My impression was she was not quite sure of herself and wanted to have the admiration of even a young squirt like myself." After Stein's death in 1946, Steward continued to make an annual trip to Paris to visit Toklas until her death in 1967. Steward also lunched with Thomas Mann, knew André Gide and Lord Alfred Douglas, and even had an affair with Thornton Wilder in Zurich and during Wilder's later visits to Chicago.

In 1934 he became a professor of English at Carroll College in Helena, Mont. Later, he taught at Washington State University in Pullman, Wash. In 1936 he was dismissed from his position as assistant professor at WSU for his portrayal of prostitution in his novel Angels on the Bough. After his abrupt departure, he came to Chicago, where he was an associate professor of English at Loyola University from 1936 until 1946 before moving to DePaul University from 1948 to 1954.

From 1946 to 1948 he was the editor of several departments for the World Book Encyclopedia. It was at this time that Steward also met and became an unofficial collaborator with the sexual behavior scientist Alfred Kinsey. He not only found contacts for the researcher; in 1949 he even performed in a bondage-and-S&M scene with a sadist for Kinsey to

One of Sam Steward's books.

film. The two remained close until Kinsey's death in August 1956. During this period Steward also submitted drawings and wrote fiction under various pseudonyms and in a number of publications, including the famous Swiss gay magazine Der Kreis (The Circle).

In 1954 Steward left DePaul, disenchanted with academia when none of the students in his incoming English class had heard of Homer. Two years earlier, Steward had become a tattoo artist, using the name Phil Sparrow lest the faculty at DePaul disapprove of the nature of his moonlighting. He then decided to do tattooing full-time and subsequently worked as a demographer in Chicago, Milwaukee and Oakland.

During this time he continued his diverse writings. In the next 35 years he released mysteries, nonfiction, literary fiction, erotica, memoirs and more. He wrote two Gertude Stein–Alice B. Toklas mysteries, Murder Is Murder Is Murder (1985) and The Caravaggio Shawl (1989), and was working on a third at the time of his death. He also edited a collection of their letters, Dear Sammy: Letters from Gertrude Stein and Alice B. Toklas (1977). Some of his other titles include Understanding the Male Hustler (1991), Chapters from an Autobiography (1981), Bad Boys and Tough Tattoos (1990), A Pair of Roses (1993), and the historical novel Parisian Lives (1984). Under the pseudonym and alter ego Phil Andros (in Greek, "philos" means "loving," and "andros" refers to "man"), he also wrote several erotic novels about the adventures of a hustler, with titles such as My Brother the Hustler, $tud, The Boys in Blue, The Greek Way, and San Francisco Hustler.

Samuel Steward died on New Year's Eve 1993 in Berkeley, Calif., of chronic pulmonary disease at the age of 84. ▼

GERTRUDE AND ALICE COME TO CHICAGO
by MARIE J. KUDA

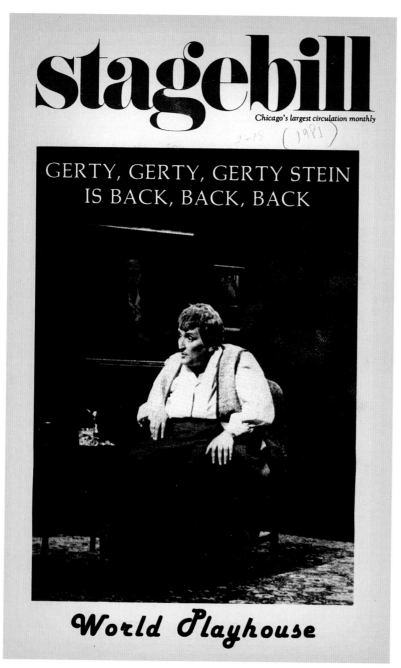

A 1981 playbill for Pat Bond starring as Gertrude Stein in Gerty, Gerty, Gerty Stein Is Back, Back, Back, *presented by Playhouse Enterprises at the World Playhouse. Courtesy M. Kuda Archives, Oak Park, Ill.*

GERTRUDE STEIN WAS THE DARLING OF RANDOM HOUSE AFTER it published her Autobiography of Alice B. Toklas in 1933. The famous expatriate writer and her lover Toklas returned to the United States in 1934 to be lionized on a national book tour. Stein made quite a stir when she hit Chicago that year.

According to critic Fanny Butcher, when Stein autographed copies of her books at Marshall Field's, "the crowds were so great the elevators couldn't stop at the book department floor. She was literally the talk of the country." Her first lecture at the University of Chicago had as many people outside the hall as attending the lecture, kept out by local fire ordinances.

She lectured at the Arts Club, rode around in a police car, and stayed at the Drake Hotel during the premiere of her opera at the Auditorium Theatre. Four Saints in Three Acts, with libretto by Stein and music by homosexual composer Virgil Thomson, opened in November 1934 with an all-"Negro" cast and cellophane scenery. The production shocked and scandalized, was laughed at and praised, and was not heard again in our city until revived by the Chicago Opera Theatre in 1993. (COT had performed its first Stein-Thomson collaboration, The Mother of Us All, in 1974.)

Stein returned during the following spring to give a special course at the University of Chicago at the invitation of Robert Maynard Hutchins and Mortimer Adler. She enjoyed "her first experience at teaching" and, while a guest in Thornton Wilder's South Drexel Boulevard apartment, wrote the four lectures in the Narration series that articulate her distinctions between poetry and prose. ▼

LESBIAN NIGHTLIFE

A 1935 newspaper report substantiates the existence of a thriving lesbian nightlife in Chicago, subject to the same political whims as male bars for their continued existence. Police Commissioner James P. Allman was ordered by Mayor Edward J. Kelly to close the Star and Garter at 854 W. Madison St. for "indecent performances."

Kelly also cracked down on nightclubs catering to women who preferred men's attire by ordering officials to revoke the licenses of the Roselle Associates Club, 1251 N. Clark St., and the Twelve-Thirty Club, 1230 N. Clybourn Ave.

Investigators sent to the clubs reported that women in male attire were nightly patrons of the places. One woman, when questioned, admitted that many of the couples were actually married, and furnished the police with the name of a "Negro" minister on the South Side who performed the marriage ceremonies, their investigators reported.

— *Marie J. Kuda*

ADOPTING NEW WAYS: ROBERT ALLERTON   by MARIE J. KUDA

ROBERT ALLERTON (1873–1964) WAS THE only son of Samuel Allerton (1828–1914), who had cornered the Chicago hog market and made a corollary fortune (Union Stockyards, First National Bank). Samuel had 40,000 acres of farm and ranch land in rural Illinois and a home on Prairie Avenue among the other civic leaders. After his wife died, Samuel married her younger sister, and Robert was raised by a stepmother barely 15 years older than he, whom he adored.

To escape the city in summer, Samuel built the "Folly" on 26 acres at the narrows of Lake Geneva in Wisconsin. Robert watched as young architect Henry Lord Gay built the imposing redwood structure. His stepmother Agnes (1858–1924) loved the Folly and, with young Robert in tow, created extensive gardens there.

Robert skipped college to go abroad with a friend and study art. At 24, he destroyed all his work and returned to the United States. Samuel gave him a few thousand acres in Piatt County; Robert had architect John Joseph Borie build a 32-bedroom Georgian mansion. He created perennial gardens, placed sculpture throughout, and set aside a 40-acre stand of virgin timber before settling into the life of a gentleman "farmer." He continued traveling extensively

to purchase furniture and art for the new house.

Robert was the first of many generous donors to enrich the collections of the nascent Art Institute of Chicago (his gifts of major 19th- and 20th-century art included Rodin's six-foot bronze sculpture, Adam). He lent sculpture and paintings from his personal collection for exhibition at both the 1893 and 1933 World's Fairs. A 1970 Art Institute guidebook states that "the original Michigan Avenue edifice was named to honor Allerton for his long service as a trustee, officer and benefactor of the museum."

In 1922 he met young John Wyatt Gregg (1899–1985) at an event at the University of Illinois in Urbana, and they decided to make a life together. They traveled extensively from Thanksgiving through the winter each year, returning to Chicago and the "farm" in the spring. As a concession to their age difference, they presented themselves as "father and son." When his stepmother Agnes died, Robert destroyed the Folly in Wisconsin and built the Allerton Hotel on North Michigan Avenue in Chicago (its penthouse club, the Tip Top Tap, had a reputation as a gay-friendly meeting place until it closed in the mid-1960s).

In the 1930s on a stopover in Hawaii, Robert fell in love with the Lawai-Kai river valley on Kauai. He

bought a 54-acre plot and constructed a house and gardens. Returning to Illinois briefly after World War II, he and John Gregg closed the "farm," donating almost 5,000 acres to the university. Part of the Robert Allerton Park is now designated a National Natural Landmark.

Meanwhile, the aging Robert explored the possibility of adopting Gregg. Under the law at the time, Illinois had no provision for adopting an adult. Apocryphal history credits Allerton with using his connections to initiate a revamp of statutory Illinois adoption law. A comprehensive reworking of the law (now known as 750 ILCS 50/0.01 to 50/24) passed in 1959 and, in part, permitted legal adoption of an adult provided the adult had lived in the petitioner's home for two consecutive years. John Gregg Allerton's oral history states that Robert Allerton was the first to adopt under the new law, in front of Judge Dighton of Monticello, Piatt County.

After Robert's death, the Kauai gardens and home and $1 million were given to the state of Hawaii. The property is now part of the National Tropical Botanical Garden. ▼

With research contributions by William B. Kelley.

1920s SENSATIONALISM: LEOPOLD AND LOEB

by RON DORFMAN

INTELLECTUALLY GIFTED BUT MORALLY STUNTED, the pampered teenage sons of two wealthy Hyde Park families, Richard Loeb and Nathan Leopold lived a secret life of petty crime. Loeb did it just for kicks, but Leopold used these adventures as a binding agent to secure sex with Loeb.

To cement their relationship, they planned what they imagined would be the "perfect crime": murdering a kidnap victim while still collecting a ransom, but covering their tracks so thoroughly they would never be implicated. On May 21, 1924, using a rented car, they picked up 14-year-old Bobby Franks on his way home from school, bludgeoned him to death, and stuffed his body into a drainpipe in a culvert near Wolf Lake. But they left Bobby's feet sticking out of the pipe.

The body was soon discovered, as was a pair of eyeglasses nearby which the police traced to Leopold. Other evidence accumulated, and the pair confessed to murder and kidnapping as well as their sexual relationship. This led to lurid psychiatric testimony and newspaper coverage that also darkly pondered their fabulous wealth, superior intelligence, and Jewish heritage. America's most famous defense attorney, their Hyde Park neighbor Clarence Darrow, pleaded them guilty to avoid trial by an enraged jury and asked Judge John Caverly for what would now be called a mitigation hearing. Darrow's extended argument against the death penalty is a classic of legal literature.

Each defendant got life plus 99 years. In 1936 a fellow inmate murdered Loeb in the shower room: The Chicago Daily News said he had "ended his sentence with a proposition." Leopold was paroled in 1958 and then settled in Puerto Rico as a hospital technician, married a local woman, took a degree in social work, and continued the ornithological studies he had pursued since childhood. He died of natural causes in 1971. ▼

Above: The accused are pictured watching as their attorney Clarence Darrow defends them.
Right: Nathan Leopold Jr. and Richard Loeb sitting in profile in a courtroom during their murder trial. Photos courtesy the Chicago History Museum.

VARIANT WOMAN: JEANNETTE HOWARD FOSTER

SCHOLAR, LIBRARIAN, EDUCATOR, CRITIC, author and poet Jeannette Howard Foster was born in Oak Park, Ill., in 1885. In 1935 she earned a Ph.D. in library science from the University of Chicago. Her monumental, pioneering book, Sex Variant Women in Literature: A Historical and Quantitative Survey, was the first scholarly work ever to study the lesbian in literature. The ripples of her influence are still being felt by the current generation of academics, writers, librarians and educators, and her contribution to the development of a lesbian culture is immense.

During Foster's long career she taught creative writing, literature, college English and library science and worked as librarian for, among other places, the special library of the Institute for Sex Research at Indiana University. She was one of Dr. Alfred Kinsey's first librarians and also served as librarian to the President's Advisory Committee on Education in Washington, D.C.

Foster's Sex Variant Women in Literature is a scholarly work that Foster originally self-published in 1956 through a "vanity" press. It discusses, chronologically, the "variant ... emotional reaction[s] among women as these appear in literature." She had difficulty in gaining access to much of the material she wished to consider for the study and wrote that "no class of printed matter except outright pornography has suffered more critical neglect, exclusion from libraries, or omission from collected works than variant belles-lettres." She spent more than 30 years pursuing rare works.

Foster's book critically examines 324 examples of "variant women" in literature in such languages as French, German and English and from the ancient writers and the Bible through the mid-20th century. The assumptions Foster made in evaluating "variant" literature presaged later feminist criticism and remain unchallenged. Her pioneer work has been recognized as a cornerstone title for a variety of gay men

and lesbians active in the counterculture as well as those interested in scholarly research, including Barbara Grier, who praised it as "essential to any collection of lesbian literature."

In 1974 Barbara Gittings presented Foster with the third annual Gay Book Award from the then Task Force on Gay Liberation of the American Library Association, sparking a resurgence of interest in Foster's work. In 1975 Diana Press and in

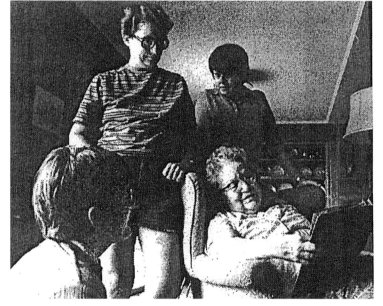

Tee Corinne, left foreground, Dr. Foster, seated, and Barbara Grier and Donna Watson standing, in a photo taken in Pocahontas, Ark., 1977. Photo by Honey Lee Cottrell. Courtesy M. Kuda Archives, Oak Park, Ill.

1985 Naiad Press brought out paperback editions of Sex Variant Women in Literature, making Foster's work more readily available to a new generation of scholars.

Historians of gay and lesbian life such as Jonathan Katz and Lillian Faderman have acknowledged Foster's work as indispensable to their own. Chicago's Gerber/Hart Library used Sex Variant Women in Literature as a guide to collection development, eventually succeeding in obtaining a grant to purchase a significant body of lesbian titles drawn from her opus. It is difficult to find a work on les-

bian literature or history that does not make some reference to Foster or her work.

Foster also contributed reviews, fiction, poetry and criticism to The Ladder under a variety of names, including her own. In 1976, Naiad published Foster's translation from the French of Renée Vivien's A Woman Appeared to Me, based on Vivien's stormy affairs with Violet Shilleto and Natalie Barney.

During the late 1970s, many well-known activists made pilgrimages to see Foster. She was praised and lionized. When her expenses began to exceed her resources, benefits and fundraisers were held around the country, further extolling her work and enhancing her reputation. Foster died in a nursing home in Pocahontas, Ark., in July 1981. ▼

This is adapted from the writings of Marie J. Kuda, including "Jeannette Howard Foster (1895–1981), Literary Pioneer: A Personal Reflection" in Outlines newspaper, Nov. 11, 1998, and her Foster entry in the book Gay & Lesbian Literature.

A LEAGUE OF THEIR OWN

by YVONNE ZIPTER

DURING THE MIDDLE YEARS OF THE LAST CENTURY—1943–54, TO be exact—women played professional baseball. Still the country's longest-running women's pro sports league of all time, the All-American Girls Professional Baseball League began as part of a larger homosocial environment that emerged as men went off to war and women were encouraged to take on traditionally male roles in service to their country.

Recruited by Philip K. Wrigley from park district and industrial softball leagues across the country and Canada, the women of the AAGPBL were not simply patriots: They were supremely conditioned athletes who played hard and took the sport seriously, despite regulations meant to avow their fundamental femininity, such as uniforms with flared skirts, mandates against short haircuts, and compulsory charm school attendance. At its height, the AAGPBL boasted 10 teams in the Midwest, and attendance figures as high as nearly a million in a single season. Even when the league ended, it provided inspiration to the next generation of women, including lesbians, who populated sandlot teams around the country until the league was all but erased from our collective memories.

When Title IX of the Education Amendments of 1972 was passed, more athletic opportunities became available to women. But the women of the AAGPBL were not given their due until 1988, when the league was commemorated with a permanent exhibit at the National Baseball Hall of Fame and Museum in Cooperstown, N.Y.; not until 1992, with the release of the movie, A League of Their Own, did the league become widely known again.

Given that lesbianism was a taboo topic during the league's heyday, it is difficult to know exactly how many players and fans were, in fact, lesbians. But the many players who "never married" (including one outed by a niece after her death [see www.thediamondangle.com/archive/aug03/deegan.html] and another survived by "one dear friend" [see www.paducahsun.com/articles/stories/public/200801/19/8bbX_obituari.html]) would indicate that more than a few of the league's members were lesbian. (Tellingly, the newspaper obituary as posted at aagpbl.org moves the "dear friend" from the top of the list of survivors to the end.)

Female athletes have long been revered by lesbians for their independence, strength and success; the women of the AAGPBL have been treasured role models, regardless of their actual sexual orientations—witness the number of lesbian jocks who tried out for roles on the teams in A League of Their Own (filmed in Evansville, Ind., and at Chicago's Wrigley Field) and the number of lesbian actresses in the film, including Rosie O'Donnell, Megan Cavanagh (as Marla Hooch, now starring in Exes & Ohs on the Logo cable network), and Kelli Simpkins (who played "tall girl Beverly" Dixon and is an Emmy-nominated co-writer of the HBO cable network film of The Laramie Project and an actress in the latter film and the off-Broadway play). ▼

Alma Wilson of the Chicago Chicks baseball team.
Photo courtesy the Chicago History Museum.

WORLD WAR II's IMPACT ON GAY CHICAGO   *by MARIE J. KUDA*

WORLD WAR II BROUGHT MANY CHANGES —mostly from the sheer influx of people, not just workers in defense plants. By the middle of the war, 50,000 to 100,000 military service people descended on Chicago for weekend leave. Parts of the Auditorium Building were taken over by the USO, and the acoustically perfect theater turned into a bowling alley. The red-light districts around the train stations flourished. Penny arcades, tattoo parlors, and burlesque joints crowded the south end of the Loop. The military police were kept hopping. Military bases issued lists of clubs that were off-limits to servicemen, who used the lists to find the kind of action they were seeking.

Novelist and memoirist Sam Steward was told of locker clubs near the bases where uniforms were changed for civvies, and the soldiers and sailors were off to the city without regard to military sanctions. Steward said you could usually identify the guys regardless of their clothes because of their haircuts and GI shoes.

The military ban on homosexuals in uniform did not go into effect until January 1943. The circumstances surrounding the ban are but a few of the details in Allan Bérubé's 1990 book, Coming Out Under Fire: The History of Gay Men and Women in World War Two. Bérubé also spoke at the Chicago Historical Society in January 1992 as part of its "Chicago Goes to War" exhibit. He read excerpts of postwar letters in which writers remembered gay ushers at Orchestra Hall, or a successfully culminated evening of cruising the Chicago Theatre.

George Buse (1924–2000) was featured in the gay documentary Before Stonewall and Studs Terkel's The Good War. Buse was a gay man who served in the Marines in WWII and often wrote about his experiences and spoke out against the gay ban. Another gay WWII veteran, Edward Zasadil (born 1924), has been active in Chicago gay veteran causes

in the 2000s, and has carried the American flag at tribute events. He and his partner Larry Simpson (1939–) have been together since 1962.

Finnie's in the Pershing Hotel had been the site of drag balls in 1939. In the early 1950s, Ebony magazine described traffic backed up for three blocks as drag versions of Josephine Baker, Billie Holiday and Lena Horne made it through the crowds. During the war years the Pershing Hotel was the official billet for Black troops on R & R. (As the war dragged on,

World War II gay vets: Marine George Buse and Army man Ed Zasadil.

troops who had seen active duty or a certain length of service were given a block of leave for "rest and relaxation.")

As in other major cities, the overcrowded conditions allowed soldiers and sailors to double up in hotel beds. A subtle system of signals developed to see if your bedmate was receptive or straight. The swankier hotel bars, three deep by late evening, became cruising places. Sources recollect the Dome at the Hotel Sherman and the Town and Country at the Palmer House as well as some of the classier gay lounges: the Haig and the 12 o'Clock Club. Gays frequented the Lincoln, Terminal, Wacker and Wabash bathhouses during this period.

In 1942 and '43 the military began anti-vice crusades that impacted every city. The Chicago City Council passed an ordinance prohibiting women from drinking in bars and especially targeted women employees in nightspots. The effect of the legislation was to encourage gay activity by all those off-duty men with no women around. In December 1942, the city fathers thought better of it and revised the law to permit escorted women back in the bars.

The war earned a certain amount of freedom for women. They could go about unescorted without censure. Women seen dancing together, going bowling or to films were commonplace. Slacks were the order of the day for factory work. Economic freedom for those who worked outside the home, particularly at jobs formerly held by men, would not be lightly relinquished at war's end. The new freedom felt throughout the country would be reflected in the desires of nascent gay "communities."

With the war winding down, "homosexual discharges" increased. As soldiers and sailors were mustered out and defense plants disbanded, many small-town men and women who had discovered their sexual orientation remained in the cities. Some of these would become the nucleus of the rights-oriented groups that would form in the 1950s and, in Illinois, succeed in urging the passage of legislation that in 1961 made ours the first state to decriminalize gay acts.

The ensuing years in Chicago would not be easy—McCarthyism was on the horizon, and machine politics were more firmly entrenched than ever. Roaring '20s–style mobsters were replaced by a more subtle underground that would extend its control into gay clubs, bars and bathhouses. But for most of us the war ended on a note of hope. We may have been different, but now we knew we were not alone. ▼

THE SEEDS OF CHANGE TAKE ROOT

From McCarthy and the Closet to Civil-Rights Demos and the Democratic Riots

IT WOULD BE DIFFICULT TO FIND ANY TWO DECADES MORE DIFFERENT than the 1950s and the 1960s in the United States. The postwar 1950s represented a repressive time for most Americans. Racial segregation, the return of Rosie the Riveter to the kitchen, the witch hunts of Sen. Joseph McCarthy, the heavy-handed and homophobic tactics of J. Edgar Hoover, and the push toward a cookie-cutter suburban life all meant that life continued to be difficult for most gay Americans. The 1960s turned the previous, rigid decade on its head, but homophobia was slow to reverse, still deeply wounding gay lives.

In Chicago, the 1955–77 reign of Richard J. Daley was marked by aggressive police tactics, raids on gay bars and a generally difficult time for those seeking reform of any kind. Yet there were already signs of change in the wind. Dr. Alfred Kinsey's sexuality books showed many people that they were not alone in their feelings. Sexual Behavior in the Human Male came out in 1948, followed in 1953 by Sexual Behavior in the Human Female. Oak Park native Jeannette Howard Foster contributed to the research for his work on women, and the Indiana-based Kinsey and his investigators came to nearby Chicago for some of their research.

Beat generation gay writer Allen Ginsberg premiered his poem Howl in San Francisco in 1955. Meanwhile, Chicago-born playwright Lorraine Hansberry was writing anonymous letters to the national Daughters of Bilitis publication The Ladder in 1957, telling them she was "glad as heck that you exist," according to Jonathan Ned Katz's book Gay American History.

The Mattachine Society was starting nationally, and Chicago's first Mattachine also began in the mid-1950s. After it folded in 1957, a new chapter was formed two years later,

A demonstration at White City Roller Rink in 1946; racial bias was becoming an even larger issue as the country entered the 1950s and 1960s. Photo courtesy the Chicago History Museum.

Opposite: Drag persona Tony Midnite. See page 57. Courtesy Windy City Times archives.

but it, too, was short-lived. Eventually a strong Mattachine Midwest was created, with its first meeting in 1965.

The 1950s also saw the thriving of gay bars, including Tiny and Ruby's Gay Spot on the South Side and Chuck Renslow's Gold Coast, the first known leather bar in the country. While Hugh Hefner was building his Playboy empire out of the Windy City, Renslow began his men's physique magazines out of Kris Studios with his partner Dom Orejudos.

Chicago writers Valerie Taylor and Sam Steward wrote gay "pulp" novels in the 1950s. Drag balls continued to be popular, including those organized in the name of Finnie's Club. Female impersonator

many. MLK had marched in Chicago to attack the entrenched racial segregation here, and his assassination caused riots in Chicago and elsewhere. His widow Coretta Scott King would come to Chicago in later decades and proclaim not only that she was in favor of gay rights, but that her husband would also have been. Gay pioneer Bayard Rustin, a key player behind the 1963 March on Washington for Jobs and Freedom, visited Chicago numerous times to promote civil rights.

The mainstream media portrayals of our community did not improve significantly. Even late-1960s articles were full of stereotypes and gay shame. Some gays would only appear anonymously, but a few

this documentation of gay issues and to the push for better portrayals in the mainstream media.

While Illinois was the first state to remove sodomy from its list of barred acts, in 1961, it would still take many years of work by activists to change the police's and society's view of homosexuals. The 1960s witnessed many major police raids on gay bars, and newspapers such as the Chicago Tribune would print the names of those arrested. This resulted in lost jobs, broken families and, in some cases, suicide. Mattachine Midwest and Chicago chapters of the Daughters of Bilitis and of ONE Inc. all mobilized to fight against such harassment. Their small cadre of activists worked on a variety of issues, not just the police, and the all-volunteer efforts were draining. The organizations, and many of those arrested in bar raids or entrapped by police in cruising areas, were assisted by attorneys including Pearl Hart, Renee Hanover, Paul Goldman, Ralla Klepak and Todd Lyster.

Chicagoans were also tied into the greater U.S. gay movement and hosted the 1968 national meeting of the North American Conference of Homophile Organizations (NACHO), held just before the Democratic National Convention. The DNC riots, and the raid on The Trip bar in 1968, were among the sparks of Chicago's own "Stonewall," creating radicalizing moments for local activists. Some NACHO delegates participated in the DNC protests and were connected to anti-war and civil rights movements. The oral histories of many gays and lesbians active in the 1960s show that they were not single-issue-focused—they connected the struggles of many communities together.

One such activist was Henry Wiemhoff, who had marched in Selma, Ala., for racial equality. He had been a student at the University of Chicago and was tired of homophobic roommates. In 1969 he placed an ad in the school's Chicago Maroon newspaper for a gay roommate; among others, lesbian Michal Brody answered the ad. The University of Chicago Gay Liberation group formed out of this chance meeting and living situation. Thus, as the 1970s approached, Chicago was on the precipice, poised to enter a brave new world of gay rights. ▼

Martin Luther King Jr. (left) and President John F. Kennedy (right) with civil-rights leaders before a 1963 march. Next to Kennedy is A. Philip Randolph. Photo courtesy the Chicago History Museum.

Tony Midnite booked the famous Jewel Box Revue.

The 1960s brought the impact of shattering national events to Chicago. The shooting of three "kings" (President John F. Kennedy, presidential candidate Robert F. Kennedy, and civil-rights leader Martin Luther King Jr.) devastated and demoralized

brave people did allow their images and words to be used, in newspapers and also in broadcast media. The Mattachine Midwest Newsletter was a key to "for us, by us" communication and laid the foundation for a boom in gay and lesbian media in the 1970s. William B. Kelley and Marie J. Kuda both contributed immensely to

— *Tracy Baim*

The Jewel Box Revue at Roberts Show Lounge in the 1950s. Photo from Tony Midnite. Courtesy Windy City Times archives.

DANCING WITH THE STARS   *by TRACY BAIM*

"DRAG" IN THE 1950s AND EARLIER WAS mostly seen as men dressed as women to perform onstage, or seen as butch lesbians in the bars. A sophisticated understanding of various kinds of gender-identity issues only started to be written about in significant ways post-Stonewall. While many people truly just wanted to entertain, others simply wanted to live their lives in new bodies altered by medical science. Two of Chicago's transgender luminaries were Tony Midnite and Jacques Cristion, both members of the city of Chicago's Gay and Lesbian Hall of Fame.

After coming to Chicago in 1951 as a female impersonator, Midnite opened a costume design studio and eventually worked 16-hour days to meet worldwide demand, according to his Hall of Fame Web site biography. His clients included Club Chesterfield performers such as Roby Landers, Mitzi Monet, Jackie Lynn, Criss Cross, Kismet, Kara Montey, and more. "During an election year, most all the strip clubs got closed and I panicked," he said. "I depended on these girls for a lot of my business and money. I still had a wig and a pair of high-heeled shoes. I got in touch with an agent and booked a pantomime show into the Kismet Club ... on State Street." After it too closed, they moved to the Blue Dahlia on West North Avenue.

He defied police disapproval of such shows in the early 1950s by booking the Jewel Box Revue for a sold-out run at Roberts Show Lounge on the South Side, which set a precedent. "The revue, billed as '25 Men and a Girl,' included 25 impersonators and a lesbian. It was booked in for two weeks with options, but stayed eight months and packed the house. Impersonators have been able to perform here since with comparatively little hindrance," according to the Hall of Fame.

In 1978, GayLife newspaper did a three-part series on Midnite and gay life in Chicago. He spoke about bar payoffs to police, early gay bars during the 1930s and 1940s, and the difficulties of cross-dressing, including discrimination by gay people.

Midnite took part in the 1977 Medinah Temple demonstration against Anita Bryant and in the Daley Center protest against police harassment at Carol's Speakeasy during Mayor Jane M. Byrne's administration. Today, Midnite is in his 80s and lives in Las Vegas.

Jacques Cristion (1936–2003) was a Chicago legend who held drag balls on the South Side for more than 31 years. He was also a dancer, costume designer and dressmaker. The decades of materials Cristion retained from his famous events were lost after his death when a landlord threw all his possessions away before friends arrived. When writer Sukie de la Croix interviewed Cristion for the January 2000 issue of BLACKlines, Cristion said that his first ball took place in 1970 at the Grand Ballroom at East 64th Street and South Cottage Grove Avenue. "My opening was 'Soulful Strut'; that was the first dance in the show. That first year it was packed," said Cristion. "There was about 1,500 people. My sister's club [The Original Thirty Ladies and Gents Social Club, where Cristion's first ball was organized] had about 40 members. Imagine each one of them selling tickets. That wasn't a gay club, just a social club."

The inclusion of trans and gender-identity issues is still a hot topic 50 years later, both in Chicago and across the United States. As Midnite and Cristion proved, their efforts have been an integral part of the community. ▼

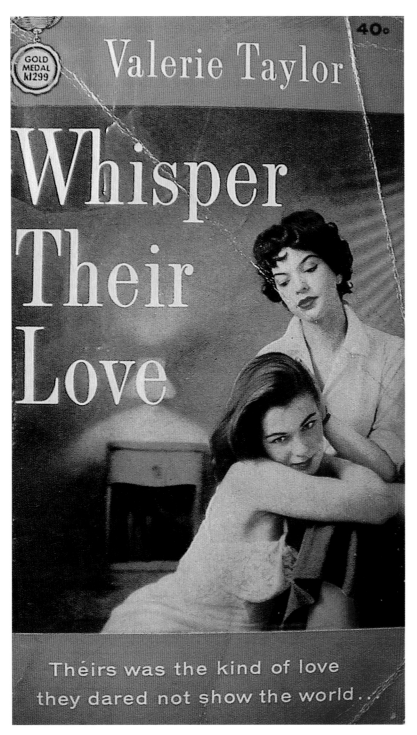

One of Valerie Taylor's pulp novels.
Courtesy M. Kuda Archives, Oak Park, Ill.

POSTWAR PULPS   *by MARIE J. KUDA*

AFTER WORLD WAR II THE PAPERBACK BOOK TRADE ACCELERATED.
Paper made of low-quality wood pulp and the books' lurid cover art connoted
genre trash titles for a disposable market. But the industry also created a niche for
cheap reprints of reputable works.

In the estimation of later lesbian feminist critics, a few lesbian genre writers stand out from the mass. Illinois natives Ann Bannon of Joliet and Valerie
Taylor of Oswego garnered loyal followings.

Bannon, nom de plume of Ann Weldy, a married academic at the time,
published five lesbian novels in the 1950s—the first, after only one visit to a
Greenwich Village gay bar. Bannon created the quintessential "butch" character, Beebo Brinker. Bonnie Zimmerman in The Safe Sea of Women: Lesbian
Fiction, 1969-1989 (1989) and others suggest that Brinker's swaggering
attitude not only became the stereotypical perception of "butches" but also
determined the behavior of a generation of gay women.

Valerie Taylor used the proceeds of her first novel to obtain a divorce from an
abusive husband and moved with her three boys to Chicago, the setting for
several of her lesbian novels. Taylor, nom de plume of Velma Tate, sold more
than 2 million copies of her first lesbian title, Whisper Their Love (1957). Five
of her novels featured some of the same characters. Taylor wrote for The Ladder
(1958-1972), the magazine of the first U.S. lesbian rights organization, the
Daughters of Bilitis.

Another notable "trash" writer of the period was Chicagoan Paul Little,
who wrote genre fiction (including lesbian fiction) under at least a dozen
names, according to his obituary.

European bestsellers such as the questionable Radclyffe Hall classic, The
Well of Loneliness (1928), which postulated homosexuals as a "third sex," and
Elisabeth Craigin's Either Is Love (1937), with its total acceptance of bisexu-
ality, were reprinted as paperbacks.

In 1972 Anyda Marchant and her partner Muriel Crawford incorporated as
Naiad Press, self-publishing two novels written under Marchant's nom de plume
Sarah Aldridge.

The women soon pooled resources with Barbara Grier (who under the pseudonym Gene Damon had retained The Ladder's mailing list as its last publisher) and
with Grier's partner, Donna McBride, and the most successful lesbian press to date
began. The new joint venture was coordinated out of the Missouri home of the latter couple. The initial Naiad brochures were printed by Chicago's Womanpress,
and early titles including Jeannette Howard Foster's translation of Renée Vivien's
Une femme m'apparut (A Woman Appeared to Me) were printed at Salsedo Press,
a Chicago printer for progressive causes. Books by Bannon, Taylor, Mary Renault,
Patricia Highsmith and others would be reprinted in the 1980s by the Naiad Press.
Taylor would continue to write novels until her death in 1997. ▼

LITERARY POWERHOUSE: VALERIE TAYLOR *by JORJET HARPER*

VALERIE TAYLOR WAS BORN VELMA NACELLA YOUNG IN AURORA, Ill., in 1913. Five years after her graduation from Elgin High School, at the height of the Depression, she attended Blackburn College in Carlinville, Ill., a "work college" where all students work as part of their educational experience. In 1939 she married and had two sons. At first a rural schoolteacher and later an office worker, she supplemented her income from the 1930s throughout the 1950s by publishing dozens of poems and short stories in magazines under several pseudonyms.

In 1953 she sold her first novel, Hired Girl, a heterosexual romance, under the name Valerie Taylor and divorced her alcoholic, abusive husband. She moved with her sons to Chicago, where they lived in a tin-sided house near a beach built for workers at the 1893 World's Fair. Taylor would later lead pickets for tenants' rights, gay rights, and anti-war groups such as Women for Peace and the Women's International League for Peace and Freedom.

In Chicago, Taylor worked as a proofreader and an assistant copy editor, and her first lesbian novel, Whisper Their Love, was published in 1957. The novel sold 2 million copies, an astonishing figure for its day. In the 1960s Taylor contributed poetry and reviews to the Daughters of Bilitis magazine, The Ladder. Jeannette Foster, the Kinsey Institute's first librarian, who self-published Sex Variant Women in Literature, visited Taylor in Chicago, and over the years Taylor would exchange letters with Foster and other writers including Elsa Gidlow and May Sarton about their work and the future of lesbian literature.

In 1962 Taylor was invited to lecture on lesbian literature by a Chicago chapter of the Mattachine Society. Taylor was about 50 when, through the chapter, she met Pearl Hart (1890–1975), then in her 70s. Attracted by Hart's intellect and passion for social justice, Taylor entered into what she felt was the most important relationship of her life. The chapter collapsed, and in 1965 Taylor, Hart and others helped found Mattachine Midwest, Chicago's first politically active gay rights organization. Taylor was soon writing and editing its newsletter. Frequently called upon to be the woman's voice of the organization, Taylor appeared with sexologists William Masters and Virginia E. Johnson on Phil Donahue's nationally syndicated TV talk show. In the mid-

1960s Midwood-Tower published four more Taylor novels set in an urban lesbian milieu: A World Without Men, Unlike Others, Return to Lesbos, and Journey to Fulfillment. In 1967, Ace Books released The Secret of the Bayou, her first in the gothic genre, under the name Francine Davenport.

In 1974, Taylor co-founded the national Lesbian Writers' Conference, held in Chicago, where the following year keynote speaker Barbara Grier persuaded Taylor to publish with Grier's nascent Naiad Press. From 1977 through 1989 Naiad released Taylor's new, more feminist lesbian novels Love Image, Prism (which she called her geriatric novel), and Rice and Beans (imbued with poverty and activism); it also reprinted three of her earlier pulps. Naiad co-founder Anyda Marchant credited Valerie Taylor's name recognition and popularity with helping to push the publishing house into the black.

Valerie Taylor in Chicago at Lake Michigan. Photo by James Albert Vaughn. Right: Taylor speaks at a pride rally in downtown Chicago, 1970s. Photo by Stephen Kulieke, GayLife newspaper. Courtesy M. Kuda Archives, Oak Park, Ill.

In late 1979 Taylor moved to Tucson, Ariz., where she continued to write novels and poetry into the 1990s. In 1992 she was inducted into the Chicago Gay and Lesbian Hall of Fame. In October 1997 she fell from her wheelchair while reaching for a book and died in hospice 12 days later at age 84. Taylor's papers are archived in the Human Sexuality Collection of the Carl A. Kroch Library at Cornell University. ▼

This article is based on materials provided by Marie J. Kuda.

Tiny Davis. Drawing by Otis Richardson.

TINY AND RUBY'S GAY SPOT

IN THE 1950s, TRUMPETER TINY DAVIS AND PARTNER RUBY
Lucas opened "Tiny and Ruby's Gay Spot" at 2711 S. Wentworth Ave.—
"light, white, brown and yellow," the femmes and the daddies all came to
see Tiny use her tongue "like Pops, and better than Bix." Tiny had been a
star performer with a wartime all-girl band, the International Sweethearts
of Rhythm. A 1986 documentary, Tiny & Ruby—Hell Divin' Women, profiled the couple. Ruby was Tiny's partner for 40 years and was herself a
drummer and pianist. They were interviewed in their North Chicago, Ill.,
home. The African American Registry's Web site lists Ernestine "Tiny"
Davis' birthdate as Aug. 5, 1907. She died in 1994. ▼

IN UNIFORM: DARBY

CHICAGOAN JIM DARBY CERTAINLY CUT A FINE FIGURE IN HIS U.S. NAVY UNIFORM. HE
served from 1952 to 1956 as a cryptographer and radioman during the Korean War. The brutal murder of
Chicagoan Allen Schindler by fellow servicemembers in 1992 prompted Darby to become an activist. By this
time a retired teacher, Darby lobbied to lift the military's gay ban and co-founded the Chicago chapter of the
Gay, Lesbian and Bisexual Veterans of America (now American Veterans for Equal Rights). James C. Darby
and his partner Patrick Bova have been together since 1963. The duo organize and participate in numerous
gay and non-gay military events. ▼

Jim Darby arrested at a demonstration for gay rights, at the White House, 1993. Photo courtesy Jim Darby.

RUSTIN IN CHICAGO

OPENLY GAY BLACK ACTIVIST BAYARD
Rustin (1910–1987)—known primarily for advising Dr. Martin Luther King Jr. and for his
work organizing the March on Washington for
Jobs and Freedom in 1963—was a pivotal figure
in the civil rights movement in Chicago as
well. His travels to Chicago are documented in
both John D'Emilio's Lost Prophet: The Life
and Times of Bayard Rustin and Dempsey Travis' An Autobiography of Black Chicago.

For the first meeting of the Chicago March
on Conventions Committee, which took place
June 21, 1960, Rustin attended with civil rights
leader A. Philip Randolph. At a National
Association for the Advancement of Colored
People (NAACP) meeting in January 1960,
Rustin discussed the importance of a large
demonstration at the Republican National
Convention in Chicago that would follow a
similar protest in Los Angeles at the Democratic National Convention.

During 1961 and 1962, Rustin (promoting his
pacifist agenda) engaged in a series of public
debates with Nation of Islam leader Malcolm X
in New York, Chicago and Washington, D.C.
While the Nation of Islam believed in racial
separation and armed self-defense, Rustin—
himself a Quaker—called for strategic nonvio-
lence and mass action.

Rustin was one of the few national public
figures to be openly gay during the 1960s. Some
scholars feel that his homosexuality restricted
his actions, while others have taken the opposite argument: that he overcame the prejudices
of others to accomplish much. While his
honesty may have cost him at least some of the
political prominence he rightly deserved, his
refusal to remain closeted in an era when homophobia was the death-knell for anyone with
political aspirations has made him an inspiration and a hero to the generations that have
followed. **— Andrew Davis**

A WOMAN IN THE SUN: LORRAINE HANSBERRY

by MARIE J. KUDA

CHICAGO-BORN WRITER LORRAINE HANS-berry (1930–1965) studied at the School of the Art Institute of Chicago and at the University of Wisconsin. Her father, real estate broker Carl Hansberry, moved his family into a neighborhood of racially restricted housing in 1939, challenging Chicago's segregation covenants. The ensuing court cases would be fought through the Illinois system to victory in the U.S. Supreme Court, effectively breaking a legal barrier to open housing. This experience gave her crucial elements for her award-winning play, A Raisin in the Sun (1959), set in Chicago. Hansberry's The Sign in Sidney Brustein's Window (1964) and her posthumously published Les Blancs (1972) both have gay characters.

Hansberry moved to New York in 1950 and married. She separated from her husband in 1957, the same year she joined the Daughters of Bilitis, an early lesbian-rights organization. The couple divorced in 1964—months before her death from breast cancer. In the August 1957 issue of the DOB magazine, The Ladder, she entered into a dialogue with Marian Zimmer Bradley (who later would become a bestselling author) on the position of married lesbians. Hansberry asked: "Isn't the problem of the married lesbian woman that of an individual who finds that, despite her conscious will oft times, she is inclined to have her most intense emotional and physical reactions directed toward other women, quite beyond any comparative thing she might have ever felt for her husband—whatever her sincere affection for him?"

In 1963, gay author James Baldwin was invited by then–Attorney General Robert F. Kennedy to discuss race issues. He invited prominent African-Americans, including Hansberry, to join him. Randall Kenan in his 1994 biography of Baldwin says Hansberry warned RFK of the "fire next time": "You and your brother [President John F. Kennedy] are

representatives of the best that a white America can offer; if you are insensitive to this then there's no alternative except our going to the streets." In Beautiful, Also, Are the Souls of My Black Sisters (1978), Jeanne L. Noble writes that Hansberry's legacy is monumental. But she wonders what activism may

Lorraine Hansberry. Drawing by Otis Richardson.

have been quelled by her early death, noting Hansberry's statement: "I think when I get my health back I shall go into the South and find out what kind of revolutionary I am."

Neil Miller in Out of the Past: Gay and Lesbian History from 1869 to the Present (1995) writes: "Her husband Robert Nemiroff noted that Hansberry's ho-

mosexuality 'was not a peripheral or casual part of her life but contributed significantly on many levels to the sensitivity and complexity of her view of human beings and of the world.'"

In 1958 DOB founders Del Martin and Phyllis Lyon, on the final leg of a cross-country trip, visited Hansberry in New York. According to Marcia Gallo in her DOB history Different Daughters (2006), Hansberry found time for them even though she was readying Raisin for its Broadway opening. She expressed regret at not being able to "get more involved" with DOB.

For his book Making History (1992), author Eric Marcus interviewed numerous people, including former DOB national President Shirley Willer. The 1990 interview took place at her home in Key West, and she recalled meeting Hansberry, possibly on that same DOB trip: "Several of us went up to see [Hansberry] in New York and asked her if she would come out openly, admit to being a lesbian. Her explanation was that she had to pick which of the closets was most important to her. And at that time it was more important for her to be a Black woman who had written a great play and book than to come out as a lesbian. We were disappointed, but we could understand it." Marcus asked how she knew Hansberry was a lesbian: "I know it's hackneyed, but it takes one to know one. I knew. The word does get around."

In the years following the production of Raisin, Hansberry would move in a circle of other closeted lesbians who shared a social life sub rosa in Greenwich Village. Novelist Marijane Meaker (who wrote lesbian pulp fiction as Vin Packer and Ann Aldrich, and children's books as M.E. Kerr and Mary James) noted in her 2003 memoir that she knew Hansberry, her lover, and her gay friends. Hansberry invited Meaker to a pre-release screening of the 1961 Sidney Poitier film version of Raisin. ▼

MATTACHINE MIDWEST: STANDING UP FOR GAY RIGHTS

by JOHN D. POLING

At a time when mainstream society did not accept gays and lesbians, Mattachine Midwest arose to fight against decades of discrimination and advance the rights of homosexuals.

IN THE SUMMER OF 1964, PRESIDENT LYNDON B. JOHNSON SIGNED THE MOST significant civil rights legislation since Reconstruction—the Civil Rights Act of 1964. As one of the crowning achievements of the explosive civil rights movement, the act secured the rights of African-Americans and outlawed employment discrimination based on race, color, sex, religion and national origin. Such protection, however, was not afforded to America's sexual minorities. In the 1950s and 1960s, most Americans perceived gay men and lesbians as a threat not only to the country's moral foundation but also to the very heart of national security in the Cold War era.

In the 1960s, large metropolitan areas, such as Chicago, afforded homosexuals a certain level of anonymity but did not shelter them completely from the nationwide persecution of gays. Law enforcement officials reflected the views of society's mainstream and held little tolerance for deviant sexual behavior.

In the chilly early-morning hours of Saturday, April 25, 1964, Cook County sheriff's deputies raided the Fun Lounge, which was owned and operated by Louis Gauger at 2340 N. Mannheim Rd. Louie Gage's, as the bar was often called, catered to Chicago's sizable gay population but was located in an unincorporated area outside city limits, probably to avoid regular crackdowns by the Chicago Police Department. As part of a campaign promise to get tough on the county's vice activity, Cook County Sheriff Richard Ogilvie had placed the club under surveillance. Ogilvie held particular scorn for the Fun Lounge, which he once called "too revolting to describe." At the culmination of a three-week surveillance operation, these deputies carried out the subsequent raid and arrested more than 100 people.

While some Fun Lounge patrons did participate in criminal activity, including underage drinking and drug possession, the sheriff's office charged most with "deviate sexual conduct" or as "patrons of a disorderly house." The following day, the Chicago Tribune reported on the "powder puffs and lipsticks" that some men carried, before mentioning the underage patrons or seized marijuana. While space prohibited the newspaper from running the names of all 109 arrested, the names of eight teachers and four municipal employees appeared in print. One of the men arrested, a junior-high teacher from Park Ridge, had already resigned before the story hit the newsstands. The following month, the charges brought against those arrested were dropped, but, of course, it was a bit late for those whose names had been included in the original news coverage.

Bar raids occurred with regularity in Chicago and other cities across America, but the large scale of the Fun Lounge raid made it unique. It went beyond the scope of previous police raids and shook the city's gay political scene out of hibernation. In addition to arresting 103 men, the sheriff's department also took six women into custody. The raid touched the lives of many in the gay community and bolstered the first successful, sustained effort to organize a gay civil rights organization in Chicago—Mattachine Midwest. In an interview years later, MM founder Ira Jones referred to the Fun Lounge raid as "the straw that broke the camel's back."

Mattachine Midwest was part of the nationwide homophile or gay-rights movement that was gaining in momentum in urban areas across the country. The movement represented the first significant, unified effort by gay men and lesbians to fight for justice and equality and against decades of oppression and discrimination sanctioned by mainstream society. Although their numbers were small, the individuals who risked ostracism for the betterment of their population won important battles in securing civil rights for homosexuals. Their actions made the homophile movement a significant achievement, regardless of the continued debate over the movement's effectiveness before the Stonewall riots of June 1969.

In 1965, Mattachine Midwest had what few other homophile organizations in the United States could boast—a legacy. Forty years before Mattachine Midwest's founding, Henry Gerber, a Chicago postal clerk, founded the Society for Human Rights to fight the persecution of "those who deviated from the established norms in sexual matters." The society was incorporated by the State of Illinois in December 1924.

Gerber, a German immigrant and World War I veteran, modeled his society on homosexual-rights groups that existed in Germany at the time. He believed that reforming legislation that criminalized homosexuality was one way to end gay discrimination.

Teacher, 1 of 8 Seized in Vice Raid, Quits

One of eight suburban teachers arrested in a vice raid early yesterday morning at the Fun lounge, a tavern at 2340 N. Mannheim rd., Leyden twp., resigned yesterday afternoon.

Norris Angel, 24, of 2025 Pine av., Des Plaines, a teacher in Lincoln Junior High school in Park Ridge, quit altho he denied any wrongdoing. Blair Plimpton, district superintendent, said Angel's resignation would be accepted.

Arrests Being Investigated

Cook and Du Page county school superintendents' offices said that the cases of seven other suburban teachers arrested along with 95 other men and six wimen in the raid by sheriff's police would be investigated.

Roy DeShane, Du Page county superintendent, said that local school districts would investigate the charges. If proved, he said, procedures for revoking the certification of the teachers would be initiated. Many of the men arrested carried powder puffs and lipsticks and some of them wore wigs, according to Richard Cain, the sheriff's investigator.

Marijuana Is Seized

Among those arrested by a squad led by Cain were a civilian employe of the Chicago police department, a deputy court clerk assigned to the Chicago board of election commissioners, and an employe of the Cook county forest preserve district.

The squad seized a supply of marijuana freshly shipped from

[Continued on page 6, col. 4]

[TRIBUNE Staff Photo]
Robert Levy, manager of lounge, as he appeared in Criminal Courts building.

Louis Gauger (left), proprietor, and Herbert Schieler, licensee of Fun lounge.

Tribune Features

Tower Ticker	Page 16
Weather	Page 22
Editorials	Page 24
World Spotlight	Sec. 1A
Social Security	Sec. 1A, p. 15
Sports	Sec. 2
Classified	Sec. 3
Business	Sec. 4
Crossword Puzzle	Sec. 5
Feature Section	Sec. 5
Travel and Resorts	Sec. 6
Magazine Section	Sec. 7
Comics	Sec. 8
Books Today	Sec. 9
Deaths and Obituaries	Sec. 1A, p. 14
News summaries on page 4	

On Sunday, April 26, 1964, the Chicago Tribune featured front-page coverage of the raid on the Fun Lounge. Photographs of the lounge's manager, proprietor and licensee accompanied the story. Courtesy the Chicago History Museum.

Left: Tom Gertz

Below:
William Kelley (below left), with Gertz at right and Roland Keith (Lancaster) and James Bradford (Osgood) in middle at an early 1970s Mattachine banquet at The Trip gay bar.

Courtesy M. Kuda Archives, Oak Park, Ill.

To this end, he wrote, printed and distributed two newsletters, the most widespread of which was Friendship and Freedom. His campaign, however, was short-lived. In July 1925, aided by a tip from the wife of a society member, the Chicago Police Department raided Gerber's apartment at 1710 N. Crilly Ct., arrested him, and confiscated his typewriter and homophile literature. Gerber eventually lost his job because of "conduct unbecoming a postal worker" and decided to reenlist in the Army. He served for 17 years and received an honorable discharge in 1945.

Although the raid brought a quick end to the Society for Human Rights, its existence was not in vain. Decades later, a lanky Californian named Harry Hay learned of the society from the lover of a former member. The notion of a gay political organization appealed to Hay, who was struggling with the discrimination and danger of being a gay man. With the help of four friends, Hay built on Gerber's idea of an organized society. The Mattachine Society, as Hay dubbed it, began in Los Angeles in 1951. Hay took the name Mattachine from Société Mattachine, said to be a secret medieval fraternity of unmarried townsmen whose masked appearance gave them the freedom to speak the truth.

Hay's Mattachine Society extended beyond the scope of a localized group and achieved greater success than Henry Gerber could have imagined in the 1920s. By 1953, as many as 2,000 gay men and lesbians met as part of various Mattachine cells throughout California, including San Diego, Los Angeles and the San Francisco Bay area. By the mid-1950s, Mattachine Society chapters were organized nationwide, including chapters in New York, Denver and Chicago. The small Chicago Mattachine chapter published a newsletter, held discussion group meetings, and volunteered to serve as subjects for a Chicago doctor who wanted to perform Rorschach tests on "non-institutionalized homosexuals"; the group urged members to take part in the test in order "to assist professional groups in filling the

void of reliable data on sexual deviates."

The leading members of Chicago's first Mattachine chapter echoed the sentiment of California groups. They believed that hope for the integration of gays into mainstream society hinged upon support from medical and psychological experts. Experts,

A Mattachine Midwest newsletter, 1969.

they believed, would make the scientific argument that sexual deviates were not a threat to society.

The prevailing notion of the era was that a sexual attraction that deviated from the norm was not only a psychological illness but also a danger to those who came in contact with the homosexual. Gay men and lesbians, it was thought, wanted to turn others

into homosexuals. Thus, Chicago Mattachine members were not encouraged to speak out on their own behalf or to question the anti-homosexual legal system. "It is not the function of this Society," one member wrote in 1954, "to deplore the enforcement of enacted laws or to make subjective guesses about their justices or injustices."

While Mattachine members strove for acceptance and integration, the overriding emotion of the group remained the fear of being exposed. In such a secretive environment, communication was a constant problem. Telephones, some with party lines, were rarely seen as safe, so most communication was done through the mail. Many of the members also used pseudonyms and often never knew the real names of their fellow members. By 1957, communication problems, along with the difficulty of recruiting new members, spelled the end of the first Chicago Mattachine chapter. These difficulties were not unique to Chicago. According to historian John D'Emilio, Mattachine groups of the late 1950s were "distressingly small in size."

Two years later, a second Chicago Mattachine group was organized. This chapter was also short-lived, but it surpassed the first group in rhetoric and tone. The second group's newsletters lashed out at the newspapers that printed the names of persons arrested in bar raids. In 1960, one Mattachine writer asked the Milwaukee Journal if it planned to give the acquittals of bar patrons "as much publicity as their arrests." The second society even had the boldness to attempt to place an advertisement in a major city newspaper to attract new members. The paper's management alluded vaguely to "the nature of the society" as the reason for its rejection of the advertisement.

In the fall of 1962, the chapter folded. With a life span of barely two years, the second group, similar to its predecessor, could not sustain the long-term effort needed to lay the groundwork for a successful gay political organization. Both groups, however, advanced the formation of a viable gay civil rights organization. The two previous Mattachine Societies had attracted members who would become instrumental in forming the ultimately successful Mattachine Midwest.

Despite the efforts of the two Chicago Mattachine Societies, circumstances remained bleak for the city's gay community in the early 1960s. The limited social outlets for gays, including bars and bathhouses, brought a risk of being arrested, which often meant the publication of one's name in a city newspaper. This, in turn, could lead to the collapse of a social network or the loss of a job. In extreme cases, the pressure could lead to suicide. Those arrested had limited opportunities for recourse, and only a handful of attorneys would represent such cases.

After the demise of the second Chicago Mattachine chapter, a small chapter of the Daughters of Bilitis remained the only gay political presence in the city. Formed in San Francisco in 1955, the DOB worked to dispel society's myths about lesbians. The DOB's focus of validation and support was more inward than that of the Mattachine Society. The group strove to help members overcome the negative images society placed upon lesbians. Besides holding meetings, the Chicago DOB also published a member newsletter, but due to the group's small size, there was little outreach to the rest of the city's homosexual community.

Plans for Mattachine Midwest began in earnest early in 1965 when Ira Jones, Pearl M. Hart and Robert Basker began organizing the new group. Jones, a local entrepreneur, and Hart, a prominent civil rights attorney, had both been involved with the earlier Chicago Mattachine Societies. Basker was a New York City transplant who had a passion for social justice. He had come to Chicago as an ency-

clopedia salesman. Despite their varied backgrounds, Jones, Hart and Basker all believed in the desperate, long-overdue need for an organization such as Mattachine Midwest.

Hart served as the legal adviser, and Jones and Basker did much of the legwork, using personal contacts and networking in bars to spread the word about the new organization. In May 1965, Jones, Hart, Basker and about a dozen others met to map

Mattachine Midwest members in the 1970s, including Valerie Taylor (back, second from left) and Roland Keith Lancaster (in glasses). Courtesy M. Kuda Archives, Oak Park, Ill.

out the agenda of MM and organize several committees, which would become the backbone of the organization.

Mattachine Midwest held its first public meeting on July 25, 1965, in the ballroom of the Midland Hotel (now the W Chicago City Center hotel) at 172 W. Adams St. The work of the publicity committee exceeded expectations, and more than 140 people attended the meeting. The group chose Basker as its first president and Roland Lancaster as secretary. Basker gave a stirring speech, pointing out not only the social injustices inflicted upon gay people but also the responsibilities that gay people must accept:

"In our time, homosexuals have been the victims of abuses winked at by the law authorities. They have been arrested without due process of law, victimized by odious police methods such as entrapment, manhandled by the police and deprived of legal redress when physically assaulted by gangs. … Our work will help many people who will never support or understand our purpose of existence. Nevertheless, those of us here tonight have the responsibility to give of ourselves … to strengthen Mattachine Midwest. It is our vehicle in this generation for advancing the rights of homosexuals."

Vowing to improve the "legal, social and economic status of the homosexual" through programming and social service, MM leaders gave those in attendance a message of empowerment that few had ever heard before. Hart further drove home the message when she addressed the group, telling them to "assert the equal rights" that were already theirs.

The first meeting of Mattachine Midwest generated an immense and heated reaction, and the group's leaders faced the challenge of keeping up the momentum. In addition to starting a newsletter and a telephone helpline and putting together a lending library for members, MM leaders organized a publicity event they called "The Homophile Movement in America" and invited several national homophile leaders to Chicago. Mattachine Midwest leaders held a news conference, arranged appearances for the guests on the Nightline radio program on WBBM and on Irv Kupcinet's television program, and organized a fundraising dinner.

By the beginning of 1966, Mattachine Midwest proved itself more than a worthy successor to the previous efforts at organizing a gay political group in Chicago. While awareness initiatives and social service efforts remained much emphasized, leadership began to cast a wider net. According to the group's "Homophile Movement" campaign, some members wanted to look beyond a support network and begin to challenge the subjective nature of law enforcement toward homosexuals. They desired to tackle the problem of gay entrapment by police—which consisted of assigning undercover officers to stake out public men's rooms. The officers were supposed to wait to be propositioned, but they often took the initiative, approaching men first. Chicago's early Mattachine groups had taken little interest in addressing this problem.

Challenging social injustice came to the forefront in the fall of 1965 when, upon Basker's resignation, Jim Bradford became the new president of Mattachine Midwest. Bradford, another New York transplant, was no stranger to leadership or to questioning authority; while in New York, he had actively protested capital punishment and the Korean War. Similar to many Mattachine members, he chose to use a pseudonym instead of his real last name. Pseudonyms offered protection not only to members who wanted to remain anonymous but also to outspoken ones such as Bradford.

Jim Bradford had no reservations about blaming the city's police force for the unfair treatment of gays in Chicago. He challenged the police department's actions toward homosexuals as no one before him had done. He had access to Mattachine's mouthpiece—its newsletter—and used it to wage a campaign to publicize his views and engage the police. Bradford's biggest complaints involved entrapment of men in public restrooms and random, informal interrogation of any man whom police deemed suspicious. Police used the "stop and quiz" method, as the practice was called, to keep track of single men who were walking or parking in suspected homosexual "cruising" areas.

Chicago's police officials did not want to talk to Bradford or the members of Mattachine Midwest about their practices toward homosexuals. Bradford made numerous attempts to arrange a meeting with the police, beginning in the fall of 1965. He also asked for a police representative to come to an MM

meeting to address police practices. He reported that the police claimed that they "had inadequate knowledge of the topic."

Through perseverance and pestering, however, Bradford finally prevailed in arranging a meeting between the police and several Mattachine officers in April 1966. While the occasion was historic, it yielded minimal results. MM representatives presented their grievances regarding police entrapment of gay men. According to a newsletter report, the police responded that the force was only a "tool of society" and that "vague city ordinances and [a] lack of court decisions" forced them to take action and justified those actions.

The meeting was not the breakthrough for which Mattachine leaders had hoped. But however tendentious the relationship remained, MM had opened a line of communication. Two years later, Mattachine and police officials met again, and during these meetings, Mattachine leaders gave police the names of specific officers accused of initiating flirtation and, at times, making physical contact in order to entice gay men into soliciting sexual acts.

Much of what is known about the group's earliest efforts to meet with police comes from accounts in the organization's monthly newsletter. Realizing that the organization had a responsibility not only to inform but also to inspire hope for gays and lesbians, MM leaders were determined to circulate their newsletter to a wider readership. Unlike the earlier Mattachine groups, Mattachine Midwest expanded and formalized its distribution methods.

Each month, members took stacks of newsletters to gay bars and gay-friendly bookstores. Distributing the newsletter, however, came with a risk. According to Ira Jones, in at least one instance, police confiscated newsletters from a bar during a raid and used them as evidence that the owner ran a "disorderly house."

The Mattachine Midwest Newsletter quickly became a source of information and a voice for Chicago's gay community. Less than six months after the group's founding, Jim Bradford estimated the newsletter circulation to be in excess of 2,000. Through membership dues and advertising sales, the newsletter continued to grow throughout the

1960s. By July 1970, the circulation was approximately 8,000.

The newsletter became a valuable forum for the city's gay liberation groups that formed following the Stonewall riots of June 1969. Stonewall proved to be the pivotal event in gay political history. The riots, which began in protest to a bar raid at New York's Stonewall Inn, became a call-to-arms for young gays. Most of the Stonewall-inspired gay liberation groups had little money to publicize their activities, so Mattachine Midwest printed their news and promoted their events in the MM newsletter.

Besides providing the gay community with monthly news, Mattachine Midwest also started the city's first telephone helpline for gay men and lesbians. The Mattachine Midwest answering service, run by member volunteers, operated for 19 years. The service gave gay people in need a number to call for a sympathetic ear and, if necessary, a referral to a professional. MM recruited doctors, psychologists, lawyers and ministers, who agreed to offer their services to anonymous callers. By the late 1960s, the answering service received 40 to 60 calls per month. Building on the success of the Mattachine service, other groups began to launch helplines in the 1970s.

Some MM members also volunteered to participate in the group's speakers bureau. A variety of groups invited Mattachine representatives, including Bradford, Tom Gertz, Bill Kelley, Marie Kuda, David Stienecker, and Valerie Taylor to speak on the topic of homosexuality and Mattachine Midwest's role in the gay community. While Mattachine speakers occasionally faced open hostility, many recalled that audiences were considerate and genuinely interested in the subject. As social mores began to ease, groups as diverse as the Cook County School of Nursing and the Lakeview Ministers' Workshop requested MM speakers.

Mattachine Midwest reached its peak in early 1970. Until that time, the organization had enjoyed an unchallenged position as the voice of the city's gay community, but following the Stonewall riots, the gay-rights movement grew rapidly and became increasingly militant. Local Gay Liberation groups began to describe Mattachine Midwest as a complacent group,

MATTACHINE MIDWEST
NEWSLETTER
NOV.- DEC. 1969

DOCTORS AND NIMH
URGE LAW CHANGE   by M. J. Kuda

The results of two studies of interest to the homophile community have received local and national news coverage. The final report of the Task Force on Homosexuality, sponsored by the National Institute of Mental Health, and a poll on sociomedical issues, including homosexuality, conducted by <u>Modern Medicine</u> magazine, concluded that homosexual acts between consenting adults "if they are carried out discreetly" are not matters of public or legal concern.

Of the 27,700 doctors responding to the <u>Modern Medicine</u> poll, the percentage of physicians specializing in psychiatry who were in favor of legalizing homosexual acts was significantly higher than the total poll result—92% versus 67.7%.

The NIMH's "Hooker Report" (after its chairman, UCLA's Dr. Evelyn Hooker), while advocating further research into the non-clinical aspects of homosexuality in our society, emphasized the necessity for the review and revamping of existing legal policy and employment practices.

Both studies stressed that their conclusions were well ahead of general public reaction but anticipated gradual changes in society's attitudes. [The Harris Poll's survey of public attitudes is reported on page 3 of this issue.] Illinois has had a "consensual" law on the books since 1961 and thus should be in the forefront of implementing the balance of proposed reforms recommended by the Task Force. These reports can be ammunition in the militant homophile's arsenal. Thinking men will find them conclusive. As <u>Newsweek</u> commented, the homosexual no longer demands "simple privacy, but full legal, economic and social integration."

TIME's clock runs backward

See VALERIE TAYLOR's article, Page 14

Mattachine Midwest newsletter, 1969. Courtesy M. Kuda Archives, Oak Park, Ill.

whose membership comprised mostly closeted, middle-aged men, and took MM to task for not taking action. In May 1970, during a meeting between Mattachine Midwest and several of the Gay Liberation groups, leaders of the old and new guards looked upon MM as a has-been. By 1971, the new groups had usurped MM's role as the city's leading gay-rights organization.

As a result, Mattachine Midwest experienced difficulties throughout the early 1970s. With a declining membership base and a large newsletter printing debt, the remaining members struggled to keep the group going. In 1971, some members offered a resolution to dissolve the group due to its inability to keep pace with the post-Stonewall movement. The membership voted against the resolution but decided to concentrate the group's energies on social service and leave political advocacy to groups such as the Chicago Gay Alliance. MM continued to operate its telephone helpline and launched new social services, including weekly discussion sessions, a support group for gay alcoholics, and a group called Parents and Friends of Gay Men and Lesbian Women, a predecessor to today's national organization, Parents and Friends of Lesbians and Gays.

With its new mission, MM's membership grew steadily throughout the 1970s, peaking at 150 in 1979. The early 1980s, however, found the organization's membership once again in decline but for different reasons. The Mattachine of the late 1970s and early 1980s encountered a gay movement that had lost its momentum and found many in the community less concerned with social consciousness.

By the late 1970s, raids on gay bars had decreased significantly, and the gay social scene had exploded. In the sexually charged atmosphere that prevailed, many members of the gay community took more interest in discos and bathhouses than in discussion groups and garage-sale fundraisers. By 1984, acquired immune deficiency syndrome (AIDS) began to radically change the sexually liberal atmosphere that

had become the community's norm. Mattachine leaders were a step behind, however, in aggressively moving into AIDS service. New groups emerged to deal with the AIDS crisis, and Mattachine leaders were forced once again to question their relevance to the community.

By 1985, Mattachine Midwest seemed to have exhausted its usefulness. Ira Jones, the group's president at the time, was single-minded in his goal to see

MATTACHINE
MIDWEST

P.O. BOX 924
CHICAGO, ILL. 60690
TELEPHONE: 337-2424
EVERY NIGHT: 7 p.m. to 7 a.m.

AUGUST '82

up•date8

August 8 — Old Town Garden Brunch —
This month's brunch for members and their friends, will be truly special. It will be at George and John's Garden, 1830 N. Lincoln Park West, from 11 a.m. to 3 p.m. The cost for members will be $3 and guests and friends $4. Cocktails as usual will be $1 each.

Hot Line Committee — Ken Turley, Chairman
Our social service station has been running continuously since 1965 under the same number. It now functions for twelve hours nightly, 7 p.m. to 7 a.m., with dedicated, all-volunteer help, every night rain or shine. Ken still needs more help, as he doesn't want to assign any one person to more than one shift every two weeks. Call him at home after 6 p.m. for further information (388-1794). We are proud that Ken will be part of the tennis tournament at the Gay Olympics in San Francisco over Labor Day . . .
We are likewise proud of ex-member Marie Kuda, who did such a dedicated job in the early days of Mattachine, when she worked on the Mattachine newsletter. In those days it consisted of several pages — this was before the Gay Crusader, followed later by GayLife and Gay Chicago began publishing . . . Marie has been appointed a staff writer for GayLife newspaper, helping to form a team of reporting staff made necessary by the resignation of Steve Kulieke. Steve has moved to San Francisco to become the news editor for the Advocate.
Also, present member George Buse has also been appointed a staff writer on the paper . . . In addition to that, Sarah Craig, who is part owner of the company which typesets this newsletter, continues as staff writer along with Chris Heim.
Added to the staff with Buse and Kuda is Paul Cotton, who will start out as the City Hall Reporter — this means, of course, that it takes three additional staff reporters to fill Steve's shoes . . . What a tribute.

Mattachine Midwest newsletter, 1982.
Courtesy M. Kuda Archives, Oak Park, Ill.

Mattachine Midwest reach its 20th anniversary and to have the milestone properly commemorated. Toward this end, he called in several personal favors, recruiting past members to come back and convincing current members to stay.

Jones got his wish when Mattachine Midwest celebrated its 20 years of service in May 1986 at a gala

at the Midland Hotel, the site of the first MM public meeting. Several past presidents, including Jim Bradford and Bob Basker, attended the event. Chicago Mayor Harold Washington made an appearance as well.

The gala was a testament to Jones' drive and tenacity and was sadly his last hurrah. Just two months later, he suffered a fatal heart attack. His death was the final blow for Mattachine Midwest.

Despite the successful anniversary celebration, there was little interest in trying to keep the group going. Some members even felt that Jones had willed the organization past its natural demise. In the end, Mattachine Midwest fell victim to the forces that doom many organizations: member apathy, lack of direction, challenging times.

Mattachine Midwest experienced great success in the months that followed the massive raid on the Fun Lounge in 1964, and this success carried the organization through the exhilarating times that rapidly followed Stonewall. MM's contributions were many, ranging from providing the gay community with a newsletter and a telephone help and referral line to speaking out against police harassment. Perhaps, though, its greatest contribution was simply that it existed.

For many of Mattachine's early members, the organization meant an end to the chronic isolation which often accompanied being a homosexual. One member recalled, "You get the feeling you are alone a lot when you're gay. Mattachine was the first inkling of community, that there were people behind you." For members like these, Mattachine Midwest was a support network long in the making. Its success represented not only the beginning of centralized gay activism in Chicago but also offered a sense of community to a population that in many ways epitomized the disenfranchised. ▼

This article is reprinted with permission from Chicago History, the Chicago History Museum magazine. Copyright © 2005 Chicago History Museum.

The Killing of Sister George, a lesbian play, was staged at the Studebaker Theatre in 1968. The next year, The Boys in the Band, a gay play, took the theater by storm. At right is the flier promoting a Mattachine Midwest benefit at the opening-night performance. Courtesy M. Kuda Archives, Oak Park, Ill.

'THE BOYS IN THE BAND' PLAY ON   *by MARIE J. KUDA*

IN DECEMBER 1969, MART CROWLEY'S PLAY The Boys in the Band opened at the Studebaker Theatre in the Fine Arts Building on South Michigan Avenue. On the eve of the Hooker Report, just months after Stonewall, and weeks after Time magazine's cover feature on "The Homosexual in America," Mattachine Midwest ran a benefit at the Dec. 2 opening, selling 300 "choice orchestra seats." Columnists and reviewers had a field day commenting as much on the audience as on the play.

In the Chicago Daily News, Jon and Abra Anderson acknowledged that the "homosexual liberty lobby is raising funds to fight the blue meanies (police harassment)" but noted that the theater was "jammed with the limp set, lads in fur, open-necked flounce shirts, leather maxicoats, plus several would-be ladies who walked funny."

Doyenne of reviewers Glenna Syse, writing in the Chicago Sun-Times, said the audience "hooted, hollered and applauded its way through the evening and almost managed to turn what is a compassionate, devastating and brilliant piece of writing into a circus."

Sydney J. Harris, in a creditable review (like the others, he lauded the performance of Paul Rudd as Donald), warned the readers of his "family newspaper" of the "raw and raunchy" language of the play, noting that his "coarser fiber" sustained him. He concluded the play was a hit; "in this bleak season, the theater has come alive with a play that involves, that deepens our insight as much as it entertains our sadly malnourished sense of humor."

The Boys is now considered by gay historians as either a landmark event (largely because of its frank, crackling dialogue) or a play that (because of its stereotypes) set gay theater back a couple of decades. ▼

THE 'INFAMOUS CRIME' AGAINST PRIVACY

Until Illinois criminal laws were finally overhauled in 1961, conviction for sodomy, "the infamous crime against nature either with man or beast," carried a one- to 10-year prison sentence—regardless of whether either party ejaculated!—and rendered the perpetrator "forever ... incapable of holding any office of honor, trust or profit, or voting at any election, or serving as a juror ... ."

Illinois became the first state in the nation to decriminalize same-sex sexual activity. That achievement owes much to the passion of Paul Goldman, a straight Chicago lawyer who had been deeply affected by discovering the suicide note of his law-school roommate. Goldman hadn't known his friend was gay; in a 1979 Student Lawyer profile of Goldman after his 50 years in the trenches, he told the writer Grant Pick he "knew nothing about homosexuals, except what I had read in toilets." Anguish over his roommate's torment led him to devote his professional life to the legal needs of homosexuals, and when the Illinois and Chicago bar associations undertook a multi-year project to modernize and simplify the criminal laws, Goldman and the Rev. James Jones, a prominent Episcopal clergyman, led lobbying efforts to eliminate the crime of sodomy.

"We weren't so much concerned about the consequences of prosecution," Goldman said. "It was more the psychological effects the law had on 'Joe and Jim,' who lived together for 25 years always in the shadow of the penitentiary."

In 2003, after 35 states had followed Illinois' lead, the U.S. Supreme Court echoed Goldman's sentiment: The liberty protected by the Constitution, the court said in Lawrence v. Texas, allows "adults [to] choose to enter upon this relationship in the confines of their homes and their own private lives and still retain their dignity as free persons." **— Ron Dorfman**

GAY POWER! *by JOHN D'EMILIO*

"MATTACHINE" IS NOT EXACTLY A HOUSE-hold word. It most often registers as "Oh, yeah, those are the people who tried to do something in the years before the Stonewall riots started the real gay liberation movement." The name itself has the ring of another era—another planet even. In those days, even the activists couldn't say "gay" or "lesbian." They came up with names like the Mattachine Society or the Daughters of Bilitis, and they called themselves the "homophile movement."

Imagine my surprise, then, when I came upon the phrase "Gay Power" in a 1966 newsletter of Mattachine Midwest. Sitting in one of the carrels at the Gerber/Hart Library, I was startled. Almost three years before Stonewall, this band of supposedly conservative, cautious activists in Chicago was using a phrase I associated with the most militant and radical queer activists. What was going on here?

Some of what was going on was the times. A spirit of rebellion was all around. In June 1966, Stokely Carmichael, a civil rights activist working in Mississippi, had used the phrase "Black Power!" in a protest march across the state. The words captured the anger, frustration and determination of many African-Americans who had experienced too much white violence and too many denials of basic human rights for way too long. Black power symbolized an unwillingness to go slow. It stood for a belief that abuses of power had to be met with at least an equal and opposite force.

These sentiments and experiences weren't confined to Mississippi. In the summer of 1966, the Rev. Martin Luther King Jr. had come to Chicago to assist in efforts to open up the housing market in the city's segregated neighborhoods. Marchers, including many priests and nuns, were met by the ugly violence of white mobs. It drove home the message that peaceful protest and efforts to negotiate reasonably weren't going to do the trick.

That year, 1966, was a particularly bad one for the city's gay men. Issue after issue of the Mattachine Midwest Newsletter reported on the latest police outrage. Chicago's police force seemed out of control. "Enticement, Entrapment, and Harassment face the homosexual every time he steps into the street," the newsletter declared.

Illinois had repealed its sodomy law in 1961, becoming the first state to decriminalize sexual behavior between consenting adults in private. In response, police stepped up their tactics against "public" sexual activity. Reports came to Mattachine of all sorts of aggressive police practices. Cops were exposing themselves in public restrooms in an effort to make lewd-conduct arrests. Plainclothes officers in "obviously seductive attire" walked the streets that gay men cruised. They'd strike up a conversation and then, when the unsuspecting target invited the officer home, arrest him for solicitation for prostitution. Or, police would hang out in gay bars and listen to the conversations around them. When they heard a pickup line, it was all they thought they needed to arrest bartenders for running "a disorderly house" and cart off patrons for being "inmates" of the house.

Early in 1966, newspapers in Chicago revealed that the police had a "stop-and-quiz" policy. If cops didn't like the look of someone—if they suspected a person even in the absence of evidence of any crime—they would stop the person; demand a name, address and place of employment; require identification; and grill them for an explanation of their presence on the street. Black men in white neighborhoods, women alone at night wearing clothes that seemed too sexy, queeny-looking guys: All faced stop-and-quiz procedures.

These were police-state tactics, but refusing to cooperate was a tricky matter. It could lead to an arrest for disorderly conduct or loitering. At least one gay man who didn't provide information on his place of employment was arrested on charges of "no visible means of support." The list of potential dangers was a long one.

Mattachine Midwest tried, again and again, to set up meetings with police to discuss the department's policies. Every time, the police declined the invitation. Meanwhile, as spring and summer wore on, Mattachine's newsletter reported a continuing series of raids on gay bars and bathhouses. It also reported the "sadistic" public exposure in the Chicago Tribune of the names of those arrested.

The anger of Mattachine members came through in the newsletter. "As children, we were told that the policeman was there to protect and help us," the editor wrote. "To the homosexual citizen such thoughts are pure nonsense." As the year wore on, Mattachine's rhetoric grew more and more heated: "'Lawless police' is a phrase which still aptly describes Chicago's cops ... the entrapments, shakedowns, brutality, and corruption continue ... no one is immune." "Quit buying the right-wing line about crime in the streets and wake up to YOUR rights. Crime is as much rampant inside the police department as elsewhere."

An unmistakable sense that folks were fed up, that they'd had enough, jumps from the newsletter's pages each month. "It's time things were changed," the newsletter told its readers. "It's time to stop running." Mattachine urged gay men to "[h]old your heads up high. Be proud of your individuality. Spend your energy fighting for equality." Finally, as the year ended, almost in exasperation Mattachine's president, Jim Bradford, burst out: "Maybe we need to form a 'Gay Power' bloc!"

Bradford's declaration is a good reminder that rebellion was in the air here in Chicago more than 40 years ago. It was percolating from the ground up, on the streets and in the bars and in the parks, wherever queers found themselves in confrontation with the law. Stonewall was one expression of that, but it didn't need to be imported to Chicago from New York to rile people up. There were more than enough homegrown grievances to start the talk about "Gay Power." ▼

MATTACHINE SOCIETY today ▶▶

RENSLOW: LEATHER MAN   *by OWEN KEEHNEN*

CHUCK RENSLOW WAS BORN IN 1929, RAISED in the Logan Square neighborhood of Chicago, and graduated from Lane Technical High School. In the late 1950s he became the famed adult photographer Kris of Chicago and ran his studio, Kris Studios, during the entire physique pictorial era from 1950 to 1979. He further advanced the genre by publishing the popular physique magazines Triumph, Mars, and Rawhide.

In 1958, he was brought to court for the distribution and possession of material with "excessive genital delineation." Unlike some gays, Renslow did not passively wait for a conviction. He and his American Civil Liberties Union attorneys fought back, including as evidence nude statues in Chicago. In 1964 the Post Office Department also brought Kris Studios up on charges of pornography. The studios did not use the more common strategy of saying the materials were art; they just denied they were pornography, and the judge agreed that the human body itself, in posing straps, was not porn.

Renslow met his longtime lover, dancer-choreographer-artist Dom Orejudos (also known as the famed gay erotic artist Etienne), in 1953. In 1958 the couple opened the legendary Gold Coast, the first gay leather bar in the United States. The popular landmark (at 501 N. Clark St. for most of its existence) soon attained international renown and reigned until 1993 as the oldest leather establishment in the world.

In the late 1970s, Renslow (who had been an official of the Amateur Athletic Union) decided to have a Mr. Gold Coast contest. It was a huge success, with crowds spilling out of the bar and onto the street. A new venue was necessary, but holding the Mr. Gold Coast contest elsewhere wouldn't work. The solution was the creation of an entirely new contest, and in 1979 the International Mr. Leather contest was born. A couple of years later, two vendors asked if they could set up booths to sell their goods. That practice evolved into the IML Leather Mart. The contest and mar-

ket have since become one of the largest gay tourist draws in the country and a large source of revenue for Chicago.

Renslow was the founder of the Second City Motorcycle Club. He was the first to have a float in the Chicago Gay Pride Parade (a flatbed, a gazebo, and

Chuck Renslow in the 1970s.
Photo courtesy Gay Chicago Magazine.

three drag queens), and his birthday celebration became the granddaddy of all circuit parties, the legendary White Party of Chicago.

For about seven years, from the late 1970s to 1986, Renslow was publisher of the early Chicago

gay newspaper GayLife. He has been a dynamic and visible presence in the business community for five decades and even started the Metropolitan Business Association. His bar and other businesses have included the Chicago Eagle, Man's Country bathhouse, Triumph Health Studios, Sparrows Lounge, Bistro Too, Zolar, The Club Baths, Center Stage and Pyramid, in addition to the Gold Coast.

In 1991 he gave back to the community in an entirely new way and (along with Tony DeBlase) opened the Leather Archives & Museum. His primary motivation was to store, preserve, and share with the public the extensive artwork of his lover Etienne (valued at well over $1 million at the time), who died from AIDS complications that year. Since then, the Leather Archives & Museum (located at 6418 N. Greenview Ave. in Chicago) has acquired thousands of photographs, papers, journals, gear, additional artwork (from such notables as Steve Masters and David Grieger), an entire set of Der Kreis, a complete set of The Leather Journal, and countless other treasures.

Renslow has also been a tireless force in both Chicago and national politics, serving the Democratic Party in a number of capacities. He was a founder of the Prairie State Democratic Club in 1980. He also served as precinct captain for eight years in the 43rd Ward, on the 46th Ward Advisory Council, and on the 48th Ward Democratic Party Advisory Board. He ran for election to the 1980 Democratic National Convention as a delegate pledged to U.S. Sen. Edward Kennedy. For more than 40 years he has been an instrumental force in helping to secure gay-rights legislation in Chicago and statewide. In 2008, he is a board member of the National Gay and Lesbian Task Force and has been a member of numerous local, national and international groups. His honors and awards are extensive and include his 1991 induction into the Chicago Gay and Lesbian Hall of Fame, The Leather Journal's lifetime achievement award, a Centurion Award as Leatherman of the Century, and others. ▼

PASSION ART: DOM 'ETIENNE' OREJUDOS

by RON EHEMANN

FAMED LEATHER ARTIST "ETIENNE" WAS born Domingo Orejudos in Chicago in 1933. A graduate of McKinley High School, he excelled in both music and art. In 1950, Domingo (or Dom, as he preferred to be known) met the first of his life partners, Chuck Renslow. At the time, Dom was already an accomplished artist.

Both Orejudos and Renslow were avid bodybuilders. Capitalizing on their passion, the two became partners in a different sense by opening Kris Studios, which produced Renslow's male photography and Orejudos' emerging male art. Their successful Triumph, Rawhide and Mars magazines are some of the nation's earliest examples of male or gay erotica. To find models, the two soon launched their second business, Triumph Gym.

Although Renslow would eventually leave the field of photography, erotic art became Orejudos' lifelong passion. To be more correct, it became one of his two lifelong passions—the other being ballet. In both, Orejudos rose to national fame.

Together with Renslow, Orejudos opened several other businesses in Chicago, most notably the Gold Coast leather bar, the Barracks Hotel, Man's Country bathhouse, International Mr. Leather contest, Zolar, Pyramid, and Center Stage, as well as clubs in other cities such as Club Baths in Kansas City and Phoenix. Each of those businesses relied heavily on Orejudos' art to promote themselves. Orejudos' fantastic imagination was turned into logos and posters and was used in advertisements.

Several of Orejudos' largest pieces of art could be found on the walls of the establishments. For 25 years, all but the first International Mr. Leather posters featured Orejudos' art. One large painting is still up inside Man's Country, and several more remain on display at the Chicago Eagle leather bar. In 2007, one of Orejudos' larger murals was included in a showing at the Chicago History Museum. A major showing of his work was presented at the School of the Art Institute's Roger Brown Study Collection Center.

One of the founding members of the "Renslow Family" (friends bound together through love and business), Orejudos inaugurated Chicago's August White Party, which in 2008 is in its 34th year. During the last two decades of his life, Orejudos maintained two residences. In addition to his home with the "Family" in Chicago, he resided with his other life partner, Bob Yuhnke, in Boulder, Colo.

Dom "Etienne" Orejudos succumbed to AIDS on Sept. 24, 1991. He was 58 years old.

The Renslow Family issued this statement after

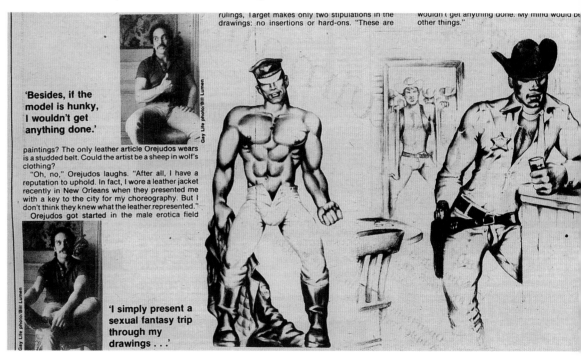

'Besides, if the model is hunky, I wouldn't get anything done.'

paintings? The only leather article Orejudos wears is a studded belt. Could the artist be a sheep in wolf's clothing?

"Oh, no," Orejudos laughs. "After all, I have a reputation to uphold. In fact, I wore a leather jacket recently in New Orleans when they presented me with a key to the city for my choreography. But I don't think they knew what the leather represented."

Orejudos got started in the male erotica field

'I simply present a sexual fantasy trip through my drawings . . .'

rulings, Target makes only two stipulations in the drawings: no insertions or hard-ons. "These are

wouldn't get anything done. My mind would be other things."

Etienne discusses his life and art in the Oct. 28, 1977, issue of GayLife newspaper.

Orejudos died: "On his death bed, Dom wanted all his fans to be aware that he in no way wanted them to actualize many of the situations that he created in his drawings and he emphasized that with fantasy anything is possible and nothing has consequences; for it's just make believe. As did Tom of Finland, Etienne felt very concerned that his fantasy stories and single works might be misinterpreted over time."

The majority of Orejudos' collective works were donated by Chuck Renslow and together with the Kris Studios' photography formed the basis of what would grow to become the Leather Archives & Museum in Chicago. LA&M dedicated its theater to Orejudos' memory.

For all his fame and notoriety as an erotic artist, Orejudos was also a very accomplished ballet dancer and choreographer. He was the recipient of three grants from the National Endowment for the Arts and the resident choreographer and principal dancer with the Illinois Ballet Company for nine years. Orejudos also earned critical acclaim choreographing ballets for almost 20 ballet companies around the United States.

Orejudos' stage credits also include dance roles in the touring companies of West Side Story, The King and I, and Song of Norway. ▼

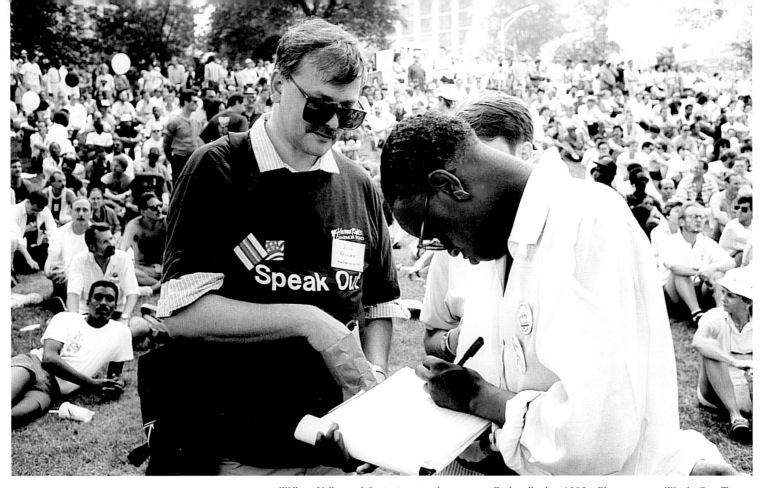

William Kelley, at left, signing up volunteers at a Pride rally, late 1980s. Photo courtesy Windy City Times.

BILL KELLEY: EYES ON THE PRIZE *by ANDREW DAVIS*

WILLIAM B. KELLEY (1942–) IS AN ATTORNEY AND ACTIVIST WHO has been a part of the gay rights movement since the 1960s. Because of his extensive knowledge about the movement, Kelley is a critical link between what transpired during that decade and modern-day activism.

Kelley helped organize the first national gay and lesbian conferences in 1966 under the name North American Conference of Homophile Organizations (NACHO), co-founded The Chicago Gay Crusader (a 1970s gay newspaper) and helped start the Gay Press Association in the early 1980s. In addition, he co-founded Illinois Gays for Legislative Action in the early 1970s; took part in the first White House meeting with gay and lesbian leaders; co-chaired the Illinois Gay Rights Task Force (which was part of the fight for the state's 2006 gay-rights law beginning in the 1970s); and was part of launching the National Lesbian and Gay Law Association in 1988.

To underscore Kelley's longevity in the movement, he has also been part of groups such as Mattachine Midwest (as far back as August 1965); Homosexuals Organized for Political Education (HOPE), formed to conduct the state's first poll of candidates on gay issues; and the Chicago Gay Alliance and the Gay and Lesbian Coalition of Metropolitan Chicago in the 1970s.

Kelley was born and raised in Dunklin County, Mo., where he witnessed and experienced racial segregation and McCarthyism. Outspoken in pro-integration letters to the editor even then, he once drew the attention of the Federal Bureau of Investigation, whose agents visited him at his farm home in an ostensible but illogical search for leads to a pro-segregationist murderer's identity.

After high school, he attended the University of Chicago and then, years later, the Illinois Institute of Technology's Chicago-Kent College of Law (graduating with high honors from the latter in 1987). In college, his interest in human rights, particularly those involving sexual orientation, bloomed. At the same time, he realized that his homosexuality was an intrinsic aspect of his personality.

Kelley became a determined activist, but he left Mattachine around 1970 because, among other things, he found the organization to be lethargic. He then co-founded HOPE.

Meanwhile, in 1966, Kelley "came out" on Jerry Williams' WBBM radio show. As far as Kelley could tell, there was no fallout from his appearance, either at his own insurance-company job or through at least one hometown official who had heard the show.

NACHO, the national conference organization, met in Chicago in 1968. The conference attendees, made up of delegates from 26 groups, talked about goals and strategy and adopted the slogan "Gay Is Good." The organization dissolved in 1970 after its annual meeting in San Francisco was disrupted by Gay Liberation–identified militants.

Later, Kelley joined the Chicago Gay Alliance as an active member until it dissolved in 1973. That organization lobbied Democrats, the City Council and the Illinois Fair Employment Practices Commission, which has since been superseded by the Human Rights Commission, to support or enact measures to forbid sexual-orientation discrimination.

By the time CGA dissolved, Kelley's lover, Mike Bergeron, started a newspaper, The Chicago Gay Crusader, and a community center, Beckman House, and Kelley joined Bergeron in both efforts. In 1976, Kelley began working in Chuck Renslow's office; Kelley saw this as an opportunity to get involved more intensively in the gay-rights movement. A few years later Renslow purchased GayLife newspaper from founder Grant Ford, and Kelley's duties included helping Renslow oversee the newspaper's operations.

The White House meeting took place in 1977. The National Gay Task Force set up the meeting through communication between Jean O'Leary, then a co-executive director of the Task Force, and Midge Costanza, President Jimmy Carter's assistant for public liaison. Kelley was invited because of contacts between Renslow and the Task Force's other co-executive director, Bruce Voeller. Kelley presented a paper about gay organizations' tax-exemption problems; participants in the meeting discussed sexual orientation–based discrimination in such agencies as the Internal Revenue Service, the Immigration and Naturalization Service, the Defense Department and the Federal Communications Commission. Among the other attendees were then–Massachusetts state Rep. Elaine Noble, activist Franklin E. Kameny and Cooki

William Kelley and his partner Chen Ooi in 2007. Photo by Hal Baim.

Lutkefedder of the Democratic National Committee. President Carter did not attend (he was at Camp David), but the meeting was still a first between gays and the White House.

In the 1980s, Kelley, now a law student, was again a part of negotiations on the city's gay rights bill, having been invited to join an attempt to craft language that would satisfy Roman Catholic critics of the ordinance, including Cardinal Joseph Bernardin. The effort failed, but in later years the local archdiocese muted its opposition to the ordinance.

Since graduating from law school, Kelley served on the board of the Chicago Access Corp., an organization that oversees public-access cable TV programming, which gave him its Spirit of Access Award. In 2008, Kelley is a member of the Cook County Human Rights Commission (he served from 1991 to 2003 as its founding chairperson) and is a member of the city's Advisory Council on LGBT Issues. Kelley was inducted into the Chicago Gay and Lesbian Hall of Fame in 1991. Since 1996, he has been what he has described as an "armchair activist."

In 2004, Kelley received a newly created annual award named for him by the Lesbian and Gay Bar Association of Chicago. In addition to his legal work, Kelley—known for his attention to detail—serves as a volunteer fact-checker and proofreader for syndicated writer Rex Wockner, whose news columns appear in LGBT publications nationwide, including Windy City Times. Kelley regards international LGBT news coverage as one of the most important factors in advancing sexual minorities' rights worldwide.

Kelley lives in Chicago with Chen K. Ooi (1952–), his partner since 1979. Ooi is an advertising creative director and a former Asians and Friends–Chicago board member. In cooperation with Lambda Legal and the organization Fair Illinois, the two were among successful objectors to a 2006 attempt to place on the Illinois ballot an anti-gay statewide advisory referendum opposing marriage and relationship rights for same-sex couples. Citing a signature shortfall that Kelley and other volunteers had verified by line-by-line scrutiny, the state Board of Elections refused to certify the petitions that sought the referendum. ▼

RENEE HANOVER: RADICAL LAWYER   by TRACY BAIM

ATTORNEY RENEE HANOVER, 82, IS ONE OF Chicago's most cherished lesbian activists. Hanover worked inside and outside the system to save and change the lives of tens of thousands of people. With her senior colleague, Pearl M. Hart, she helped overturn the Chicago "zipper" law banning cross-dressing (see page 91) and worked on numerous cases of gay men arrested by police in public spaces.

Hanover, a powerful presence in any meeting, was a traditional anti-war leftie, always challenging the government. In July 1961, she took part in a

ileges for the well-to-do unless we acted for the most vulnerable, most easily victimized queers. Long-time lesbian lawyer Renee Hanover, who had struggled for years already as an advocate of union and leftist communities in Chicago, was one of the maybe 20 of us in the freezing sleet on Chicago Avenue that day."

That was Hanover—you could count on her in the boardroom, in the courtroom, or on the streets with ACT UP protesters or draft-resisting revolutionaries. She also took on the gay establishment, fighting for African-American lesbians kept out of

consisted in large part of defending underdogs—aliens, alleged subversives, homosexuals, prostitutes, among others," Hanover said when Hart died. One could say the same about Hanover.

Hanover's work on women's issues was also important to her and to Chicago. She helped anti-rape efforts, the Women in Crisis Can Act hotline, Women Employed, Lesbians in the Law, Chicago Lesbian Liberation, Daughters of Bilitis, Lesbian Community Cancer Project, the National Organization for Women, Chicago Women's Liberation Front, and dozens more.

But she was also involved in numerous legal efforts, including the National Lawyers Guild, the Chicago Lawyers Committee to End the War in Vietnam, and even the ACLU. She was very much a co-gender activist, working with Mattachine Midwest, Beckman House, Chicago Gay Alliance, Gay Liberation Front, ACT UP and Illinois Gay and Lesbian Task Force campaigns. She was in mainstream groups, Jewish organizations (gay and non-gay), progressive groups, and dozens more too numerous to list. The Chicago Gay and Lesbian Hall of Fame has a more detailed roster of her involvement, and many of her personal papers are maintained by the Lesbian Herstory Archives in New York.

What is most important to remember about Hanover is not just her work, but Hanover as a person. She is

Renee Hanover on the front lines of a protest at the U.S. Supreme Court in 1987, right before her arrest. At right, Hanover in 2007 in Los Angeles, where she currently lives. Photos by Tracy Baim.

"freedom wade-in" at the South Side's Rainbow Beach to help desegregate Chicago's beaches.

Ferd Eggan, who died in 2007, wrote of Hanover in an essay titled "Dykes and Fags Want Everything: Dreaming of the Gay Liberation Front": "I remember best a demonstration [in the early 1970s] against the beating and killing of a Black drag queen by the Chicago Police Department. … We came to understand that our gay rights would be nothing but priv-

women's bars. During the 1987 March on Washington weekend in D.C., the 61-year-old Hanover was among those arrested at a protest in front of the U.S. Supreme Court.

For more than 40 years, she was involved in a wide range of causes. As an out lesbian attorney as long ago as the 1960s, Hanover made history alongside very few out colleagues. Her practice with Hart inspired Hanover's own work. "Her legal career

short and mighty, a mentor and friend, an amazing force for change of both individuals and institutions. She was out and proud and unapologetic, well before that became the norm. She was a role model for so many Chicagoans and others around the United States—lawyers, activists, politicians. Her retirement to Los Angeles was a sad blow to the Windy City; Chicago may never see the likes of Renee Hanover again. ▼

MARIE JAYNE KUDA: WORKING WOMAN

by JORJET HARPER and JUDITH MARKOWITZ

BORN IN 1939, MARIE J. KUDA HAS MADE an indelible contribution to Chicago's cultural and political life as an independent scholar, publisher, lecturer, archivist, writer and grass-roots activist.

Among her many accomplishments, in 1974, Kuda founded Womanpress, a short-lived small press dedicated to lesbian literature. She has edited and published works that have been essential reading in lesbian literature and scholarship, including Two Women: The Poetry of Jeannette Howard Foster and Valerie Taylor, and Women Loving Women: A Select and Annotated Bibliography of Women Loving Women in Literature. Kuda organized the Lesbian Writers' Conferences held in Chicago from 1974 to 1978—the first gatherings of lesbian writers anywhere in the United States.

Beginning in 1973, Kuda served for 16 years on the American Library Association's Task Force on Gay Liberation, working closely with Barbara Gittings. Kuda was the first open lesbian to write reviews for ALA's Booklist (used as a guide by school and academic libraries for new acquisitions), contributing over 200 reviews of lesbian and gay books from 1990 to1994.

Completely Queer: The Gay and Lesbian Encyclopedia cites Kuda as "a leading chronicler of lesbian and gay life, particularly as it unfolded in the Midwest." Kuda shared the information she found not only through her writings but also through hundreds of visual presentations on lesbian and gay literature and history—long before the emergence of gay and lesbian academic studies, and long before the Internet. "In the years before we had our own published histories, a bunch of us, like Greg Sprague, Tee Corinne, JEB [Joan E. Biren] and Allan Bérubé, were itinerant storytellers going around with our slide projectors, sharing our history whenever queers were gathered," Kuda recalls. She continues to assist scholars, students and others in their LGBT research.

The part that Kuda has played in the gay movement cannot be calculated solely according to her awards and achievements; her work conveying positive images of our culture has inspired many others, especially lesbians. Over the years her listeners have extended her contributions and her conviction that LGBT history was as important to document as to create. She gave many women the courage to come out. She gave gays and lesbians crucial information they didn't even know they needed about the lives of gays and lesbians of the past and, for some, the tools they sought to make sense of their own lives.

Kuda talked about the links between historical figures in a way that showed not only that gays and lesbians in the past fully understood who they were, but that many of them were well aware of each other. Her inspirational slide shows and lectures covering a wide range of topics on lesbian and gay history, in particular, proved—sometimes to the astonishment of her audiences—that "we are everywhere" was not just a catchphrase but an actual reality.

For the first time, we heard that many of our lesbian foremothers were women of amazing courage, generous heart and breathtaking accomplishment. ▼

Marie J. Kuda. Photo by Tee A. Corinne. Courtesy M. Kuda Archives, Oak Park, Ill.

VERNITA GRAY: TIRELESS WORKER FOR CHANGE *by TRACY BAIM*

UBIQUITOUS: "BEING OR SEEMING TO BE everywhere at the same time." That could be one definition of Vernita Gray, born in 1948, who has worked for more than three decades on gay and lesbian rights.

As a young woman, Gray headed with lesbian friend Michal Brody to Woodstock, N.Y., for the concert of a generation. That 1969 watershed event helped inspire Gray to become more involved in the gay movement. "In the middle of all of that mud and dirt, there was a little table with some information about an event called Stonewall (the New York gay riots had been just a few weeks earlier). And my friend got that information and she said to me, 'When we get back to Chicago, we're going to get active in the gay movement,'" Gray said. When they returned home, Gray and others set up a phone number, FBI-LIST, as a gay support line, operated out of their Hyde Park apartment.

"The civil rights movement had touched me when I was still in high school," Gray said in 2007. In the 1960s, when Dr. Martin Luther King Jr. moved to Chicago to fight racial segregation, "he lived about three blocks away from where I lived ... [My] friend Susan said to me, 'We're not going to let this go by us.' And as with many teenagers, I was just caught up in the peer pressure, and I was, like, 'Oh yeah. Absolutely. We're going on demonstrations.' So that was the beginning of my activism as a Black person in America. We were still very oppressed. I can recall going shopping with my mother at Field's. At that time, it was the policy to wait on white people before you waited on Black people."

Since that time Gray has been involved in a wide range of lesbian, co-gender, African-American and political work. She was part of the Women's Caucus of the Chicago Gay Alliance and wrote for the lesbian newspaper Lavender Woman in the 1970s. She also performed her poetry, including performances at Mountain Moving Coffeehouse, and wrote a chapbook, Sweet Sixteen (published in 1986 by Mona Noriega). She helped organize Lesbians of Color Nights of performers, which grew out of the work of Cravolinajong (Rhonda Craven, Florencia Carolina and Lola Lai Jong).

Gray's political involvement has included IMPACT, the gay political action committee, as well as campaigning for numerous gay and pro-gay candidates.

She owned Sol Sands, a popular restaurant on

Left: Vernita Gray at a 1980s Horizons conference. Photo by Lisa Howe-Ebright. Right: Gray in 2007. Photo by Hal Baim.

West Montrose Avenue near North Broadway, for eight years before becoming a GLBT specialist in the Cook County state's attorney's office. Over her many years at the state's attorney's office, she has held various positions helping gay and lesbian crime victims, or the families of murdered gays and lesbians. The work is both mentally and physically draining: Gray sees the brutal results of anti-gay crimes and same-sex domestic violence. In response, she educates thousands of students annually about hate crimes.

Gray is not afraid to challenge the community from within on sexism, racism, classism, and now ageism, and she has worked tirelessly to change organizations. She has volunteered her time for numerous causes and, as a cancer survivor herself, has been a longtime supporter of the Lesbian Community Cancer Project.

Gray has also been a prominent representative of the community in the mainstream media and a columnist for the gay media, including Nightlines and Outlines newspapers. As a bold, out African-American lesbian, she has been a role model to many generations and an inspiration to her fellow Chicago activists. ▼

CHICAGO'S STONEWALL: THE TRIP RAID IN 1968

by MARIE J. KUDA

IN THE 21ST CENTURY, "STONEWALL" IS THE ACCEPTED buzzword for the beginning of the gay liberation movement in the United States. It conjures up a vision of bar-raiding Greenwich Village cops terrorized inside the Stonewall Inn by a bunch of angry queens outside, tossing rocks, bottles, a Molotov cocktail and shouts reminiscent of Network ("I'm not going to take this anymore!").

But in Chicago, the events of that June day in 1969 barely made a ripple. The riot was not immediate national news. A few local gay papers existed around the country, but there wasn't any real national gay press. When word from New York finally reached here, it was recorded in July's Mattachine Midwest Newsletter with the same emphasis as was given to the item on vigilante residents of the borough of Queens who, in a campaign against homosexuals reportedly frequenting a neighborhood park, had cut down dozens of its trees. According to the writer, William B. Kelley, "The New York Times ran at least three days of stories, one editorial and one letter on the subject. They were against cutting the trees."

Chicago gays chose to challenge the status quo in the courts instead of the streets. In a city coming out of 1968 with a nationwide reputation for police brutality, discretion was indeed the better part of valor. The Trip case, challenging bar closings, went to the Illinois Supreme Court; the case of Mattachine Midwest Newsletter editor David Stienecker involved defending him against charges brought by an officer who arrested gays in tearooms (public washrooms). While slower and more low-key than Stonewall, these two cases led Chicago gays to become proactive instead of reactive in their fight against oppression and discrimination.

THE TRIP CASE

Chicago's equivalent to Stonewall began 40 years ago with a police bust at The Trip, a gay-owned restaurant-bar complex at 27 E. Ohio St. The Trip had a main-floor restaurant, a second-floor cabaret and a third-floor playroom with pool table and pinball games. At midday, because of its location just west of North Michigan Avenue, the restaurant catered to luncheon crowds of shoppers, often featuring women's fashion shows. The area was undergoing an upswing; a few gritty hotels with questionable clientele remained, but new upscale

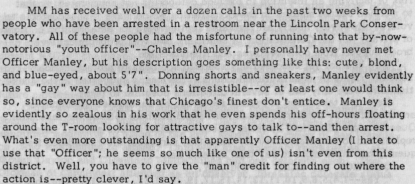

Officer Manley on the March
A GAY DECEIVER - OR IS HE ??
by David Stienecker

MM has received well over a dozen calls in the past two weeks from people who have been arrested in a restroom near the Lincoln Park Conservatory. All of these people had the misfortune of running into that by-now-notorious "youth officer"--Charles Manley. I personally have never met Officer Manley, but his description goes something like this: cute, blond, and blue-eyed, about 5'7". Donning shorts and sneakers, Manley evidently has a "gay" way about him that is irresistible--or at least one would think so, since everyone knows that Chicago's finest don't entice. Manley is evidently so zealous in his work that he even spends his off-hours floating around the T-room looking for attractive gays to talk to--and then arrest. What's even more outstanding is that apparently Officer Manley (I hate to use that "Officer"; he seems so much like one of us) isn't even from this district. Well, you have to give the "man" credit for finding out where the action is--pretty clever, I'd say.

Officer Manley is evidently so concerned about protecting the public from whatever it is he's protecting it from that it appears he has jumped the gun--well, you know what I mean--a few times. A couple of reports go like this: A young man goes into restroom to relieve himself--you know, urinate. Apparently place is empty; aha, Officer Manley lurks behind door; zap--young man is arrested. Tactic #2: You walk into john to do you-know-what; Manley thinks you look like a hot prospect; oops! in he comes and starts chatting, looking in that clever disguise of his like he's really a nice guy interested in the weather. Finally, you and Manley walk out arm in arm--handcuffed, that is.

The general after-arrest annoyances occur--you know, those little things that tell you who's boss (shades of S&M). No chance for making call--"use a quarter, fag." Handcuffs so tight they'd like to break your wrist, and "wait until I'm ready before you call anybody."

The more I think about it, the cleverer this gets. If I were gay and didn't want anybody to know, and if I felt very, very guilty, I think I might get a job where I could cruise in the public interest. After relieving my sexual tensions in some weird sort of way, I could get rid of my guilt by arresting the other party. Very clever indeed, but I'm not suggesting . . .

Oh, yes, there's one other aspect of this whole affair. Manley has a helper. Now get this: sometimes he works with a woman (at least we think it's a woman). She watches through a window while he does his thing. Explain that one if you can.

At any rate, our advice to you is to stay out of the restrooms in Lincoln Park, at least this one. What if you have to go? Well, I think your chances are better behind a tree--unless, of course, you want to get a look at a cute blue-eyed, blond-haired cop.

SUPPORT THE AMERICAN CIVIL LIBERTIES UNION — This respected organization has produced numerous court decisions that have brought new meaning to civil liberties. We urge you to support their activities. Inquire at A.C.L.U. 6 South Clark Street Chicago, 60603. Telephone: 236-5564.

3

David Stienecker's September 1969 Mattachine article on "Charles" Manley (corrected the following month). Courtesy M. Kuda Archives, Oak Park, Ill.

businesses were mediating the fringes of adjacent Rush Street nightlife. On the borderline, The Trip became quite gay after the dinner hour, and on Sundays it operated as a private club.

One Sunday in January 1968, police raided The Trip, arresting 13 patrons on charges of public indecency and soliciting for prostitution. A plainclothes officer had gained entry by using a membership card obtained illegally during an unrelated arrest and made the charges after observing members dancing together as same-sex couples.

When the case came to court in March, attorney Ralla Klepak defended, and charges against patrons and management were dismissed. The Mattachine Midwest Newsletter, reporting on the incident, saw it as an illustration of further harassment by police, noting that dancing was not illegal per se and that the ACLU would welcome an opportunity for a test case. (In 1970 The Trip would become one of the first venues to have same-sex dancing, even before Chicago Gay Liberation picketed bars for that right.)

A second raid in May 1968 by two plainclothesmen resulted in the arrests of one patron and one employee; but, more significantly, the local liquor authorities issued an emergency closing order pending appeal on the revocation of The Trip's liquor license. This was common practice in Chicago and a kiss of death for gay bars. If they appealed the order (the appellate process could drag on for months) they had to remain closed pending a decision; meanwhile their clientele moved on and they were effectively put out of business. The Trip had barely been open a year, the bad publicity from the earlier raid had ruined its luncheon business, and owners Dean Kolberg and Ralf Johnston were not about to see their investment tank.

The Trip hired attorney Elmer Gertz to mount a case against the License Appeal Commission of Chicago after it upheld the license revocation. The Mattachine Midwest Newsletter reported that no gay bar had previously challenged being shut down before The Trip case. It took a significant amount of time for the case to wend its way to the Illinois Supreme Court. The final decision (a complete reversal) was in Johnkol, Inc. v. License Appeal Commission of Chicago, 42 Ill. 2d 377, 247 N.E.2d 901 (1969).

Meanwhile, even though closed during 1968, The Trip hosted a variety of movement events. The North American Conference of Homophile Organizations (NACHO), a coordinating group made up of delegates from 26 organizations, met there for its third annual nationwide conference, just days before the Democratic National Convention riots. Mattachine Midwest also held its monthly public meetings there while the business was closed.

A police arrest during the riots outside the 1968 Democratic National Convention. Photo courtesy the Chicago History Museum.

Mattachine Midwest was an independent corporation created in 1965 after years of failure to sustain local chapters of the West Coast–headquartered organizations Mattachine Society and Daughters of Bilitis. The impetus for the new organization was a particularly brutal raid on the Fun Lounge, a rather sleazy suburban bar that packed in a queer clientele on weekends. The Chicago Tribune led off the report in its April 26, 1964, edition with a headline indicating eight teachers had been seized in a "vice raid" that also netted 95 other men and six women. The article listed names, addresses and occupations of those arrested (a common practice of the time) along with asides that "many of the men carried powder puffs and lipsticks" and that a quantity of "freshly shipped" marijuana had been seized. Subsequently there were reports of job losses and a rumored suicide.

Though The Trip had been allowed to reopen, the police still visited; in 1971 a patron was arrested on the old-standby charge of public indecency, but the charge was dismissed. The owners became overly protective of their business, allegedly refusing to call police when a Mattachine officer was robbed at gunpoint while at a meeting with an out-of-state activist on the third floor. In a 1972 on-site interview with the owners, Chicago Today columnist Barbara Ettorre noted the bar was full, with men from all walks of life, all ages, every manner of dress. The bar's management told her that weekends were "crowded wall-to-wall" and that they had a uniformed Andy Frain company usher to check IDs. They were going to make certain none of their patrons would be subject to arrest.

CHICAGO IN 1968

In 1968, Chicago was going through critical times, well beyond the constant harassment of the gay community. In addition to reports on bar raids and park arrests, Mattachine Midwest's referral service received many calls from draft resisters; the anti-Vietnam War movement was well under way. Gays could not serve if identified when drafted: Few wanted to go, but no one wanted to be branded with a stigma that would affect their economic and social lives.

After Dr. Martin Luther King's assassination in April 1968, Chicago's West Side erupted in four days of anguished riots and looting. The police and National Guard were called out; the notorious "shoot to kill" order was given. Then Bobby Kennedy, seen as the Democrats' likely candidate for president, was murdered. The Democratic Party's nominating convention was to be held in Chicago that August. Anti-war activists, a variety of New Left groups, old-line hippies, Yippies, and others were calling for people to come to Chicago and stage demonstrations at the convention site. Abe Peck, now self-described as "hippie-rad editor turned journalism professor," tried to dissuade misguided flower children from coming to the city, warning them in his counterculture newspaper The Seed about the potential for violence here.

In addition, many civil rights groups (Black, women's, gay) had been infiltrated by the FBI's COINTELPRO, a counterintelligence program whose goal was to disrupt, disorganize and cause internal dissension in an effort to neutralize a group's activities. The program originated in the Cold War anti-communist 1950s and perfected its "dirty tricks" down through the Nixon administration. Its informants planted derogatory stories (they had been responsible for labeling former Illinois Gov. Adlai Stevenson "gay" during his bid for a presidential nomination); they used anonymous letters and surveillance, embedded "moles," opened mail, blackmailed, and by other devious means invaded the rights of U.S. citizens.

Chicago police also had their covert group, the Red Squad. This group in various incarnations had its origin all the way back in the days following the Haymarket labor riot of 1886 in which seven policemen were killed and dozens injured. The objects of the squad's covert activities switched over the years from anarchists, to communists, to any left-leaning organizations of the civil rights era.

In the early 1970s when attorney Rick Gutman of the Alliance to End Repression (of which Mattachine Midwest was a member) was about to challenge the Red Squad in court on constitu-

tional grounds, the squad reportedly destroyed thousands of files. Activist John Chester, who in 1972 was the first open gay on the Alliance's Steering Committee, reports that he "replaced a woman who was a Red Squad spy." Historians have speculated many of the threats that Mayor Richard J. Daley said (after the convention protests) had prompted him to order the police and National Guard to clamp down on demonstrators were "planted" by one of the embedded groups (COINTELPRO or the Red Squad) and then reported by the other as fact.

Red Squad records are sealed at the Chicago History Museum (until 2012), but when finally disbanded, the squad was reported to have accumulated files on more than 250,000 individuals and 14,000 organizations. As part of the settlement of the suit against the Red Squad, it was learned that the squad had also obtained information at the first gay political convention, called in Chicago in February 1972 to develop demands for a gay plank to be presented at the major party conventions.

The 1968 NACHO convention at The Trip was held Aug. 11 through 18. Activists from around the country converged and passed a "Homosexual Bill of Rights." One item demanded a national policy that had been law in Illinois since 1961, that sexual acts by consenting adults in private would not be held to be criminal. A motion by pioneering activist Franklin E. Kameny made "Gay Is Good" the slogan of the movement.

Meanwhile, the National Mobilization Committee to End the War in Vietnam (the MOBE) and other protest groups were arriving daily. On Wednesday, Aug. 21, the MOBE failed in its attempt to get an injunction against the city in U.S. District Court to preclude the refusal of permits for a variety of activities, and the ban against sleeping in the parks.

Late Thursday, Aug. 22, on Wells Street in the Old Town area just west of Lincoln Park, two young runaways were being pursued by police. One, Jerome Johnson, a 17-year-old Native American from South Dakota, allegedly produced a handgun and was shot and killed by Youth Officer John

COPS, BARS AND BAGMEN

A 1972 article in the Chicago Sun-Times noted federal indictments of police Capt. Clarence E. Braasch, former commander of the East Chicago Avenue District, and 23 policemen who had served under him as vice investigators, for taking kickbacks from bar owners. A second article reported the names of bars that the indictment alleged were shakedown victims of the cops between 1966 and 1970. A number of gay bars were included in the list, among them the Gold Coast, the Baton Lounge, the Haig, the Inner Circle on Wells, the King's Ransom, New Jamie's, the Normandy, and Togetherness.

The old mayor, Richard J. Daley, had bowed to pressure from reformers in 1960 when he had hired a new superintendent of police, O.W. Wilson, who was supposed to clean house in the department. James B. Conlisk Jr. served as superintendent after Wilson retired in 1967 and was in office during the West Side riots and Democratic National Convention police riots of 1968. Corruption was the norm in the city; no one believed that, if they really wanted to, the brass couldn't find evidence of what most bar patrons knew.

When bars were busted (in the days when attorneys were not allowed to advertise) it was common for district cops (who got a percentage) to hand out business cards for attorneys who knew how to get arrestees off for a fee.

But that was only half the battle. The other side of doing business in Chicago in those days was dealing with the wiseguys. If you were "in the know" you could tell which bars were "connected" to the mob (translate: didn't want trouble, like having the bar busted up) by what brand of beer was on tap, what company had the towel and toilet-paper concession, whose jukebox was installed.

Others had their hands out, too; there were the ward heelers, legmen for the ward bosses and aldermen. Ignore them, and inspectors from departments you never heard of would find violations and close a bar. Chicago has always had a helluva record for corruption, and it's only in recent memory that so many politicians and court officers have found their way to jail.

"The situation would not have become the profitable venture that [it] apparently was had bars and other establishments refused to go along with the pay-off system in the first place. This break-through now should liberate everyone—bars, bar employees and individual gays—to assert their right to pursue their happiness unmolested by authorities. Anyone who is bothered unlawfully, either by false arrest or extortion attempt should say 'never again,'" stated Chicago gay activist Jim Bradford in the Mattachine Midwest Newsletter for January 1973.

Gays were outside the mainstream. It wasn't until the spring of 1972—when kids from Gay Liberation and Mattachine old-timers demanded dancing in the bars (it wasn't illegal), drinks that weren't watered, safety, and even brighter lights—that things began to change.

They called for bar boycotts and held a dance at the old Coliseum. The establishment tried to block that, too: permit problems, insurance hassles. But attorney Renee Hanover stepped in, insurance was obtained from a Black-owned company, and 2,000 gays (and what may have seemed like almost as many cops) came to the party. Challenging the economic base of the system opened the door to change all down the line.

— *Marie J. Kuda*

Manley of the Damen Avenue District. An April 1970 article by Ron Dorfman in the Chicago Journalism Review reported it as "the only fatality remotely connected with the Democratic National Convention of 1968 ... touching off the first angry rally in the park the week before the convention." Word spread quickly and a memorial march was held.

After the rally on Sunday, Aug. 25, as poet Allen Ginsberg and a group of gays were "omming" peacefully in Lincoln Park past the 11 p.m. curfew, police weighed in with batons swinging. The Chicago Tribune Magazine later called this the "beginning" of the convention riots, the first large-scale police-public confrontation.

THE DAVID STIENECKER CASE

David Stienecker had come to Chicago originally from the small town of Climax, Mich. In the mid-1960s he met Bill Kelley and Ira Jones, who were active in Mattachine Midwest; they prevailed upon him to join the organization. In 1966 Stienecker heard New York activist Craig Rodwell speak at an MM public meeting. Rodwell was a native Chicagoan who would return to New York and later open Oscar Wilde Memorial Bookshop, the country's first gay bookstore. Stienecker said he was "blown away by his frankness and activism" and they had a brief affair; Stienecker followed Rodwell to New York.

On Wednesday, Aug. 28, 1968, Stienecker, still in New York, watched the fateful televised report of the police beating demonstrators across from the Conrad Hilton Hotel, convention headquarters. He returned to Chicago in December to find Mattachine Midwest embroiled in a variety of actions to ward off increasing police harassment. President Jim Bradford and attorney Renee Hanover were meeting with police commanders in attempts to mitigate the violence. Stienecker became editor of the MM Newsletter and joined in reporting and pursuing the issues.

Throughout 1969, activism also continued around the trial of those charged during convention week: the "Chicago Seven," as they became known after Black Panther Bobby Seale was bound, gagged, and subsequently removed from court for protesting the legitimacy of the trial. When U.S. Attorney Thomas A. Foran characterized the convention riots as "a freaking fag revolution," Chicago gay activists printed up buttons with the phrase. MM and its officers individually wrote protest letters to the mainstream press.

The number of entrapment arrests escalated in the parks and tearooms. "You have to remember that at this time in Chicago the only way you heard about things was by word of mouth," Stienecker told John Poling in 2002 during an interview for Poling's thesis on Mattachine Midwest. The organization's answering service and newsletter were the only game in town. Members and the gay grapevine reported on the increased police activities.

Stienecker thought that one zealous officer with a reputation for physical violence merited particular attention and that the community should be warned against him: "It wasn't a matter of hearing about one incident, but rather hearing almost weekly about another Officer Manley entrapment that finally made us realize this was serious and something had to be done. People's lives were at stake, not necessarily physically, but every other way. ... I think there was something seriously wrong with Manley, but I'm not sure what it was. I wanted to get under his skin and we all wanted these incidents to stop."

Draft resistance and the anti-war movement had also been increasing in intensity. A popular film comedy, The Gay Deceivers, centered on two straight guys passing as gay to avoid the draft. It didn't sit too well with gays for whom this was a critical issue.

But when Stienecker wrote about Manley in the September 1969 MM Newsletter (see image, page 79), he titled his article "A Gay Deceiver, or Is He?" Describing Manley and his arrest techniques, Stienecker suggested that he enjoyed his work too much, and posited that it would be a great way for a closeted cop to get his rocks off and still come out smelling like a rose. The article mistakenly used "Charles" instead of "John" as the officer's name. In the October 1969 issue Stienecker ran a correction, with a brief follow-up and a photograph of Sgt. John Manley.

In early 1970 a newly formed gay group at the University of Chicago learned that Sgt. Manley was scheduled to speak Feb. 25 on "Youthful Offenders" to the Women's Bar Association of Illinois. In the Feb. 6 issue of the Chicago Maroon and a concurrent Gay Liberation Newsletter, Step May, Nancy Garwood, and Bill Dry signed an article calling for a picket and leafleting of the WBAI protesting Manley's appearance. May and Garwood were later "outed" to their parents in anonymous letters with a veiled warning about messing with a Chicago po-

lice officer. (Dry was not a UC student and would go on to be a founder of Gay Liberation at Northwestern University.) On the day of the demonstration when they saw Manley in person at the WBAI picket, one UC student, Alice Leiner, recognized him as having attended a planning meeting and passing himself off as an out-of-town gay activist named Mandrenas.

On the morning of Feb. 7, 1970, Manley himself showed up at David Stienecker's third-floor apartment with a warrant for his arrest on the charge of "criminal defamation" (Chapter 38, Section 27-1, Illinois Revised Statutes, since repealed). Stienecker told Poling: "I wasn't sure if I was going to go to jail or be taken for a ride and beaten up. (That was not uncommon in those days.) So, yes, I was scared."

Perhaps validating his earlier assessment of Manley, Stienecker also said the cop "insisted on watching me dress in the bathroom." (In a later Chicago Journalism Review article, "Mattachine editor arrested," Ron Dorfman noted that the warrant for Stienecker's arrest had been issued in October 1969, shortly after the second Manley article had appeared.) Stienecker told Poling that although Manley suggested he just plead guilty and the judge would give him "a slap on the wrist," he insisted on calling an attorney: "I mention this because it shows the attitude of the cops at the time. They never believed a gay person would fight a charge."

The March 1970 MM Newsletter headlined Stienecker's arrest, railed against Manley's contempt for freedom of the press, and noted this was "the first case … in which an official of a homophile organization has been arrested for writing an article." MM President Bradford wrote that he regarded Stienecker's arrest as a sign of Mattachine Midwest's effectiveness in the fight against police abuse. Both the MM and UC-CGL newsletters called for any information on Manley, urging anyone willing to testify to come forward. Attorney Renee Hanover represented Stienecker, and the case was eventually dropped because the prosecution hadn't made a case and Manley failed to make three court dates.

As their trial dragged through federal court, one of the Chicago Seven and other activist leaders, including Stienecker, were asked to speak at a rally at the Logan Monument in Grant Park. In its coverage of the event, the Chicago Tribune devoted a couple of paragraphs to Stienecker. His employer, World Book Encyclopedia, had seen the item, and a couple of months later he was fired (as investigation indicated, because he was gay). Stienecker wanted to sue "but the ACLU didn't think we had a good case because I quickly got a better job. I would also have to involve gay people [from World Book] who were very closeted, and it would have ruined their lives."

CONCLUSION

It would be naive to conclude that these two cases (The Trip's and Stienecker's) on their own changed the treatment of gays in Chicago overnight. But they certainly gave notice for the first time, to the city and the police, that it wasn't going to be the same old, same old anymore.

More importantly, disparate gays alone, and in groups, understood that they too could stand up and fight for their rights. By mid-year there were gay groups on all the major college campuses in the area. New organizations (CGA, IGLA, IGRTF) began polling and political action. Lesbian and gay newsletters popped up everywhere. Former members of MM dispersed throughout the new organizations. Instead of just the Mattachine referral hotline there were now directories, newspapers, clinics, a lesbian center with a bookstore and library, social service organizations from Rogers Park to Hyde Park—Beckman House and Gay Horizons, and a gay community center on West Elm Street.

In 1971 the president of the Chicago Gay Alliance presented the Judiciary Committee of the City Council with its first demand that amendments be added to existing housing and employment laws to include "sexual orientation" in the list of prohibited forms of discrimination. In just a few years, with the old guard as midwives, a citywide community had been born. ▼

With research contributions by William B. Kelley.

The 'gay' life in Chicago

Homosexuals today refuse to remain submerged and oppressed by the 'straight' world

By Paul Sampson

CHICAGO TRIBUNE, 1970.

The ever-evolving mainstream media coverage of gays. Courtesy M. Kuda Archives, Oak Park, Ill.

FIFTY CENTS •   OCTOBER 31, 1969

TIME

The Homosexual in America

TIME, OCTOBER 1969.

THE GREY CITY JOURNAL

The "Problem" of Homosexuality

By Henry Weinhoff

GAY ACTIVIST HENRY
WIEMHOFF IN THE GREY CITY
JOURNAL, JANUARY 1970.

Homosexuals cry out for acceptance

By Barbara Emeric

CHICAGO DAILY NEWS, JUNE 1972.

IN THE NEWS   *by JOHN D'EMILIO*

THESE DAYS, WE TAKE FOR GRANTED THE newsworthiness of LGBT topics. Gender identity gets left out of the latest Employment Non-Discrimination Act bill, and the ensuing battle for trans inclusion becomes a mainstream news story. Same-sex marriage; don't ask, don't tell; the use of the "F" word as a slur by a television star: These stories are splashed across the pages of print media or become fodder for nighttime television commentary.

It wasn't always so. In 1951, when Donald Webster Cory (a pseudonym) published the book The Homosexual in America, he identified what he called a "conspiracy of silence" that blanketed the nation's press. Gay and lesbian life wasn't considered a fit subject matter for the "family newspaper" that millions of Americans picked up on their way to work in the morning or had delivered to their homes each day.

Of course, editors selectively enforced this silence. The Chicago Tribune had no compunction writing about the dangers posed by "men of perverted sex tendencies." The Chicago Defender felt free to claim that lesbians controlled the city's prostitution

trade. But articles that simply described life as it was experienced by gay men and lesbians? That allowed them to speak in their own words and set the terms of the coverage? Not on your life.

When did this journalistic state of affairs begin to change? Historians love the concreteness of dates, and in this case we have a precise one—Dec. 17, 1963. On that day, The New York Times, whose motto is "all the news that's fit to print," carried this headline: "Growth of Overt Homosexuality in City Provokes Wide Concern." The accompanying article described a flourishing male homosexual underground as the city's "most sensitive open secret."

Perhaps because the Times presents itself as the "newspaper of record" in the United States, this article provided journalistic permission for other papers to follow suit. Over the next couple of years, copycat articles appeared in city newspapers around the country. Atlanta, Denver, Washington, D.C., and Seattle were just some of the cities where reporters decided to expose the gay world to their readership. Chicago's turn came on June 20, 1966, when the now-defunct Chicago Daily News began a four-part series.

To our contemporary sensibilities, the content of the series would be enough to make thousands of angry queers spontaneously storm the headquarters of the publisher and sit in until apologies were issued and the evil deed rectified by providing space for rebuttal. In the series, a judge described homosexuals as "sick people." James O'Grady, the police lieutenant in charge of the anti-prostitution detail (who was to become police superintendent briefly in 1978), talked about "fag bars" and "queers." The doctor who directed the Municipal Court's psychiatric unit referred to homosexuality as "socially distasteful." The reporter described gay men as "disturbed" and as "deviates."

The headlines and section headers that the Daily News employed were just as bad: "Twilight World That's Tormented"; "Cops Keep Watch on Deviate Hangouts"; "Homosexuality a Sickness? 'No' Say the Deviates"; "His Bizarre Double Life."

But our contemporary eyes are not the best ones for judging how these articles were viewed at the time. In the context of 1966, they represented progress, a journalistic opening wedge of sorts. Why?

THE CHICAGO GAY CRUSADER
WROTE ABOUT PERCEIVED
ANTI-GAY COMMENTS
BY MIKE ROYKO (1974) AND
ANN LANDERS (1973).

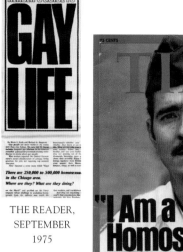

THE READER,
SEPTEMBER
1975

TIME, SEPTEMBER 1975.

SUN-TIMES,
SEPTEMBER 1979 SERIES.

CHICAGO TRIBUNE MAGAZINE,
FEBRUARY 1993.

Because "tormented" and "deviate" and "disturbed" and "affliction" were not the only points of view expressed in the series. I wouldn't go as far as to say the articles displayed balance—if by balance we mean equal weight to anti-gay and pro-gay sentiments. Reporter Lois Wille, who had already won a Pulitzer Prize for a 1963 series on refusal to provide contraceptive services to poor women, allowed dissenting opinions to be heard. She found ways to insinuate that there was more than one viewpoint about homosexuality, thus legitimizing a debate about homosexuality where, before, there was nothing but a negative consensus.

She did this in different ways. Sometimes she posed questions, such as these in the opening article: "Can and should deviates be 'contained' to keep them from spreading further? ... Or are these disturbed, misunderstood men needing help, understanding and the freedom to live in their way?" She also suggested that the gay world was made up of all kinds of people. Yes, there were "the dregs of the invert world," but there were also those who led "happy lives" and who made "good neighbors."

Wille held public policy up for criticism. A major topic in the series was police behavior. She wrote at length about the crackdown against gay bars, the raids and the closings, and the mass arrests. But Lt. O'Grady's defense of police activity did not go unchallenged. Wille interviewed Pearl Hart, whom she described as a lawyer with 52 years of practice in civil liberties law. Hart called police conduct unethical and said the raids and arrests were a waste of time and taxpayers' money. "It just doesn't make sense to go after homosexuals," she told Wille.

The series also let it be known that some homosexuals were challenging the way things were. Sometimes this took the form of organizations, such as Mattachine Midwest, whose president Wille approvingly described as "a tall rugged-looking businessman."

Sometimes more spontaneous forms of resistance appeared in the article. Wille described a wonderful scene in court where a well-dressed defendant began shouting at the judge: "I'm happy. Are you happy? Well, I am. ... Don't tell me I'm sick." According to Wille, this kind of response was becoming typical as

gay men no longer listened meekly to what prosecutors and judges had to say.

The Daily News articles were as revealing for what they left out as for what they contained. There was not a single mention of lesbians. This was a series about male homosexuals, and lesbians never entered the discussion. There was no mention of their bars, no mention of their social circles, and no mention of any difficulties they faced. The articles also had no racial descriptors. This effectively coded the discussion as one about white men, implying that gays are all white. By and large, the locations Wille identified for gay bars and cruising areas were North Side locations, reinforcing the sense this was a white social phenomenon.

These silences were not surprising, but they were especially unfortunate. At a time when silence in the press was more the rule than not, a series such as this one was something of a road map. For the very closeted, these articles offered information. They named bars. They named locations. In other words, the articles provided hope to the very isolated that they might find others. But that hope, alas, didn't extend to everyone. ▼

OUT OF THE
closets
INTO THE
streets

Harold
Washington
For-Chicago

GAY
RIGHTS
NOW

EQUAL
RITES
for
WOMEN

NATIONAL MARCH FOR LESBIAN AND GAY RIGHTS
GAY LESBIAN PRIDE
80
OCT. 14

MAYOR
DALEY
'95

CATANIA
COOK COUNTY
BOARD

OPEN
PAC
ORGANIZATION TO
PROMOTE
EQUALITY
NOW

Gay &
Lesbian
Pride
'78

DYKE

THE GAY 90'S
10% of the Century for
10% of the Population.
It's only fair.

LARRY
McKEON
FOR STATE
REPRESENTATIVE
CHICAGO 199

TIM
DRAKE
STATE
REPRESENTATIVE

THE
**MORAL
MAJORITY
IS NEITHER**

CAROL
MOSELEY
BRAUN
DEMOCRAT U.S. SENATE

NO
MORE!
Witch Hunts
Resist Now

GAY
'76
REVOLUTION

COME OUT

LESBIANS
IGNITE

PEOPLE
LIKE US

**EQ
IL**

LESBIANS IN LEATHER
CHICAGO

NATIONAL GAY RIGHTS
RIGHTS ARE NOT WON
ON PAPER:
THEY ARE WON
ONLY BY THOSE
WHO MAKE THEIR
VOICES HEARD
—HARVEY MILK
MARCH
WASHINGTON, D.C.
OCTOBER 14, 1979

GAY
RIGHTS
ARE
HUMAN
RIGHTS

GAY
LIBERATION

THE
NAMES
PROJECT

CHICAGO '71
**GAY
PRIDE**
CELEBRATION

WOMEN UNITE!
take
back
the
night
SEPTEMBER 5R, '7_
ILLINOIS

LESBIAN PRIDE WEEK
AUG 1-8 '76

MOTHER
NATURE
is a
LESBIAN

GARY
NEPON
FOR
STATE REP.

THE WE DECADE

Chicago's community saw its largest growth during the post-Stonewall 1970s

CHICAGO'S GAY COMMUNITY BURST WIDE OPEN IN THE 1970s. Building on the 1960s movement created by organizations like Mattachine Midwest, and emboldened by a new generation of college-age activists, the explosion out of the closets was unprecedented. The bar raids and Democratic National Convention riots, combined with the civil rights and women's movements, fostered the creation of radical and more conservative gay groups.

From the formation of Gay Liberation in 1969 at the University of Chicago came the splinter group Chicago Gay Alliance (CGA) in 1970. Both organizations wanted gay rights; they just represented different paths to achieve success. This would parallel similar schisms in the community that still exist in 2008. Then, as now, some splits were based on conservative vs. liberal philosophies, others on personality and style.

Many lesbians, disappointed with the sexism they perceived in gay groups, formed their own organizations and publications. Gays of color also created their own groups, including Third World Gay Revolutionaries. Gay organizations, including the Illinois Gay and Lesbian Task Force, sprouted from mainstream progressive organizations, and activists trained in the ways of civil disobedience from the Vietnam War used their skills in new gay and lesbian groups.

CGA and others started working on political issues, and began asking candidates their positions on gay issues and lobbying for city and state protections for gay people. But social events were also important, and Gay Liberation sponsored the first citywide dance at the South Side's Coliseum April 18, 1970, with 2,000 gays and lesbians in attendance. The ACLU worked with activists to make sure police knew that same-sex dancing was not illegal in Illinois. Even some gay bars believed this to be the case, and at least one was picketed until it allowed same-sex partners to dance there.

The poster for the International Mr. Leather 1979 contest. Courtesy Chuck Renslow and the Leather Archives & Museum, Chicago.

Opposite: Buttons from the 1960s–1990s. Courtesy M. Kuda Archives, Oak Park, Ill., and Nancy Katz.

Chicago's first major gay political actions happened in 1970, less than a year after the Stonewall riots in New York City. On Feb. 25, gays protested the appearance of anti-gay police officer John Manley at a Women's Bar Association luncheon. In April 1970, on tax day (April 15), about 100 gays and lesbians marched with other non-gay Moratorium Week activists down State Street to the Federal Building to protest the use of tax dollars in Vietnam. On April 16, about 250 people gathered in Grant Park for Gay Liberation Day, which was also being celebrated in other U.S. cities. Activist Step May had the Student Mobilization Committee designate the day, and despite not having a permit, Gay Liberation held the event.

That summer, Chicago's first commemoration of the Stonewall riots was held. There were several social and political events, and on June 27 there was a rally at Bughouse Square downtown. More than 150 people attended the event, which ended with a march to the Civic Center Plaza (now the Daley Center Plaza). The Pride Parade has been held every June since; today, it attracts more than 400,000 spectators and participants.

In the early 1970s, Kathleen Thompson started Pride & Prejudice, the city's first feminist bookstore, at 3322 N. Halsted St. It later became The Women's Center, and in 1974 it was renamed the Lesbian Feminist Center (and Bookstore) and moved to a new location, 3523 N. Halsted St.

In early 1971, Chicago boasted its first gay community center. A Chicago Gay Alliance (CGA) member leased a two-story brick building at 171 W. Elm St. After renovations, the space housed CGA and was open to others to host meetings, rap groups and other events.

Beckman House, a community center, opened in early 1974 at 3519½ N. Halsted St. The center was named for lesbian activist Barbara Beckman, who died in a car crash in 1972. The Tavern Guild of Chicago, which started in the 1970s, created the Rodde Fund in 1977 to found the city's next community center. The Rodde Center operated at 3225 N. Sheffield Ave. for several years, but funds from the sale of that property were squandered on rents during a failed several years of fundraising to start a new center. Chicago would not get a community center for nearly two more decades; eventually, Horizons changed its name to Center on Halsted, opening a massive new building in 2007.

A gay and women's lib dance flier, early 1970s.
Courtesy Hannah Frisch.

While the passage of city and state gay rights legislation was years away, Chicago did see some important changes in the 1970s. The American Psychiatric Association removed homosexuality from its categories of illness in 1973. In that same year, Pearl Hart and Renee Hanover successfully challenged the city's law against cross-dressing (until that point you could be arrested if you were not wearing at least three items of clothing considered appropriate to your gender).

A coalition of Chicago gay and lesbian groups was created out of anger at two women who, the groups felt, had tried to "exploit the issue of gay marriage in a publicity stunt." In October 1975 Nancy Davis and Toby Schneiter tried to get a marriage license at the Cook County Clerk's office. The newly formed Gay and Lesbian Coalition of Metropolitan Chicago included representatives of most major community groups, businesses and publications, including the Illinois Gay Rights Task Force, The Chicago Gay Crusader, Gender Services of Chicago, Dignity/Chicago, Mattachine Midwest and Gay Horizons, and opposed the women's action. The coalition felt the ill-prepared attempt would hurt efforts to pass the city's gay-rights bill.

Chicagoans were very connected to other regions and helped raise funds for the battle against the California Briggs Initiative; the survivors of a devastating fire at a New Orleans gay bar; and the quests of Leonard Matlovich and Miriam Ben-Shalom to stay in the U.S. military. In March 1977, Chicago's William B. Kelley was among a select group of 14 gays and lesbians who attended the first-ever gay meeting in the White House.

When Anita Bryant, pop-singer-turned-conservative-crusader, helped roll back gay rights in Dade County, Fla., Chicagoans quickly reacted. During her appearance at the Medinah Temple on June 14, 1977, several thousand people surrounded the building in what became a huge spark for the Chicago gay movement. Thirty years later, activists who attended that protest say it was among the most important events in Chicago's gay history.

Gay, lesbian and feminist media played a critical role in the community's growth in the 1970s. Dozens of newsletters and newspapers were started. Some lasted a short time, some lasted into the 1980s, and one founded at that time

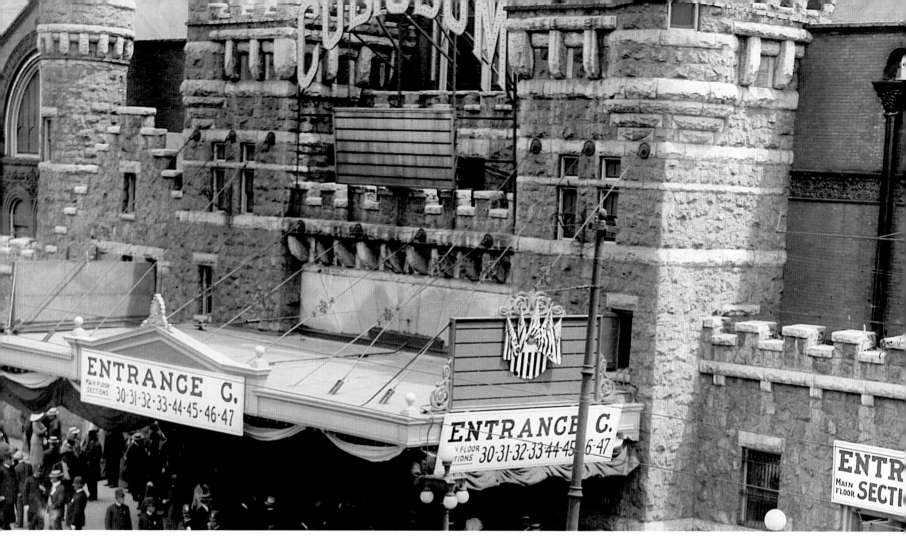

Gay Liberation sponsored the first citywide dance at the South Side's Coliseum April 18, 1970, with 2,000 gays and lesbians attending. This picture is from the 1912 Republican National Convention. Both the Democrats and Republicans used the venue for national conventions. Courtesy the Chicago History Museum.

still publishes in 2008: Gay Chicago Magazine. For about a decade, Gay Chicago also hosted popular awards programs for the community, piggybacking on its Mr. Windy City pageant. The community's media publishers and reporters often pushed an activist agenda, editorializing for gay-rights bills and demonstrations and providing a critical analysis of difficult issues facing the community. The mainstream media continued their tainted coverage of the community, but there were exceptions, as some print and broadcast journalists tried to cover the community in a more balanced way. Gay groups protested mainstream media outlets, and gays working inside those companies tried to change things from within.

There were scandals in the 1970s, but none more difficult for the community than the case of John Wayne Gacy. The media frenzy around Gacy, who was convicted and executed for killing 33 young men and boys, threatened to destroy progress on gay issues. Gay people were quick to recognize that despite the

slogan "Gay Is Good," not all gay people are good. Acknowledging this fact was key to the maturing of the movement. There were other hate crimes in the 1970s, and killings by lovers and ex-lovers. There were also tragic suicides, some for personal reasons, and others for political causes.

Family of Woman, the first out lesbian rock band in the country, was started in Chicago in the early 1970s. Singer Linda Shear was out and proud in the media, speaking about her bandmates and their impact on the community. The women's festival and music movement was just beginning, and many Chicagoans were part of the national push to secure more roles for women in the music industry. Mountain Moving Coffeehouse, Women in Crisis Can Act, women's shelters, Artemis Singers and numerous other organizations started in the 1970s, and many carried on well into the 1990s and even 2000s. While the feminist Jane Addams Bookstore did not survive past the mid-1980s, Women & Children First Books, which started in the late 1970s, still is open in 2008.

Women were finding their voices in literature as well, and Marie J. Kuda hosted several important Lesbian Writers' Conferences in the 1970s. She and others, such as Metis Press and the Women's Graphics Collective, were also part of a critical national Women in Print movement. Chicago also hosted the American Library Association's annual meetings several times and frequently hosted the ALA's Gay Liberation Task Force book awards.

The fight for Illinois to ratify the Equal Rights Amendment was pushed by many lesbians, and some gay men joined the cause as well. But Illinois-based anti-gay activist Phyllis Schlafly's campaign against the measure was successful, and Illinois was unable to join other states in an effort to put the measure over the top. The ERA never passed as a constitutional amendment.

On the social scene, disco was the name of the game. Many dance clubs sprouted up, some fueled by liberal drug use and drinking in the community. Some gay and lesbian bars that opened in the 1960s were still around, but a new wave of bars opened in the 1970s, some of which are still open in 2008. With the rise of disco also came the rise of the dance-music disc jockey as celebrity, and Chicago's Frankie Knuckles, credited with being the founder of house music, still is among the hottest DJs in the world.

In the 1970s, Jim Flint's Baton Show Lounge, which started in 1969, built a loyal following among gays and straights who wanted to see the female impersonators; Chilli Pepper was just starting her 30+-year career as a female performer, winning the title of Miss Gay Chicago 1974.

Gay bars were often not gay-owned, however, and the mafia's control was stifling, to say the least. The police collected payoffs to prevent bar raids, but they often raided them anyway, especially close to election time. Jim Flint was among those who helped break up the payoff schemes, risking a lot by testifying in court.

Unfortunately, the racial divisions in Chicago were (and are still) visible within the gay and lesbian community. Some gay bars were accused of excessive demands for identification from African-American patrons. Patricia McCombs was so upset by the extra carding at one lesbian bar that she worked with attorney Renee Hanover to fight the bar's liquor license. McCombs was joined by dozens picketing the bar, and other efforts were made to protest similar carding at gay clubs around the city. The Black gay community was beginning to create separate spaces for pride as well. The "Rocks" along the lake near Belmont Av-

Frankie Knuckles spins at the Gay Games VII 2006 Opening Ceremony. Steve Becker photo.

enue became the site of an annual Black gay pride celebration; it later moved to the lakefront at Montrose Drive.

Religious gay groups were also growing strong, including Dignity/Chicago for Roman Catholics, Congregation Or Chadash for Jews, and the congregations of the Universal Fellowship of Metropolitan Community Churches, for those seeking another way to worship.

Chuck Renslow's leather and business empire expanded in 1979 with the founding of the International Mr. Leather contest. In 2008, the contest will celebrate its 30th titleholder, attracting contestants and spectators from around the world.

While lesbians and gay men played sports in city leagues and even had all-gay teams in the 1960s in straight bowling and softball leagues, Lincoln Park Lagooners was Chicago's first gay sport and social group, incorporated in 1977. By 1978, the Gay Athletic Association (later the Chicago Metropolitan Sports Association) was formed to host 16-inch softball leagues for men and women. The growth of sports teams and leagues soon took off, including the Windy City Athletic Association, the Women's Sports Association and individual gay teams in straight leagues. Eventually, Chicago's gay sports infrastructure was strong enough to host Gay Games VII in 2006.

The issue of parents' and families' supporting their gay and lesbian children also began to be addressed in the 1970s. Gay activist Guy Warner was looking for support for his mother, and when he found nothing he started his own group. Parents, Families, and Friends of Lesbians and Gays (PFLAG) did not exist yet, so he worked with Mattachine Midwest to start Parents of Gays in March 1977. PFLAG's Chicago chapter later grew out of this organization.

Lionheart Theatre also began in the 1970s, creating groundbreaking works and fostering the work of gay and lesbian playwrights into the 1990s. The work of Jeff Hagedorn (who wrote One, the first play about AIDS in the United States), Nick Patricca, Rick Paul and many others was featured.

The people of Lionheart and other activists and cultural pioneers were inspired by an event that ended the 1970s with a bang: the Oct. 14, 1979, National March on Washington for Lesbian and Gay Rights. An estimated 100,000 people attended that first of several similar Washington, D.C.–based national marches. Chicagoans who drove, took the train or flew to D.C. for the weekend's events came back forever changed. That renewed energy was needed, because the movement was about to face a new and terrifying opponent: AIDS. ▼   — *Tracy Baim*

CROSS-DRESSING LAW STRUCK DOWN *by MARIE J. KUDA*

On Sept. 21, 1973, three Chicago daily newspapers had the following headlines:

> *"Transvestite Law Held Illegal;*
> *4 Juveniles Freed"* – CHICAGO SUN-TIMES

> *"Cross-Sex Dress Ban Overruled"*
> – CHICAGO TRIBUNE

> *"City Ordinance KOd: Judge Upsets Ban*
> *on Transvestism"* – CHICAGO DAILY NEWS

ATTORNEY RENEE HANOVER DEFENDED four juvenile transvestites who were arrested Aug. 21, 1973, on charges of cross-dressing and underage drinking. The young men, aged 17 to 20, said they had entered a tavern at 2200 W. 21st Pl. to buy cigarettes; one used the women's bathroom. An altercation with patrons ensued and the four were beaten up, but police from the 10th District arrested only the youths. They were charged with violating Section 192–8 of the Chicago Municipal Code, which prohibited someone from appearing in a public place in clothing of the opposite sex "with the intent to conceal his or her sex."

The ordinance had originally been enacted by the City Council long prior to 1943, but in that year it was amended to include the "conceal" language. At the height of the war years, the ordinance may have been seen in some way as a protection for military personnel. Sailors from the Great Lakes Naval Training Station flooded the city on weekend leave. Companion ordinances prohibited women from serving drinks in bars or tending bar (unless they were owners) and prohibited unescorted women in such establishments, effectively turning the jam-packed bars all-male.

Appearing before Judge Jack Sperling (a former City Council member) in North Boys Court, the defendants—Melinda, Mona, Tanya and Tammie, as they preferred to be called—wore blouses and miniskirts, lipstick, rouge, and wigs, and they carried purses. Hanover said the unisex fashions and hairstyles of the time made it difficult to tell the difference between men and women. Hanover followed her law partner Pearl M. Hart's advice and argued

While it was fine for lawyers who were part of the Chicago Bar Association to dress in drag for their annual follies show (like these men in 1952), those same lawyers and future judges may have ruled against gays, lesbians and transgender people for doing the same in that era. Photo courtesy the Chicago History Museum.

the case on purely constitutional grounds; since not all transvestites are gay, homosexuality was not to be an issue.

Hanover's defense resulted in Sperling's decision that the ordinance violated the constitutions of Illinois and the United States by not affording transvestites equal protection under the law. He cited federal court opinions in cases that held government dress codes unconstitutional, stating that people's right to present themselves as they chose was guaranteed by the 14th Amendment.

Sun-Times reporter Larry Weintraub ended his coverage of the case: "Ms. Hanover was clad in a blouse and a knit, striped slack suit. Mooradian [the city prosecutor] was attired in a striped sports jacket and slacks. The judge wore a floor-length black robe."

Because the case was decided by a trial-court judge rather than an appellate court, it had little or no weight as precedent in any other court. In any event, the police could use anti-gay discretionary enforcement of other laws if they chose.

Earlier, in July 1973, Alderman Clifford P. Kelley and nine co-signers had introduced what has become popularly known as the "gay rights bill." At public hearings on the proposed bill held by the City Council's Judiciary Committee on Oct. 10, Hanover was one of 24 who testified on discrimination against gays. She used the case of the four to call for repeal of the cross-dressing ordinance, arguing that since Judge Sperling's decision was not binding on other criminal court judges, repeal was necessary to eliminate further arrests.

In a Nov. 2 article in the Chicago Reader newspaper, Nancy Banks reported that Hanover's testimony had noted further consequences to the arrest of the four: "[T]he day before the court hearing, the home of defendant Mona Garcia was burned. The day after court, Tanya Williams, who appeared on television, was fired from her job, and the following day Melinda Balderas was evicted from her apartment." ▼

With research contributions by William B. Kelley.

THE REVOLUTION ... WILL BE REPORTED ON

 *by TRACY BAIM*

The cover of Killer Dyke, 1971. Below: Lavender Woman, September 1972, The Original Lavender Woman, July 1974, and Blazing Star, November 1977. Courtesy M. Kuda Archives, Oak Park, Ill.

THE FIRST KNOWN GAY PUBLICATION IN the United States was the newsletter Friendship and Freedom, published in the 1920s by the short-lived Illinois-based Society for Human Rights. No copies of the publication are known to exist. The next big media venture was the extremely important Mattachine Midwest Newsletter, which was packed full of news and information during the 1960s through the early 1980s. Marie J. Kuda, William B. Kelley, Jim Bradford, Valerie Taylor and David Stienecker were among its key contributors.

The first known gay Chicago newspaper-format publications arrived in the early 1970s, including Killer Dyke, Chicago Gay Pride, and The Paper. This section could be its own book, given that there were likely more than 100 media efforts by the Chicago community in recent decades, from newsletters to radio shows, TV to the Internet, newspapers to magazines. This article is an extremely brief overview of the media movement, but more details are available on www.ChicagoGay History.org, including scans of many of the publications mentioned here. Subsequent chapters also deal with some media issues, including The 10% Show on cable and LesBiGay Radio.

LESBIANS

Women in general were taking control of the media in more ways than ever in the 1970s, including starting newspapers, magazines, printing presses, graphics collectives and literary conferences. In Chicago, the first known lesbian publication was the short-lived Killer Dyke (1971), produced by Northeastern Illinois University students and based on the design of the liberal Seed newspaper. Killer Dykes and Freakin' Fag Revolutionaries put out three newspapers with government funding available for "any group that could put together a paper," as Margaret "Skeeter" Wilson remembers, and then for two more years produced mimeographed copies. For decades to come, women would continue to start new media endeavors, from newspapers to Web sites.

The gender wars of the 1970s meant that some

lesbians wanted to create their own media, while others preferred to work on joint ventures with gay men. In a July 1988 Outlines article, Marie Kuda wrote: "Chicago lesbians have contributed and/or published no less than 28 periodicals since the late 1960s."

In August 1971, members of the Women's Caucus of Chicago Gay Alliance pooled money to publish the first issue of The Feminist Voice. One page, devoted to the Women's Caucus, was called The Lavender Woman. By November, Lavender Woman (LW) broke off as its own publication and had a national impact. It ran 26 issues at irregular intervals, according to Kuda's article, through July 1976.

Eventually the Chicago Lesbian Liberation (CLL) group split from LW. It published its own newsletter in 1973–74, since LW was published irregularly. When LW pulled the one-page CLL space over a controversial cartoon, CLL countered with publication of two issues of The Original Lavender Woman in September and October 1974. "It was the first really nasty split in the community and it would have a long-lasting effect," Kuda wrote. Michal Brody wrote about Lavender Woman in her 1985 book, Are We There Yet? A Continuing History of Lavender Woman, a Chicago Lesbian Newspaper, 1971–1976.

Some members of the Chicago Women's Liberation Union started Blazing Star, a newspaper, in 1975. It changed formats a few times and continued through January 1980, when it became an insert in GayLife newspaper. Eventually, it disappeared, and GayLife began an insert called Sister Spirit in 1984. Later, Windy City Times and Outlines both had women's sections.

Kuda, Thelma Norris, Fran Heron, Judy Brabec and Pam Chamberlain were involved in the late-1976 start of Women's News … for a Change. It was not identified as lesbian but included information about lesbians; it lasted only a year.

Lesbians contributed to general gay media, and they also played a role in the mainstream media, even if they were closeted. Both Lavender Woman

Top: In 2006, Frank Robinson reviews his gay Chicago publications from the early 1970s. Photo by Tracy Baim.
Left: Chicago Gay Pride newspaper in 1971, and The Paper in 1972. Courtesy M. Kuda Archives, Oak Park, Ill.

The Chicago Gay Crusader, 1974, and GayLife, 1984. Courtesy M. Kuda Archives and Tracy Baim Archives.

At age 21, Michael Bergeron and his partner, activist William B. Kelley, started The Chicago Gay Crusader, which ran from May 1973 through April 1976. The impact of the Gay Crusader is immeasurable: It was a serious newspaper covering the community during critical years, and it was known for its inclusive coverage of men and women alike. Every issue of the Crusader was packed with news, interviews, features, entertainment, photos, and more—a treasure trove of details about a wide range of topics. The pre-AIDS years were not without tragedy, as most issues reported on deaths, whether by fire, car accident, violence, suicide or natural causes.

Bergeron was a unique leader who also created a community center, Beckman House, started a crisis and information telephone line (929-HELP, still in use by Center on Halsted), and encouraged the creation of a women's hotline to handle the calls his Crusader line was getting from lesbians. Bergeron also published what may have been the earliest gay guides, the Chicago Gay Directory, from the early to mid-1970s. The Up North bar on North Western Avenue was a key sponsor.

GAYLIFE AND WINDY CITY TIMES

In his June 1975 Gay Crusader column, Pride activist Rich Pfeiffer noted that a new local paper was to begin in Chicago: GayLife. Grant Ford was the publisher in its early years, but he eventually sold it to Chuck Renslow. Once the Gay Crusader folded, GayLife became the main newspaper in the community. While Gay Chicago Magazine primarily focused on the social scene (see separate entry), GayLife covered all parts of the community. Some women objected to the more graphic male ads, but GayLife did have a decent reputation for covering both men and women.

As the AIDS crisis grew in the early 1980s, GayLife was a critical early place for information about the epidemic. The political scene was also heating up, with candidates, organizations, and a renewed commitment to city and state gay rights bills.

When I graduated from Drake University in 1984 with a degree in news-editorial journalism, my

and Blazing Star were considered vital links for the 1970s lesbian communities. In the 1980s, HOT WIRE continued the trend, but it was a national journal of women's music and culture, not a Chicago lesbian newspaper. There would never again be as vital, or volatile, a media community for lesbians, because by the 1980s, with the AIDS crisis looming, gay men and lesbians collaborated more comfortably on co-gender publications.

GAY AND LESBIAN MEDIA

While lesbians were creating their own media in the 1970s, gay men and lesbians were also working together on gay publications.

In 1971, Frank M. Robinson started the city's first tabloid-size gay newspaper, Chicago Gay Pride. It continued as the organ of the Chicago Gay Alliance from February 1972 through June 1973, but Robinson did not stop there. In the summer of 1972

he started The Paper, which focused on entertainment and gay culture. It was a slick tabloid written for both men and women. According to Kuda, only two issues ever were published.

Robinson is a Chicago legend. He served in the Navy in World War II and the Korean War, worked at Science Digest, wrote the advice column for Playboy magazine, and became a very prolific writer. He collaborated with the late Tom Scortia on a novel, The Glass Inferno, which became a film classic under a slightly different name: The Towering Inferno. He has numerous books to his name, but his critical role in early gay media has gone mostly unacknowledged. After he moved to San Francisco in the mid-1970s, he became a speechwriter for Harvey Milk, and Robinson wrote some of Milk's most important speeches, as documented in The Mayor of Castro Street: The Life and Times of Harvey Milk, by Randy Shilts.

BLACK LINES

FEBRUARY 1996 Vol. 1, No. 3   FREE   EXPRESSIONS FROM BLACK GAY, LESBIAN, BISEXUAL AND TRANSGENDERED LIFE

PREMIERE EDITION

MAKING HISTORY
past present future

2nd UNITY CONFAB
Feb. 24

Also:
Seraiah Carol, Donna Rose
Calendar of events
Hot pics
Poetry

Windy City Times
Chicago's Gay and Lesbian Newsweekly
Windy City Times Vol. 1, Number 1   Thursday, September 26, 1985

Mayor's committee named
Gay and lesbian activists chosen

By Tracy Baim

The appointments to the 15-person mayor's Committee on Gay and Lesbian Issues were announced Monday late afternoon by Mayor Harold Washington's liaison to the gay and lesbian community, Kit Duffy.

In addition to the 15 slots there will be symbolic positions for closeted gays and lesbians. One of the 15 positions will be a 'job share' between Women & Children First Bookstore owners Linda Bubon and Ann Christophersen.

The 16 people slated include eight women and eight men. Three blacks and one Hispanic were selected.

Washington announced the formation of the committee the day after this year's Gay and Lesbian Pride Rally. At the June 30 rally, Washington had been scheduled to make the announcement but failed to remember to do so.

Duffy released the committee names on Monday after Washington approved her recommendations. Duffy made each of the choices herself, despite original notice that a selection committee would choose the committee. She said because of potential controversy surrounding such a selection process, she made the decision herself based on numerous interviews with community members.

Accompanying this article is a list of the 16 people. In next week's Windy City Times, there will be full backgrounds on

Duffy explained that the committee will examine critical issues in the gay and lesbian community. This will include areas such as city funding, purchasing and grant requirements, and how the city can better meet human and health services needs.

It is possible, Duffy explained, that the committee will subdivide to coincide with city committees, such as those on economic development or human services. One specific action could be a seminar on purchasing and grants, especially for women and minorities. Basically, the committee can possibly assist gays and lesbians in hooking into the city process, she said.

The specific power of the committee members is limited. They make recommendations and members will serve as activists within the community. However, to avoid losing credibility, the committee will not be able to direct legislative lobbying.

About 40 people applied for committee positions. Duffy said she viewed the formation as a whole with the many community persons in mind. She was cognizant of geographical representation, but the people who applied did not come from all areas. She said she definitely tried to have as many women as possible on the committee.

One major qualification was the ability

willingness to work and "get their hands dirty." She stressed that the people selected see this appointment as working on behalf of the community, not as a mere status symbol.

strata. But the number grew as Duffy found it difficult to leave some names off. Even though it was expanded, however, many could not be chosen. Duffy realizes there may be some upset feelings. As a

Committee on Gay and Lesbian Issues

Carolyn Bay: Professional community organizer and ACTION co-chair.
Caryn Berman: Social worker with organizing background.
Art Brewer: Doctor, experienced in health issues, particularly AIDS.
Ann Christophersen and Linda Bubon: Co-owners of Women & Children First Bookstore.
Chris Cothran: Metropolitan Business Association, National Coalition of Black Gays. Co-owner Tangible Type.
Rhonda Craven: Communications and art background.
Ted Hoert: Small business owner, Far North Side activist.
Marie Kuda: Long-time active feminist, one of founders of Chicago Mattachine.

Achy Obejas: Latina community and political organizer, communications.
Rich Pfeiffer: Community activist, Gay and Lesbian Pride organizer.
Linda Rodgers: Paris Dance co-owner, community activist.
Larry Rolla: Attorney, active in wide variety of issues, including civil rights.
Ron Sable: Part of Cook County Hospital Sable/Sherer Clinic, community organizer.
John Simmons: Executive director of Joseph Holmes Dance Theatre.
Bill Young: Harris Foundation, expertise in private funding.
Symbolic position To represent the closeted gay and lesbian community.

Top right is the top half of the first edition of Windy City Times (WCT), Sept. 26, 1985. Eventually WCT co-founder Tracy Baim split off to start Outlines, and that first issue is shown middle, below, June 4, 1987. Below right is WCT in 2008, the combined forces of Outlines and WCT. Far left are other Windy City Media Group products over the years: BLACKlines and En La Vida both published for 10 years before becoming Identity, an online-only publication. Nightlines, now Nightspots, continues in 2008.

En La Vida
No. 15 Sept. 1997 voces de lesbianas, gays, bisexuales y transgéneros latinos

LLEGO REACHES OUT ACROSS U.S.

Martin Ornelas-Quintero (left), head of the National Latino Lesbian and Gay Organization, speaks on LLEGO's goals.
See page 6.

Also inside:

'Thank You, Cristina!'
See page 16 for a salute to talk-show host Cristina, who has been honored for her open-minded shows on gay issues.

Nightlines
WEEKLY
No. 228

DANCE FOR LIFE AUG. 13

...871-7610, 1115 W. Belmont, 2-D, Chicago, IL 606...
...La Vida, Nightlines, BLACKlines, OUT!, CLOUT!...

August 3, 1994

Nightspots
Giving Good Face

Sal-E and JoJo Baby are the subjects of Bernard Colbert's photo show "Getting Into Face" page 14

Chicago Outlines
The Voice of the Gay and Lesbian Community ● Vol.1 No.1 ● June 4 1987

Coping with AIDS: PWAs seek support

By William Burks

Last year after "Mark" (some of the names in this article have been changed to protect privacy) was hospitalized for tuberculosis and diagnosed with AIDS, he experienced "anger, fear, self pity—very intense doses of emotion," he said, sitting on an apartment balcony overlooking a becalmed Lake Michigan on a recent spring evening.

"But at some point I realized I wasn't dead yet. I was going to get out of the hospital, and I had to get on with my life," he continued. Mark began to look at what kind of support systems are available for people with AIDS in Chicago, and although he has been able to find the support he has needed so far, the ever growing number of AIDS cases—a record 47 in Chicago last month—calls into question whether such support will continue to be available.

One of the ways Mark chose to cope was to request a "support manager"—someone to help him deal with the emotional, physical, and practical needs he might experience—from Howard Brown Memorial Clinic.

"It took awhile before Bob was assigned to me, but my experience has been really good with him. I think there's probably a shortage of people who are willing to do this," Mark suggested as a reason for the delay.

In fact, support managers are in short supply at Howard Brown, with 115 managers—some of them very recently trained—serving 200 clients with AIDS. Just three and a half months ago, the clinic served 90 PWA clients.

Mark also inquired about joining a weekly support group for PWAs sponsored by Howard Brown. "I joined a group because I hadn't met anyone with AIDS before," he explained. I met a lot of people who looked remarkably healthy, and hadn't given up. So where I'm at now is not really bad at all."

He also investigated free legal services from one of the clinic's volunteer attorneys. However, he decided not to wait until someone could get to him (the attorneys are often helping people with more urgent needs), and hired a lawyer on his own. Far, he chosen to wait, he could have received free services such as preparing a will, power of attorney, or living will from a volunteer lawyer.

According to Bob Rybicki, head of Howard Brown's Social Services Department, Mark could also request through the clinic a PWA peer counselor with whom he could share experiences and receive emotional support, resource management such as help in applying for Public Aid or disability or entering a hospital or hospice, financial assistance, or professional counseling or therapy.

Mark could even get a free haircut from Howard Brown volunteers, or arrange for massage therapy if he wants it. There are support groups for significant others

Other agencies and organizations in the city–such as Cook County Hospital, Chicago House and Social Service Agency, Kupona Network, AIDS Pastoral Care Network, AIDS Assistance Association, Gay and Lesbian Horizons, and the American Civil Liberties Union–also provide such services as support managers or "buddies," housing, clothing, food, furniture, support groups, pastoral care, case management, and legal assistance for PWAs.

Mark had few complaints about the health care he received while hospitalized, and although his insurance covered the bill, which amounted to more than $20,000, he has still been unable to get an itemized accounting of where the money went. "People say, 'Don't worry, it's covered by your insurance,' but someone is paying for it. Bob's [his support manager's] insurance may cost 10 cents more a month; then he's paying for it too. I feel that I have the right–no, the duty–to be concerned about the cost of medical services."

Mark's insurance also took over the $900 per month cost of his AZT treatment when the federal Food and Drug Administration gave its approval for the drug in March. He had been receiving the drug free because of

Turn to page 6

Brian Hamilton (right), who has AIDS, with his support manager/buddy Rick Tessmann. Photo: William Burks

---

Last S.F. bathhouse shuts doors

By Charles Linebarger

Faced with jail terms and fines, owners of the 21st Street Baths agreed to drop the plug recently. The last operating gay bathhouse in San Francisco closed Monday, M...

In return, San Francisco Attorney Louise... agreed to drop legal action against the three bath... owners. Renne had threatened up to 70 days in jail, $14,000 fine. Renne charged the owners with viol... December, 1984 court order banning contact sex related establishments. A hearing had been set for... 11 on Renne's request for a contempt-of-court c... but has now been cancelled.

Tom Steel, the attorney for the 21st Street Baths, "I negotiated with Renne through one of her assistants. And frankly it's my belief that it's the mayor who's behind the decisions in this case. She was the one who behind the original bathhouse closure move."

The 21st Street Baths is owned by John Act..., William Estep and David Anderson. The three ha... charged with violating a 1984 court order issued by Superior Court Judge Roy Wonder. The order sp... the rules under which gay bathhouses could ope... the city must operate in an attempt to curb the spre... AIDS.

The bathhouse owners were accused of not p... monitoring the bath's patrons, thus allowing the... engage in high-risk sexual activity.

The city sent private investigators from the Hal... Service on Pacific Avenue into the bathhouse to s... on sexual activity.

The Lipset private eyes said in a report that "h... sex," as defined by the court order, was taking p... the 21st Street Baths. Wonder's order defines h... sex as any contact of the penis or anus of one... with the mouth or penis of another.

Last in a Line

A superior court judge in Los Angeles, re... nearly identical sex ban rules there, declared th... unconstitutional and threw them out of court... maintains several operating gay bathhouses.

Randy Stallings, former president of the ... Toklas Democratic Club, and a consultant for... Street Baths, decried the closing of the last gay... in the city.

Stallings recounted the history of bathhous... for Bay Area Reporter, a San Francisco gay new... At the time when Mayor Dianne Feinstein be... crusade to close the bathhouses under the bo... stopping the spread of AIDS, the city had at leas... baths and sex clubs.

Stallings reeled off their names: "There was... House, Sutro, Liberty Baths, Dave's, Ritch Stre... Baths, 21st Street, the Cauldron, Animals, the...

Turn to...

The Real Joe Orton
Page 17

Internat'l Mr. Leather
Page 25

Kate Clint at Mus... Fest...
Page 16

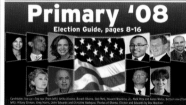

WINDY CITY TIMES
THE VOICE OF CHICAGO'S GAY, LESBIAN, BI AND TRANS COMMUNITY SINCE 1985
JANUARY 30, 2008 ● VOL 23 NO 20

Know Your Candidates

BY LISA KEEN
KEEN NEWS SERVICE

For gays in states with the largest gay populations, like California and Illinois, it's decision time in the 2008 presidential race. From the evidence available—anecdotal and indirect—most gays are trying to choose between the top two Democratic candidates—Hillary Clinton and Barack Obama. For those who will consider only a Republican, the choice appears to have also narrowed to two, also—John McCain, whose record has been relatively moderate on gay-related is-

sues, and Rudy Giuliani, whose record has been relatively supportive but whose campaign is relying on a sort of "Wait, Rudy" strategy that started in Florida Jan. 29.

What's problematic for the LGBT community at this juncture in the presidential contest is that the gay vote—which has politely favored candidates with a significant and reliable voting bloc in the past—is in danger of being marginalized by record turnouts.

The Las Vegas Sun reported that more than 10 times the number of Democrats turned out for that party's caucuses Saturday than attend-

ed four years ago. As many as one-third of the crowd were newly registered Democrats. Records were broken similarly in Iowa and New Hampshire for the Democrats.

Exit polls in the 2008 and 2004 general elections have found about four percent of voters willing to self-identify as gay nationwide, and what few surveys that have been conducted, indicate that the vast majority of gays are already registered.

But while the gay vote may seem diminished

Turn to page 4

Tunney Talks Committee page 8

POW-WOW Marks Five page 26

Heath Ledger: A Look Back page 22

Primary '08
Election Guide, pages 8-16

Candidates (top row from left): Anita Alvarez, Barack Obama, Deb Mell, Howard Brookins, Jr., Mark Pera and Aaron Weiss. Bottom row (from left): Hillary Clinton, Greg Harris, John Edwards and Christine Radogno. Photos of Obama, Clinton and Edwards by Rex Wockner.

Mary York, 52, Dies
BY TRACY BAIM

Chicago attorney Mary York died Jan. 23 after a long battle with renal cancer. She was 52.

York was among the most respected attorneys in Chicago, serving in legal support and advisor to countless gay and lesbian individuals, organizations and businesses. As part of the firm Holz-igian and York, she was inducted with her legal partner Rosemary Mulryan into the Chicago Gay & Lesbian Hall of Fame in 2006.

York also volunteered her time extensively in the community, including as president of the board of the Lesbian Community Cancer Project. She also served on the board of the Heartland Alliance for Human Rights and needs, and for more than 15 years provided legal services with out charge to such organizations as Gerber/Hart Library, Horizons, Mountain Moving Coffeehouse

and many more.

Mary York was also the attorney for 40 years for Outlines and when Outlines purchased Windy City Times in 2000, York oversaw the merger.

Mulryan and York opened in 1989 and they were among the first firms to be openly lesbian-owned. Their focus in on LGBT families, relationships and institutions, and also real estate issues. York gave advice and also lobbied for legal change, and also served as a role model for many law students and community activists. The firm also donated time to many people living with HIV/AIDS, to help plan their estates.

During York's long battle with cancer, Leberta Bailey (her partner of more than 10 years) and many friends and family members rallied to help her.

"My heart is broken but through your support and love we will be sustained during this time," Bailey wrote to friends the night York died.

"I met Mary in 1985 at a party and we im-

Turn to page 7

Mary York. Photo by Nel Reine.

www.WindyCityMediaGroup.com

Publishers row, from left: Ralph Paul Gernhardt, Dan Di Leo, Jeff McCourt and Chuck Renslow in the late 1980s. Di Leo died in 1989, Gernhardt in 2006 and McCourt in 2007. Below left: Publisher Tracy Baim receiving the Studs Terkel Award, in 2005. Below right: Outlines co-founder Nan Schaffer with Mayor Daley at her 2004 Hall of Fame induction. Photos from Gay Chicago and Windy City Times archives.

hope was for a way to be openly lesbian and be a journalist—not an easy choice in the 1980s, or before. When my mom heard about a part-time reporting job at GayLife, I jumped at the chance. Because I could also run the typesetting machine, take photos, and work cheap, I was hired.

I soon moved up in the ranks, as attrition was rampant in those days, and became managing editor of GayLife in June 1985 at age 22. I liked working for Renslow because he was hands-off, but the economic struggles were hard, and some in the community also did not trust Renslow's coverage of AIDS and political issues: He owned a bathhouse and was involved in politics.

Renslow never censored me—but I knew perception was reality. Meanwhile, Bob Bearden, our sales manager, was a man I also respected, and he and his partner, Jeff McCourt, were working with Art Director Drew Badanish to buy GayLife or start a new paper. When the purchase deal fell through, I was torn. It still ranks among the most difficult decisions of my life.

I left GayLife to start Windy City Times with those three men, and our first issue was published in September 1985. We worked out of McCourt and Bearden's apartment, a third-floor walk-up on West Melrose Street near Lake Michigan. The typesetting machine was in the cold basement. Within a few weeks, Bearden became sick, and soon we learned he had AIDS. He locked himself in his room for weeks on end. McCourt's behavior was erratic, and most of us could not stand the environment. But my partner, friends and volunteers plugged along, keeping the community in mind.

Eventually we moved to 3225 N. Sheffield Ave., with McCourt on one floor and me on another. After Bearden died, I knew I could not stay. I tried to buy the paper anonymously with funding support from Nan Schaffer, Scott McCausland and my dad, Steve Pratt, but when McCourt learned I was the buyer, he reacted angrily. We gave two weeks' notice, put out two more issues under very stressful circumstances, and 90% of us walked out to start Outlines newspaper in June 1987.

Outlines and Windy City Times went head-to-

The first version of the pocket-size Gay Chicago, April 1978 (in 2008 it is a four-color glossy magazine), and other 1970s covers, including Chuck Renslow with Leonard Matlovich and Mother Carol.

head from 1987 to 2000. Outlines became a monthly by early 1988 because of financial constraints. Soon, Outlines added sister publications—Nightlines (which is now Nightspots), a weekly bar guide; BLACKlines and En La Vida (both eventually became Identity online); and the OUT! Resource Guide. We purchased LesBiGay Radio in 2001 and changed its name to Windy City Radio.

McCourt's WCT experienced another near-total staff walkout in 1999, and those staff members started Chicago Free Press (still publishing in 2008). After 12 years of silence, McCourt and I finally spoke; he was devastated by the second walkout. He and his former employees had fought each other in the courts and on the streets for a year.

In 1998, Outlines became a weekly once again, so for a year, from mid-1999 to mid-2000, there were three weekly gay newspapers in Chicago. This was bound to be short-lived; by the summer of 2000 McCourt shut down WCT. When I called to buy the name Windy City Times, I knew it was a risk, but I felt the brand alone was worth it. The purchase allowed McCourt to get out of huge legal and tax debts, and Outlines merged into Windy City Times, using Outlines' own strong community reputation to combine with McCourt's mainstream name recognition. Today, WCT is the oldest weekly gay and lesbian newspaper in Chicago. (See more on media in later chapters.)

The media landscape in Chicago is ever-changing. There are other print media such as Boi and Pride magazines. Today, Internet-based media are prevalent, including Web sites Chicago Pride.com and DykeDiva.com, and most print media have Web sites as well. Just as 1970 saw a new rise in community media, in the 2000s we are finding different ways to communicate with one another.

GAY CHICAGO SETS THE PACE

Ralph Paul Gernhardt started Gay Chicago News in 1976 as a free-circulation newspaper covering both news and entertainment. In 1977, he and co-publisher Dan Di Leo started Gay Chicago Magazine together. Di Leo had worked for the newspaper as typesetter and news editor, bringing a serious sense of journalism to Gernhardt's publication. They clicked as business partners, and remained so until Di Leo's 1989 death from AIDS at 51. Gernhardt died of lung cancer in 2006 at age 72; he was preceded in death by Michael A. Williams, his partner of 23 years, who died of AIDS.

Gernhardt's first gay business enterprise was a telephone information line in 1976, which easily led to the newspaper and then the magazine. Gernhardt and Di Leo also tried their hand in several regional gay media enterprises, including Midwest Times, Gay Milwaukee, Gay Detroit and Gay Ohio.

"The early years were rough, to say the least," Gernhardt wrote after the passing of Di Leo, "but even with the added success of our product, the last few years have been much more painful. As opportunistic illnesses began to affect his body, Dan fought them off one by one, succeeding, according to authorities, beyond their expectations. Yes, Dan, living with AIDS, was a fighter."

Gay Chicago Magazine was home to the early careers of several important Chicago writers, and it often featured prominent local celebrities on its covers. While the magazine has aways been primarily male-focused, it did also cover women's issues—especially those related to women's bars. An early masthead shows it was home to Jon-Henri Damski's columns, as well as Richard Cooke and many more writers. Gernhardt left the magazine strong and in competent hands in 2006, and it remains the longest-running gay publication in Chicago history. ▼

LET'S DANCE   *by JOHN D'EMILIO*

"IF I CAN'T DANCE, I DON'T WANT YOUR revolution." At some point in the 1970s, it seemed like every third person I knew had a poster emblazoned with these words. Attributed to the early 20th-century anarchist Emma Goldman, the sentiments captured the exuberance of some of that era's lesbians and gay men. (As it turned out, Goldman never said this, but that's a whole other history tale.) In discos, at women's music festivals, on college campuses, and at street fairs, queer folk looked as if we were dancing our way to freedom. Unlike the dour images of men storming the citadels of power, the gay revolution was going to be fun.

I suspect that for some politicos—straight or queer—the association of dancing and revolution is evidence of just how trivial gay liberation is. But, if so, they don't know much history.

In Chicago in the 1950s and 1960s, the prohibition on same-sex dancing was pretty nearly complete. The CPD might make an exception for a Halloween or New Year's masquerade ball, particularly if most of the dancing couples looked to be of opposite sexes. But the bars did their own serious policing, not just of dancing but of any form of touching. An arm around someone's shoulder or a playful squeeze of someone's butt could be enough to send lurking plainclothes officers into action, and arrests for public indecency would follow. Same-sex dancing in this kind of climate? Not likely.

Folks from that era who went regularly to the bars loved them and were loyal to them, but it was a bittersweet love. "The bars are the only place for Gay people to go to get together outside of home," one of them wrote. And then, in the next line: "There is no question that they were for shit." No wonder that, when gay liberation groups started forming at the end of 1969, creating new gay and lesbian spaces—and opening up those spaces for same-sex dancing—would be high on the list of priorities.

The first group in Chicago to take on the name of "gay liberation" was on the South Side, in the Hyde Park neighborhood, and included a number of University of Chicago students. At first they met mostly to talk, but talking soon led to action. One of the first actions, in January 1970, was to attend a campus mixer (a "mixer" was a dance in the lingo of the '50s and '60s) and dance together. Fewer than a dozen gay men and lesbians showed up for the action and, according to Step May, one of the participants, "we were all scared to death." But nothing bad happened, so that, emboldened, they decided to hold the first out-of-the-closet same-sex dance on campus.

Because some Chicago Gay Liberation members were University of Chicago students, they had access to campus facilities. They reserved the dining hall in Pierce Tower, a dormitory, for a weekend night in February. But who would come? Was it too big a space? Would they feel foolish if only two dozen campus queers showed up? So they did a "real leafleting blitz," as May recalled, going to gay bars on both the South and North sides. Vernita Gray, who was there, remembered that folks came from all over the city, not just from the campus.

"Black, white, brown, straight, gay, male, female—600 liberated people danced freely to live music," one of the attendees reported. "Even the security guards seemed to enjoy the scene." The crowd was mostly "young" and "hip." One can just imagine the long hair on the men, the women with granny glasses, and bell-bottomed jeans on everyone.

It was too much fun not to do again. In April, there was a second dance, this time in Woodward Commons, a women's dorm. More than a thousand showed up. Not to be outdone, lesbian and gay students at Northwestern and at Circle Campus (today's UIC) scheduled dances, too, for later that spring. The dancing bug was proving contagious.

Bold as all this was, these actions were still, in one sense, cautious. After all, campuses by the late 1960s had come to seem like another world; wholly different standards of morality, politics and values held sway. Of course these radical environments would embrace these queer celebrations. Could same-sex dancing happen off a campus, in Chicago proper? People were scared.

Chicago Gay Liberation decided to find out. It rented the Coliseum, a structure near East 16th Street and South Wabash Avenue that, in bygone days, had once hosted professional hockey and basketball, roller derby and major political conventions. It was public space in every sense of the word. This was pushing the boundaries and taking a big risk.

Would the police invade the place? Was there the danger of a "giant bust"? Renee Hanover, the lawyer for the gay groups, pressed hard on the police to make sure nothing would happen. The police did show up and patrol the area on April 18, but there were no arrests and no interference.

The dancing crowds didn't quite fill the place, but 2,000 people came, making it probably the biggest queer gathering in Chicago history up to then. "The dance floor was filled with laughing faces," reported Mattachine Midwest's newsletter. Its writer waxed eloquent about the dance. It "introduced freedom as the remedy that will end the closet as a way of life. The faggots came out for their public, the band was great, the vibes were beautiful. ...The revolution has just begun, and the dances are part of it."

The heady pleasures of a few dances led straight to the door of a popular local bar. The weekend after the Coliseum dance, gay and lesbian liberationists showed up with picket signs outside the Normandy Inn, a gay bar near East Chicago Avenue and North Rush Street. The fliers they distributed listed their demands: "Gay people can dance both fast and slow ... no arbitrary dress regulations ... no discrimination against women."

The Seed, a local alternative radical newspaper, reported that the Normandy was "nearly empty" that weekend, as protesters kept patrons away and "convinced the owners they would have to take the wishes of Gay people seriously." The owners caved in, and other bars responded as well. For queer Chicagoans, dancing had come to stay. ▼

Gay Liberation sponsored the first citywide dance at the Coliseum in 1970. This picture is from the 1912 Republican National Convention, held in that same historic space. Courtesy the Chicago History Museum.

CREATING COMMUNITY   *by TRACY BAIM*

IF YOU THINK THE DIVISIONS WITHIN THE gay community today are strong, imagine the 1970s, when the nascent movement was full of passion and energy. People were just learning how to work together. Some people came to the movement from radical groups and wanted to dismantle all institutions, while others were interested in focusing primarily on gay rights and changing the system. There were leaders and worker bees, marchers and organizers. And new groups cropped up seemingly every month to deal with new issues, new personalities and new crises.

Chicago Gay Liberation (CGL) was among the new breed of groups in the early 1970s, formed out of the work of University of Chicago gays and lesbians. Its members wanted to be more revolutionary than Mattachine Midwest, whether throwing public dances or protesting injustice. They held large dances at the Aragon and the Col-

iseum in 1970, and rallies at Bughouse Square and other locations. Soon, Chicago Gay Alliance (CGA) broke off from what had become the Gay Liberation Front (GLF). CGA wanted to work on political issues and was considered the more conservative group. Among others, civil rights activist Jesse Jackson told CGA in 1970 that he supported homosexual rights.

Women and people of color formed their own caucuses of CGA and broke off entirely into Chicago Lesbian Liberation (CLL) and Third World Gay Revolutionaries, respectively. While many of the white men in GLF and CGA wanted to support women and people of color and even backed such efforts as the Equal Rights Amendment in Illinois, there was often a lot of other emotional baggage among the good intentions, and sometimes nerves were just too raw. There was even a separate lesbian Pride Week in 1975. For more

than three decades now, African-Americans have celebrated Pride Day with their own celebration, first on the Belmont Rocks and now on the lakefront at Montrose Drive. In recent years there have also been Black gay pride celebrations in July (in 2008, two separate Black gay pride celebrations are planned).

AIDS in many ways forced men and women to work together more; some people question whether men would have come to the aid of lesbians had AIDS impacted that community, but that is an impossible debate. Most lesbians helped with AIDS issues, but not all lesbians (or even all gay men) came together during the AIDS crisis. The 1970s were a training ground, a time of new hope and big dreams; the 1980s brought a harsh reality, but also forced open more closet doors than ever before. The difficult lessons learned in the 1970s helped us prepare for the decades to come. ▼

THE 'CENTER' OF THE GAY COMMUNITY *by TRACY BAIM*

CHICAGO HAS A LONG HISTORY OF GAY, lesbian and feminist community centers. Most served for a few years and then closed or merged with other agencies. Burnout was high as most of the centers operated on volunteer power, and sophisticated black-tie fundraising galas were years away. Passion was also at a fever pitch, and that sometimes meant personality conflicts and political clashes.

The first known community center was in operation sometime prior to 1966, as a project of the Daughters of Bilitis' (DOB) Chicago chapter, which existed from about 1961 to 1966. (DOB was briefly active in another form later, as reported in a 1970 community newsletter, with a post office box in Northlake, Ill.) A November 1972 essay by Jody Lynch in Lavender Woman newspaper (Vol. 1, No. 6) looks back at the DOB center, but does not state exactly the years of operation and location, although it was "in an old building located at North and Clybourn." A few women renovated the property, and once it opened "we had anywhere from 50 to 60 women at our social gatherings." Lynch was writing to members of the Chicago Lesbian Liberation (CLL) group as a warning to learn from the past, to better plan for a CLL Center. There was a CLL Center at Liberty Hall, 2440 N. Lincoln Ave., and they later moved to another North Side location.

"Community Center a Reality!" screams the front-page headline of the February 1971 Chicago Gay Alliance newsletter. That issue of CGA's publication (Vol. 1, No. 4) featured a full-page photo of the building at 171 W. Elm St., a two-story brick dwelling downtown, one block south of West Division and North Wells streets. The seven-room CGA space was being remodeled and was to become home for CGA and other groups needing space to meet.

Gary Chichester was president of CGA when the space was secured. "We had just as much going on there as any community center to this day. We were kind of advanced for our age. We had a library. We did meetings. We had potluck dinners. You could bring people with no place else to go into the com-

munity center. We had a help line. Out of that era, it's kind of amazing to look back and see how different organizations, from Howard Brown to Horizons and Center on Halsted ... you could see stemming from that seed that we planted on Elm Street," Chichester said in 2007. The center closed because of funding problems on Sept. 15, 1973.

In the early 1970s, Kathleen Thompson rented space from gay activist and playwright Nick Patricca at 3322 N. Halsted St. to open Pride & Prejudice, the city's first feminist bookstore, and a Women's Center that provided many services, including pregnancy testing and abortion counseling, a lesbian artists' collective, a lesbian counseling service, and directories of resources for women. The center eventually changed its name to the Lesbian Feminist Center and relocated to 3523 N. Halsted St.—just a short distance from today's Center on Halsted, which opened in 2007 at 3656 N. Halsted St. The LFC was women-only and included a bookstore, the Counseling Resource Center and the New Alexandria Library for Women.

Later, Michael Bergeron, the energetic young activist who also founded The Chicago Gay Crusader newspaper, opened Beckman Housse. In the March–April 1974 Crusader (issue No. 11), Beckman House was announced as "the first in a series of new gay community centers projected for Chicago." Located at 3519½ N. Halsted St., two doors south of the women's center, the new space was named for Barbara Beckman, "a lesbian activist who participated in several groups of gay men and women until her death in a 1972 car accident while moving from Chicago to Iowa." The Gay Switchboard, which had been founded in the apartment shared by Bergeron and fellow activist William B. Kelley, was moved to Beckman House, but out of a desire "to keep the center less inhibited and free from dominance by any one group" no gay groups met there. Bergeron financed the center from the newspaper and personal funds, and he also received community support, including money from the Baton and Up North bars.

Kathleen Thompson in the 1970s and in 2007. 1970s photo courtesy M. Kuda Archives. 2007 photo by Hal Baim.

By the Crusader's next issue, May 1974, Bergeron announced that Beckman House was expanding next door; a coffeehouse would be part of the new space, and the other half "will become a boogie room for small dances." The switchboard number, 929-HELP, is still in operation today—it was inherited by Gay Horizons, which is now Center on Halsted. On Oct. 1, 1974, Bergeron's Oscar Wilde's Children group had turned over control of the center to Gay Horizons, and by 1975 the center was planning to move.

The April 1974 edition of the Crusader (the same issue that announced the death of legendary lesbian attorney Pearl Hart) reported that Gay Horizons and ONE of Chicago, a local chapter of the national gay group ONE Inc., were working together to purchase a building for a new center.

A neighborhood community center belonging to the Loyola–Rogers Park Gay Students Association eventually became the Rogers Park Gay Center and later the Rogers Park/Edgewater Gay Alliance. Grad student Richard Stern had first tried to get funding from Loyola to start the group, but when the school refused, Stern added Rogers Park to its name. The group began by meeting at the short-lived gay bar David's Place, and then at Alternatives, a space on North Broadway used as a day-care center during daytime hours. The parents soon got the gay group kicked out, according to Mark Sherkow, a member. Stern, Sherkow and Laura Hathaway then found a space at 7109 N. Glenwood Ave. and opened it as a gay drop-in center Nov. 24, 1974, eventually renaming it the Rogers Park Gay Center. In their second year, they posted the name on the door, and twice a window was broken with a rock, Sherkow said. After the second attack the landlord forced them to move out. The center relocated to 6920 N. Glenwood Ave. (with no name on the door) for two years. Their final location was at 5823 N. Ridge Ave., when they took the name the Rogers Park/Edgewater Gay Alliance and remained there for another two years. Under its three names, this Far North Side center lasted a total

The first gay community center is announced, in 1971. Gary Chichester (pictured above in 2007, with his 1971 pride flag), was head of Chicago Gay Alliance when the center opened. Newsletter courtesy M. Kuda Archives. Photo by Hal Baim.

of six years, providing a hotline, a library, drop-in nights, events, art shows and more.

In 1977, Chicago's Tavern Guild, a group of bar personnel, formed a building fund in memory of Frank M. Rodde III, a gay bartender murdered in April of that year. The Tavern Guild raised money for several years, eventually enough to buy a building complex at 3225 N. Sheffield Ave. A photo in GayLife newspaper's April 14, 1978, edition shows Tavern Guild members on the first anniversary of the Rodde Fund announcement. Those pictured include Chuck Rodocker of Touché, Paul Little, Bruce Wertin, Cesar Ubalde, Jim Rains, Ben Allen, Gary Martin, Rene Van Hulle, Tyrone Sinclair, Bobby Lee Smith and Karen Richardson.

In the late 1980s, the Rodde Center was facing a string of controversies. Many in the community believed that the Sheffield Avenue building had been sold for well under market value and that, without an immediate plan for a new home, the money was squandered on rent in the Uptown Bank Building at 4753 N. Broadway while the Rodde board tried to raise funds. Facing a high level of skepticism from business owners and donors, the Rodde Center eventually disintegrated under the weight of big plans and a dwindling bank account. The Rodde Center was not just a victim of mistakes, but also a sign of the times in the early 1990s, when a lot of activism and fundraising were focused on HIV and AIDS.

While at the Uptown building, there had been high hopes for smaller community agencies who used the facility there and were looking to eventually share quarters in a new center. The "incubator"-like environment included space for the

Left: Rogers Park activist Mark Sherkow in the 1970s. Right: Phyllis Athey and Mary Jo Osterman of Kinheart. Photo by Tracy Baim.

short-lived Lesbian Chicago group (which had moved from Montrose Avenue to the Rodde location in November 1991). Lesbian Chicago was seeking to create its own community center, a dream never realized.

In 1982, Evanston gained a space for lesbians: the Kinheart Womyn's Center at 2214 Ridge Ave., in the Wheadon United Methodist Church. Founded by partners Phyllis Athey and Mary Jo Osterman, the center flourished for many years, providing cultural events, counseling services, and educational programs on homophobia. The two women had met at Garrett-Evangelical Theological Seminary; Athey was later denied ordination as an open lesbian. Osterman had begun teaching on a verbal contract with Garrett, but when she was discovered to be a lesbian, that contract was broken. Unfortunately, Athey took her own life on May 23, 1988. Kinheart continued on for years, and when it closed, former members created a new organization, Kindred Hearts, to host community events and programs.

By the mid-1990s, no community center that served both gay men and women existed in Chicago. However, over the years, many other types of spaces had acted as community centers, including the Jane Addams Bookstore, Women & Children First bookstore, Left Bank Bookstall in Oak Park, Platypus Books in Evanston, People Like Us Books, Unabridged Bookstore and the Gerber/Hart Library and Archives.

On the South Side, Affinity Community Services opened a space for Black lesbian and bisexual women in the mid-1990s at 5650 S. Woodlawn Ave. Located in a church basement, Affinity has sponsored and co-sponsored a wide range of programming, entertainment, and educational events.

Churches have also served as de facto community centers for many years, whether associated with a specific gay religious denomination or renting out space to gay groups and events. Church of the Open Door, the now-defunct African-American gay and lesbian church on the Southwest Side, was the first gay church in the area to own its own building.

Besides events and meetings at bars, another important home for the community from the 1980s through the 2000s has been Ann Sather restaurant on Belmont Avenue. In 2007 the business moved a few doors east, but for two decades 929 W. Belmont Ave. was home not just to future Ald. Tom Tunney's restaurant (purchased in the 1980s from Ann Sather herself), but also hundreds of community meetings, dances, political rallies and fundraisers. A famous 1989 confrontation with Mayor Richard M. Daley occurred upstairs at Ann Sather, and huge lesbian and gay dances and a rally for U.S. Senate candidate Carol Moseley Braun were held in the parking lot.

As the 1990s came to a close, community leaders were frustrated that a city as large as Chicago was not part of the national movement of strong community centers. Horizons, which long ago had shuttered Beckman House, returned to the community center-business more emphatically, announcing a long-term goal of opening a facility to serve the needs of the growing Chicago gay community. Horizons had dropped "Gay" from its name years before, and in February 2003 it changed its name again, to Center on Halsted. Government, foundation and community funders eventually lined up behind the agency as the natural choice to establish a center—because it already served many of those needs through helplines, youth groups, counseling services, and much more.

Affinity was founded in 1995. Pictured above left is the founding meeting. Photo by Tracy Baim. Above right are some of those same women in 2007 (from left): Chris Smith and her mother Barb Smith, Teresa "Ted" Dobbins and Lisa Pickens. Photos by Hal Baim.

The 2005 sketch released for the future Center on Halsted.

In 2007, after years of fundraising, a state-of-the-art facility opened at 3656 N. Halsted St. The $20 million, 65,000-square-foot building is environmentally friendly; has a unique partnership with Whole Foods as its first-floor tenant; features a 165-seat theater, a gym, an outdoor patio, meeting rooms, and youth and senior spaces; and houses the offices of Center on Halsted and several small community groups. The building has hosted hundreds of community events, theater productions, concerts, benefits, memorials, book signings, support groups, and much more.

Hundreds of people played a role in the growth of Horizons and the gay community center movement. For Center on Halsted, those key people were Patrick Sheahan, Marcia Lipetz, Evette Cardona, Vicki Raymont, Julio Rodriguez, Robbin Burr, Modesto "Tico" Valle, Robert Kohl, Michael Leppen (and his aunt Miriam Hoover), Martin Gapshis, Denise Foy, Dan Foy, Dave Halverson, Robert Bell, Ald. Tom Tunney, former Ald. Bernie Hansen, and many more. More than 2,000 individuals, businesses, foundations and government entities contributed. Mayor Richard M. Daley and tennis legend Billie Jean King served as honorary co-chairs of the capital campaign, and the rooftop garden and gym are named for each, respectively. As we move into this new century, we should "build on" the past, not forget it, in order to leave a lasting legacy for the next generations.

"We must be bold enough to dream; naive enough to believe, and tenacious enough to make it happen," said Board President Patrick Sheahan at the June 2007 public unveiling of the center. Sheahan joined the board in 1998 and assembled and chaired the building Project Steering Committee. He chaired the Horizons/Center board from 2003 to 2005 and stepped down in December 2007 after nine years of service.

"We can now be proud of bricks and mortar, not just who we are," said community activist Art Johnston.

And as philanthropist Michael Leppen, a huge booster of the center, said: "In the past, we would go to gay bars that had unmarked doors with darkened windows so the world could not see in and we would feel protected. Now we have an incredible glass building, highly visible to the street and the rest of world. A place to feel welcome, feel safe and still be part of the everyday world without hiding who we are and what we believe in."

The Center is truly a building that can be called "out and proud." As the Center plans for the future, it will increasingly deal with the demographic shifts of its clients, and the changing character of the Boys Town neighborhood.

"I'm so proud to have been a part of the creation of the Center," said Burr, who was executive director until the opening in 2007, when she turned over control to Valle. "Like the other 160 LGBT community centers across the country, it will undoubtedly have storms to weather, but for those of us who were intimately involved in bringing it into existence, I can testify to the love, pride and passion we stirred into the bricks and mortar." ▼

(For more Center on Halsted photos, turn to page 214.)

THERE'S A PLACE FOR US

Following are a few milestones at Horizons, which is now the Center on Halsted.

1973: Gay Horizons begins as a volunteer-run information clearinghouse and a meeting place. The help line starts, and a youth coffeehouse begins at Liberty Hall, 2440 N. Lincoln Ave.

1974: Some volunteers form an organization to provide medical services (which later separates and becomes Howard Brown Memorial Clinic). Gay Horizons moves into Beckman House, 3519½ N. Halsted St., where it continues operation of the Gay Switchboard (929-4357).

1975: Gay Horizons moves to 2745 N. Clark St., above the Astro Restaurant.

1976: Gay Horizons begins to shift more from social activities to providing mental health and social services, including the Gay People's Counseling Service.

1977: Gay Horizons moves to a one-room basement space at 920 W. Oakdale Ave.

1978: Gay Horizons' first Youth Group of fewer than 10 people meets. The precursor to Gay Horizons' Speakers Service is started as part of the Gay People's Counseling Service.

1979: Horizons Youth Program begins. Gay Horizons moves to 3225 N. Sheffield Ave.

1980: Gay Horizons' Youth Group opens a coffeehouse and becomes affiliated with a gay parents group 1978. Horizons becomes affiliated with Lambda Resource Center for the Blind, founded in late 1979. Horizons begins responding to the AIDS crisis.

1982: Gay Horizons begins recruiting volunteers to participate in an AIDS services project co-sponsored by the Howard Brown Memorial Clinic. The Lambda Resource Center and Gerber/Hart spin off from Horizons.

1984: Gay Horizons hires its first paid staff (part-time, Chuck Cushing).

1985: Anti-Violence Project starts. Youth from Gay Horizons appear on The Oprah Winfrey Show. The name is changed to Horizons Community Services, Inc.

1986: Horizons now has two full-time staff: an executive director, Bruce Koff, and an administrative assistant, Nancy Sorkow.

1988: Anti-Violence Project becomes first federally funded gay anti-violence program.

1989: Horizons achieves full membership in United Way—the only gay and lesbian agency in Illinois, and one of five in the U.S.

1990: Horizons moves to 961 W. Montana St. It begins conducting LGBT-sensitivity training for Chicago police officers.

1997: Horizons begins programming and advocacy for older LGBT adults.

1999: The Anti-Violence Project begins assisting LGBT survivors of domestic violence.

2000: Chicago Park District property at the corner of North Halsted Street and West Waveland Avenue becomes available.

2001: Center on Halsted project launched.

2003: Horizons Community Services changes its name to Center on Halsted.

2005: Construction for the Center building kicks off with a groundbreaking ceremony.

2006: Center on Halsted announces new funding for its expanded Just4Adults program, which will be renamed SAGE.

2007: Center on Halsted moves into its new facility at 3656 N. Halsted St. in May.

TREATING OUR OWN

by SUZANNE DEVENEY

IN THE BEGINNING, THERE WAS A COFFEEPOT, A portable kitchen table, a room above an old grocery store at 2440 N. Lincoln Ave., and four medical students. The members of the Chicago Gay Medical Students Association believed there was a need for a safe and confidential place where gay men and lesbians could get empathetic psychosocial counseling and sexually-transmitted-disease testing and treatment without political, professional or personal implications or intrusions.

The students and Gay Horizons volunteers met above the store across from the Biograph Theatre almost every night in 1974. The informal but well-organized clinic was born. It moved in early 1975 to 1250 W. Belden Ave.

Soon, volunteers left Gay Horizons to work on health issues. By 1976, the first board formed and named the clinic Howard Brown Memorial Clinic after Dr. Howard Brown, a native of Peoria, Ill., a founder of the National Gay Task Force and New York City's first Health Services Administrator, who came out in 1973.

During the late '70s, Howard Brown providers identified a high rate of hepatitis B among its patients, which led to the agency's participation in several important studies and vaccine trials. This work resulted in a major scientific breakthrough: the development of the hepatitis B vaccine.

When early warning signs of the impending AIDS epidemic became widespread in the early '80s, Howard Brown was quick to react. By 1985, Howard Brown helped develop and implement the city of Chicago's AIDS Hotline. In 1984, 1,102 sexually active gay and bisexual men volunteered to participate in the Multicenter AIDS Cohort Study (MACS) at Howard Brown and several other sites across the country.

The capital campaign was launched in 1995. Howard Brown was the first gay organization in the Midwest to complete a capital campaign, resulting in a $3.5 million, state-of-the-art facility. Oct. 4, 1997, was opening day for Howard Brown Health Center's new home at 4025 N. Sheridan Rd.

Howard Brown opened the Broadway Youth Center in 2004 in collaboration with Children's Memorial Hospital, Teen Living and the Night Ministry. In 2006, Howard Brown was selected by the National Gay and Lesbian Task Force to lead a collaborative effort in developing a new initiative for LGBT and vulnerable older adults. ▼

QUEER THINKER: JON-HENRI DAMSKI *by OWEN KEEHNEN*

JON-HENRI DAMSKI WAS BORN IN 1937 AND raised in the Seattle area. He received his Bachelor of Arts degree in English from Whitman College, his master's from Brandeis University in the history of ideas, and his Ph.D. from the University of Washington in classics. He briefly taught Latin and Roman history at Bryn Mawr College.

After moving to Chicago in 1975, Damski began his extensive career as a columnist at Gay Chicago Magazine and GayLife before moving to Windy City Times in 1985 and Nightlines and Outlines in the early 1990s.

At the time of his death in 1997, Damski had written more than 700 columns and was believed to be the longest-running columnist on gay and lesbian issues in the United States—and he never ran out of topics. His subject matter was radically diverse, with topics ranging from neighborhood and community profiles, reviews, national news, philosophizing, politics, and his beloved Chicago Cubs baseball team (he was almost always seen with his signature Cubs hat). Anything and everything was fair game for one of his columns, which were pounded out on his Underwood manual typewriter from his single-room-occupancy residence in the Belair Hotel on West Diversey Parkway.

Damski was a true man of the people. He was a familiar face in the Lake View neighborhood, roaming the streets daily, stopping for coffee, dining or holding court at the Wheel Around restaurant, chatting, and befriending a truly diverse cross-section of the public. He knew all the politicians, the homeless, the hustlers and almost everyone else. His "business" card said it all—a caricature of the man alongside the words "Gay Writer/Queer Thinker."

Damski's political importance to the GLBT community was strong. As a member of the Gang of Four (along with Laurie Dittman, Rick Garcia and Arthur Johnston), Damski's lobbying efforts helped pass the Chicago human rights ordinance in 1988 (banning discrimination on the basis of sexual orientation in housing, employment, public accommodations and credit transactions).

In 1989 he received the Liberty Bell Award from the Chicago Bar Association for his efforts in getting the human rights ordinance passed. He was an original inductee into the Chicago Gay and Lesbian Hall of Fame in 1991. Damski was also a founding member of the Illinois Federation for Human Rights, now known as Equality Illinois.

Damski's collaboration with Firetrap Press produced X-Ray Reports (a collection of poetry) and

Here are some of Damski's own words, about a friend, from the Oct. 27, 1978, issue of Gay Chicago magazine: "I wasn't surprised when I heard he had OD'd and died. I always said he had a life expectancy of zero. Jesus, what can you expect, when you look like Mick Jagger and try to live like Keith Richard. … But still, to die at 18. I had forgotten his age. 18. That shocked me. 18, not even old enough to fight

Above: Jon-Henri Damski (left) marches with Ald. Luis Gutierrez (now U.S. representative; he is wearing a shirt for LLENA, a Latina lesbian group at that time) and Mayor Daley in the 1989 Pride Parade. Photo by Antonio Dickey for the Mayor's Office. Inset: Damski on his business card.

Damski to Go, with Damski's sage and pithy remarks (and graphics by Vernon Huls) printed on rainbow slips of paper in a Chinese to-go container. Firetrap Press also published Angels into Dust, a selection of his columns, just prior to his death. A few years later, Firetrap released Dead/Queer/Proud, a collection of diverse Damski essays over the years, with an introduction by Neal Pollack, who wrote, "I didn't always understand everything Jon-Henri said, or everything he wrote. Like his schizo mind, his writing sometimes goes off on odd tangents. Secret shards of knowledge burst out, seemingly disconnected to the previous paragraph. Popular references get knocked off-center by the obscure, by what was unspoken."

in one of our stupid wars, but old enough to die on one of our stupid streets."

Jon-Henri Damski died of complications from malignant melanoma on Nov. 1, 1997, at the age of 60. The year prior to his passing, friends gathered to give him a farewell party at the AIDS Care chapel. It was perfectly in character. If Damski was going to have a memorial service, he wanted to be part of the celebration.

As an appropriate epilogue to Damski's life, the first queer punk band in Chicago, Boys' Entrance, released an Internet-only single in November 2000 called "Jon-Henri Damski (Queer Thinker, Queer Thoughts)," which featured a mix of Damski's voice. He would have loved it. ▼

PRIDE PARADE GROWS TO 400,000+

by RICHARD PFEIFFER

THE ANNUAL CHICAGO PRIDE PARADE started in 1970 as a march with 100 to 150 people from the Near North Side to downtown.

In its second year it became a parade with decorated vehicles as well as marchers and moved to the gay-friendly East Lake View neighborhood (then called New Town, now Boys Town). Over the years, the number of registered entries, participants and spectators has steadily increased, as more people become out and proud.

A noticeable boost in both viewership and participation in the parade occurred in 1977, shortly after anti-gay singer Anita Bryant was picketed by more than 5,000 people at Medinah Temple.

One of the largest increases in numbers of participants and spectators took place during the 1982 parade. That year, a group of anti-gay neo-Nazis decided that they were going to protest by holding a rally beforehand and then marching down the street to confront the parade procession head-on. Although their rally took place, the direct confrontational march by the neo-Nazis did not. However, the parade that year brought out thousands more gays and allies who either registered for the parade, lined the parade route or attended a counter-rally near the neo-Nazi rally. In fact, some city statistics at the time indicated that spectators may have doubled from the previous year. The number of parade participants increased dramatically as well.

Another increase was noted in 1984. Up until that time a local state representative and an alderman had been the only elected officials in the parade. After Mayor Jane Byrne lost her bid for re-election, she decided to thank the gay communities for supporting her. When word got out that she was

Opposite page: From 1970s Pride parades and rallies. Photos courtesy Rich Pfeiffer. This page, top: From the 15th Pride Parade in 1984. Photo by Tracy Baim. Below, middle: Rich Pfeiffer and Mayor Jane Byrne. Bottom: Pfeiffer (right) with Dewey Herrington and Kit Duffy. Photos courtesy Rich Pfeiffer.

going to be in the parade that year, elected officials began contacting PRIDEChicago in large numbers to register for the parade, continuing a tradition that lasts through today. Some spectators said that they came to see the first "major" Chicago politician to appear in the annual Pride Parade. Later, Mayor Harold Washington spoke at a Pride rally, and political marchers have included Richard M. Daley, Barack Obama, Jan Schakowsky, and dozens more.

For a number of years, the Pride Committee also sponsored downtown rallies at the Civic Center Plaza (now the Daley Center Plaza) during Pride Week. The Illinois Gay and Lesbian Task Force took over managing those rallies in the 1980s, and the rallies were gone by the 1990s, as were the bureaucratic barriers to use of the plaza that the original rallies had meant to challenge. Those rallies were more political in nature than the Pride Parades, with speakers and protest signs. Also for many years, after each Pride Parade had ended, rallies coordinated by PRIDEChicago were held in the parks. In later years, they were discontinued, in part because of neighborhood noise complaints and many competing events, including dances, Black gay pride celebrations, and bar parties.

Now, the annual Pride Parade contains a predetermined 250 registered parade entries featuring floats, decorated vehicles and marching units. Entries represent organizations and local and national businesses. Crowd estimates of the parade each year are between 400,000 and 450,000. It's quite a change from that first step down the street in 1970. ▼

Rich Pfeiffer is coordinator of PRIDEChicago.

BY THE NUMBERS

The following parade statistics are for spectators (not participants), as estimated by several sources including police, city officials, PRIDEChicago (the parade organizers), and mainstream and gay media.

1970:	"several hundred"
1971 to 1977:	"several thousand"
1978:	10,000
1980:	10,000
1982:	30,000
1986:	60,000
1987:	75,000
1989:	90,000
1990:	100,000
1991:	110,000
1992:	120,000
1994:	160,000
1995:	175,000
2000:	350,000
2003:	400,000
2007:	450,000

Participants have been estimated at 100-150 for 1970, and 5,000 for 2007.

ORIGINS OF A NATIONAL GAY POLITICAL STRATEGY: THE GAY RIGHTS PLATFORM OF 1972 *by MARIE J. KUDA*

THE FIRST NATIONAL CONFERENCE TO SET a gay political strategy was held in Chicago Feb. 11–13, 1972, at a North Side church. Co-sponsored by Chicago Gay Alliance (CGA) and New York's Gay Activists Alliance (GAA/NY), the conference drew more than 200 delegates from 80 organizations. A 17-point "Gay Rights Platform in the United States" specifying demands on federal and state governments was adopted on Feb. 13. Platform demands covered amendments to existing federal and state legislation, repeal of some laws, and enactment of others; topic areas included immigration, cross-dressing, child custody and parental rights, insurance, and sex education in schools.

Executive orders prohibiting discrimination in hiring, promoting, security clearances, and military service and discharges were also part of the platform. It demanded the release of all persons detained or incarcerated because of their sexual orientation, "the immediate destruction of all existing data" in government dossiers and databanks, and initiation of new controls on the "compiling, maintenance and dissemination of information on individual sexual preference and behavior." A proposal dealing with redrafting marriage laws was noted as being problematic.

The final plank of the platform, "Repeal of all laws governing the age of sexual consent," was hotly contested; arguments centered on reinforcing the perception of homosexuals as child molesters. While some held that the plank would become a lightning rod for critics of the movement, it narrowly passed by an eight-vote margin. The delegates debated this point in their post-conference discussions, and CGA President John Abney reported that his organization voted against ratifying this plank.

Dr. Benjamin Spock, the People's Party candidate for president, addressed the conference. Delegates included several who would continue in the movement for decades: Franklin Kameny, who ran as the first openly gay candidate for the House of Representatives; Steve Endean, later with GRNL, NGTF and HRCF; Rich Wandel, who would found the National Archive of Lesbian and Gay History; and Chicago activist William B. Kelley.

When interviewed by Dudley Clendinen and Adam Nagourney for their book Out for Good: The Struggle to Build a Gay Rights Movement in America, Endean reported his feeling that among the delegates were "agents provocateurs." Kelley noted that at the time of winning the case against the Chicago police "Red Squad," among the documents allowed to be seen briefly by groups or persons surveilled was one related to the 1972 conference. The document contained a list of attendees at the conference, annotated with the local FBI office for each—with one exception. Kelley speculated that the exception was a "mole." In their notes to Out for Good, the authors cite rumors "repeated in stronger forms in a number of interviews" that New Yorker Jim Fouratt was the agent: They also note Fouratt's denials.

The delegates did not endorse any candidates, but passed a resolution to demonstrate at the Republican National Convention in San Diego and to demand 10% representation at the Democratic convention. The first openly gay delegate to do so, Jim Foster of San Francisco, addressed the Democratic National Convention in Miami on July 12, 1972. But it would be 1980 (with Jimmy Carter and Walter Mondale as its candidates) before the Democratic Party would adopt a "gay rights" plank. ▼

With research contributions by William B. Kelley.

Photos on these two pages from the 1972 first national conference to set a gay political strategy, held in Chicago. Among the speakers were gay activist Frank Kameny (top) and presidential candidate Dr. Benjamin Spock (bottom). Photos courtesy M. Kuda Archives, Oak Park, Ill.

A SEAT AT THE POLITICAL TABLE *by TRACY BAIM*

WITH THE CHICAGO GAY ALLIANCE (CGA) pushing for political changes through legal and electoral means, it was only a matter of time before openly gay people ran for office. A lot of the gay activists of the early 1970s were quite radical, but the true political diversity of the community soon was obvious. There were left-wing candidates and eventually conservative Republican gays seeking office by the end of the 1970s.

In 1972, charismatic activist Michael Bergeron, age 20, campaigned to become an at-large delegate to the Democratic National Convention. As Marie J.

Feminist Lesbian Party, Transvestite Legal Committee, Advocates of Gay Action, HOPE: Homosexuals Organized for Political Education, and university groups.

CGA also surveyed candidates on gay issues and held political forums for the community, including a March 14, 1972, "Gay '72" event at Lincoln Park Presbyterian Church dealing with candidate positions on fair employment, police harassment, income tax inequities, child custody and more.

In 1974, two radical gays tried unsuccessfully to run for alderman, Don "Red Devil" Goldman in the 44th

the gay rights bill, helped stop police harassment of gay bars, and issued an executive order on June 18, 1982, banning anti-gay bias in all city departments.

The first gay political action committee in the city was the Organization to Promote Equality Now (OPEN/PAC). It donated money to candidates to show the clout of the gay community; it folded in the 1980s and was the predecessor to IMPACT, founded in the late 1980s.

In 1979, Grant Ford, publisher of GayLife, ran unsuccessfully for 44th Ward alderman after Dick Simpson, the last independent to hold the seat, retired. With each successive race, gay candidates were treated more seriously.

Another important group still in operation today is what is now known as the Independent Voters of Illinois–Independent Precinct Organization (IVI-IPO). Longtime IVI-IPO activist David Igasaki points out that in 1973–74 Glynn Sudbery was the first gay chief executive of that group; later, Igasaki held the post himself. Sudbery, who coordinated field operations for the campaigns of state Sen. Dawn Clark Netsch and state Rep. James M. Houlihan and for William S. Singer for mayor, all in the early '70s, was among the first Chicagoans to die of AIDS, and IVI-IPO honored his name for many years with an annual award given out in his memory.

As the 1970s drew to a close, gays were active in both gay-specific and mainstream organizations. Many became active in Jesse Jackson's 1984 and 1988 Democratic campaigns for president and in John Anderson's 1980 Republican run for the White House. In fact, gay activist Timothy E. Drake, active in the Illinois Gay and Lesbian Task Force and the Chicago Area Republican Gay Organization, was the first openly gay Chicagoan to win an election, as a convention delegate for Anderson's presidential race. ▼

  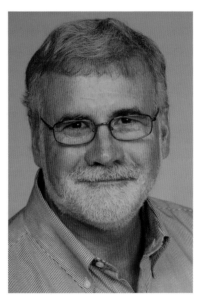

Left: Michael Bergeron interviewed for The Paper gay publication in September/October 1972. Courtesy M. Kuda Archives, Oak Park, Ill. Middle: Grant Ford runs for office. Photo courtesy Gay Chicago Magazine. Right: Tim Drake in 2007. Photo by Hal Baim.

Kuda wrote in the September-October 1972 edition of The Paper, "It was the first time in Illinois history that an avowed homosexual ran for political office." While he didn't win, his efforts created a new visibility for gay political activism. Bergeron, who later founded The Chicago Gay Crusader newspaper and the Beckman House community Center, had been endorsed by the Gay Liberation Front, Fiery Flames,

Ward and Nancy Davis in the 43rd.

Gary Nepon, age 28, mounted a more serious campaign for office in 1977, running for state representative from the Mid-North Side's 13th District. He faced strong opposition in a liberal district; his opponents also supported gay rights.

When Mayor Jane M. Byrne took office in 1979, gays finally felt there could be change. She supported

GL COALITION: CAN WE ALL GET ALONG? *by TRACY BAIM*

THE GAY AND LESBIAN COALITION OF MET- ropolitan Chicago was formed out of a conflict but eventually turned into an important link between diverse parts of the activist, business, and nonprofit communities. On Oct. 20, 1975, two women, Toby Schneiter and Nancy Davis, staged a sit-in at a Cook County Marriage License Bureau facility and were arrested.

Many activists believed this event would hurt more mainstream efforts to pass a city gay-rights law and that the fight for marriage was years away. They feared a media backlash, especially since one of the women, Schneiter, was still married to a man. The women joined forces with Jeff Graubart and called themselves the Chicago Gay Rights Action Coalition, claiming to represent the community and espousing socialist views. Some activists believed the whole thing was a publicity stunt for a book, Heterosexual, that Schneiter and Davis had written. Bill Kelley wrote in The Chicago Gay Crusader that media reaction was actually generally favorable.

"This political action was done at a time when the Illinois Gay Rights [later: Gay and Lesbian] Task Force was working closely with Ald. Clifford Kelley to get a gay-rights bill passed in the City Council, and many gay and lesbian activists felt their efforts were undermined by the sit-in and subsequent arrest of Davis and Schneiter," said Mark Sherkow, who from 1974 to 1979 represented the Rogers Park Gay Center (which later became the Rogers Park/Edgewater Gay Alliance) as its delegate to the Coalition. (In 1978 he was the secretary of the Coalition's executive committee.) "Worse, the two protesters had issued a flier proclaiming they spoke for and represented the gay and lesbian community of Chicago."

Organizers of the Coalition issued a press release denouncing the sit-in and formed an organization that lasted several years. Its first major public meeting was called for Jan. 13, 1976, at the Good Shepherd Parish Metropolitan Community Church, 615 W. Wellington Ave. Chris Riddiough and Guy Warner were early leaders of the Coalition.

"In my work with IGLTF and the Coalition, I grew to admire many of the people who made up the community, from Renee Hanover to Guy Warner to Al Wardell and many others," Riddiough said in 2007. "At the time, Chicago seemed in some ways to be more 'backward' than some of the gay

A mid-1970s Coalition leadership photo included Delilah Kenney, Guy Warner, and Chris Riddiough. Warner and Riddiough are pictured middle and right in 2007. Photos courtesy Gay Chicago Magazine, Hal Baim and John Fernez.

meccas like New York City and San Francisco, but in many ways I think we were able to build a more solid and diverse community, in part because we needed each other more. Indirectly I think the Chicago organizing tradition also helped solidify the community."

Trying to bring so many diverse voices and interests to the table was difficult. "There had been a number of complaints that African-Americans were being discriminated against by bars by being asked for five IDs at the door and then being denied admittance to the bar," Sherkow said. "The Coalition discussed this issue in the second or third year of its existence. Most of the bars present did not want the Coalition to form the committee, and many of them left the Coalition after the decision was made to form the committee. The committee eventually issued a report which suggested that such discrimi-

nation probably did exist. The Coalition continued to exist for a year or two, but eventually disbanded."

But Sherkow said the impact of the Coalition is still felt today: "It was an important meeting place for Chicago gay and lesbian activists. ... It was also a place for representatives of businesses to interact with representatives of organizations. We got to know one another and work with one another, and this interaction probably spurred all of us in our activism. Its membership is too numerous to mention, but a few members stand out in my mind: Guy Warner of Mattachine Midwest; Jim Bussen of Dignity; Marie Kuda and Renee Hanover; Gary Chichester of Man's Country and Chuck Renslow of the Gold Coast and Man's Country; David Boyer of Touché and Marge Summit and Delilah Kenney; Jim Edminster of Integrity; as well as Chris Riddiough, Bill Kelley, Rene Van Hulle, Michael Harrington, Max Smith, Al Wardell, Ira Jones, Ron Helizon, Joe Murray, Elaine Wessel and Chris Cothran. The Coalition was one of those places in time where a lot of people got together and reinforced each other in their activism, and probably set the stage for the working together and community-building that, in my mind, has been a hallmark of the Chicago GLBT community since that time." ▼

DON'T STOP THE MUSIC: DJS AND ENTERTAINERS *by JEFF BERRY*

ASIDE FROM BEING THE TITLE OF A MEDIOCRE MOVIE THAT starred the Village People, "Don't Stop the Music" was the mantra of the Chicago club scene back in the late 1970s and early 1980s. At the end of a busy evening at popular dance spots such as Dugan's Bistro or Carol's Speakeasy, the late-night crowds would roar in approval and stomp their feet until granted an encore performance from their favorite DJs such as Lou DiVito or Mark Hultmark, always wanting the music to go on and on.

And music to our ears it was. These artisans and many other gifted DJs from that era understood the most important thing about DJ-ing: how to weave the music together to tell a story. Most songs were uplifting, unlike most of the club music of the 2000s, which has a much harder, grittier feel to it.

Ground zero for the club scene back then was downtown at 420 N. Dearborn St., the site of Dugan's Bistro, run by Eddie Dugan (born Edward Davison, 1946–1987). Bistro was the Studio 54 of the Midwest. On any given night you might bump into members of the Rolling Stones, Joseph P. Kennedy II, Bette Midler, Sylvester, Barry Manilow, Elton John or Rudolf Nureyev, among others. All could be seen rubbing elbows on the dance floor or in the VIP lounge with newly liberated members of Chicago's gay community, as well as straight folks from the suburbs. At the same time you would be entertained by beefy dancers and the Bearded Lady, and mesmerized by the lighting wizardry of T.L. Noble under snow machines and NERF cannons.

Within walking distance of the Bistro were many other memorable joints: Ozone; Sunday's, which then became the Annex; the Gold Coast, with its infamous "Pit"; the Baton, which still remains; the Redoubt; the New Flight for those into "gay for pay"; and, of course, for late-night "snacks," Jumbo Jarry's and the Machine Shop (depending on which type of tube steak you were in the mood for). A little farther up North Wells Street in Old Town was Carol's; Alfie's on North Rush Street was always hopping after work and late into the evening with DJ Michael Graber; and over in Lincoln Park at Le Pub you'd be jumping to the sounds of Peter Lewicki.

The Butterfly (later known as the Iron Butterfly), a raucous and fun hangout on North Wells Street, always had a great party or benefit going on.

Up farther on North Broadway in New Town (now Boys Town) you could go bar-hopping, starting at Crystal's Blinkers and any number of smaller, cozier bars and pubs in the neighborhood. Most nights, people ended up at Broadway Limited, with its bleacher seats, lighted dance floor and resident DJ, Mark Vallese. Farther still, there was the Up North on North Western Avenue, which hosted many community benefits. There was nothing on North Halsted Street back then except Little Jim's, and then later Bushes—in fact, it was kind of a rough neighborhood—but if you ventured a little farther you'd eventually wind up at Coconuts on North Sheridan Road, where Frank Lipomi worked his magic on the turntables.

And of course, if all of that wasn't enough (and it usually never was), you'd continue on to after-hours clubs such as the Warehouse or Columns to be seduced by the sultry sounds of Frankie Knuckles, where house music was born; or to David Shelton's Medusa's, to bounce to the beats of Mark Stephens and Teri Bristol.

Other great clubs came and went, including Paradise, Trianon and Center Stage, all of which paved the way for what ultimately became the Halsted Strip. Ralphi Rosario came into his own during that time as well (as well as many other talented DJs too numerous to mention in the space of this article). Over the years, Lora Branch and DJ Sheron Denise Webb have been inducted into the Hall of Fame. Modern-era DJs also include DJ Psycho Bitch, DJ Larissa, DJ Harry T and Peter Mavrik.

Popular women's bars, some with dance spaces, have included Lost & Found, Augie's, CK's (Augie's and CK's later merged), Marilyn's, The Patch, Swan Club, Ladybug, Suzi B's, Off the Line, Paris Dance, Razzmatazz, Temptations, the mixed bars His 'n Hers, Opal Station, The Closet, Berlin (including the long-running Women's Obsession), Big Chicks and more.

In addition to private house parties and social clubs, such as Sons of Sappho, longtime South Side bars include Jeffery Pub, 7041 S. Jeffery Blvd., and Club Escape, 1530 E. 75th St., both still in operation in 2008. Other famous clubs have included Edyie's Banquet Room (aka The Connection Club), 6403 S. King Dr., and Martin's Den, 5550 S. State St. Promoter Otis "Heavy Diva" Mack has been hosting popular shows for more than 16 years.

The 1980s changed the dynamics of the club scene in dramatic ways, not least because of the AIDS-related losses of so many promoters and bar owners. The post-Stonewall, pre-AIDS 1970s and 1980s were like "another day in paradise": a bubble fueled by youth and sometimes drugs. ▼

HELPING HAND

Gay bars in Chicago helped raise money for causes outside their own backyards. In 1973, a suspected arson fire at the Upstairs Lounge, a New Orleans gay bar, killed 32 people. The event tugged at Chicago's heartstrings, and bars here opened their doors for benefits. The 1970s-era California battles against the anti-gay Briggs Initiative and in favor of Harvey Milk's campaign for San Francisco supervisor also sparked concern in Chicago, and community members opened their wallets for their West Coast peers.

Top, from left: Marky Mark brought his Funky Bunch to the Vortex, early 1990s. Sylvester at the Bistro, late 1970s. The Bearded Lady, 1970s. The Tavern Guild, a group of bar personnel, holds up funds raised for the Rodde Center. Below: Big Red and Quentin Crisp. Chilli Pepper. Jim Flint as Felicia. Ron "Polish Princess" Helizon. And David Boyer with Colt model Ed Dinakos. Photos courtesy Gay Chicago Magazine and Outlines/Windy City Times Archives.

THAT'S ENTERTAINMENT *by TRACY BAIM*

MANY TOP ENTERTAINERS HAVE COME OUT of Chicago or have visited the Windy City and its gay clubs over the years. Disco divas, cabaret professionals, puppet masters and drag shows have been a part of our gay club history. The Man's Country bathhouse attracted top-name entertainers in the 1970s and 1980s, and special events such as the Lincoln Park Lagooners' Cruisin' the Nile featured top performers.

For example, legendary fan dancer Sally Rand was a guest performer at the Man's Country Music Hall in February 1975. Eddie Dugan's Bistro attracted gay disco diva Sylvester, among many top names. The Village People played in area clubs, and in the 1980s and 1990s former disco queens joined the dancing queens for special numbers at gay clubs.

Chicagoans Bruce Vilanch, The Bearded Lady and Phyllis Hyman were joined by Madame and Wayland Flowers, Andy Warhol, Holly Woodlawn, Divine, Eartha Kitt, Liberace, Quentin Crisp, Rip Taylor, Pudgy,

Judy Tenuta, and even Marky Mark and the Funky Bunch at gay and gay-friendly clubs. Many top names also entertained at gay galas in the later years, including Chaka Khan, Patti LaBelle and more.

Chicago's "female performers" have spent decades entertaining both the gay and mainstream community, and no club compares to The Baton, which opened in 1969. Some performers have been dancing in heels since the 1970s, including Chilli Pepper. A 1975 Chicago Gay Crusader article has a picture of Baton owner Jim Flint as "Felicia" with some of his "girls": Chilli, Peaches, Audrey Brian, China Nuyen, Jan Howard and Shawn Luis. Since that time, many more Baton performers have become legends, including Mimi Marks, Ginger Grant, Sheri Payne, Maya Douglas, Leslie Reginae, Regine Phillips, and Victoria LePaige. The Baton's "Tops of the Nation Revue" has been visited by (the real) Joan Crawford, Sammy Davis Jr., Carol Channing,

Dinah Shore, Kirk Douglas, Robert Wagner, George Chakiris, Stephanie Powers, Lauren Bacall, Shirley MacLaine, Joan Rivers, Madonna, Janet Jackson, RuPaul, Da Brat, Tim Curry and Chris Farley plus professional athletes Dennis Rodman, Steve Kerr, Luc Longley, Jimmy Connors, Gayle Sayers and more.

While lesbians in male drag have never been as big, there were contests in the 1970s and many top drag-king shows in the 1990s and 2000s, including shows by the Chicago Kings.

Wanda Lust (Stephen Jones) was another important 1970s personality. Wanda promoted venereal disease testing (as it was called then) in a nurse's uniform, accompanying the VD testing van as it made its rounds to gay bars. On Feb. 19, 1980, Jones was stabbed in a Kansas City movie theater and died in his lover's arms. Other interesting 1970s personalities were Tilly the Dirty Old Lady and Mother Carol (Richard Farnham, who ran Carol's Speakeasy). As we moved into the 1980s and 1990s, other personalities included Feathers, Cesar Vera (Ubalde), Michael Shimandle, Sophie, Ron "The Polish Princess" Helizon, Miss Ketty, Memory Lane, Angelique Munro, and Miss Foozie.

The International Mr. Leather contest started in the 1970s and continues today, and many other contests were also the rage in the 1970s. Gay Chicago Magazine sponsored the annual Mr. Windy City awards featuring handsome young men, accompanying the event with the Gay Chicago Magazine awards for community businesses, organizations and individuals. Jim Flint and his Baton bar helped host the contests and awards. In the 1980s, many Mr. Windy City winners used their fame to help fight against AIDS and for anti-violence causes; Paul Adams and Alyn Toler were among the best-known. Flint's annual Miss Continental contest, which has been going strong since 1978, has attracted top names from around the country for many years. ▼

See later chapters for more on the entertainment and club scenes.

Top: An early 1990s reunion of bar owners, mostly of women's bars. Photo by Lisa Howe-Ebright. Left: Signs for Augie & CK's and Paris Dance.

Photos courtesy Outlines archives.

A SNAPSHOT: BARS OF 1974 A list from the Chicago Gay Directory, published by Michael Bergeron.

ADRON'S, 41 S. Harlem Ave., Forest Park
ALAMEDA, 5210 N. Sheridan Rd., Chicago
AUGIE'S, 3729 N. Halsted St., Chicago
ANNEX, 2865 N. Clark St., Chicago
ANOTHER PLACE, 7300 S. Cottage Grove Ave., Chicago
BATON, 436 N. Clark St., Chicago
BISTRO, 420 N. Dearborn St., Chicago
BLUE PUB, 3059 W. Irving Park Rd., Chicago
BOYS AT SEA, 642 W. Diversey Pkwy., Chicago
BRADBERRY, 7101 N. Clark St., Chicago
BROADWAY SAM'S, 5246 N. Broadway, Chicago
CHAIN, 7860 S. Cottage Grove Ave., Chicago
CHECKMATE, 2546 N. Clark St., Chicago
CHEZ RON, 4210 N Lincoln Ave., Chicago
CLOSET, 3325 N. Broadway, Chicago
COMING OUT PUB, 2519 N. Halsted St., Chicago
EPISODE, E. 77th St. & S. Cottage Grove Ave., Chicago
GATE, 650 N. Dearborn St., Chicago
GLORY HOLE, 1343 N. Wells St., Chicago
GOLD COAST, 501 N. Clark St., Chicago
HAIG, 800 N. Dearborn St., Chicago

HIDEAWAY II, 7301 W. Roosevelt Rd., Forest Park
HITCHING POST, 13101 S. Cicero Ave., Crestwood
IN BETWEEN, W. 63rd St. & S. Harlem Ave., Chicago
JAMIE'S, 1110 N. Clark St., Chicago
JEFFERY PUB, 7041 S. Jeffery Blvd., Chicago
JESSIE'S, 1012 W. Lawrence Ave., Chicago
KING'S RANSOM PUB, 20 E. Chicago Ave., Chicago
KITTY SHEON'S, 745 N. Rush St., Chicago
KNIGHT OUT, 2936 N. Clark St., Chicago
LE PUB, 1936 N. Clark St., Chicago
LEVIN'S INN, 3526 N. Lincoln Ave., Chicago
LOST AND FOUND, 2959 W. Irving Park Rd., Chicago
MIKE'S TERRACE LOUNGE, 1137 W. Granville Ave., Chicago
MIKE'S ARAGON, 1113 W. Lawrence Ave., Chicago
MARK III, E. 73rd St. & S. Cottage Grove Ave., Chicago
MR. B'S, 606 State Line Rd., Calumet City
MS., 661 N. Clark St., Chicago
MY BROTHER'S PLACE, 111 W. Hubbard St., Chicago
NAME OF THE GAME, 2616 E. 75th St., Chicago
NITE LIFE, 955 N. State St., Chicago
OFFICE, 4636 N. Broadway, Chicago

OUR DEN, 1355 N. Wells St., Chicago
PARKSIDE, E. 51st St. & S. Cottage Grove Ave., Chicago
PATCH, 155th St. & Wentworth Ave., Calumet City
PEANUT BUTTER AND JELLY,
    659 W. Diversey Pkwy., Chicago
PENGUIN, E. 74th St. & S. Yates Ave., Chicago
PEPPER'S, 1502 W. Jarvis Ave., Chicago
PIT, 501 N. Clark St. (basement), Chicago
POUR HOUSE, 103 155th Pl., Calumet City
RITZ, 937 N. State St., Chicago
SHARI'S, 2901 N. Clark St., Chicago
SHORELINE, 7650 S. South Shore Dr., Chicago
SHIRLEY'S SET LOUNGE, 6539 Roosevelt Rd., Berwyn
SNAKE PIT, 2626 N. Halsted St., Chicago
SUE AND NAN'S, 3920 N. Lincoln Ave., Chicago
SUNDAY'S, 430 N. Clark St., Chicago
TRIP, 27 E. Ohio St., Chicago
TWENTY-ONE CLUB, 3042 W. Irving Park Rd., Chicago
UP NORTH, 6244 N. Western Ave., Chicago
WILLOUGHBY'S, 1608 N. Wells St., Chicago
YO-YO, 3909 N. Ashland Ave., Chicago

LOST ... AND FOUND: LONGTIME BARS *by TRACY BAIM*

THE CHICAGO AREA BOASTS SOME OF THE oldest gay bars in the country, if not the world. The Jeffery Pub, 7041 S. Jeffery Blvd., has been operating (under various owners) since 1964, and is likely the city's oldest continuously operating gay bar. It predominantly serves African-American gays and lesbians.

Several gay bars in suburban Calumet City lasted more than 30 years, including the famous Pour House and The Patch. In Chicago, Jim Flint opened The Baton in 1969, and in 2008 it is still going strong with a female impersonator show seen on Oprah and known around the world. Little Jim's has operated since 1975 as the first gay bar on North Halsted Street. On West Irving Park Road, on a small block west of North California Avenue, two small neighborhood bars served drinks and music for decades—Lost & Found (most recently at 3058 W. Irving Park Rd.) and Legacy 21, formerly called the 21 Club (3042 W. Irving Park Rd.; it closed in the early 2000s).

Lost & Found opened in 1965, making it the oldest lesbian bar in Chicago and possibly in the United States. (In early 2008, Allen was expected to announce the sale of Lost & Found—it would remain a bar, but for gays and non-gays, not just for lesbians.) It has been a mainstay for lesbians, sponsoring numerous sports teams and a dart league, and holding benefits for a variety of causes and individuals. Some 43 years since it opened, you still have to be buzzed into the place, and many longtime customers are known to have their "own" bar stools.

L&F was started by Shirley Christensen. Allen joined as both her domestic and business partner in 1973. The couple resisted police harassment and anti-gay laws banning women from wearing "men's" clothes. Christensen died of cancer in 1986, and Allen made sure the bar did its part to raise money for many health causes, including an "Adopt-An-Angel" program with the Lesbian Community Cancer Project, which honored Allen for her efforts.

Allen, Jim Gates (owner of Little Jim's), and Jim Flint (owner of The Baton) have all been inducted into the Chicago Gay and Lesbian Hall of Fame for their business contributions. Baton performer Chilli Pepper is also a Hall of Famer. Gay bars, especially from the 1930s to the 1980s, were the central meeting places for the community, and some of those owners took that calling seriously, helping to raise funds for the community and to host meetings.

Other bars or bar owners inducted into the Hall

Left: Chuck Rodocker of Touché bar. Courtesy Gay Chicago Magazine. Middle: Rose Pohl and Judy Petrovsky, owners of The Closet, a bar open since the 1970s. Photo by Hal Baim. Right: L&F owner Ava Allen in early 2008. Photo by Tracy Baim.

of Fame include Marge Summit (His 'n Hers); Buddies' (George Brophy, Martin Enright, and their manager, the late Michael Shimandle, himself a legend in the bar business); Sidetrack (owners Art Johnston, Pepe Peña and Chuck Hyde were inducted as individuals); Elizabeth Tocci (The Patch in Calumet City); Arlene Halko (an important activist who also owned Piggen's Pub in the 1980s—she died in 2007); Paris Dance owner Linda Rodgers; Star Gaze bar (Mamie Lake and Dusty Fermin); and bar legend Chuck Renslow. Adrene "Big Red" Perom (1935–2000) was inducted into the Hall of Fame as

a Friend of the Community. Her Big Red's bar was a key spot for gay events and fundraisers, especially during the AIDS crisis, and she sponsored many sports teams. The Closet bar on Broadway started in the 1970s and is going strong in the 2000s as a co-gender neighborhood bar. Other popular long-time bars along the Halsted Street strip include Spin, Circuit, Lucky Horseshoe and Roscoe's.

Chuck Rodocker moved his long-running Touché leather bar from its original North Lincoln Avenue location to North Clark Street, next door to Jackhammer. Also important were individual party promoters who may not have had a bar but who hosted events and benefits. Those include Pat Mc-Combs and Vera Washington of Executive Sweet; Rene A. Van Hulle Jr. (Tavern Guild and numerous other causes—he died in 2007); promoter, fundraiser and top clown Gary Chichester ("Buttons T. Clown"); the late Samuel Davis Jr. (Dëeks, Pangea and Clubhouse); businessman Roger "RJ" Chaffin; DJ Frankie Knuckles; DJ Sheron Denise Webb; and the late Chef Tania Callaway. ▼

JIM FLINT: BATONS TO POLITICS   *by OWEN KEEHNEN*

BORN IN MASON CITY, ILL., IN 1941, JIM Flint grew up with 13 brothers and sisters in public housing in Peoria. He left home at 14 and, at 17, joined the U.S. Navy, serving from 1959 to 1962. In 1964 he moved to Chicago and soon got a job bartending at gay bars: the Annex (2865 N. Clark St.), the Chesterfield (2828 N. Clark St.) and Sam's (1205 N. Clark St.), before moving on to the Normandy (744 N. Rush St.), which he designed and opened. In 1969, Flint opened The Baton Show Lounge (436 N. Clark St.) in the then very seedy River North area.

In a 2008 WTTW interview, Flint had this to say about the opening of The Baton club: "So I thought, 'We'll start a drag show, like the Chesterfield.' So I got a kid named Lady Baronessa, Samantha George, Jody Lee, and myself, and we put down about 16 beer cases, put a little curtain around it, and a little spotlight. And we started the show. The place got packed on Friday night."

Flint's character, Felicia, was more comic than serious drag (he retired her in 1985). As to the origin of the name The Baton: It was a skill and a sure way to draw a crowd. "I was a drum major in high school, and I would start twirling back and forth across the street on roller skates, and then I would stand in the middle and twirl my baton." Almost 40 years later, The Baton Show Lounge still features top female impersonators playing to packed houses. Flint is also the founder and owner of the Miss Gay Continental Pageant, a national female impersonator contest that annually draws a crowd of nearly 1,500 and is franchised in numerous cities across the United States and Canada.

Flint's experience in the gay bar scene of the 1960s is fascinating. At that time, several Chicago-area gay bars had rear entrances with no markings except for the address. Touching or dancing with a member of the same sex could prompt a raid, with everyone loaded into paddy wagons and the names of those arrested printed in the newspaper. This common police practice randomly ruined hundreds, and possibly thousands, of gay and lesbian lives.

During this time and into the early 1970s, raids and

Jim Flint with Mr. Baton of the late 1970s. Photo by Tom Coughlin from the Gay Chicago Magazine Archives.

incidents of police harassment were routine. If a bar wanted to remain open, payoffs had to be given to both the police and the mafia. In 1971, he says, gay bars banded together against continued extortion from officers. As a result of the ensuing investigation, dozens of offending officers were jailed.

Flint and many others thought that era was finally over. When it seemed to begin again in 1980, Flint helped organize a demonstration in which thousands of protesters marched to Daley Center Plaza and demanded an end to police harassment. In his WTTW interview, Flint says that he told then-Mayor Jane Byrne, "I don't think you or anyone else knows that we can mobilize. And I don't think you think we're really going to go through with this, but we are not gonna tolerate police harassment anymore." After that, the police harassment stopped, for the most part.

It was several years earlier, in 1971, that Flint says he decided he was no longer going to pay off anyone, and that included the Mob. However, that was not the case with other gay bars. In the late 1970s, owners of Carol's Pub, the New Flight, and the Glory Hole worked with federal agents on an undercover sting operation against organized crime. When the case over extorting funds from gay bars during 1978–79 finally came before a grand jury in 1984, Flint says he testified about his refusal to make protection payments to the Mob and that evidence showed that, in fact, he had refused to make the $500 monthly payments. He recalls that one of the defendants remarked, "He's got balls, that Jimmy Flint," about his refusal to make payments. The trial resulted in one of the five indicted defendants being found guilty.

Flint was also one of the founding members of the Windy City Athletic Association, giving gays and lesbians the opportunity to participate openly in amateur sports leagues. In 1979 Flint helped organize a 12-inch softball league. It was wildly successful from the start. The following year, bowling was added to the roster, and then basketball. Since that time, Flint has served as the Windy City Athletic Association's commissioner more than once, and has sponsored dozens of teams.

Flint's political activism includes leadership of the 1980s–era Prairie State Democratic Club and running a very close race for election to the Cook County Board in 1987—when the elections were citywide, not by district. In 1977, Flint was a key part of the march around Medinah Temple where homophobe ("God made Adam and Eve, not Adam and Steve") Anita Bryant was appearing.

In the late 1970s and into the early 1980s, Flint was also president of the Chicago Knights MC, a leather and Levi's club that raised money for Toys for Tots. In the mid-1980s, he helped organize community forums that eventually led to the establishment of Chicago House, a hospice residence for people with AIDS. He was vice president of the 46th Ward Democratic Organization from 1984 to 1986. He is a member of the International Gay and Lesbian Travel Association and an active member of Dignity/Chicago. He was inducted into the Chicago Gay and Lesbian Hall of Fame in 1991, and in 2000 Flint was the first Chicagoan to be inducted into the North American Amateur Gay Athletic Alliance Hall of Fame for contributions to gay softball.

In addition to The Baton, he has also owned such businesses as Annex 2, Annex 3, Redoubt, Redoubt Atlanta, and River North Travel. He is a member of the Rainbow Coalition, the Independent Voters of Illinois–Independent Precinct Organization (IVI-IPO), the Lake View Citizens' Council, and Operation PUSH.

Flint's activism and visibility have resulted in his being arrested 16 times. Clearly, that defendant was right to comment that Jimmy Flint has balls. And all 16 times, he has been found not guilty. ▼

Andy Warhol with Richard Cooke in the 1970s. Photo by David Veltkamp.

Courtesy Richard Cooke.

COMING OUT IN THE BARS

In the summer of 1968, when I first came out, I quickly learned that the place to be was the local gay bar. Until then I was forced to cruise North Pine Grove Avenue near West Oakdale Avenue at night. From 10 p.m. on, there were dozens of gay men standing in the dark shadows of Pine Grove. The street was overgrown with trees that blocked out the moonlight, so it was easy to hide when the police drove by. This could be dangerous because the police would constantly swoop down in their many raids.

Eventually I learned that there were three gay bars in the neighborhood. All three were located on North Clark Street near West Surf Street: Ruthie's, the Annex and Shari's. I had to get in.

One evening, being young and dumb, I tried to get into the Annex. The girl who worked the coat check, Diane Kasper, whispered to me to come over by her. She said "Honey, let me see your ID." I handed her my driver's license, and she chuckled, noticing I was only 20 years old. "Honey," she said, "Let me give you a tip: If the door person asks you for ID and you're under 21, say you left it at home." She let me in anyway, and we became quick friends.

The two guys who ran the bar were fat, bald, 40ish and straight mafia types. Eventually I filled in for Diane, and she let me work the coat check on her days off. Occasionally a police car would pull up, and one of the owner-managers would run out with an envelope for them. Sometimes this wasn't good enough (especially during election season), and they would raid the bar. The management would shut off the music and turn on the bright overhead lights. The police would walk around picking a couple of people out to arrest. If they didn't like the way you looked, you were arrested. Of course, before they entered the bar you could hear the sound of pills hitting the floor like raindrops. You didn't want to get caught with drugs.

My experience at the Annex got me a job doing the coat check at Ruthie's. Again, my job was to signal Ruthie (Herman R.) whenever the police pulled up; he would give the bouncer an envelope of cash to give to the police.

Eddie Dugan, who later opened the Bistro, was a bartender there, and I became his roommate. Ruthie, the owner, used to sit at the bar every night watching the bartenders. He used to say of Eddie, "I know he's stealing from me. I just can't figure how." All the bartenders were presumed to be stealing. — **Richard Cooke**

GAY AMERICAN PSYCHO: SERIAL KILLERS

by RON DORFMAN

GAY CHICAGO IN THE 1970S AND '80S CAME OUT OF THE closet and quite literally found its skeletons strewn all about. Three homicidal maniacs with serious sexual issues targeted boys and young men in the area, claiming at least 70 victims. Years later, Andrew Cunanan came to town.

First revealed was John Wayne Gacy Jr., a building contractor on the Northwest Side. In 1972 he picked up his first murder victim at the Greyhound bus station; during the next six years, he tortured, raped and murdered 32 more youths, burying most of them in a crawl space under his house. Gacy was tried for murder in 1980 and executed in 1994.

Larry Eyler was a studly leatherman who had complex living arrangements with a gay professor in Indianapolis and a bisexual family man in Lake View. His prey were mostly young hustlers and teen runaways; their mutilated or dismembered corpses turned up in trash at sites along U.S. 41 in Illinois and Indiana starting in 1980. Arrested for one murder but released on bond, Eyler killed again, carelessly; the body was found in the trash behind Eyler's Chicago apartment. He confessed to more than 20 murders and died in prison of complications from AIDS in 1993.

For sheer operatic monstrousness, it's hard to top the story of Jeffrey Dahmer of Milwaukee, who picked up some of his 17 victims at Chicago gay bars and the Pride Parade. He drugged them, had sex with their comatose or dead bodies, butchered them, and told some interrogators he ate their flesh. Some he tried to dissolve in vats of acid; others' heads and body parts were stored in Dahmer's fridge. Convicted of 15 murders, Dahmer refused protective custody and was killed in 1994 by a fellow prisoner who said he was doing "God's will."

And then came Cunanan. On May 4, 1997, the body of Chicago real estate developer Lee Miglin was found in the garage of his Gold Coast townhouse. Andrew Cunanan, a 27-year-old gay party boy and gigolo from San Diego, wanted for a double murder in Minneapolis, was soon implicated. By the time the story was over in July, three more people were dead—including Cunanan, by suicide, and his last victim, the fashion mogul Gianni Versace, gunned down in front of his Miami Beach mansion. In contrast to the slummy world of Dahmer's and Eyler's down-and-out victims, media coverage of Cunanan introduced Americans to the upscale gay generation gap he navigated—affluent, out young business and professional people on the one hand, and closeted older men on the other who could afford Cunanan's company and discretion. New York magazine snapped that Cunanan wasn't nearly elegant enough for Manhattan's A-list closet cases. ▼

The Aug. 30, 1984, GayLife coverage of Eyler's murders.

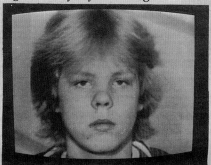

A LOVE THAT SEEMED SO MUCH LIKE DEATH
Part II of story by Jon-Henri Damski—Section X

GayLife
CHICAGO'S GAY AND LESBIAN NEWSWEEKLY

SOUND AND SPIRIT IN A 'CITY OF WOMYN'
9th annual Michigan Womyn's Music Fest—pullout Section X

CHICAGO • VOLUME 10, NUMBER 9 | THIS ISSUE IN TWO SECTIONS | THURSDAY, AUGUST 30, 1984

2-YEAR TRAIL OF SEX KILLINGS LEADS TO MURDER OF UPTOWN TEEN
Body identified as Danny Bridges; Larry Eyler charged

Accused sex slayer Larry Eyler (right) walked out of Lake County jail last February after evidence against him was ruled inadmissable. With Eyler are his mother and attorney David P. Schippers, who defended Eyler against charges that he murdered Uptown resident Ralph Calise. (Photo: Paul Cotton/GayLife)

Now Eyler has been charged with the dismemberment murder of Danny Bridges, 16, seen here as he appeared on an NBC News report about teenage prostitution. Bridges had also been a key witness in the Joe's Juice Joint case in April 1982, in which three men were found guilty of charges involving sex with minors. Bridges' body was found in a Rogers Park dumpster Aug. 21. (Photo courtesy NBC/WMAQ TV, Chicago)

By PAUL COTTON

A two-year trail of vicious sex murders of young men may have ended, police believe, with the discovery of 16-year-old Daniel Bridges' body and the arrest of Larry Eyler for Bridges' murder.

Eyler, 31, who had walked out of Lake County (Ill.) Jail on $1,000 bail Feb. 6 after evidence linking him to another murder was tossed out on a technicality, is being held in isolation at Cook County Jail, awaiting his Sept. 19 arraignment on charges of murder, armed violence, aggravated kidnaping, unlawful restraint, and concealment of a homicide. The penalty could be death.

Bridges' body was found in eight pieces in garbage bags in a dumpster behind the apartment building next to Eyler's building, 1628 W. Sherwin on Chicago's far North Side. Like most of the 24 other murder victims linked by police to Eyler, Bridges, a prostitute, had been tied up, sexually assaulted, and stabbed repeatedly.

Police say they have gathered a "mountain" of evidence against Eyler in the Bridges case. A witness allegedly saw Eyler with a teenager resembling Bridges driving in Eyler's pickup truck Sunday night, Aug. 19. A janitor said he saw Eyler carry the garbage bags containing Bridges' body to the dumpster. Blood matching Bridges' type was found splattered under the just-painted walls throughout the apartment that Eyler, a house painter, had lived in for two months.

The relatively new technique of spraying the chemical Luminol, which interacts with iron oxide in the blood to give off a dark green glow,

See MURDER, page 3

TRUMAN CAPOTE: The chameleon passes on

Truman Capote, 1924-1984

By ALBERT WILLIAMS

"...so fierce is the world's ridicule we cannot speak or show our tenderness; for us, death is stronger than life, it pulls like a wind through the dark, all our cries burlesqued in joyless laughter; and with the garbage of loneliness stuffed down us until our guts burst bleeding green, we go screaming round the world, dying in our rented rooms, nightmare hotels, eternal homes of the transient heart."
—From *Other Voices, Other Rooms*, by Truman Capote (1948)

Truman Capote, in his own eye and the public's, was a self-styled chameleon of America's cultural life. From the start of his career, there were at least two Truman Capotes. There was Capote the artist,

who blended a decidedly "special" sensibility with what this week's *New York Times* obituary rightly called a prose style that "shimmered with clarity and quality." And there was Tiny Truman, celebrity court jester to the jet set, whose impish behavior and waspish, frequently self-deprecating humor could hardly conceal a morbid undercurrent of despair.

Somewhere in between there was Truman Capote, the man. He died Saturday, Aug. 25.

* * *

When Americans thought of gay people in the years following World War II, they almost invariably thought of Truman Capote. This was as true of gay people themselves as it was of heterosexuals. Especially after *In Cold Blood* made him a major celebrity, he became the quintessential amusing pansy of the TV talk shows, with his high-pitched lisp, sultry Southern drawl, androgynous figure, and flair for bitchy gossip.

Unfortunately, Capote lived out another, crueler stereotype of the male gay. As the spoiled, sissified, social-climbing, self-destructive, drug-addicted old queen, going "screaming round the world," squandering his brilliant talent and toadying up to the rich, Capote built an image that was as pathetic as it was laughable.

He had burst upon the literary scene in 1948 as a girlishly pretty youth, photographed lying languidly on a sofa making bedroom eyes for the dust-jacket of his first novel, *Other Voices, Other Rooms*. ("I was a beautiful little boy," Capote said later, "and everyone had me—men, women, dogs and fire hydrants." The sex kitten was another of Capote's public/private personae.) In its elegantly written story of a sensitive, precocious 13-year-old's observations on the world around him, *Other Voices* presented the reader with a gay outsider's viewpoint on life while

"playing it safe" by keeping the boy prepubescent, though a secondary character in the novel is a gay man who speaks eloquently of gay love turned grim by "the world's ridicule." *Other Voices* marked Capote as a writer of exceptional talent; the dust-jacket photo made him an easy mark for critics who sought to rid American literature of the "taint" of homosexuality.

In 1980, for the jacket photo of what would be his last book, *Music for Chameleons*, Capote repeated his *Other Voices* pose. The beautiful boy of 1948 had been ravaged by age, illness, and a self-abusive lifestyle laced with

See CAPOTE, back page

ACTION seeks support for gay rights bill

More than 500 letters have been sent to both gay and non-gay organizations in Chicago by ACTION (Ad-hoc Coalition To Impel Ordinances Now) in an effort to gather support for the pending gay and lesbian civil rights ordinance in the City Council.

In the mailing, which went out last Saturday, a form letter was enclosed asking support for the ordinance, which would prohibit discrimination in jobs, housing, and public accommodation on the basis of sexual orientation. Letters that are returned will be presented by ACTION to members of the City Council, Charles said.

Also enclosed in the mailing was a letter from Mayor Washington's gay community liaison, Kit Duffy, explaining the ordinance.

Charles said the mailing went to every gay organization in the city as well as to non-gay groups such as chambers of commerce, social services, social groups, and unions. Charles specifically said solicitations of support had been sent to black and Hispanic organizations.

ACTION will hold meetings Thursday, Aug. 30, and Tuesday, Sept. 4, at 7 p.m. at the Wellington Avenue United Church of Christ, 615 W. Wellington.

On Thursday, Sept. 6, at 9 a.m., ACTION will hold a "passive, peaceful" vigil at Daley Plaza supporting the ordinance in hopes of offsetting the effect of a planned anti-gay rally organized by the Rev. Hiram Crawford, a Moral Majority supporter who has staged demonstrations against gay rights in the past.

Ed Asner hosts AIDS: Portrait of an Epidemic, a PBS documentary airing this weekend on Channel 11. Featured in the program is Dr. Renslow Sherer, who, with Dr. Ron Sable, operates the Sable/Scherer Clinic for AIDS patients at Cook County Hospital. See story, page 5.

GAYS AND THE POLICE

The police have long tried to control and suppress dissident movements and marginalized communities—labor organizers, civil rights workers, hoboes, hippies, the homeless, immigrants and African-Americans, among others. Of course, they have other duties as well—protecting lives and property, directing traffic, and investigating crimes. There's always some tension between those roles, which is proportionally reduced as dissidents achieve respectability and marginalized groups move into the mainstream.

It would be unthinkable now, not to mention pointless, to raid a gay bar or bathhouse as Chicago police often did well into the 1970s. Dozens of people would be arrested for alleged disorderly conduct, with their names, ages, addresses and occupations listed in the next day's Chicago Tribune. Listing these individuals by name in the newspaper to embarrass them, ruin their reputations and thereby instill fear among all gays about socializing together was probably the real objective of such raids in the first place.

By 1978, when young thugs carried out a number of attacks on gay men in Lake View, the cops did the right thing. Grant Ford, then publisher of GayLife, told Time magazine: "The community groups came to our help right away. They saw us as neighbors rather than gays. The police were even more amazing. They were totally cooperative."

The Gay Officers Action League (GOAL) in the 2007 Chicago Pride Parade. Photo by Tracy Baim.

Gays and lesbians have also been part of the community policing program. When Chicago's first lady Maggie Daley, wife of the mayor, stood with Coretta Scott King, widow of Martin Luther King Jr., and other dignitaries at the 25th-anniversary luncheon of the Lambda Legal Defense & Education Fund in the Palmer House Hilton in March 1998, security was provided by a phalanx of out lesbian and gay Chicago police officers.

The last big bar raid was at Carol's Speakeasy on North Wells Street in the mid-1980s, but that was by law enforcement groups not associated with the Chicago Police; it was roundly attacked. While police harassment of gays continues in some measure by individual officers in the 2000s, the organized attacks have stopped. This change came because of outside pressure from activists, and also because courageous officers began to come out of the closet.

Dorothy Knudson, Chicago's first out police officer, joined the force in the early 1990s. As a recognized fraternal organization, the Gay Officers Action League (GOAL) of Illinois advocates for its members within the department and mediates issues that arise between the police and the gay community. Members of GOAL now even march in uniform in the Pride Parade to loud applause and support from the crowds of bystanders.

— **Ron Dorfman**

VICE COP: MANLEY *by RON DORFMAN*

AS U.S. SEN. LARRY CRAIG (R-IDAHO) LEARNED IN AN AIRPORT men's room, a good-looking stranger giving off come-hither signals just might be an undercover cop. In the late 1960s in the Lincoln Park area, one handsome devil in particular, Sgt. John Manley Jr., was responsible for so many arrests that the Mattachine Midwest Newsletter published his picture and warned the community about his tactics. It also suggested that Manley might be a closet case.

"I'm honored that they feel I have the compelling personality to induce people to commit public indecency," the pugnacious policeman told a reporter. Turns out he did indeed have issues: In 1994, as a police captain and watch commander at the Foster Avenue District, Manley was the first ranking officer to face departmental charges of sexual harassment.

"He called virtually every woman a bimbo," a female lieutenant testified, including his policewoman wife and "the women he was sleeping with." He also called them bitches and whores, made crude references to their genitals, and invited various sexual activities, women complainants said. Manley was dismissed from the force in 1995 and appealed unsuccessfully through state and federal courts on a variety of grounds, all the way up to the U.S. Supreme Court, which refused to hear his case in October 1999. A month later, the city settled the women's lawsuit. ▼

June 24, 1977, coverage of Chicago's anti-Anita Bryant protest.

Photos courtesy GayLife Archives and M. Kuda Archives, Oak Park, Ill.

THE FRUITS OF HATE SPEECH: ANITA IS PROTESTED *by TRACY BAIM*

BY FAR THE WATERSHED EVENT FOR GAY rights in Chicago during the 1970s, still mentioned most often by local activists today, was Chicago's march against Anita Bryant on June 14, 1977. Bryant ignited a national firestorm after her successful opposition to a Dade County, Fla., law protecting gay people, and the national gay movement became galvanized in protest.

Bryant was a former Miss Oklahoma, a singer, and a spokesperson for Florida orange juice who was outspoken in her anti-gay rhetoric. Her highly publicized homophobic remarks sparked activists to launch a successful orange-juice boycott and motivated gays in a way that the anti-gay Rev. Fred Phelps has done in more recent years. She was scheduled to speak that evening at Medinah Temple, 600 N. Wabash Ave., and activists including Chuck Renslow helped organize the opposition. "I got an

anonymous call that day from a woman who worked at the limousine company driving Anita," Renslow recalled in 2008. "She was the dispatcher, and she told me where and when Anita would be arriving, so that we could plan our pickets. She said we have to stick together."

Organizers said an estimated 5,000 gays and lesbians circled Medinah Temple (police said 2,000), called together by the Gay and Lesbian Coalition of Metropolitan Chicago and the Committee for Gay Rights. Although the event had been sold out, it was estimated that only about one-third showed up to hear Bryant. Only a few arrests were recorded.

"Media coverage of the march was extensive, with front-page coverage in the daily newspapers as well as on several television stations," said veteran Pride Parade organizer Rich Pfeiffer in 2008. "Two weeks later, the annual Pride Parade with the theme

'Gays and Lesbians in History' saw an increase in participants as well as spectators. It was a fitting theme because history was made that night at the Medinah Temple with the largest GLBT demonstration to that date in Chicago history."

At 9 p.m., protesters marched to Pioneer Court, the plaza south of the Chicago Tribune building, where speakers addressed the crowd under Tribune windows. "Anita Bryant is not our enemy; she only represents the enemy," said GayLife Publisher Grant Ford in his newspaper's June 24 edition. "This is only the first time we will meet like this. All our good works will be undone if we go home tonight and forget that we will march again and again and again, until we have our rights. We will be free."

More than 30 years later, those at the event are still inspired by what it meant for the Chicago gay and lesbian community. ▼

THE WOMEN IN PRINT MOVEMENT   by MARIE J. KUDA

IN 1976 AN EXTRAORDINARY CONFERENCE with far-reaching effects brought together existing feminist and lesbian presses (publishers and printers), periodicals and women's bookstores from all over the United States, including Chicago. The moving force behind the first Women in Print conference was Texas heiress and author June Arnold, who founded Daughters Press in 1973. In addition to publishing three of her own novels over time, Daughters' initial offerings included a reprint of The Treasure (1903), by Selma Lagerlöf, the first woman writer to win the Nobel Prize in literature, and a book that would become a lesbian blockbuster, Rita Mae Brown's Rubyfruit Jungle (1973).

One hundred thirty women representing over 80 venues met, by invitation, at Camp Harriet Harding outside Omaha, Neb. The eight-day conference was planned to network, share skills and discuss strategies for everything from raising capital to bill-collection techniques in the context of feminist politics.

Security and paranoia were strong. These were the days when the FBI was hunting alleged bomber Susan Saxe in every lesbian venue in the country. Only months before, lesbian poet Camilla Hall (Miz Moon) was shot and others burned to death during a Los Angeles Police Department shootout in which the FBI was involved at the Symbionese Liberation Army house in Los Angeles where kidnapped heiress Patty Hearst had been held.

At the very least, most women at the conference felt they were in the business of reclaiming, promoting and preserving a heritage that had been hidden from history. Some had the feeling of being on the cutting edge of a revolution against the patriarchy, and that the freedom of the press did indeed belong only to those who owned the presses. Over 30 movement periodicals covered the conference; a post-conference feature ran in The New York Times Magazine.

Booksellers, periodicals and presses joined Chicago women in establishing a Midwest presence among their bicoastal counterparts at Women

in Print. Posters from the Chicago Women's Graphics Collective filled the walls and windows of the dining hall. Metis Press co-founder Chris Johnson, who also worked with Chicago's small-press feminist literary journal, Black Maria, would later be joined by Nancy Poore of Helaine Victoria Press, an Indiana letterpress feminist postcard publisher. Womanpress was a publisher-printer that

panded their horizons. Mary Wings, who developed a market for her feminist comic books, went on to write great mystery novels. Carol Seajay opened Old Wives Tales bookstore in San Francisco and began publishing the Feminist Bookstore News. In a 1995 issue she reprinted June Arnold's prophetic 1976 warning about the need for alternatives because of the ability of the Establishment, with its

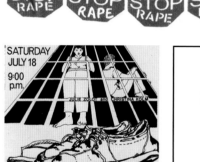

Left: From the Women's Graphics Collective of Chicago. The STOP Rape T-shirt raised funds to help bail out graphics activists Julie Zolot and Christina Kolm, who in the late 1970s were arrested for putting STOP Rape stickers on Chicago stop signs. At right: Metis Press marks 10 years. Images courtesy M. Kuda Archives, Oak Park, Ill., Julie Zolot and Chris Johnson.

also sponsored the annual Lesbian Writers' Conference in Chicago.

After the conference, women went back to their communities re-energized and reinforced in their commitments and skills. An alternative distribution company was founded by Cynthia Gair and Helaine Harris. The Women in Print Newsletter went out from Chicago for a year. Printers from WIP formed their own group and newsletter. Two more conferences were held.

Former Chicagoans who attended in 1976 ex-

immense markets, to co-opt lesbian writers: They "will publish some of us—the least threatening, the most salable, the most controlled, or the few who cannot be ignored."

By the mid-1990s the megamart bookstores installed "Gay & Lesbian" and "Women's Studies" sections, pushing small specialty stores out of business. After releasing hundreds of titles in the 1970s and 1980s, only a handful of publishers, a few magazines and fewer than a dozen bookstores survived nationwide. ▼

PUTTING WOMEN & CHILDREN FIRST *by JORJET HARPER*

FEMINIST BOOKSTORES HAVE PLAYED AN important part in the cultural life of lesbian communities around the country. Women who launched bookstores specifically catering to women were often motivated by feminist ideals as much as business goals, because feminism had changed their lives. This was just as true in Chicago as elsewhere.

In the 1970s, Kathleen Thompson opened Pride & Prejudice on North Halsted Street, and Nancy

Nov. 13, 1986, at Women & Children First Bookstore's 1967 N. Halsted St. location, from left: Lucy Moynihan, Julie Parsons, Starla Sholl, and co-owners Ann Christophersen and Linda Bubon (with her son Max). Photo: Windy City Times/Outlines archives.

Finke and Flora Faraci opened the Jane Addams Bookstore in the historic Fine Arts Building on South Michigan Avenue in the Loop. Both bookstores were focal points for the nascent Chicago women's community, but relatively short-lived. The bookstore that took root and became a true home for the lesbian-feminist imagination was Women & Children First.

Inspired by a feminist criticism group at the Newberry Library and prompted by the difficulties they had experienced during the 1970s in finding books by women authors in bookstores, Ann Christophersen and Linda Bubon decided to open their own. From its inception, the owners thought of the bookstore in political terms as a way to join with and support those in Chicago working to further the rights and well-being of women and children, and to contribute to the growing international feminist movement.

"The mission of Women & Children First was to provide books, periodicals, music and programming that reflected the lives, experiences, ideas and art of women in all our diversity and with all our commonality. It was also to nurture a love of reading in children of all ages by providing the best children's books available, with special attention to books with strong girl characters and all kinds of families, races and cultures," says Christophersen.

"It was like we were creating a library. We even built all the shelves ourselves," recalls Bubon, "and I guess we didn't think that we would actually make money because we hadn't bought a cashbox, cash drawer or cash register. The night before we opened, it suddenly dawned on us that we didn't have anything to put cash in if anybody actually came in and bought a book."

Women & Children First opened its doors on West Armitage Avenue in the DePaul neighborhood on Nov. 10, 1979, and quickly built a loyal clientele. At that time, one small shelf contained the store's entire lesbian section, almost all of it from small presses. Today a whole wall in the store is dedicated to LGBTQ books, approximately 80 percent of them published by major presses and university presses. In the early days, appearances by authors such as Mary Daly, Rita Mae Brown, Judy Grahn and Maya Angelou helped create the aura of excitement about the growing body of literature and feminist theory by women.

Five years after its founding, Women & Children First moved to a larger nearby location on North Halsted Street south of Armitage. In 1990 it moved to its present location on North Clark Street in Andersonville, becoming one of the first business anchors for the influx of that area's lesbian and gay residents.

Almost three decades after they started the venture, Christophersen and Bubon still co-own the bookstore. Their political activism through the years has always been a natural extension of their commitment to the community. Bubon and Christophersen were both on the city's first Advisory Council on Gay and Lesbian Issues, appointed by Mayor Harold Washington. Christophersen later became its president. She served for eight years on the board of the Crossroads Fund. She was a vice president of IMPACT, a board member of Gerber/Hart Library, and president of the American Booksellers Association. Bubon has served on the boards of the Independent Booksellers of the Chicago Area, the Andersonville Chamber of Commerce, and the Chicago Women's Health Center. ▼

BOOKSTORES OF NOTE:

Women & Children First, Andersonville

Unabridged Books in Boys Town

CLOSED:

Pride & Prejudice, Chicago, 1970s

Jane Addams Bookstore, Chicago, 1970s–80s

Stonewall Memorial Bookshop, in the
   Knight Out bar, 2936 N. Clark St.
   in Chicago, 1970s

People Like Us Books, Chicago

Left Bank Books, Oak Park

Pride Agenda, Oak Park

Platypus Books, Evanston

Prairie Moon Books, Suburban

Third Annual Lesbian Writers Conference
September 17, 18 & 19   Chicago, Illinois

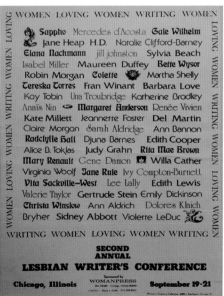

WOMEN LOVING WOMEN WRITING WOMEN

Sappho Mercedes d'Acosta **Gale Wilhelm**
Jane Heap H.D. Natalie Clifford-Barney
Elana Nachmann jill johnston **Sylvia Beach**
Isabel Miller **Maureen Duffey** **Bette Wysor**
Robin Morgan **Colette** **Martha Shelly**
Tereska Torres Fran Winant **Barbara Love**
Kay Tobin Una Troubridge Katherine Bradley
Anaïs Nin **Margaret Anderson** Renée Vivien
Kate Millett Jeannette Foster **Del Martin**
Claire Morgan Sarah Aldridge **Ann Bannon**
Radclyffe Hall Djuna Barnes **Edith Cooper**
Alice B. Toklas **Judy Grahn** **Rita Mae Brown**
Mary Renault Gene Damon **Willa Cather**
Virginia Woolf **Jane Rule** Ivy Compton-Burnett
Vita Sackville-West Lee Lally **Edith Lewis**
Valerie Taylor **Gertrude Stein** Emily Dickinson
Christa Winslow Ann Aldrich **Dolores Klaich**
Bryher **Sidney Abbott** Violette LeDuc

WRITING WOMEN LOVING WOMEN WRITING

**SECOND
ANNUAL
LESBIAN WRITER'S CONFERENCE**

Chicago, Illinois   WOMANPRESS   **September 19-21**

LESBIAN WRITERS' CONFERENCES: SHARING WORDS

by JORJET HARPER

The following is adapted by Jorjet Harper from "Women Loving, Women Writing: A Brief Look at the Lesbian Writers' Conference, Chicago, 1974–78," by Marie J. Kuda, Outlines newspaper, Sept. 30, 1998.

IN 1974 CHICAGO WOMEN CREATED THE first lesbian writers' conferences ever held anywhere in the world. At the time, few lesbian writers were aware that they were not writing alone or that there were hundreds of books by and about lesbians buried in the published works of the past.

Novelist Valerie Taylor, writer Marie J. Kuda, Susan Edwards and Rebecca Hunter of Lavender Press, and Pauline (Polly) Adams of Mattachine Midwest together spearheaded the creation of the first conference. Sandy Szelag secured the location for the conference near the University of Chicago in Hyde Park, including the Blue Gargoyle (which was also the first meeting place of Chicago Gay Liberation).

Lesbian writers from all over the country and Canada attended—women whose writings would contribute to the creation of contemporary lesbian culture and aesthetics. The success of the first conference led to its continuation annually for a total of five years, all in Chicago, through 1978.

The weekend-long format featured a keynote address on Friday night, followed by a coffeehouse and chance to view displays or buy books; a full day of workshops on Saturday, with free entertainment in the evening; and on Sunday afternoon, readings by participants from their own works. Valerie Taylor presented the first year's keynote address, an irreverent history of lesbian writers. The keynote speaker at LWC II was Barbara Grier, who, as Gene Damon, had edited the national lesbian magazine The Ladder and reviewed hundreds of books in her "Lesbiana" column. Academic anthologist Beth Hodges, who had edited a special issue of Margins on lesbian writing and publishing (and would later edit two such issues for Sinister Wisdom), spoke the following year.

At LWC IV in 1977, Alma Routsong keynoted. Under her pen name Isabel Miller, Routsong had written and self-published Patience and Sarah in 1969; it was picked up by McGraw-Hill and became a Literary Guild selection. By the time of her appearance at the Lesbian Writers Conference, her book was a lesbian classic. The keynote speaker at the last conference was Yvonne MacManus, who wrote pulp fiction under the name Paula Christian.

Scholars and artists as well as writers benefited from the conferences. Women's studies had barely gained a foothold on university campuses, but some of the workshops offered at LWC read like a graduate course in lesbian studies. Workshops were also given each year for those needing the skills to get their own work into print.

Representatives from women's presses presented the fundamentals of production and design, keyline and paste-up of camera-ready copy, and other self-publishing information from copyright to finished publication. Women from local feminist publishing ventures such as Blazing Star, Metis Press, and Black Maria offered fiction-writing and magazine tips. At a time before lesbian history or art books were available, these conferences offered visual history in a variety of slide presentations by artists and scholars such as Maida Tilchen, Max Dashu, Tee Corinne and Marie Kuda.

Feminist and separatist controversies and other crises arose around the gatherings, but alternative press coverage for the conferences, both local and national, was extensive and glowing. Many Chicago lesbians volunteered their time to keep the conference alive. By the fifth year, however, pressure was being placed on organizers not to have the conference in a state that had refused to ratify the Equal Rights Amendment—though it proved not possible to move it elsewhere—and mainstream publishers had begun to co-opt the new lesbian market, so the fifth LWC was the last. ▼

Posters for the 3rd (top) and 2nd annual Lesbian Writers' Conferences.
Courtesy M. Kuda Archives, Oak Park, Ill.

SARAH LUCIA HOAGLAND

Sarah Hoagland. Photo by Tracy Baim.

Through many of her writings, Sarah Lucia Hoagland has deeply explored lesbian community and lesbian connection. She was born in 1945 in Denver, Colo., and came to Chicago in 1977. At that time, women's liberation groups around the country—including the Chicago Women's Liberation Union—had split apart, and Hoagland realized that "collective work, which we came to politically as a way of giving meaning to our lives, had shifted to ethical assertions of obligation and duty."

Out of this came her 1988 book, Lesbian Ethics: Toward New Value, expressing her perceptions about the importance of lesbian focus and lesbian community to women's existence as lesbians: "My thesis was that the norms we absorbed from Anglo-European ethical theory undermine rather than promote integrity and agency; they promote dominance and subordination through social control thereby legitimating oppression by redefining it as social organization. As a result these norms undermine rather than encourage lesbian community."

Lesbian Ethics had an immediate impact, encouraging women to think about lesbian issues in new and radical ways. As a result of the book's publication Hoagland gave talks and workshops all over the United States, as well as Montreal, Ottawa, Vancouver and London. Lesbian Ethics was translated into several languages, leading to speaking invitations around the world. She spoke at the Fifth International Feminist Book Fair in Amsterdam and later in Rome for a seminar organized by feminists who had met for a year and translated Lesbian Ethics into Italian.

Hoagland is a professor of philosophy, women's studies, and Latino/a American studies and has been on the faculty of Northeastern Illinois University since 1977. She has co-edited For Lesbians Only: A Separatist Anthology, with Julia Penelope (1988), and Feminist Interpretations of Mary Daly, with Marilyn Frye (2000). Her writing has appeared in such journals as Sinister Wisdom: A Journal for the Lesbian Imagination in the Arts and Politics; Hypatia: A Journal of Feminist Philosophy; and Trivia: A Journal of Ideas.

In Chicago, she has been an active and frequent organizer and participant in workshops, panels and community gatherings, and is a founder of the Institute of Lesbian Studies. Hoagland continues to write, teach and engage in various communities. "My concern remains," she says, "how marginalized peoples meet each other, ways we animate or resist animating dominant logic with regard to each other, how we form community, and how we come to see each other through difference, rather than through commonality that erases the richness of differences." — **Jorjet Harper**

THE AGONY AND THE ECSTASY: LESBIAN SEPARATISM

by JORJET HARPER

LESBIAN SEPARATISM HAS, FROM THE 1970S ONWARD, BEEN a volatile subject both within and outside the lesbian community. "The premise of separatism is simple," wrote Bonnie Zimmerman in the March 1974 issue of Chicago's Lavender Woman. "Male supremacy is the oldest, most pervasive, root cause of all oppression. Men benefit from and perpetuate the system; women suffer from it. Men are therefore the enemy."

Other separatists pointed to the institution of patriarchy, not actual men, as "the enemy." Others said lesbians should forget about assigning blame and focus on the empowerment of women, lesbians, or both. Individual attitudes toward separatism usually hinged on whether one's experience of separatism felt exhilarating, divisive, or a combination of the two.

Many prominent lesbian and feminist spokeswomen around the country had separatist sympathies, and one of the most basic tenets of separatism was the creation of "women-only space." A woman-centric vision that was not necessarily separatist but was fueled by separatist energy became a driving force for women's music festivals, most notably the Michigan Womyn's Music Festival and the East Coast Lesbians' Festival.

Chicago was a center of lesbian separatist activity in the United States during the 1970s and 1980s. Two Chicago-based bands were early advocates of women-only audiences. The Chicago Women's Liberation Rock Band, a dance band founded in 1970 that included Susan Abod, Shelly Jenkins, Patricia Miller, Fania Montalvo, Suzanne Prescott and Naomi Weisstein, performed for women-only audiences, and Family of Woman, founded by Chicago vocalist, pianist and songwriter Linda Shear with Ella Szekely and Joan Capra in 1972, began performing in Chicago specifically for lesbian audiences.

While these concerts produced an atmosphere of "palpable excitement," recalls Shear, "Women-only, lesbian-only performances were always an issue. The notion of women or just lesbians gathering seemed powerful but was met in the community with very mixed reactions, trying to create community and getting the opposite in some cases. There was a range of orthodoxies. Some women involved in separatism had many other community connections at the same time, and others shunned association with straight men, gay men, and straight women as much as possible."

The impetus of separatism led to discussions of idealized visions of the "ancient matriarchy" that was thought to have preceded patriarchy, calls to lesbian mothers to "give up" their male children, arguments about the relative oppressions of racism, sexism, and classism, political lesbianism versus cultural lesbianism, whether sadomasochism was incompatible with separatism, strategies of how to "withdraw" from patriarchy, even arguments about whether orgasms were a form of patriarchal oppression—all variously eliciting creative ideas, newfound confidence, anger, angst, hope, despair, humor and ridicule, depending on one's perspective.

Women-only space engendered feelings of elation at creating something genuinely new, at the same time separatism was plagued by an ever-more-rigid dogmatism. As finer and finer lines were drawn defining who was "separatist enough," hostilities grew toward other women, other lesbians and other separatists. The first Lesbian Writers' Conference in Chicago, for example, was picketed by separatists because one of the presenters was known to be bisexual. Motherhood, male children and transsexuals were perennially contentious issues, and there were also heated debates about how to keep lesbian cultural products such as books and music in the hands of lesbians only.

Despite the schisms, there was certainly a hunger for lesbians to be alone among their own, and a feeling that women-only space, however defined, was valuable and fragile. Reacting against male-dominated groups in the gay movement and on the Left, as well as the homophobia in many feminist organizations, lesbian separatism was a logical outgrowth of a community trying to define itself. Out of this foment, lesbians made decisions about how they would conduct their political and social lives, and where their allegiances lay. In Chicago, Mountain Moving Coffeehouse was a central hub of separatist activity (see page 127). Collectively run, its events spanned everything from women's music to radical lesbian discussions to poetry readings. Many lesbians who cared nothing about separatist theory loved this woman-only space simply because they had a good time there; the atmosphere fostered feelings of freedom and community that they felt nowhere else.

Many small, local newsletters with varying leanings toward separatism were produced, but probably the most substantial work on separatism appeared in 1988: For Lesbians Only: A Separatist Anthology, edited by Chicagoan Sarah Lucia Hoagland and Julia Penelope. HOT WIRE magazine, a separatist publication focused on the positive aspects of lesbian feminism, maintained a policy of being published by, for and about women. ▼

JACKIE ANDERSON

Second-generation Chicagoan Jacqueline Anderson was born in 1942 into a middle-class African-American family who started her on her path of lifelong activism. "I felt strongly that there was an obligation to pay back the debt I owed to other Black folks who made me possible," she recalls.

As a young woman she joined the Young People's Socialist League and read leftist politics and philosophy: "I understood what racism was really about through reading Plato's Republic, so I studied philosophy because it made things make sense. My relationship to philosophy is to some degree radical. I feel that philosophy is relevant, it's useful as a way of doing analysis." From 1975 until her retirement in 2007, Anderson taught humanities and philosophy at Olive-Harvey College, one of the City Colleges of Chicago, and has published in such journals as Signs: Journal of Women in Culture and Society.

Jackie Anderson's devotion to creative social empowerment has had a major impact on the Chicago lesbian community and demonstrates how much one person can do to effect change. Her long list of volunteering in the gay and lesbian community includes playing pivotal roles in the founding of several important organizations. She was on the first board of the Lesbian Community Cancer Project (LCCP) and helped to establish an LCCP clinic on Chicago's South Side. She was on the board of Les-BiGay Radio, and was a central figure in the beginnings of Affinity. In the 1980s, she founded Yahimba, a monthly newsletter, as a way of connecting people and events beyond the bar scene in Chicago, and her leadership of the Yahimba organization resulted in at least two citywide conferences specifically addressing needs of African-American lesbians. She has been a supporter of the Institute of Lesbian Studies and the Gerber/Hart Library, and a collective member of Mountain Moving Coffeehouse. She is a past board president of Performers or Writers for Women on Women's Issues (POW-WOW), an African-American lesbian community organization dedicated to supporting the arts and providing safe space for women from vulnerable communities.

Jackie Anderson. Photo by Hal Baim.

A tireless and well-respected activist, fundraiser and organizer, Anderson has been a constructive and inspiring role model in the community for many years. — **Jorjet Harper**

TWO WOMEN
AND
THEIR MUSIC

an evening with
MARGIE ADAM
&
GINNI CLEMMENS

Monday, November 3, 1975

Admission: $3.00   Performances: 7:30 & 9:30

Advance tickets available at Old Town School Of Folk Music, 909 W. Armitage

Second City
1616 North Wells
Information: 337-3992

A.S.K. productions

Left: Toni Armstrong Jr. (right) with Melissa Etheridge at the 1993 March on Washington. Photo courtesy Toni Armstrong Jr. Right: A 1975 women's concert flier. Courtesy M. Kuda Archives, Oak Park, Ill.

WOMEN'S MUSIC TAKES CENTER STAGE *by JORJET HARPER*

THE LESBIAN-FEMINIST MUSIC SCENE THAT began in the early 1970s was a grassroots movement of music by, for and about women. For the most part it was consciously created with the idea that women would be the controlling force in every step of the process—not only the artistic aspects, but also the business and technical aspects. The term "women's music" actually encompassed an enormous range of cultural activities, businesses and art forms in addition to music. Women's music itself was never one musical genre or style; it was defined as much by its audience as by its artists. That audience was overwhelmingly lesbian, but many bisexual women and some straight feminists were also enthusiastic supporters.

Chicago was a major concert destination for women's music performers. In addition to local musicians such as Ginni Clemmens, Linda Shear and the band Surrender Dorothy, nationally known women's music pioneers such as Meg Christian, Holly Near, Margie Adam, Mary Watkins, Cris

Williamson and Kay Gardner performed to large crowds in Chicago.

Mountain Moving Coffeehouse was a regular venue for women-only concerts, and early on, producers such as Thelma Norris arranged concerts of nationally touring artists at rented church and university halls around the city. Women & Children First Bookstore in Chicago and Val's Halla in Oak Park offered recordings of lesbian artists at a time when they were unknown in the mainstream. Windy City Times and Outlines newspapers gave extensive coverage to women's music events. HOT WIRE: The Journal of Women's Music and Culture was produced in Chicago, as well as the Women's Music Plus Directory, the trade publication for the women's music industry. Chicago, and the Midwest in general, became a linchpin in the national network of women's culture built by the momentum of women's concert events.

Part of the philosophy of the movement was to offer women the opportunity to learn music-industry skills, since women were largely locked out of the

mainstream music business. Ignored when not openly vilified by society at large, lesbians turned to each other for encouragement and appreciation, and music was a natural way of expressing lesbian experience, solidifying friendships and building community. This we-can-do-it-ourselves spirit led some women to consider, for the first time, professions such as sound, lighting, media distribution, and production.

The National Women's Music Festival, the first women's festival in the nation, was founded in 1974 by Kristin Lems, a straight feminist singer-songwriter; it took place in Illinois and later at other Midwest locations. The women-only Michigan Womyn's Music Festival was founded the following year. Both are still held annually. Many of the workers at these festivals came from Chicago and its suburbs, and technicians who trained on women's music stages in Chicago went on to become sound engineers and other staff members at these large festivals.

As it grew, women's music came to involve not only women-identified performers, concert producers, and technicians, but also photographers, cartoonists, filmmakers, visual artists, craftswomen, record labels, festivals, theater troupes, choirs, recordings, record distributors, radio women and the Women in Print movement, with its expanding roster of writers, periodicals, feminist bookstores, writers' support groups, conferences and publishing ventures. In Chicago, concert producers took overtly lesbian music into mainstream music venues such as Park West.

Inclusivity and accessibility were central tenets of the movement. For example, women's music leaders initiated the idea of presenting signers onstage during concerts and other events, a practice that was later introduced into the mainstream. Concerts and festivals offered a safe, nurturing environment where lesbian and bisexual women could see out lesbians onstage, forge new alliances and gain the courage they needed to deal with homophobia in their lives. The movement empowered women to come out at their jobs and to their families, and to accomplish more than society led them to believe they could.

Around the country, many of these women became activists who went on to create new organizations in their home communities that were not specific to the music. Moved by their firsthand experience of being among other lesbians in a joyous, intensely lesbian cultural setting, they embraced the message that "you are not alone" and also saw confirmation of the feminist notion that "the personal is political."

The women's music movement generated independent artists, local production companies and independent record labels long before MP3s and the Internet. Starting with a handful of musicians and other women dedicated to creating and distributing woman-identified music despite the hostility of society, the power of the huge music industry machinery, and the indifference of popular culture, the women's music network grew to include hundreds of performers and many thousands of fans. Chicago played a crucial role in that growth.

"At a time when it was difficult to be taken seriously as a female artist or musician, and lesbians had a difficult time finding halls that would rent to them, printers that would print openly lesbian fliers, and most lesbians were afraid to come out of the closet, the women's music movement created spaces to celebrate women's lives, lesbianism and feminism," recalled HOT WIRE publisher Toni Armstrong Jr. in a 2005 interview with Queer Music Heritage. "And it created its own festivals and its own publications and its own recording labels and its own everything. It became more professional, more encompassing, and eventually larger and more mainstream."

The Chicago History Museum, in fact, became the first mainstream historical society to acknowledge the impact of lesbian-feminist music and culture upon American culture and politics, hosting a daylong celebration of women's music with speeches, panels and performances in 2004 as part of its Out at CHM gay program series. ▼

MOVING MOUNTAINS

Mountain Moving Coffeehouse for Womyn and Children was the longest continuously operating women-only concert venue in the United States. It was founded in 1974 by a group of lesbian activists, including Beth O'Neil and Nancy Katz, who also ran Women In Crisis Can Act (WICCA), a women's crisis hotline. Named for the Mountain Moving Day album recorded in 1972 by the Chicago Women's Liberation Rock Band and the New Haven Women's Liberation Rock Band, the coffeehouse was, from its inception, a women-only space, conceived as a safe space where women could socialize and enjoy woman-identified, feminist entertainment. As a drug-free, sober space, it provided an important alternative to the bars as a place to meet other lesbians.

Though "coffeehouse" might seem to imply a cafe-type storefront operation, Mountain Moving Coffeehouse was in fact a rented, once-a-week gathering space in a local church. In its heyday from the late 1970s to the early 1990s, MMCH presented up to 40 shows a year, often featuring local lesbian talent but also offering to touring musicians, comedians and well-known lesbian-feminist authors a venue in which to appear before Chicago's lesbian audiences.

A large, enthusiastic collective of members was responsible for booking

MMCH *flier. Courtesy M. Kuda Archives.*

acts, organizing publicity and running the coffeehouse space during events.

Its weekly women-only concerts sometimes attracted large crowds, especially for headliners of the burgeoning women's music movement or for its Lesbians of Color nights. The coffeehouse also sponsored panel discussions, offered readings of lesbian plays and poetry, and put on an annual Midwinter Minifest holiday fair featuring arts and crafts by local lesbian craftswomen.

In the late 1980s, pressure was sometimes put on the coffeehouse to admit men, and beginning in the 1990s its door-policy restrictions aroused the ire of some male-to-female transsexuals, but the coffeehouse staunchly maintained a right to admit only "women-born women." Although it moved locations several times over the years, at times experienced high turnover and philosophical disputes among collective members, and in its last years presented fewer shows, the coffeehouse nevertheless continued to provide Chicago lesbians with a showcase for lesbian talent for a remarkable 31 years before closing its doors in 2005. The last women's music artist to perform there, on closing night, was Deidre McCalla.

The final MMCH collective members were Kathy Munzer, Jackie Anderson, Luanne Adamis and Cheryl Pattin. — *Jorjet Harper*

MEN IN BLACK: INTERNATIONAL MR. LEATHER *by RON EHEMANN*

INTERNATIONAL MR. LEATHER (IML) WAS founded by business and life partners Chuck Renslow and Dom "Etienne" Orejudos in 1979. Then co-owners of the Gold Coast leather bar, the pair were looking for a larger venue for their popular Mr. Gold Coast Contest, which had outgrown its namesake.

Working together with Gold Coast manager Patrick Batt, they moved the contest to the Grand Ballroom of Chicago's Radisson Hotel, changing the name to International Mr. Leather. In 2008, celebrating 30 years, IML is the oldest and largest contest-weekend event of its kind.

In 1979, there were 12 contestants from six states. Four hundred people packed the audience. Fast-forward 30 years: The 2007 IML contest boasted 53 contestants from 23 states and four foreign nations. As for spectators, 1,800 filled the historic Chicago Theatre to watch the 2007 contest. Countless more attended one or more of the official and unofficial events surrounding IML that stretched over five days and nights. One of the more popular official events, the post-contest victory celebration, has developed a life of its own on the circuit-party scene. To accommodate the extra volume, recently two victory parties have been held simultaneously—one at the House of Blues and one at the host hotel.

Most recently, the host hotel has been the 2,100-room Hyatt Regency. In prior years, the Palmer House Hilton, the Congress Hotel, the Lake Shore Hotel (now demolished), a Days Inn on North Lake Shore Drive (where the W Chicago Lakeshore hotel is today), and the Executive House hotel have hosted. In most years, the host hotel adds bars (and sometimes dance floors) to its lobby, effectively creating the world's largest leather bar, if only for the weekend.

While contestants spend their days Friday and Saturday in private prejudging interviews, everyone

else visits the Leather Market, which boasts upward of 300 vendors and artisans.

On Saturday night the official function is physique judging, the leather equivalent of a "swimsuit competition." The next night, physique and prejudging interview scores are combined to pare the contestants down to 20 semifinalists.

Sunday night, semifinalists are announced. They appear in another "swimsuit" parade as well as one in

1981 IML poster, courtesy Chuck Renslow and Leather Archives & Museum.

"total leather look." In addition, each of the competitors addresses the audience for up to 90 seconds on a topic of his choice related to leather. Often these set the tone for the winner's agenda as a titleholder.

Titleholders are selected by a panel of nine judges. With the exception of years one and two, the retiring titleholder has always served as one of the judges. Until his untimely death in 1991, co-founder Orejudos served as chief judge. West Coast leather journalist Mr. Marcus was another perennial member of the judging team for many years. Today he remains a "judge emeritus." The last of the "recurring judges" was Thom Dombkowski, who served as chief judge from 1992 through 2001. (He died in 2006.)

These days, a different panel of judges is selected

to pick the titleholder each year, with an eye toward diversity in such varied areas as geography, sex, race, age and even sexual orientation. Indeed, the invitation to judge IML is often made to effect or acknowledge social change within the leather communities. The first International Ms Leather, Judy Tallwing-McCarthey, judged the 2003 contest. Mistress Diamond, the author and noted straight dominatrix, was the first non-gay judge, joining the panel in 1998.

Historically, IML has provided entertainment to fill the time between the parades of contestants. In 1979, the comedian Pudgy became the first IML headliner. Other performers have included Judy Tenuta, Hal Sparks, Scott Thompson, Bruce Vilanch, Bronski Beat, the Village People, Linda Clifford, Linda Imperial, Jeanie Tracy, Jo Carol, Vicki Shepard, Bonnie Pointer, Erin Hamilton and Thelma Houston. Chicago groups such as the Righteously Outrageous Twirling Corps (R.O.T.C.), the Chicago Meatpackers, the She-Devils, the Joel Hall Dancers, and the Midnight Circus have performed on IML's stage.

IML Weekend ends on Monday night with the infamous Black and Blue Ball. During IML's formative pre-AIDS years, this official event was held inside Man's Country bathhouse and billed as a "Roman orgy." Today, in homage to its roots, it is a high-energy dance party primarily populated by throngs of shirtless and half-naked people who just don't want the weekend to end. For at least seven years the Black and Blue Ball has been held at Excalibur nightclub.

The first IML titleholder was David Kloss, sponsored by the Brig in San Francisco. The next year, IML lived up to its grandiose name; IML80 was Patrick Brooks, Mr. Leather Australia from Sydney. He won a motorcycle, which cost more to ship home than its retail value. Texan Coulter "Colt" Thomas won the 1983 title and passed it on to Denver's Ron Moore,

IML's first Black titleholder. By 1985, AIDS entered the communities' consciousness, a fact reflected in the contestants' speeches and the winner's agenda. Titleholder Patrick Toner (Chaps, San Francisco) made AIDS-related fundraising his mission. Sadly, in coming years Colt Thomas, Ron Moore and Patrick Toner would succumb to the disease. IML87, Thomas Karasch (Mr. Leather Europe, Hamburg), took the American concept of free condoms back to Europe. Others invested their time in bridging gaps they perceived in the leather communities.

A Philadelphian, Scott Tucker, won the title in 1986 in part because of his contest speech urging unity between leather men and women. That year IML was asked if it objected to another organization's adopting a variation of IML's name: Subsequently, International Ms Leather was born.

Harry Shattuck set up as a bootblack at the 1992 Leather Market. A contestant in the first IML, then again in 1986, Shattuck sought to establish bootblacks in a contest of their own. The following year, 1993, he accomplished that goal, and the International Mr. Bootblack competition and title have become a part of IML Weekend.

IML depends upon the entire community (local, national and international) to succeed. The 2007 IML Weekend required more than 300 staff members, virtually all of whom are volunteers. Among the many who have contributed to IML's growth and success are Jim Dohr, Jon Krongaard, Harley McMillen, R.J. Chaffin, Gary Chichester, Doug Newitt, Bill Stadt and this writer, Ron Ehemann.

Early after-parties were always held in community bars until their numbers grew unmanageable. As word of the weekend in Chicago spread, people began to pour into the city each year. Today, IML attracts more than 15,000 people to Chicago each year.

For more information, see International Mr. Leather: 25 Years of Champions, edited and written by Joseph W. Bean, Nazca Plains Corp. (2004); Leather Archives & Museum, 6418 N. Greenview Ave., Chicago, Ill. 60626, www. leatherarchives.org. ▼

Images from past IML weekends. Courtesy Leather Archives & Museum and Gay Chicago Magazine.

LGBT THEATER IN CHICAGO   *by JONATHAN ABARBANEL*

GAY MEN ALWAYS HAVE BEEN PART OF THEATER; JUST READ MARY
Renault's The Mask of Apollo. Often harder to track, lesbian women probably have been part of theater since women were given professional access, from the mid-17th century on.

Until recent times, however, gay and lesbian theater was a matter of influence or suggestion rather than anything overt. Social reformer and Hull House founder Jane Addams was a lesbian, but that didn't make the notable Hull House theater program LGBT. Indeed, it was a wholesome contrast to Chicago's infamous First Ward Ball, an annual drag gala at the turn of the last century that drew many local theater folk. Circa 1900–60, gay men and women used "gaydar" to understand performances and performers who were PLU ("people like us") or sympathetic, among them Lillian Russell, Noël Coward, Clifton Webb, Tallulah Bankhead, rival opera divas Maria Callas and Renata Tebaldi and the plays of Tennessee Williams. It was a period when artists such as Langston Hughes and Lorraine Hansberry (A Raisin in the Sun) sharpened their writing skills in Chicago without revealing their sexual identities.

Stonewall, the great dividing point of LGBT history, was the stimulus that lesbian and gay theater artists needed to openly announce their sexuality and to create theater that spoke directly to their themes and issues. By the early 1970s, Chicago could claim several pioneering "gay" theaters, among them the Godzilla Rainbow Troupe (1971–74) of Garry Tucker (aka Eleven), who introduced Theatre of the Ridiculous, genderfuck and the midnight curtain to Chicago; the Artemis Players (mid-1970s), a lesbian-oriented women's theater company; and the Drama Shelter (circa 1972–80), the storefront theater of lovers Daryl Hale and Ron Hitchcock.

The Drama Shelter did some straight plays but made its fame on gay fare, notably the plays of Robert Patrick. By decade's end Rick Paul's Lionheart gay theater (1979–94) assumed primacy, eventually producing more than 100 plays by writers such as Jeff Hagedorn, Lawrence Bommer and Nicholas Patricca. Hagedorn earned a footnote in drama history by writing the first play produced on the subject of AIDS, One, which premiered in Chicago.

As Chicago's off-Loop theater industry grew, the pioneer troupes were succeeded by a number of LGBT companies, among them Theatre Q, Zebra Crossing, A Real Read (an African-American group including Byron Stewart, Sanford Gaylord and C.C. Carter) and the Pansy Kings, a mid-1990s vaudeville-style showcase for gay male performers that nurtured a number of important artists such as solo performers David Kodeski and Edward Thomas-Herrera, video artist and poet Kurt Heintz, novelist Robert Rodi, writer Dave Awl and songwriter Eric Lane Barnes.

The progress of the last 25 years has been so significant that Chicago gay and lesbian artists and troupes scarcely need special theatrical identities today. Out theater artists and managers are integrated in every possible facet of Chicago's booming

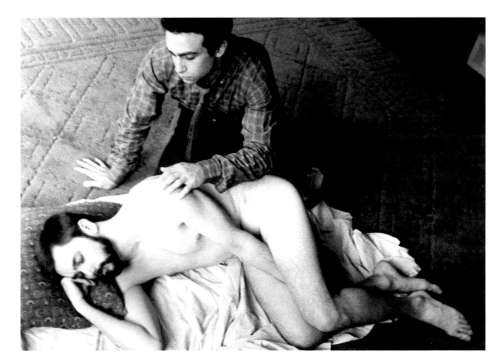

Left: A scene from the play Johns, which opened June 24, 1982, by Party Productions Company. Right: I Am My Own Wife premiered at Chicago's About Face Theatre in 2003, starring Jefferson Mays. It went on to win the 2004 Tony Award. Windy City Times archive photos.

theater industry from producers to ushers, playwrights to prop masters, and academics to theater critics.

Among Chicago theaters today that self-identify as LGBT-specific are About Face, Bailiwick, Easy Street Players, GayCo, Hell in a Handbag, Hubris, Ludicrous, Mid Tangent Productions and the People's Theatre. An additional number of troupes boast female-centered identities without being specifically lesbian, among them Babes With Blades, Footsteps (now defunct), Rivendell, Stockyards Theatre Project, Sweat Girls, Teatro Luna and 20% Theatre Company. More-casual performance programs also address specifics of gay and particularly lesbian sexuality, including the Drag Kings of Comedy, Dyke Mic, Chick Magnets and Bailiwick's Second Sex series. Perhaps more importantly, more than three dozen local professional theaters have LGBT founders and artistic or managing directors, among them several of the largest commercial and nonprofit companies.

Chicago has been the birthplace of a number of nationally prominent works that reflect LGBT history or issues, such as David Dillon's much-produced Party; Doug Wright's I Am My Own Wife; Patricia Kane's Pulp; the Alfred Kinsey musical comedy Dr. Sex; and Loving Repeating, the Gertrude Stein musical fashioned by Frank Galati and Stephen Flaherty. The late Scott McPherson's Marvin's Room—first produced at the Goodman Theatre—may be the single most important LGBT work to emerge from Chicago. Although not gay in its story, the play was McPherson's passionate and profound response to the AIDS crisis that took his life too soon.

In addition to those already named, a woefully incomplete list of Chicago LGBT theater artists who have made an impact over the last 25 years must include playwrights Claudia Allen, Sarah Gubbins, Joel Drake Johnson, Dwight Okita, Barbara Lhota, Paula Berg and John Logan (Never the Sinner); producer Vicki Quade (co-creator and producer of Late Nite Catechism); directors L.M. Attea, Frank Carioti, Scott Ferguson, Gary Griffin, Patrick O'Gara, Tina Landau, Eric Rosen, L. Walter Stearns and David Zak; writer-director-actors Michael Martin, Bev Spangler and Amy Matheny; designers and stage managers too numerous to name; and a string of performers who have achieved national success such as Alexandra Billings, Cherry Jones, Denis O'Hare, Maripat Donovan and David Sedaris.

Long-time partners Steve Scott and Ted Hoerl are integral parts of the theater scene, Scott as an associate producer at Goodman Theatre, along with teaching positions, and Hoerl as an actor and director, as well as an adjunct instructor at Roosevelt University.

Of special note are Malik Gillani and Jamil Khoury, co-founders of the Silk Road Theatre Project, who are respectively of South Asian and Middle Eastern ethnicity. Openly a couple, they rapidly are becoming nationally known for the diverse range of sexual and nonsexual issues raised by their productions, and for fostering growing recognition of diverse Asian theater artists and audiences. ▼

An early 1900s skit by Little Club, with men in drag and "blackface," a white performer playing a Black person. Contrast that with A Real Read (right), a gay performance group of the 1990s. Photos courtesy the Chicago History Museum and Byron Stewart from A Real Read.

Claudia Allen in 2007. Photo by Hal Baim.

SHE LIKES GIRLS BEST: CLAUDIA ALLEN

by JORJET HARPER

CLAUDIA ALLEN IS PERHAPS THE MOST PROLIFIC CONTEMPORARY writer of lesbian-themed plays. Born in 1954, she grew up in Clare, Mich., and moved to Chicago in 1979. Of Allen's repertoire of 24 produced plays, 11 have either a lesbian relationship as the central focus or a major character who is lesbian or bisexual.

Allen is playwright in residence at Chicago's Victory Gardens Theater and has been associated with that playhouse for more than two decades, but her plays have also been produced at many other Chicago venues and at theaters around the country. Her works are wide-ranging and always contain elements of humor; Allen describes a recurring central theme as "people finally getting the nerve to do what they want."

"I wrote lesbian-themed plays because I wasn't seeing what I wanted to watch," she recalls. "I started writing them thinking I was never going to make any money at them but that they were important stories to tell. My plays are a gift to me as much as to anybody, and it's been interesting to watch the world catch up, because I was writing years ago about things people were scared to do. The directors and actresses in those early productions were also pioneers, because it was not many years ago that so many actors just wouldn't play lesbian and gay roles, out of fear."

Movie Queens, about two rival actresses who were in love years before, when they were both closeted Hollywood movie stars, originally premiered as a one-act play at Stonewall Repertory Theater in New York, then was expanded into a full-length play for Chicago's Zebra Crossing Theater in 1990. Hannah Free premiered at Chicago's Bailiwick Repertory Theatre in 1992 and is still Allen's most frequently produced lesbian-themed play, about a lifelong rocky lesbian love affair. "I wanted to put a human face on some legal issues that lesbians and gays have—particularly end-of-life issues," she says. Her very popular and amusing sendup of soap operas, Gays of Our Lives, was presented at Zebra Crossing and has been done in a number of other cities, including Los Angeles and San Diego. Raincheck, Roomers, Dutch Love, A Gay Christmas Carol, and a musical comedy called Xena Lives are also among her works. At Victory Gardens in 2001, renowned actress Julie Harris starred in the premiere of Fossils, a two-character play about 70-year-old women—a schoolteacher and a retired college professor—who meet at a bed-and-breakfast and fall in love.

Chicago magazine chose Allen as Best Playwright in 1999. She has won two Joseph Jefferson Awards and five Jeff nominations. She was given the Trailblazer Award from the Bailiwick Repertory Theatre "for demonstrating excellence in playwriting, and for moving lesbian plays from the theatrical fringe to the artistic center."

Allen teaches playwriting at Victory Gardens and has also taught at the University of Chicago and Lake Forest College. Four of her lesbian-themed plays were published as a collection, She's Always Liked the Girls Best, in 1993, by Chicago's Third Side Press. ▼

Left: A Lionheart flier. Center: Playwright Nick Patricca circa 1973. Right: Rick Paul (second from left) with Lionheart members, circa 1980 at the Pride Parade. Images courtesy M. Kuda Archives, Oak Park, Ill., Nick Patricca and GayLife newspaper.

HEART OF A LION   *by TRACY BAIM*

RICK PAUL'S LIONHEART GAY/LESBIAN Theatre Company, also known as Lionheart Gay Theatre, operated from 1979 to 1994, producing more than 100 plays, including the first produced AIDS-subject play, One, which premiered in Chicago.

"I stopped counting at 100 deaths of friends, acquaintances, and co-workers," said Paul in 2007. "We did the world's first play (and theatrical benefit) about the AIDS health crisis and the first plays that came to be called 'the second wave' of AIDS plays. Many of the actors who did Jefferson Hagedorn's One at the Edinburgh Festival and in Manchester, U.K., as well as Chicago and the New Orleans World's Fair eventually died of the disease, yet they were out there warning the gay world. I'm eternally proud of all of them. True pioneers."

Paul said he feels he "truly helped gay and lesbian actors and playwrights come out and present Chicago and Midwest stories, [and] not be dependent on New York, London, San Francisco to define gay life." He also said he feels he showed that "everything theatri-

cal can be of direct financial assistance to the community."

In 2007, Paul recalled a train ride to the 1979 March on Washington for gay rights: "George Buse, a wonderful journalist and actor who I worked with a bunch of times ... we were in the bar car of the train. ... George started regaling us with stories about his time in World War II, at Iwo Jima, the flag raising. When he was finished, we were so enthralled by his tales, that I said, 'George, you're a writer and you're an actor. Why don't you write a play of that and I'll produce it.' And within about a year, I formed Lionheart and we started doing only plays by Chicago gay and lesbian playwrights, because that was part of the spirit of what came to be called the Off Loop Chicago theater movement. ... We never had our own home base, no. So many theaters owed me money [Paul recently retired from a 40-year career as a scene designer for stage and film] I'd say, 'Give me an off night, or give me a weekend when you're not doing a show,' and we'd barter that way."

Nicholas A. Patricca is among Chicago's most treasured gay playwrights, and he was among those early Lionheart pioneers. He is a playwright in residence at Victory Gardens Theater and has been active in the Chicago theater movement since the mid-1970s. Among his works is Oh, Holy Allen Ginsberg, which deals with the struggle of a gay Roman Catholic priest in Chicago to be honest about his sexuality while remaining faithful to his church.

Patricca's play The Examen was performed at Victory Gardens in 1980 and was among the first gay plays at a mainstream venue in Chicago. "The Examen was kind of prophetic in that it described the life of a man who became pope almost by accident, who was homoerotic but did not have a sexual relationship with anyone. More importantly, he has a vision of how the church should change. And he died one month after being in office. This was uncanny, because in 1979 that actually happened, and I had written about it in 1977. In 1979 it actually happened to John Paul I." ▼

Chicago Gay Men's Chorus in the Pride Parade, 1988, photo by Lisa Howe-Ebright. At right, CGMC's Encore! group.

SINGING OUT: THE CHORAL MOVEMENT   *by JORJET HARPER*

CHICAGO'S FIRST GAY CHORAL GROUP, Windy City Gay Chorus, premiered Dec. 16, 1979, during the first Chicago Gay Pride Band concert, "Don We Now..." at Stages Music Hall. The chorus was formed by Jerry Carlson, Gordon Chiola, Matt Wycislak, and Don Heering, who had all been members of the band. Although WCGC's first director, Richard Garrin, would conduct the group until 1995, that first performance of 37 singers was conducted by Carlson, who later became conductor of the Gay Men's Chorus of Los Angeles.

At that first concert, WCGC announced its mission "to create, nurture, and maintain performing arts ensembles of the highest level of artistic quality for the purpose of engendering gay and lesbian pride." The chorus offered primarily serious choral works and was known for its musical

excellence. It quickly became a cultural ambassador for both the city and the gay community.

Three years after its founding, the WCGC had 72 members, and its campy offshoot, the Windy City Slickers, had 17. It was the first gay chorus to enter the Great American Choral Festival, where it won first-place awards. On Feb. 14, 1982, WCGC sang at Avery Fisher Hall in Lincoln Center as part of a memorable joint concert with the New York City Gay Men's Chorus. "For many years we performed at least one concert a year in another city, bringing gay people out into various arts groups. It had that kind of impact," says Mark Sherkow, who joined the chorus in 1982 and is currently its manager.

Chicago's lesbian chorus, Artemis Singers, is the first lesbian chorus in the nation. The group's initial meeting took place in June 1979. Joel Carothers,

who was inspired by her work in the Gay Pride Band, was among those at that first meeting. By December 1980 Artemis was formally introduced at the "Don We Now ... II" concert, with Susan Schleef conducting. In 1986 Artemis hosted the Third National Women's Choral Festival in Chicago, which included women's choruses from Minneapolis, Kansas City, Lansing, Milwaukee, Cincinnati, St. Louis and Madison. Always smaller than the gay men's choirs, Artemis has nevertheless survived and continues to perform at lesbian, LGBT and women's events 28 years after its founding. (In early 2008, current and former members joined together to honor longtime Artemis member Michaeline Chvatal, who had died of cancer at age 60.)

The first gathering of gay and lesbian choruses was Come Out and Sing Together (COAST) in

1982, out of which grew today's international organization Gay and Lesbian Association of Choruses (GALA). At the gathering, held in New York City at Alice Tully Hall in Lincoln Center, Chicago was represented by 15 members of Artemis and a group of about 40 men, mostly members of WCGC. Among all the men's and mixed choruses, Artemis was the only lesbian chorus to perform, and the other groups were so supportive that Artemis received a standing ovation even before they began to sing.

The event also proved important for the Chicago men's group, as this core group of singers—including Kip Snyder, Phil Steward, Danny Kopelson and a number of others—returned to Chicago to found the Chicago Gay Men's Chorus (CGMC) in 1983 with an initial roster of 80 singers. CGMC leaned toward more popular, less classical music than WCGC. Because of its origins at COAST, the CGMC became the opening chorus at all GALA concerts. Unlike the WCGC, the CGMC did not hold auditions; any gay man who liked to sing could join. Kip Snyder directed the group for 15 years, with Patrick Sinozich as accompanist; Sinozich has now been the CGMC director for a decade. Performances have included original musical revues, popular productions, full-length book musicals, and traditional choral concerts. CGMC has traveled extensively across North America, representing Chicago in cities including Montreal, New York, Los Angeles and New Orleans.

Both CGMC and WCGC have recorded several CDs of their music. All of Chicago's community choirs, including Artemis, have shared the stage for AIDS benefits at the Park West in 1985 and the Chicago Theatre in 1987. Chicago's men's choruses have been particularly hard-hit by deaths from AIDS.

The success of each chorus led to other choral endeavors. Windy City Performing Arts, the umbrella organization of the WCGC that also includes Windy City Slickers, formed Unison, a mixed chorus of men and women, in 1992, and then the women's group Aria. CGMC formed Encore! as a lively small ensemble, and the mixed Chicago Gay and Lesbian Chorus.

Recalling the early days of the choral movement in Chicago, Kopelson reflected: "Before all the choruses there was not a lot of opportunities for gays and lesbians to be together. They gave a creative opportunity to people who all loved music and theater in high school but never went on with it as a career. The beauty of it was, it brought diverse groups and people of different ages together who never would have met in bars." ▼

Windy City Gay Chorus in a publicity photo.

Artemis Singers in the 1980s, and the group's logo. Photo courtesy Vada Vernee.

Toddlin' Town Performing Arts Inc.
presents

Chicago Gay Pride Band
and Windy City Gay Chorus

Simple Gifts
a Spring musical celebration

April 19,1980

Left: An early 1980s fundraiser for Toddlin' Town Performing Arts with members from both the Chicago Gay/Lesbian Community Band and Windy City Gay Men's Chorus. The brass quartet members are Joel Carothers and Scott Buchanan on trumpet, Don Dayhoff on euphonium and Edgar Borchardt on tuba. Courtesy GayLife archives. Right: A 1980 program book. Courtesy Alfredo Gomez, Jr.

PRIDE BANDS: 76 TROMBONES IN THE BIG PARADE

by JORJET HARPER

THE GAY BAND MOVEMENT WAS BORN from the desire to have marching bands in the annual Pride parades. Trombone player and music teacher Alfredo Gomez, inspired by word that other bands had formed in San Francisco and Los Angeles, called a meeting at his home in early 1979. The group named itself the Chicago Gay Pride Band and began rehearsing weekly. There were no auditions, but the ability to read music was important. Mary Peck spearheaded the band's debut in the Pride parade that June, where they performed the National Emblem March and March "Grandioso," with Carl Forsberg as drum major.

"We saw it as an outlet for personal freedom, as a way to share something meaningful with other musicians, and to show that you can express yourself in every way that you are," says Gomez. "And

we wanted the community to see that gays were much more than a bunch of drunken queens falling off of floats in the Pride parade." The band performed concerts as well. In December 1979, the first "Don We Now ..." concert was presented at Stages Music Hall, 3730 N. Clark St., with Marvin Carlton conducting 28 musicians. They played a mix of classical and popular music and some holiday favorites. Chicago's first gay chorus, the Windy City Gay Chorus, was introduced at that concert.

Many concerts followed. A spring concert in 1980 featured 32 musicians. The WCGC again performed at the band's "Don We Now ... II" concert the following December along with the more pop-oriented Windy City Slickers. The concert introduced the Artemis Singers, conducted by Susan Schleef. Program notes for that concert

commented that the band "has engendered a new sense of respect and pride in ourselves as well as in the gay community." The band's name was changed after the second concert to the Chicago Gay and Lesbian Community Marching Band (CGLCMB).

In October 1982, Chicago hosted and was the founding organization of the first national conference of GLBT bands from around the country, in what would become the LGBA—Lesbian and Gay Bands of America. Seven bands were represented. Members of other gay bands who were in town made guest appearances at the CGLCMB's fall concert, which coincided with the conference, along with the Orpheus Ensemble and the Windy City Jazz Band. By December 1982 the CGLCMB had also performed at other community events and civic events around Chicago.

"When you get a bunch of gay men and women together you can really have a lot of fun," recalls trumpet player Joel Carothers. "We became more focused as time went on. We made good music, had many good musicians, and that was always a thrill."

Despite its momentum, however, the CGLCMB only lasted three years as an organization. In September 1988, a new group, the Great Lakes Freedom Band (GLFB), formed "for the purpose of providing a creative musical outlet for its members and to serve as a cultural, social, and educational vehicle for the benefit of the gay and lesbian community and the community at large." It debuted on Dec. 10, 1988, with Marvin J. Carl-ton, a veteran of the earlier band, as conductor and artistic director. The GLFB included several chamber music groups made up of band members, and a number of musicians who had been in the CGLCMB.

Chicago's current marching band, the Lakeside Pride Freedom Band (LPFB), is now more than a decade old. Drum major Jon Dallas, who marched in Chicago's Pride parade in 1997, served as catalyst for the LPFB's formation. Initially under the name Chicago Black Lesbian & Gay Marching Band, five people attended the first organizational meeting on July 8, 1997, and by September they were rehears-ing at Preston Bradley Center, 941 W. Lawrence Ave. Under the new name Lakeside Pride Freedom Band, the group debuted on Dec. 1, 1997, outside the Ann Sather restaurant on West Belmont Avenue. It successfully expanded to include an associated Color Guard in what is now called the Lakeside Pride Music Ensembles. This umbrella organization includes not only the marching band and color guard but also the Lakeside Pride Symphonic Band, Lakeside Pride Orchestra, the jazz ensemble Shout!, and small ensembles including brass and clarinet choirs, a saxophone ensemble, a women's ensemble, a polka band (Queer as Polka) and the holiday-season Lakeside Pride Toyland Band. The groups have a total active membership of more than a hundred musicians, and their Web site is www.LakesidePride.org. ▼

Lakeside Pride in the 2007 Chicago Pride Parade. Photo by Tracy Baim, taken from the roof of the Center on Halsted.

"don we now..."

PFLAG in the Pride Parade, from 1980s, to 1990s, to 2006. Photos by Tracy Baim and Lisa Howe-Ebright.

POWER OF LOVE: PFLAG IN CHICAGO *by JOHN CEPEK*

DURING CHICAGO'S PRIDE PARADE IN 1981, THE CROWDS cheered the first banner of Parents and Friends of Lesbians and Gays (PFLAG; Families was added later), and every year since, the acclaim has compounded. To the community, PFLAG is a symbol. In a world that can be hostile, PFLAG represents the power of love and acceptance when family and friends embrace the wonder of sexual diversity. Simply stated, the purpose of PFLAG is to change the world, one person at a time.

Chicago had no group for parents of gays when Guy Warner was looking for support for his mother. Finding none, he started a group. PFLAG did not exist yet, but under the auspices of Mattachine Midwest, Guy founded Chicago's Parents of Gays in March 1977 "to serve the needs of those in need." It soon became clear that the friendship and understanding of other parents can be the biggest help of all. By December 1978, the group had about 50 members and attracted parents of various social and religious backgrounds from all over the city and suburbs.

Warner's group soon became part of the national PFLAG movement. A vital presence for more than 30 years, Chicago PFLAG lives on. Thousands of families and individuals—gay and straight alike—have been touched, directly and indirectly, by the folks who gathered there. Vigorous chapters and ever-expanding activities continue throughout the Chicago area. By 1990, PFLAG Suburban had formed in Hinsdale, followed by another chapter in Glenview in 1994. Now there are chapters in Aurora, Oak Park, Palatine, and Woodstock. A Spanish-speaking chapter, Entre Familia, has also formed. Chicago-area PFLAG groups have consolidated administrative functions and larger advocacy projects into the PFLAG Council of Northern Illinois.

PFLAG has grown over the years, and its work has expanded as well; it is America's largest gay-straight alliance. In addition to supporting parents, PFLAG has become more involved with advocacy, including participating in lobby days in Springfield, Ill., and Washington, D.C. Locally, PFLAG members attended the hearings at the Crystal Lake Park District in support of the Gay Games rowing event in 2006. They also hosted the Midwest regional PFLAG conference and board of directors meeting in November 2006.

In short, PFLAG Chicago chapters welcome everyone: gay, lesbian, bisexual, transgender, and straight. In the words of the PFLAG motto, "You have a home in PFLAG." ▼

John Cepek is a leader in the local and national PFLAG movement.

MILITARY MIGHT: GAY AND LESBIAN VETERANS ACTIVATE

by TRACY BAIM

THE FIGHT FOR GAYS AND LESBIANS TO BE allowed to serve openly in the U.S. military started long before the "don't ask, don't tell, don't pursue" compromise of President Bill Clinton's first term in office. More than 12,000 servicemembers have lost their jobs since that law came into place in 1992, but thousands more were discharged from the military in earlier decades.

There were several high-profile cases prior to 1992, including one anti-gay murder, that had Chicago connections. Because of their proximity to the Great Lakes Naval Training Station, Chicago bars saw an influx of service personnel during wartime, and many of them stayed in Chicago after leaving the military. Great Lakes allegedly had purges of gays and lesbians over the years, and there are rumors that women were especially targeted.

Staff Sgt. Miriam Ben-Shalom, born in 1948, fought through several forums to keep her post in the U.S. Army Reserve. The case eventually came to the U.S. District Court in Milwaukee, and in May 1980 Judge Terence T. Evans ruled that her discharge violated the Constitution (including the right to free speech, because the discharge was based on her statement, not her acts). The Army ignored the ruling, and the 8th U.S. Circuit Court of Appeals in Chicago affirmed the decision and forced the Army to allow Ben-Shalom to re-enlist, so in 1988 she became the first openly gay servicemember to be reinstated. Eleven months later she lost a ruling in the Chicago federal appeals court; she appealed to the U.S. Supreme Court, which in 1990 refused to hear her case.

Tech. Sgt. Leonard Matlovich (1943–1988), a Vietnam War veteran, was another gay person who just wanted to serve his country. A Purple Heart and Bronze Star recipient, he traveled around the country raising funds to fight his U.S. Air Force discharge.

He was on the cover of Time magazine on Sept. 8, 1975. He came to Chicago several times, speaking at benefits and rallies. He died of AIDS complications.

Staff Sgt. Perry Watkins (1949–1996) was another gay veteran kicked out of the Army after serving in Vietnam. He came to Chicago several times to raise awareness, but he, too, died of AIDS complications before he would see his country allow gays to serve openly. Allen Bérubé (1946–2007), whose book Coming Out Under Fire includes

admit the details. Schindler had actually asked for a transfer because of the hostile climate on his ship. The 23-year-old was killed in a public toilet while docked in Nagasaki, Japan. Every year, local gay veterans pay tribute to Schindler at his south suburban gravesite, and his mother, Dorothy Hajdys-Holman, is right by their side. She continues to lobby to keep her son's killer, Terry Helvey, in prison, by testifying at his parole hearings. The other attacker, Charles Vins, was allowed to plea-

Staff Sgt. Miriam Ben-Shalom, photographed by Sue Burke, and murdered Navy man Allen Schindler. Windy City Times/ Outlines newspaper archive photos.

Chicago's George Buse (a World War II veteran featured in this book), also visited Chicago, promoting his work and the efforts to lift the gay ban.

Probably the most tragic examples of bias in the military are murders of servicemembers at the hands of their own colleagues. Chicago-area native Allen Schindler was killed by fellow Navy personnel on Oct. 27, 1992. The brutal murder almost went unreported, but the military was eventually forced to

bargain and was out of jail (and the Navy) within a few months.

With so many gay and lesbian veterans in Chicago, there is a strong chapter of the American Veterans for Equal Rights and visibility for the national Servicemembers Legal Defense Network. On June 22, 2004, Mayor Richard M. Daley established an annual "Salute to LGBT Veterans," the only ceremony of its kind in the United States. ▼

MEETING RELIGIOUS AND SPIRITUAL NEEDS *by WILLIAM BURKS*

DIGNITY/CHICAGO AND AGLO

Founded in Los Angeles in 1969, Dignity had expanded nationally, including the formation of a Chicago group, within four years, and the organization held its third Biennial Convention (its first international convention) in Chicago in September 1977. St. Sebastian Church, then at 824 W. Wellington Ave., was filled for the convention's Mass, concelebrated by 100 priests, as the organization notes on its Web site's Highlights of Dignity/USA's History.

St. Sebastian was host to Dignity/Chicago's Sunday evening Mass for 16 years, but the group's initial support from some areas of the Roman Catholic Church changed to conflict when, in 1986, then-Cardinal Joseph Ratzinger (now Pope Benedict XVI) of the Congregation for the Doctrine of the Faith in Rome issued a Letter on the Pastoral Care of Homosexual Persons. The official pronouncement declared homosexuality an "intrinsically disordered" condition and forbade bishops to allow church property to be used by organizations not adhering to the church's official position. Dignity's long-standing and publicly expressed view, that "gay, lesbian, bisexual and transgender persons can express their sexuality in a manner that is consonant with Christ's teaching," was seen as in conflict with the church's clear pronouncement that homosexuals must remain celibate.

Chicago Cardinal Joseph Bernardin responded to the Vatican's position by pre-empting the weekly Dignity Mass, declaring in May 1988 that henceforth archdiocesan-appointed priests would celebrate a Sunday evening Mass at St. Sebastian for the gay and lesbian community, under the auspices of the Archdiocesan Gay and Lesbian Outreach (AGLO). The result was an acrimonious schism between AGLO and Dignity, with a part of the GLBT Catholic community viewing the officially sanctioned Mass as a step forward in acceptance, while others were unwilling to toe the line of church teaching on homosexuality and homosexual behavior or disband their 16-year-old organization.

Adding fuel to the fire was Bernardin's 11th-hour letter the previous year to members of the Chicago City Council urging it not to pass a human rights ordinance that included sexual orientation as a protected class. The cardinal's letter was widely credited with derailing passage of the legislation.

Dignity/Chicago began holding its Masses at a nearby Lutheran church and currently holds them at 3334 N. Broadway. The AGLO Mass moved to Our Lady of Mount Carmel Church, 708 W. Belmont Ave., after St. Sebastian was destroyed by fire in 1991. Both organizations continue to offer Sunday evening Masses for the GLBT community, and Dignity will mark its 36th anniversary as a national organization in 2008.

GOOD SHEPHERD PARISH MCC

Begun in Los Angeles in 1968 by the Rev. Troy Perry, the Universal Fellowship of Metropolitan Community Churches spread a message of acceptance for gays and lesbians, boosted by publication of Perry's autobiography, The Lord Is My Shepherd and He Knows I'm Gay. In 1970, Good Shepherd Parish Metropolitan Community Church was founded in Chicago by the Rev. Arthur Green—the fourth MCC congregation organized and the first church to minister specifically to Chicago's gay community.

Providing gays and lesbians a safe and welcoming home for worship was a priority, but in the mid-1970s, Good Shepherd Parish began a more "outward-looking" ministry under the Rev. Kenneth Martin. It sued the Illinois Department of Corrections for access to minister in state prisons, according to The Chicago Gay Crusader. The church also participated in the East Lake View neighborhood's Night Ministry program and in speaking on gay and lesbian issues at other Chicago churches, while maintaining its 24-hour telephone hotline.

By then, Good Shepherd Parish had moved to share Wellington Avenue United Church of Christ's building, 615 W. Wellington Ave., which was to become the MCC congregation's home for 26 years. Membership boomed in the '70s to about 250, and the AIDS epidemic brought new forms of ministry, with a weekly Eucharist celebrated at Illinois Ma-

sonic Hospital for 15 years. Membership declined until only one member was under the age of 40. The church held its final service on July 8, 2007.

A new MCC-sponsored church, achurch4me, less traditionally structured than the previous congregation, meets on Sundays at the Center on Halsted, 3656 N. Halsted St., with the Rev. Kevin Downer, formerly a Good Shepherd Parish deacon, as lead pastor. Three MCCs continue to operate in Illinois: Holy Covenant MCC in Brookfield, MCC of the Fox Valley in Elgin, and Heartland MCC in Springfield.

JEWISH SUPPORT

Congregation Or Chadash (Congregation of New Light) was founded in 1976 to serve the Jewish gay and lesbian community of Chicago. It has done so in a wide variety of ways, including regular services, special holiday events, educational programming, visibility at Pride parades and much more.

Or Chadash's mission statement says it will "[r]emember that it was founded as an answer to the prejudice that gay and lesbian Jews experienced in other synagogues; [s]trive to ensure that no Jew experiences prejudice within our community; [m]aintain affiliations with the Union for Reform Judaism and [the] World Congress of Gay, Lesbian, Bisexual, and Transgender Jews: Keshet Ga'avah; [and] [b]uild strong ties within the greater Jewish community of the metropolitan Chicago area," besides dedicating itself to "basic obligations of Jewish life."

In the 1980s, several Jewish lesbians broke off to form their own group, concerned about perceived insensitivity by some men in Or Chadash. Those who helped to found Havurat Achayot include Elaine Wessel, Dillie Grunauer and Renee Hanover. It continued for a few years.

Or Chadash has had rabbis over the years, most recently Laurence Edwards, who teams with cantorial soloist Judith Golden. The congregation has also "spearheaded groundbreaking changes that allowed gay men and lesbians to be accepted in Jewish synagogues and institutions," according to the Chicago Gay and Lesbian Hall of Fame's profile of the group.

INTEGRITY/CHICAGO

Chicago was at the forefront of acceptance for gay Episcopalians, convening the first chapter of Integrity before a national organization was incorporated. Less than a year after a national gay and lesbian Episcopal organization was first brought up in discussion, Chicago's St. James Cathedral on North Wabash Avenue hosted Integrity's first national convention.

The August 1975 meeting drew 187 attendees, with seven chapters having been established and nine others in formation, according to a contemporary report in The Chicago Gay Crusader.

Integrity's founding was in the form of a newsletter written and published in Georgia by Dr. Louie Crew, but the Chicago chapter was, in fact, the first chapter formed, according to a history written by Crew. The presiding bishop of the Episcopal Church issued a statement of support. The initial convention addressed such issues as "Problems in Counseling for Gays," "Gay Community: Cultural, Social and Religious Involvement and Responsibility," and "Problems of Gay Parents," the Crusader reported.

Symbolic of the level of acceptance within Chicago's Episcopal Church, the diocese's assistant bishop celebrated the organization's Eucharist, which drew 300 attendees on a Saturday morning. Dr. W. Norman Pittenger, a noted Anglican theologian who had taught at General Theological Seminary in New York and at King's College, Cambridge, gave the convention's keynote address. Pittenger wrote several of the earliest works urging acceptance of committed gay relationships in the Anglican Communion.

CHURCH OF THE OPEN DOOR

The first Chicago gay-focused church to own its own property was Church of the Open Door, at 5954 S. Albany Ave. on Chicago's Southwest Side. From the mid-1990s to the early 2000s, Open Door served the African-American gay and lesbian community through services, special events, and opening its doors to other organizations. Its founders, the Rev. Karen Hutt and the Rev. Alma Crawford, welcomed many key activists to events inside the church doors, including Chicago Black Lesbians and Gays' annual Martin Luther King Jr. tribute breakfast.

UCC AND OTHER OUTREACH

Ronald Wadley, who describes himself as a same-gender-loving man, is active in Trinity United Church of Christ, a prominent African-American mainstream church of which U.S. Sen. Barack Obama (D-Ill.) has been a member. Wadley is a leader in that church's Same Gender Loving Ministry, an important group in a church that is among Chicago's largest, at 400 W. 95th St.

Wadley, Sherri Jackson, the Rev. Juan Reed and the Rev. Deborah Lake (of Sankofa Way) and others are working to change Christian churches, and their efforts have helped to pave a new path to providing gays a seat at the church table.

Rick Peterson and the Rev. Wayne Bradley, part-

ners since 1984, are active in the United Church of Christ (UCC) denomination as well—Peterson as a regional leader, and Bradley as minister of music for the First Congregational Church of Forest Glen UCC, 5400 N. Lawler Ave. Bradley previously was a clergyman in the Metropolitan Community Churches, but he turned to UCC as a way to make change within a mainstream denomination. UCC is widely believed to be one of the most accepting denominations for gays and lesbians.

Over time, most major religions have had some gay support groups, or AIDS outreach. For many

Dignity/Chicago in the 1980s: Jim Bussen (left, president of Dignity/USA, from Chicago), Bill Seng (president of Dignity/Chicago), and Jim Pilarski (secretary of Dignity/USA), greeting Catholic theologian Dr. Rosemary Ruether after her speech to the local Dignity.

years, there was an Interfaith group that held joint services with several of the gay religious organizations, especially around Pride Month. Another important Chicago-based resource for religious issues is produced by the progressive Chicago Theological Seminary: The LGBT Religious Archives Network, at the Web site www.lgbtran.org. ▼

With contributions by Tracy Baim.

TRADES FOR WOMEN

Chicago Women in Trades (CWIT) was founded in 1981 to respond to the issues facing women in the male-dominated fields of construction and manufacturing. Co-founder Lauren Sugerman has held a leadership position in the group throughout its existence. An open lesbian, Sugerman started as an elevator mechanic; her leadership of CWIT has helped thousands of women, gay and straight, get training, assistance and higher-paying jobs. The construction and manufacturing industries are still working environments fraught with sexism and homophobia, and many lesbians have reported horrible abuse and physical threats and dangers. All the while, CWIT has continued to lobby politically for change. Sugerman has been honored for the impact she and CWIT have had locally, nationally and internationally.

Lauren Sugerman in the Pride Parade, 2006. Photo by Tracy Baim.

Vera Washington (left) and Pat McCombs in 2007. Photo by Hal Baim.

RACIAL PROFILING: FIGHTING GAY CLUBS by TRACY BAIM

GAY BARS ARE A REFLECTION OF SOCIETY, so it should be no surprise that some bars have been accused of racism or sexism over the years. Various attempts to fight this bias, including surveys and random spot checks, have been met with resistance, or ignorance.

When African-American lesbian activist Pat McCombs saw her Black and Latina friends face this bias in December 1974 at CK's lesbian bar by being asked for more identification than white customers, she fought back in the way she had learned as a civil-rights activist—both in the streets and in the courts. She and others formed the Black Lesbians Discrimination Investigation Committee, picketing in front of CK's, 1425 W. Diversey Pkwy. She called for a boycott, putting out posters and getting white lesbian attorney Renee Hanover to help. White lesbians also joined the picket lines, and the state liquor commission investigated.

On March 10, 1975, the Illinois Liquor Control Commission gave the bar a citation, according to The Chicago Gay Crusader, requiring owner Carol Kappa to appear before the commission to "show cause why her license should not be suspended or revoked." The commission dismissed the citation April 15 after Kappa and Hanover entered into an agreement for the complainants, calling for Kappa to serve all customers equally and to clearly post her identification policies.

The carding policies of CK's (which later merged with Augie's to become Augie & CK's at 3726 N. Broadway, now the site of the bar Charlie's Chicago) were not unique. Dozens of gay bars over the years have been accused of keeping out people based on race or gender, having a "quota" so as not to tilt the balance in their bar. The Gay and Lesbian Coalition of Metropolitan Chicago, a 1970s group of organizations and businesses, faced an internal struggle because bar owners did not want the Coalition to investigate such bias. Even in the 2000s, some gay businesses have been accused of racism, sexism and even bias against older people. However, few patrons fight back as McCombs and Hanover did.

McCombs also responded to such bias in other ways. Executive Sweet, an African-American lesbian social events group, was started around 1979 by Pam Terrell and DJ Sheron Webb. McCombs became involved, and she and Vera Washington took over operations in 1982. It is still operating in 2008 as an alternative to bars. ▼

DANCING FOR LIFE

by TRACY BAIM

ALL THE CREATIVE ARTS WERE DEVASTATED by AIDS, with a generation of stars struck down in their prime—never to write another opera or play, sing on another stage, play another piano or organ or paint another masterpiece. The dance world was particularly hard-hit, with many gay male choreographers and dancers lost to the disease.

In Chicago, one of the earliest losses was of Joseph Holmes, the head of Joseph Holmes Chicago Dance Theatre. Holmes left his mark on many who followed, including Randy Duncan, who took over the company after Holmes died, and dancer Keith Elliott. Elliott nurtured the idea of an annual Dance for Life benefit, bringing together Chicago's top dance companies in a fundraiser for AIDS organizations and individual dancers. Like Season of Concern, which helps those in theater affected by AIDS, the Dance for Life Fund helps people meet their basic living requirements.

Danny Kopelson, Harriet G. Ross and Duncan have all played critical roles in the Dance for Life annual gala, which is still operating in the 2000s. Duncan has been honored widely for his choreography, and Elliott has expanded his work to producing many benefits for gay and AIDS groups.

Joel Hall is another important part of Chicago's dance scene. A native Chicagoan, Hall co-founded Chicago City Theater Company in 1972 and, as part of that effort, created the Joel Hall Dancers and Joel Hall Dance Studios. Hall has an international reputation as a choreographer, and his company has toured the United States and other countries.

Elliott, Kopelson, Duncan and Hall are all members of the Chicago Gay and Lesbian Hall of Fame for their important cultural and philanthropic work. ▼

Clockwise from top left: Randy Duncan, Joel Hall, Keith Elliott and Danny Kopelson, all in 2007. Photos by Hal Baim.

SILENCE = DEATH

A Generation Responds to AIDS by Acting Up and Fighting Back

THE 1980S CAME IN WITH A THUD—THE OMINOUS ELECTION OF A former actor to be the president of the United States. Ronald Reagan's administration was marked by arrogance and ignorance, denial and destruction. His refusal for many years to even say the word "AIDS," and his inaction in the early years of the crisis, can be morally linked to the deaths of tens of thousands, if not millions.

On July 3, 1981, buried in the back of their news sections, The New York Times and the Los Angeles Times both carried articles about strange cases of pneumocystis carinii pneumonia and Kaposi's sarcoma in gay men. Many gay men today recall reading The New York Times story and feeling a sense of doom. It was just the beginning of the plague years, a war with an invisible enemy that was aided by homophobia.

The response to what was eventually called AIDS was not swift, even within all of the gay community. But by 1984–86, communities in cities nationwide, including Chicago, were witnessing the wide path of destruction. Some people lost hundreds of friends within a few short years. Some people died within days or weeks of diagnosis, while others hung on for a few years. It took years for medications to come onto the scene, and even those were often toxic and high-priced. A generation of major community leaders was lost to AIDS— thousands of Chicago men in their prime, invaluable to our movement's political, cultural and social future.

The resulting lack of help, combined with draconian legislation, sparked the rise of ACT UP chapters in various cities, including Chicago. AIDS created new leaders: angry, mostly younger people who wanted to take control of their health care and force society to deal with them equally. The ACT UP demonstrations against Cook County Hospital, the

Opposite: A 1990 ACT UP/Chicago AIDS protest in downtown Chicago. Photos by Lisa Howe-Ebright.

Harold Washington at Chicago's Pride Rally after the 1987 parade. Photo from Outlines newspaper.

IMPACT button and Dr. Ron Sable's 1991 campaign button. Courtesy Nancy Katz.

federal government, pharmaceutical companies, the Chicago Transit Authority and other institutions are legendary in the Chicago community.

The growth of AIDS also resulted in the formation of numerous AIDS service and support organizations, many of them still operating in 2008. These include AIDS Foundation of Chicago, Chicago House, AIDS Legal Council of Chicago, Test Positive Aware Network, Project Vida, and Open Hand/Vital Bridges. In addition, existing institutions such as Howard Brown Memorial Clinic (now Howard Brown Health Center), Horizons (now Center on Halsted) and others incorporated the fight against AIDS into their missions. Howard Brown became one of the most important research centers for the epidemic because it already had been collecting samples from gay men for earlier disease research. A NAMES Project quilt display in 1988 created a somber, reflective time for those fighting on the front lines.

Parallel to the fight against HIV and AIDS, the community was also maturing its "suit-and-tie" activism. There were two complementary approaches taken to getting our rights—those of the street activists and those of others who were willing to sit down with influential, powerful officeholders like Mayor Harold Washington and Gov. James R. Thompson. In addition, some wanted to take a seat at the table as elected officials, and a strong movement was behind the candidacy of Cook County Hospital physician Ron Sable for alderman. He came within a few votes of defeating then-incumbent 44th Ward Ald. Bernard Hansen, and his race served as a training ground for future political candidates.

Lobbying also continued in earnest for both city and state gay-rights laws. The Illinois Gay and Lesbian Task Force worked tirelessly on the statewide gay bill, including the organizing of lobby days in the capital, but it would take many more years, and a new

organization, to eventually win gay rights legislation in Illinois. In Chicago, activists pushed for a defining vote on the gay bill in 1986, to find out who was truly with us and who was truly against us. The anger that sprang from that bill's defeat caused a new wave of protests, starting with the singing of "We Shall Overcome" in the City Council chambers and at a Daley Center rally. After Mayor Washington died in office, new Mayor Eugene Sawyer was at first slow to act for his gay constituents. Eventually, however, he supported the bill. And after one more defeat, in September 1988, that was fueled by opposition from the Roman Catholic archdiocese, the bill did pass in December of that year.

Formal gay political groups were also taking shape, including the first gay political action committee, OPEN/PAC (followed in the late 1980s by IMPACT), the Prairie State Democratic Club, the Chicago Area Republican Gay Organization, the Lesbian and Gay Progressive Democratic Organization, and gay leadership in the Independent Voters of Illinois–Independent Precinct Organization and the Chicago chapter of the National Organization for Women.

Some of the spark for late-1980s activism came from a second National March on Washington for Lesbian and Gay Rights, held Oct. 11, 1987, on what would later become known as National Coming Out Day. There was a massive display of the NAMES Project Quilt, and there were arrests at the U.S. Supreme Court. Chicago had a well-organized contingent in that march and at its related events, and thousands of activists returned to the Windy City newly invigorated for the fight against AIDS and for gay rights.

Lesbians were a strong part of ACT UP, but they also started to create energized action groups of their own, including the Lesbian Avengers and Women's Action Coalition. The Chicago Women's Health Center helped provide artificial insemination for lesbians wanting to build families, and Mountain Moving Coffeehouse, Women & Children First Bookstore, and social organizations helped provide support for lesbians. Paris Dance and Suzi B's were popular women's bars, and Lost & Found continued its reign as the oldest lesbian bar in town (it was still operating in 2008, but was expected to change owners soon).

HOT WIRE, a women's music journal, started in Chicago, joining a burgeoning gay and lesbian media scene. GayLife did not last the decade, giving way to Windy City Times, from which sprang Outlines. Gay Chicago Magazine lost one of its founders to AIDS in 1989 but continued strong as a bar guide to Chicago. The 10% Show brought gays to cable television in town, while the mainstream media were still slow to learn how to cover the community. They assigned gay "beat" reporters at the Chicago Tribune and Chicago Sun-Times, but it was still difficult to keep homophobia out of the media coverage, especially around the topic of AIDS.

One group was created to keep the media on its toes: the Coalition Against Media/Marketing Prejudice (CAMMP), formed in 1988 soon after the originally New York-based Gay and Lesbian Alliance Against Defamation (GLAAD). CAMMP started with a push against the bias at Stroh Brewery Co. and moved on to the Kellogg Co. to attack homophobic ads for its Nut & Honey breakfast cereal.

Bar raids continued into the 1980s, but a major raid at Carol's Speakeasy was nearly the final blow in that war of law enforcement officers against gays. Soon, lesbian and gay police officers started to change the system from within, while gay activists pushed for reform from the outside through forums and political clout.

A new form of corporate and business activism was also springing up. In the 1970s, the Tavern Guild of Chicago was a lobbying group for bar personnel. Later came the Metropolitan Business Association in the 1980s, and the Chicago Area Gay and Lesbian Chamber of Commerce in the next decade. Starting in the 1980s, the trend for gay employee groups pushing for rights inside companies was strong, and two bar owners in Chicago started a Gay Dollars campaign that revealed the economic clout of the gay community.

People of color were creating safer spaces, whether in social or cultural groups or around political issues. Latino, African-American and Asian groups provided support and a training ground for future leaders. Youth groups at Horizons and other agencies also played an important role for those facing bias at home and in school.

Sports organizations experienced their biggest

Mayor Daley, Mike Savage and Larry Rolla at a heated November 1989 meeting with Daley and the gay community. Daley's relationship with gay activists was initially quite tense. Photo by Lisa Howe-Ebright.

growth in the 1980s, with the boom in gay-specific leagues for softball, football, basketball, volleyball and bowling, and the creation of individual sport support, including groups for running and swimming. These sports organizations also provided a great base for fundraising against AIDS, with such events as Strike Against AIDS and Proud to Run raising much-needed dollars. The clubs were also an important partner for AIDS groups, with bars such as Little Jim's, Berlin, Sidetrack, His 'n Hers, Opal Station and others offering space for benefits.

At the same time the community fell prey to the nightmare of AIDS, there was another awareness that brought people together in new, healthy ways: the idea that something more than oppression united them. The question was being asked with some urgency: Is there another definition for gay people, other than the sexual?

Many cultural groups sprang up in the 1980s out of a yearning for more than a sexual connection, and this yearning was a strong motivating force for cultural growth in various segments of the community. New bands, choral groups, theaters, festivals, films and writers were emerging. Gay and lesbian culture was gaining momentum, creating new art, showcasing new talents, and building intergenerational and cross-gender friendships through cultural activities. The community was developing confidence that it had actual substance beyond sexuality, and that gay people could depend on each other.

The cultural scene saw the start of Reeling, the lesbian and gay film festival, still going strong in 2008. Writers such as Achy Obejas, Lola Lai Jong, Vernita Gray and Mark Richard Zubro were making their mark in Chicago, part of a national trend of openly gay authors. Literary Exchange began in the 1980s to support African-American women writers. The creation of new music, art, dance, drama, nonfiction, poetry, comedy and connections with each other all became our allies in the battle for our lives against the silence that equals death.

In part because of HIV and AIDS, the community was becoming stronger, more sophisticated and experienced. Those skills made for better fundraising, more clout in the political and corporate spheres, and eventually resulted in quicker access to experimental AIDS medications. By 1990, the community was founding new organizations almost weekly, dealing with a wider array of issues including violence, cancer, custody, gender identity and student issues. While burnout and death caused some organizations such as ACT UP to implode, they were replaced by new leaders and organizations taking up the call for gay rights, health care and equality. ▼ —*Tracy Baim*

AIDS: THE PLAGUE YEARS   *by TRACY BAIM*

WHERE WERE YOU WHEN YOU FIRST HEARD ABOUT AIDS? IF YOU ARE OF AN OLDER generation, and especially a gay man, you probably remember reading or hearing about a July 3, 1981, New York Times article reporting on a strange series of illnesses striking gay men in East Coast and West Coast urban areas. Just 12 years after the Stonewall riots in New York, the decade of love and liberation had come to a crashing end.

There were some signs of distress earlier than 1981. Doctors and nurses, especially those with many gay patients, began to notice obscure illnesses cropping up. Gay health groups did screenings for venereal diseases, which were spreading rapidly.

But it was the summer of 1981 when the U.S. Centers for Disease Control's Morbidity and Mortality Weekly Report (MMWR, June 5 and July 3) first reported that a new disease might be in our midst. It could have been around for years, but was just at that time starting to exhibit itself.

The individual illnesses striking these young gay men were otherwise rare—pneumocystis carinii pneumonia and Kaposi's sarcoma, the latter manifested as purple lesions. These and other strange illnesses had started to be diagnosed some 30 months prior to the 1981 MMWR reports. In January 1982 the syndromes together began to be called GRID, gay-related immunodeficiency, and the acronym stood until July of that year, when it was renamed AIDS, or acquired immunodeficiency syndrome.

The rumors and media reports, including those in the gay press, only trickled out for many months. But by 1983–84, it was clear a major epidemic was at hand, one that struck more than gay men.

In Chicago, while existing organizations such as Howard Brown Memorial Clinic (now Howard Brown Health Center) and Horizons (now Center on Halsted) tried to cope with new legal, psychosocial, and health issues facing the community, more support would be needed.

Within three years, major institutions were founded, many of them still in existence today. These included AIDS Foundation of Chicago, Chicago House, Open Hand (now Vital Bridges), Test Positive Aware Network, Stop AIDS, Kupona Network, AIDS Legal Council of Chicago, Chicago Women's AIDS Project, and dozens more. Eventually, more than 100 agencies dealt with some aspect of AIDS, from fundraising events, such as AIDS Walk and the AIDS Ride, to service groups, research and prevention organizations.

In many ways, the quick rise of activism and empowerment, the goals to "help our own," came out of the 1970s gay liberation movement. Women had been taking control of their own health and well-being (founding women's crisis lines and shelters and learning with the book Our Bodies, Ourselves), and gays and lesbians were already creating community centers and support structures outside the mainstream. Gay doctors were starting to come out, and those same doctors would be on the front lines of medical research and care during the AIDS crisis. Both lesbians and gay men took leadership roles in the new AIDS infrastructure, heading small organizations that would become multi-million-dollar agencies respected nationally for their pioneering work.

Part of the response was due to the fact that mainstream doctors and agencies were quick to spout anti-gay feelings and even push for AIDS-phobic acts such as quarantining and contact tracing. Families ostracized their own sons and daughters, and schools tried to keep out HIV-positive children, including a boy named Ryan White (a federal AIDS funding bill is named for him). There was a huge backlash in the United States, and gay men and women were first to recognize that we had to find solutions from within. We could not rely on a homophobic culture to save our lives. Soon, allies would come to our side. But even in 2008, abstinence-only funding takes precious resources away from AIDS work, despite studies that show those programs do not work.

BY THE NUMBERS

While the disease in Chicago and other U.S. cities was initially reported as mostly affecting white gay men, it was quickly clear that its path would grow wider and would have an impact on the entire world.

The Chicago Department of Public Health began tracking what would later become known as AIDS in 1980. The statistics for those early years show fewer than five cases in 1980 and 1981, but a jump to 16 in 1982 and 42 in 1983. It should be emphasized that these were cases reported to CDPH, since not all doctors may have known what signs to look for (especially in the early 1980s).

Among the 16 cases in 1982, 13 were among "men who have sex with men," otherwise known as MSM, and three were MSM who were also injection drug users (IDU). Nine of the cases were white, six Black, and one Latino. All were male. In 1983, 28 of the 42 cases were MSM, 24 were white, 13 Black, fewer than five Latino and fewer than five "other." (Note that CDPH only lists "fewer than five" cases as grouped together to avoid revealing confidentiality in any category.)

In 1984, CDPH reported 112 cases of AIDS, with 89 MSM, seven MSM-IDU and eight IDU. Sixty-eight of the cases were white, 33 Black, 10 Latino and fewer than five others. Among those, 104 were men, and eight were women.

In 1985, the cases continued to nearly double, at

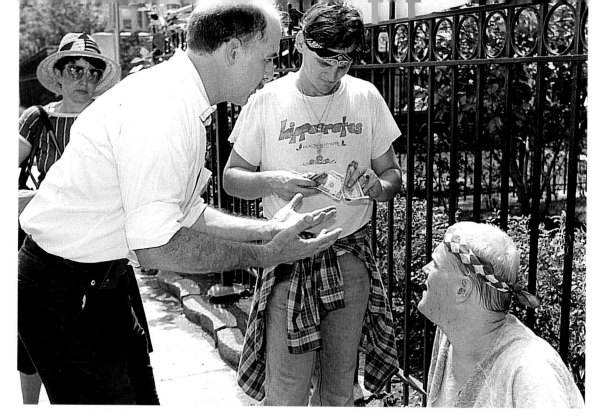

Dr. Ron Sable (left) speaks with activist David Bell (right), who had chained himself to the fence of Gov. Jim Thompson's home to protest draconian state AIDS legislation in 1987. Hundreds of people marched on Thompson's home. Both Sable and Bell later died of AIDS. Photos from Outlines archives.

Left: ACT UP in Chicago Pride circa 1990. Photo by Lisa Howe-Ebright. Above: A June 1991 protest. Photo by Genyphyr Novak.

Above left: AIDS Foundation of Chicago in the mid-1980s, with Marcia Lipetz (upper left), executive director; Roger Hansen, board president; and Caryn Berman, chair of the Service Providers Council. Photo by Lisa Howe-Ebright.

At right, the huge 1987 AFC gala featuring Angela Lansbury, Oprah Winfrey, Peter Allen, the gay and lesbian choral groups and more. Photo by David Miller, Outlines/Windy City Times.

Mary Patten, Saundra Johnson and Debbie Gould on a "Freedom Bed" protest downtown. Photo by Steve Dalber, courtesy Mary Patten.

221. Of those, 173 were MSM, 18 MSM-IDU, 16 IDU and the rest spread among several risk factors. Of the total, 131 were among whites, 64 Blacks, 23 Latinos, and fewer than five others. Seven of the total were women.

The next year, 1986, saw 371 cases: 298 among MSM, 26 MSM-IDU, 26 IDU and the rest with other risk factors. Of the total, 195 were white, 132 Black, 42 Latino. Nine were women.

In 1987, there were 602 cases: 454 MSM, 28 MSM-IDU and 79 IDU. Of the total, 304 were white, 214 Black, 80 Latino. Thirty-four were women.

Skipping ahead to 1990, the racial statistics start to shift. There were 1,142 AIDS cases in 1990: 730 MSM, 71 MSM-IDU, 238 IDU and 43 from heterosexual contact. Of the total, 444 were white, 528 Black, 161 Latino and nine other. There were 104 women.

Overall, from 1980 to the end of 2007, the CDPH reported 23,530 AIDS cases. It also shows 10,596 cases of HIV (the city started tracking HIV separately in 1999). The total is not achieved by adding those numbers, because if someone progressed to AIDS in a subsequent year, that person would be in both totals.

Of that overall AIDS total, 11,766 were MSM, 1,552 MSM-IDU, 6,022 IDU, 2,203 heterosexual-contact, and nearly 2,000 other or unknown. Of the 23,530 cases, 6,724 were white, 13,075 Black, 3,423 Latino and 292 other. Females made up 4,019 cases, males 19,507.

Of the HIV total, 4,849 were MSM, 382 MSM-IDU, 1,734 IDU, 1,443 heterosexual-contact and more than 2,000 other or unknown. Racially, 2,766 were white, 5,939 Black, and 1,537 Latino. There were 2,573 females and 8,023 males diagnosed as HIV-positive since 1999.

Among the 23,530 AIDS cases CDPH reported from 1980 to 2007, 10,987 were still living with AIDS as of the end of 2007. Most of those diagnosed with HIV (tracked separately since 1999) are still living. The Illinois Department of Public Health reports on AIDS-related deaths show the following statistics for Chicago, by year: 1994, 990; 1995, 1,030; 1996, 833; 1997, 402; 1998, 372; 1999, 362;

2000, 304; 2001, 348; 2002, 317; 2003, 269; and 2004, 256.

The deaths by year are interesting to note, because the figures show that while the new AIDS drugs introduced in the mid-1990s appear to have slowed progression of the disease, there were and are still many people dying. In addition, some of the drugs appear to be toxic in the long term, so as people with AIDS age, they are experiencing an earlier onset of diseases that are common among the elderly.

As for the geography of AIDS, CDPH tracks the disease by neighborhood. Its 2006 geographic report shows high concentrations in the following areas: Rogers Park, West Ridge, Edgewater, Uptown, Lake View, Near North Side, Humboldt Park, West Town, Austin, Near West Side, South Lawndale, South Shore, Roseland and Grand Crossing.

When speaking with gays and lesbians who were out in the 1980s, almost all report having felt the impact of AIDS, through their friendship circles, their families, the deaths of partners, or even their own HIV diagnoses. But what is striking is the vastly different experiences. In some cases, individuals may have lost literally hundreds of people from their circle of friends. Yet another person of the same age, in the same city, was relatively untouched, attending few funerals and giving few memorials. Many lesbians lost their gay brothers to AIDS, while some gay men lost no one close to them.

The change in the demographics of Chicago AIDS cases has also caused friction over the years in terms of access to resources. The AIDS Foundation of Chicago (AFC) has effectively juggled the needs of the crisis, bringing together groups from all parts of the region. The first AIDS Walk in Chicago was seen as not funding representative groups. It later collapsed, and was recreated by AFC as a new funding source for a wide range of groups.

But the bottom line for AIDS funding is that groups need to fight for a larger pie instead of fighting among each other for slices of an ever-shrinking one. The disease's demographics are shifting. That does not mean that prevention and services for white gay men should stop. It means that prevention and

services should expand overall. It is also not a "Black and white" issue. While many people segregate based on race in Chicago, some whites live south, and many Blacks live on the North Side or prefer to receive services at places such as HBHC or TPAN.

The next years of the epidemic will continue to see these struggles for funding. A new presidential administration may add to AIDS funding and may divert funds from abstinence-only sham programs, but the needs will continue to increase. The AIDS drugs have provided some relief, but there is still no cure. And there is no guarantee, even if a cure comes, that it will be made affordable to all those in need.

THE 1980s: ACTING UP

Gay men and lesbians interviewed for the Chicago Gay History Project saw the rise of AIDS in the mid-1980s as both a curse and a potential blessing. AIDS caused the voluntary and involuntary outing of thousands of gay people, from Rock Hudson to colleagues and family members. With death on the line, many gay men were emboldened to come out and live a quality life, not a closeted one. The American public had never seen so many gay men and lesbians "coming out" all within a short period of time.

But it was mostly a curse.

In 1984, Jerry Soucy and Katie Sprutta were part of the AIDS Action Project of Howard Brown Memorial Clinic, one of the first places people with AIDS could go. An article for GayLife on Nov. 8, 1984, reported that there were 50 surviving people with AIDS in Chicago at that point. The duo bemoaned a general apathy within the gay community about AIDS. Soucy said he thought some portions of the community didn't want to deal with persons with AIDS. He added: "They think there will be a cure soon. … The crisis is not over and it is not going to be over soon."

Chicago for Our Rights (C-FOR) was an organization that already existed prior to its morphing into a Chicago chapter of the national ACT UP (AIDS Coalition to Unleash Power) movement in 1988. C-FOR was a name originally chosen by the group of Chicagoans arrested at U.S. Supreme Court demonstrations after the October 1987 March on Washing-

ton. It was a radical group of street protesters unafraid of police and included gay men with HIV or AIDS, lesbians fighting for their friends, straight allies, and both younger and older people. There had actually been a radical group prior to C-FOR, called Dykes and Gay Men Against Repression (DAGMAR) (alternate uses of the "R" were Right Wing, Reagan, etc.). DAGMAR had marched in Pride parades and responded to the KKK presence there. DAGMAR and C-FOR merged and became Chicago for AIDS Rights (C-FAR), which later became the Chicago ACT UP chapter.

Some early AIDS demonstrations, like a June 30, 1987, protest at Federal Plaza, were sparsely attended. Among those at the protest was Lori Cannon, a longtime AIDS activist still working on AIDS issues in 2008. Chants included "Reagan, Reagan, you can't hide! We all know it's genocide!"

In August 1987, activists David Bell, Maryon Grey, Carol Jonas, Don Maffetore, Darral Pugh and Ferd Eggan tied themselves to the fence outside the Chicago home of Illinois Gov. James R. Thompson to pressure the governor not to sign homophobic AIDS legislation. An estimated 400 people participated in the DAGMAR-sponsored march and protest. A 24-hour vigil was held, with no arrests. (Bell died soon after from AIDS complications, and Eggan died in 2007.)

On June 16, 1988, C-FAR occupied the Chicago office of the regional director of the Food and Drug Administration to push for more AIDS research and drugs in the pipeline. C-FAR members Eggan and Paul Adams (who also died of AIDS) commandeered two phones and began dialing the national FDA office to issue their demands. The demonstrators demanded that drug companies be banned from "extorting huge profits from people with AIDS." Eight protesters were handcuffed by security officers, some of whom wore rubber gloves. All were later released.

However, not all AIDS activists were on the streets risking arrest. There was a very deliberate move to have both an "inside" and an "outside" approach. Existing groups such as the Illinois Gay and Lesbian Task Force and the Chicago Area Republican

Gay Organization met with government officials, while ACT UP, C-FAR and others protested in the streets. City and state health departments were feeling the political pressure, and Gov. Thompson, after pressure from activists, needed to meet with the gays in "suits and ties." Among those who met with Thompson were Tim Drake, Gail Schiesser, Al Wardell and Paul Varnell.

Each of these battles was being fought on many fronts: the work to stem the tide of bad AIDS legislation, increase AIDS funding, allow safer-sex messages on buses and trains, push for access to low-cost AIDS drugs and fight for more AIDS beds for women. Chicago hosted national AIDS demonstrations, stopping traffic in the streets along march routes and laying down beds in front of the Cook County Building. Chicago activists also traveled around the country to protest at the 1988 Democratic National Convention in Atlanta and at events in Washington, D.C., New York and San Francisco. Meanwhile, political gays worked the corridors of power.

When Richard M. Daley took over as mayor, he inherited a community already on edge about failed health department policies and people. Daley was seen as not acting fast enough to increase AIDS spending, and protests occurred at City Hall and at a dramatic 1989 community meeting at the de facto community center, the Ann Sather restaurant on West Belmont Avenue. Danny Sotomayor, Lori Cannon and other AIDS activists confronted Daley wherever they could, and 46th Ward Ald. Helen Shiller and others were able to fight for more city AIDS funding. Daley eventually repaired his reputation among most gays; however, many AIDS activists, including Sotomayor, did not live long enough to see that happen.

But no matter how media-savvy and creative ACT UP became, the divisions in the community and within organizations were similar to those in society. ACT UP meetings were often long and heated. There were people living with AIDS and people fighting for them. Diverse voices all came to the movement with their own agendas, and many could not separate out AIDS as their only cause. ACT UP

was a very loose coalition, and members could choose what events they wanted to stage. More issues were added on, including national health care and pro-choice activism. Prominent members such as Danny Sotomayor became telegenic media stars, able to use their charisma to help the cause. But despite, or maybe because, of the amazing dedication of these activists, there was bound to be burnout. The energy could not be sustained. Some activists died, and others could not maintain the fever pitch. By the end of the 1980s, ACT UP was about to give way to Queer Nation, which itself was short-lived.

RAPID RESPONSE

Among other responses to AIDS was the important work of two doctors at Cook County Hospital, which saw a large proportion of the early cases in Chicago. Dr. Ron Sable, an openly gay physician, and his straight colleague, Dr. Renslow Sherer, founded the Sable/Sherer Clinic in 1983 to focus on treatment for people with AIDS as well as what was known at the time as AIDS-related complex (ARC). The nurse who helped was Jim Lovette, now living in San Francisco. Sable, who unsuccessfully ran for office, later died of AIDS complications. Sherer, meanwhile, has continued to work for many years on issues related to AIDS. He was also a key ally in the years when the state legislature was considering draconian measures to stem the epidemic. As a straight, married man with children, he was happy to play a role for the community, someone to whom the elected officials could relate, but Sherer's opinions on the bills coincided with those of gay activists.

"It's an obvious fact to me that while the rest of the world did almost nothing and ignored AIDS—in fact, consciously looked the other way—best symbolized by the fact that our president [Ronald Reagan] didn't utter the word until September 1986 … people did nothing, with the exception of the gay community," Sherer told Outlines reporter William Burks in July 1987.

Gay doctors David Blatt and David Moore, partners in life and in their medical practice, were also on the front lines, treating hundreds of people with

AIDS from their base at Illinois Masonic Hospital's Unit 371.

People with AIDS, or even those thought to have AIDS, were losing their jobs, and organizations such as the ACLU, Lambda Legal (which eventually opened a Chicago office in the 1990s) and individual attorneys and firms fought for their return to work. In 1987, a Cook County Hospital doctor was removed from treating patients because he had AIDS. After protests and a review, he was allowed only limited practice, according to ACLU attorneys. Airlines discriminated against ill passengers—or even those thought to be gay and "carriers." People were afraid of gay waiters. It was a very difficult time, and there were battles on dozens of major front lines. Dentist Larry Spang lost his job at a federal prison, which led him to found a Chicago clinic for low-income HIV-positive people.

In Chicago, the bathhouse controversy never reached the same crescendo—or outcome—as the closing of the baths in San Francisco. Chicagoans connected with the political establishment made it clear that unsafe sex was going on in many places, and that the goal was to educate men wherever they were—and that bathhouses were safer than parks and other cruising areas, because condoms could be handed out and safer-sex information posted.

People with AIDS also needed personal and individual support in many aspects of their lives. These included legal issues (losing apartments, writing wills), basic needs (housing, food, dog walking), psychosocial needs (support groups, counseling) and much more. Specific agencies took on targeted areas, while others were wider in their scope. Prevention was also important, and free condoms (including those from the Reimer Foundation), safer-sex literature, and safer-sex demonstrations were the rage. Gays protested the Roman Catholic Church's attempts to stifle condom use. Lesbians even held a blood drive.

The need to raise money for all these endeavors also opened up a new era of more sophisticated fundraising than the gay community had ever seen. In combination with support from straight allies, gay and AIDS groups began hosting black-tie galas, tag nights at bars, fun social benefits and more. AFC hosted a huge gala Sept. 27, 1987, at the Chicago Theatre, raising more than $1 million for AIDS groups. The event featured Angela Lansbury, Peter Allen, Jerry Herman, Colleen Dewhurst, Chita Rivera, Lily Tomlin (via a film clip), Leslie Uggams, Oprah Winfrey, Mayor Harold Washington, U.S. Sen. Paul Simon, all of Chicago's gay and lesbian choral groups, and others. This "Show of Concern" was a co-benefit for AFC and the American Foundation for AIDS Research. Beverly Blettner, a Chicago socialite, chaired the entire event, which was sponsored by Marshall Field's, Outlines newspaper and others.

Other fundraisers that provided support included the annual Strike Against AIDS bowling events, the Proud to Run race, golf benefits, pie tosses, croquet tournaments, drag shows, bike rides and more. While there is no longer an AIDS Ride (because of fundraising controversies), there are shorter bike benefits, a new and reinvigorated AIDS Walk, and a benefit for AIDS that piggybacks the Chicago Marathon. Foundations such as WPWR (now Alphawood) and Crossroads provided key early funding.

IMPACT ON CULTURE

There was also a cultural response to AIDS. In 1982, the Lionheart gay theater company presented the world's first AIDS play, One, by Jeff Hagedorn (who died of AIDS in 1995). The School Street Movement's Sex Police dancers educated people about AIDS. Keith Elliott, Danny Kopelson, Randy Duncan and others worked on an annual Dance for Life benefit for AIDS groups, an event still staged in 2008. Chicago Gay Men's Chorus and Windy City Gay Chorus both were devastated by AIDS, and they performed at many funeral services for their own singers and at benefits for AIDS groups.

Members of every creative profession, from photographers to filmmakers, dancers to choreographers, musicians to actors, were affected. Visual artists were also taken in their prime. Jon Reich and Gabor were two prominent local artists who were lost to the disease. Sotomayor was an editorial cartoonist who used

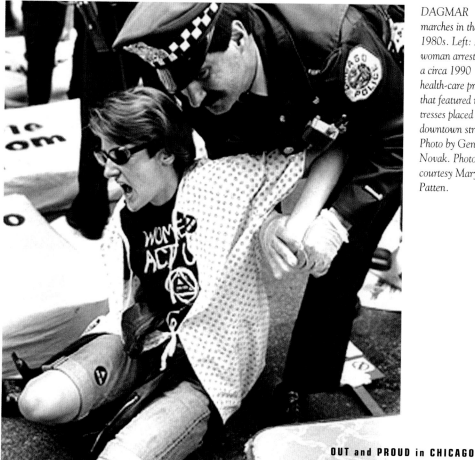

DAGMAR marches in the 1980s. Left: A woman arrested at a circa 1990 health-care protest that featured mattresses placed on downtown streets. Photo by Genyphyr Novak. Photos courtesy Mary Patten.

The AIDS crisis is not over, and these people have been working on AIDS issues in some cases for more than 20 years, each. Top, from left: Drs. David Blatt and David Moore (Illinois Masonic Medical Center), Lora Branch (Chicago Department of Public Health), Sid Mohn (Heartland Alliance), and Lori Cannon (Vital Bridges) with art by Danny Sotomayor. Below: Larry Spang (a dentist who sued for the right to practice), Steve Wakefield (active in numerous Chicago groups, now working on worldwide AIDS issues based in Seattle), and David Munar and Mark Ishaug of the AIDS Foundation of Chicago. Photos in 2007 by Hal Baim.

his anger and wit to create cartoons that cut to the heart of AIDS issues in the late 1980s, in Gay Chicago Magazine, Windy City Times, and Outlines. He died in 1992, shortly before his partner, nationally renowned playwright Scott McPherson (Marvin's Room), died of AIDS as well.

Among dancers lost to AIDS was Joseph Holmes, whose Chicago dance company continued after his death in 1986. At first his family did not want it to be known he had AIDS, so no mention of it was made at his huge South Side funeral service. Keith McDaniel, who had gone from Chicago to stardom in the Alvin Ailey American Dance Theater, died in 1995 at age 38.

Thing magazine publisher Robert Ford was also

a pioneer in publishing, heading a 'zine that played a vital role for the African-American gay community in town. Ford died in 1994, shortly after his induction into the Chicago Gay and Lesbian Hall of Fame.

In the design community, the Design Industry Foundation Fighting AIDS (DIFFA) had a strong fundraising community, bringing straights and gays together to raise funds for a variety of groups. Season of Concern did the same among theaters and theater patrons, raising money at benefits and during special nights at various shows.

There are also many cultural pioneers still living with HIV and AIDS, although the disease takes its toll on their creative energies.

SHOWING THEIR NAMES

Another major event for the city was the first display in town of the NAMES Project AIDS Memorial Quilt panels, July 9–11, 1988, at Navy Pier (well before that space was renovated to be a tourist attraction). While the quilt returned in later years, the 1988 display was seen as a pivotal coming-together of people from all communities and stood as a symbolic and somber reminder of those lost. Readers of the quilt's names included the Rev. Willie Barrow of Operation PUSH, who lost her son to AIDS, and Mayor Eugene Sawyer.

The coordinator for the local NAMES Project chapter, Peggy Shinner, told Outlines reporter Rex Wockner: "People look at this quilt and it brings the political and social issues surrounding AIDS to a very different level. … [The] quilt clearly functions as a consciousness-raising tool."

Organizers of the NAMES display stood in solidarity with C-FAR in refusing to take a $2,000 contribution from the drug company Lyphomed, the embattled maker of the drug pentamidine, at the time the most common treatment for the pneumonia striking persons with AIDS. The company had a monopoly on the drug and had raised the price 400 percent, sparking protests at its Chicago-area facility in suburban Rosemont.

The support of other corporations was welcomed, including WPWR-TV (Channel 50), WSNS-TV (Channel 44) and the Navy Pier management itself. AFC and the Illinois Department of Public Health

were hosts for the event. The Ann Sather restaurant and Marshall Field's placed some quilt panels in their windows during the display.

More than 1,000 volunteers helped with the display, which included nearly 3,000 panels. An estimated 20,000 people attended. Donations totaled $50,000, shared among local AIDS service providers.

The Chicago display was part of a national tour that ended in Washington, D.C, in October 1988, on the anniversary of the quilt's first full display during the 1987 March on Washington. The quilt has returned to Chicago in small sections and in one more large showing in 1998, the quilt's largest-ever indoor display. NAMES Project founder Cleve Jones, of San Francisco, has returned to Chicago many

times to promote the need to remember the names of those lost to AIDS.

The volunteer infrastructure that supported all these activities numbered in the tens of thousands. Whether it was sitting by someone's bedside in the Illinois Masonic Medical Center's Unit 371, delivering a meal for Open Hand, picketing the CTA, getting arrested at the Cook County Building or the American Medical Association, lobbying in City Hall or Springfield, coming out among the "Faces of AIDS" for a photo exhibit or book, or simply donating money, the effort to cope with AIDS in Chicago was a herculean task. Not every Chicagoan could rise to the occasion, and many thousands died. As a whole, the community accomplished much to be proud of. ▼

The 1988 display of the NAMES Project AIDS Memorial Quilt in Chicago, at Navy Pier. Photo by Lisa Howe-Ebright.

ONE PERSON CAN CHANGE THE WORLD: SOTOMAYOR

by OWEN KEEHNEN

DANIEL SOTOMAYOR WAS BORN IN 1958 and grew up in poverty in the Humboldt Park area of Chicago. Initially he wanted to be an actor and studied his craft at Center Theatre. He also graduated with a degree in graphic arts from Columbia College.

Sotomayor's life changed dramatically with his AIDS diagnosis in 1988. In autumn of that year, after experiencing the power of ACT UP/New York at the Food and Drug Administration demonstration in Rockville, Md., Sotomayor returned to Chicago transformed. Along with Paul Adams, Lori Cannon and many others, he helped create the Chicago chapter of ACT UP (the AIDS Coalition to Unleash Power), and Sotomayor soon became a highly

visible member of the organization. His colorful HIV-awareness and safe-sex T-shirts, buttons and protest posters helped give the fledgling organization a visual identity and raised needed funds.

Sotomayor also gained notoriety in the activist community for his tireless confrontation of Mayor Richard M. Daley on the issue of AIDS rights and funding. His relentless protests of the mayor's policies included frequent verbal challenges and even the unfurling of a banner at a black-tie gala that read, "Daley, Tell the Truth About AIDS." Daley once said of him, "Why is that man always screaming at me?" Sotomayor's unrelenting tactics are considered a major factor in Daley's significant increase

in AIDS funding during the early 1990s.

On April 24, 1990, ACT UP/Chicago sponsored the National AIDS Action for Healthcare demonstration, a daylong event that consisted of 5,000 to 6,000 protesters clogging the downtown area and targeted the practices of the American Medical Association and the insurance industry in regard to the AIDS epidemic. Sotomayor, Adams, Tim Miller and Billy McMillan emerged with banners flying atop a balcony of the Cook County Building on Clark Street to the cheers of the crowd on the street below.

Eventually Sotomayor and ACT UP/Chicago parted ways. Sotomayor contended that AIDS was the group's primary focus and opposed widening its

> "You just have to do what you can do and don't give up, because one day there are going to be survivors."
> — Danny Sotomayor

Left: Sotomayor circa 1990. Photo by Lisa Howe-Ebright. Right: A 1989 Sotomayor cartoon, courtesy Lori Cannon.

focus to include class, gender and race issues. Sotomayor continued his activism with a new direct-action group, Cure AIDS Now.

Sotomayor's in-your-face methods and ongoing struggle for his own life as well as the welfare of other persons with AIDS (PWAs) was the subject of the Public Broadcasting Service documentary film Short Fuse. His life was also chronicled in a Chicago Reader cover article, "The Angriest Queer." In the Reader piece, Sotomayor remarked, "This isn't a popularity contest, you know. I really don't care whether people like me, or whether they approve of my style or my methods. The question is whether I'm right and whether we're making progress. Because if we are, then fuck 'em."

That focus and that combative nature were also apparent in Sotomayor's cartoons. In 1989 he became the first nationally syndicated, openly gay editorial cartoonist. During his three-year career with such publications as Gay Chicago, Windy City Times, Outlines, Heartland, the Bay Area Reporter, the San Francisco Sentinel, OutWeek, and Au Courant, Sotomayor contributed more than 200 cartoons that cut to the heart of matters with acerbic prowess, tackling such issues as bureaucratic red tape, government indifference, pharmaceutical company greed, the health care system, insurance companies, the demonizing policies of the church, and numerous other issues faced by PWAs.

In the midst of his ongoing struggle with outside forces, Sotomayor's own AIDS battle continued. Through much of 1991 and into 1992 Sotomayor and his partner Scott McPherson (author of the acclaimed play Marvin's Room) cared for each other with the help of Cannon and other close friends. Sotomayor eventually succumbed to AIDS at Illinois Masonic Medical Center on Feb. 5, 1992.

Since his passing there have been several retrospectives of Sotomayor's activism, life, and work—most recently, marking the 15th anniversary of his death, the tribute "When There Were Heroes: The Life and Times of Daniel Sotomayor" at Bailiwick Repertory Theatre and, in April 2007, "Unrelenting Dawn: The Editorial Cartoons of Danny Sotomayor" at Gerber/Hart Library. ▼

McPHERSON: LIFE CATCHES UP TO ART

by OWEN KEEHNEN

SCOTT MCPHERSON WAS BORN IN COLUMBUS, OHIO, IN 1959. HE BEGAN ACTING in high school and went to Ohio University, where he majored in theater and dance. It was there that he first had a play produced, a one-act version of his slapstick farce 'Til the Fat Lady Sings. Since his death, Ohio University has named a theater space in McPherson's honor.

Moving to Chicago in 1981, McPherson wrote for local television and acted with four theater companies, performing in productions such as Larry Kramer's The Normal Heart, The Shrew, and The House of Blue Leaves. A new version of his earlier play, 'Til the Fat Lady Sings, was produced in Chicago by Lifeline Theatre.

McPherson wrote Marvin's Room when he was first diagnosed as HIV-positive but was still healthy. He wrote it on the back of commission reports at his day job. Marvin's Room is a unique blend of absurd humor and powerful emotion centering on the plight of Bessie, a woman diagnosed with leukemia after having spent much of her adult life caring for her sick father, Marvin, and her dotty aunt, Ruth. It is about a caregiver suddenly finding herself in need of care. The dark comedy resonated deeply in the era of AIDS without ever mentioning the disease. It was produced in Chicago at the Goodman and Victory Gardens theaters, both of which have since established playwriting awards in McPherson's name. Marvin's Room was then performed at Hartford Stage in Connecticut before moving to New York City, where it was produced at Playwrights Horizons and eventually the Minetta Lane Theatre.

Scott McPherson

Frank Rich of The New York Times called it "one of the funniest plays of this year as well as one of the wisest and most moving." Marvin's Room received numerous accolades including the Outer Critics Circle Award for Outstanding Off-Broadway Play, the Outer Critics Circle's John Gassner Playwriting Award, the Drama Desk Award for Outstanding New Play, the Dramatists Guild of America's Hull-Warriner Award, and even Outer Critics Circle, Drama Desk and Obie awards to Laura Esterman for her performance in the play.

McPherson was living every writer's dream, and by this time he was also living with AIDS. Oddly, Marvin's Room had become almost a foreshadowing of his own life as McPherson began caring for his ailing lover, the activist and political cartoonist Daniel Sotomayor, while dealing with his own AIDS diagnosis and failing health. "It was like my life was catching up to the play," he said. Yet despite his illness and despite the eventual death of his partner, McPherson never became bitter. Instead, he struggled through his illness with a strength, humility and humor reflective of his work.

After the success of Marvin's Room, McPherson was contracted by Norman Lear's Act III Broadcasting for a script, the screwball farce Legal Briefs. Before his death, McPherson also finished a draft of the Marvin's Room screenplay for Robert De Niro's Tribeca Productions. The film was released in 1996 and starred Diane Keaton, Meryl Streep, Leonardo DiCaprio, and De Niro.

When McPherson died from AIDS-related complications on Nov. 7, 1992, at the age of 33, the theater was robbed of an extremely talented and vital young playwright. ▼

HOLLIS SIGLER: PAINTING THROUGH THE PAIN

by CATHY SEABAUGH

THERE ARE MANY WAYS CHICAGO ARTIST HOLLIS Sigler (1948–2001) can be remembered. Her oil paintings, watercolors, drawings and prints are on view in galleries and collections around the country. Her work is in the permanent collections of the Art Institute of Chicago, the National Museum of Women in the Arts in Washington, D.C., and the Smithsonian American Art Museum. Sigler taught Columbia College students for more than a decade. She lived openly as a lesbian and often was referred to as a distinguished feminist artist. She touched many people.

Sigler's paintings have a delicate dreamlike quality. Her interior scenes and landscapes depict recognizable objects in new, fantastic semiabstractions. She often incorporates borders and frames as integral elements of the painting, sometimes with written text surrounding the images. Hollis Sigler's Breast Cancer Journal, published in 1999, shares a vibrantly colored and emotional diary of what the artist endured as the disease, originally diagnosed in 1985, recurred in 1991 and finally took her life on March 29, 2001. That 10-year battle inspired Sigler to produce thought-provoking pieces such as Etiquette for Dying, Causes and Cures and Dancing on Death's Door. She was just 37 when doctors gave her the diagnosis that her mother and great-grandmother had also faced. This initiated the Breast Cancer Journal painting series, "Walking with the Ghosts of My Grandmothers," exhibited at Chicago's Museum of Contemporary Art in 1994. Sigler had completed more than a hundred works in this series by the time of her death.

Sigler tended her soul by maintaining a large garden behind her Prairie View home, which she shared with her loving, longtime partner, jeweler Patricia Locke.

"For 20 years, it was my privilege to share my life with Hollis," said Locke, whose unique designs have a devoted and growing clientele. "We were home to one another. And out of that we both did a lot of creative work. It was a gift."

Sigler's impact on students, the art community, the breast cancer community, on anyone who encounters her life's work, endures.

"I didn't want people to look at my paintings and think, 'She draws so well,'" Sigler said in a 1994 interview. "I wanted them to look at my work and feel something." ▼

Above: Hollis Sigler's We Have Sold Our Souls to the Devil, 1996, oil on canvas, from her book Hollis Sigler's Breast Cancer Journal. Courtesy Patricia Locke.

Right: Sigler in the 1990s. Photo by Cathy Seabaugh.

ART HISTORY OF GAY CHICAGO

CHICAGO HAS A LONG HISTORY OF BOTH TRADI-tional and daring art, and gays and lesbians have played a critical role in the development of its art scene. Whether through exhibits at the Art Institute, the Museum of Contemporary Art, or other museums, galleries and exhibits in town, gay artists of all kinds have had an impact on the visual beauty of Chicago.

These include photographers who have documented the movement, painters who have inspired the community, and graphic designers who have created the buttons, logos and slogans. Danny Sotomayor's ACT UP posters and editorial cartoons are still relevant 20 years after he created them. The Women in Print movement used vibrant images to provide motivation. The NAMES Project's AIDS Memorial Quilt used art as a way to remember. Critical exhibits have been held at gay-owned or gay-friendly places such as Aldo Castillo Gallery, Leigh Gallery, Catherine Edelman Gallery, Randolph Street Gallery, Woman Made Gallery, and many more. Judy Chicago's Dinner Party exhibit in the 1970s made an important contribution to the feminist movement here and elsewhere.

Graphic designers and companies including Super Gurl, Brad Cawley, Julie Zolot, Firebelly Design, Materville Studios, Dr. Graphix, Toolbox Inc., McKnight Kurland Baccelli, WildeC3 Design, Eric McCool, and David Lee Csicsko, who did the logos for several AIDS groups and Gay Games VII, have donated innumerable hours to help create logos, designs and Web sites for nonprofits.

Individual artists have held important exhibits, such as World AIDS Day or the Faces of AIDS, featuring dozens of photographers, Richard Gray's African-American photo series, Israel Wright's portraits, Lisa Howe-Ebright's photo documentations, Jerry Pritikin's political and sports images, Bob Klunk's detailed art, Jorjet Harper's jewelry and paintings, Michael Bonfiglio's paintings, Erik Sosa's innovative paintings, and more. In the 1990s and 2000s, Juarez Hawkins and Otis Richardson have contributed to the images reflecting African-American gays and lesbians. Riva Lehrer's work takes a penetrating look into queerness and disability. Other artists include Jason Messinger and photographers Steve Becker, Betty Lark Ross, Gary Ward, Rick Aguilar, Terry Gaskins, Bret Grafton and Kat Fitzgerald. The community also lost many important artists to AIDS, including Jon Reich and Gabor.

In the 2000s, queer artists and photographers started GLANCe, the Gay and Lesbian Artist Network of Chicago. ▼

The work of Riva Lehrer (left), and Juarez Hawkins with one of her paintings. Photo at right by Hal Baim.

Artists Jon Reich (left) and Gabor in the 1980s. Photo at right by Lisa Howe-Ebright.

THE 10% SHOW: A FIRST ON CHICAGO TV
by JOHN "JACK" RYAN

THE 10% SHOW WAS CHICAGO'S FIRST TELE- vision program dedicated to the political, social, entertainment and cultural goings-on of the city's LGBT community. The idea for the show started at the Second National March on Washington for Lesbian and Gay Rights in 1987. Just like a lot of people around the country, I returned home energized and inspired. After learning that the march was covered by a group in New York City called the Gay Cable Network, I soon met with Lou

until I was finally able to find the right people with the right skills, the dedication and the dependability to make the show finally take off.

Our first program hit the air in the spring of 1989, and we continued monthly until 1992. Our "funding" was basically the generosity of my partner, Dr. Thomas Stephens (1940–1992), who was a highly esteemed physician and pathologist. Eventually we were also fortunate enough to get some monthly underwriting from

Paul Gernhardt, International Mr. Leather and International Ms Leather contestants, Miss Continental contestants, Dawn Clark Netsch, Lee K, Sandy Duncan, drag queen wrestlers, the Dancing Queens, Bruce Koff, and Gregg Araki.

One of our most exciting programs involved our coverage of a 1989 community meeting with Mayor Richard M. Daley at the Ann Sather restaurant on West Belmont Avenue. The mayor abruptly left the stage, muttering to his liaison. The next day, my voice mail was jammed with requests from

John Ryan (far right in photo) and some of his volunteers and crew for The 10% Show.

Maletta, who created the program, and asked him about opening an office in Chicago.

I found out that local cable-access rules dictated that we create our own programs devoted to Chicago. I had planned to do so eventually, but the rules caused us to jump ahead and make our own programming. The studios and equipment of the nonprofit Chicago Access Corp. were available, but we were never allowed to run advertising. Finding funds and volunteer staff was daunting; I went through generations of volunteers over a period of two years

the new bar at the time, Roscoe's, as well as an old U-matic videocassette recorder from Sidetrack.

The unique thing about The 10% Show was that we never produced anything in the studio: We took our cameras right to where the action was. Over the years we interviewed many high-profile members of the gay community and everyday people as well. People profiled on the show included Phranc, Alix Dobkin, David Leavitt, Marie Kuda, Daniel Sotomayor, The Weather Girls, Linda Clifford, Jon-Henri Damski, Chuck Renslow, Jim Flint, Ralph

virtually every channel in the city for our footage of the confrontation. I spent the whole day being driven to newsrooms, where they copied our coverage for their newscasts.

Our program started in Chicago, but eventually we produced episodes to run in other markets. Along with being shown on five cable systems in Illinois, we had requests from Cincinnati, Louisville, Los Angeles and New York. We might not have had the best program with the biggest budget in the country, but we did have some great people doing some great work, considering all our limitations. We actually had a name for our production company: SBC Productions, which stood for "shitty but cool." ▼

CHICAGO CLOUT: GAY DOLLARS CAMPAIGN   *by JORJET HARPER*

Frank Kellas and Marge Summit were named Gay Chicago Magazine organizers of the year in 1987 for their Gay Dollars campaign. Right: A September 1987 Gay Dollars campaign anniversary event, with Deja Vu Big Band. Photo by Jill Burgin. Photos from the 1987 Windy City Times/Outlines archives.

FOR THE BETTER PART OF A YEAR, GAY PEOPLE STAMPED THEIR money with a red stamp that said simply, "GAY $." During 1987, the bills were turning up everywhere in town. The Gay Dollars Campaign was the brainchild of bar owners Marge Summit of His 'n Hers and Frank Kellas of the Gold Coast. According to Summit, it had three objectives: It proved you don't get AIDS from being around gay people or touching something gay people have touched; it showed that gays and lesbians had financial clout; and it forced straight people "to hand a bill to somebody that said 'Gay' on it and they'd look at you like you're queer—because then you'd know what we feel like, all the time. And it worked."

Summit said that she and Kellas thought up the Gay Dollars idea after a successful local action against the Evergreen grocery at West Belmont Avenue and North Broadway when the store posted signs advising customers to use disinfectant and avoid gay men because they might contract AIDS through casual contact. At the time, the fight to pass a Chicago gay-rights bill was stalled, as city aldermen insisted they had no gay people in their wards. "We had to show them that we're everywhere," Summit recalled. "So I went to my stamp guy and got a stamp that said 'Gay' with a dollar sign, and a red ink pad."

Summit's bar, His 'n Hers, became the base for the money-stamping activity, and soon other gay bars began participating in the project. Eventually 600 stamps were made and sold at cost. "People were sending me letters from out-of-state requesting more stamps," said Summit.

The Secret Service sent a letter to Summit and Kellas demanding they "cease and desist" the marring of federal money. At a City Hall news conference about the matter, Summit and Kellas vowed to continue the project until the gay-rights law was passed. "We were scared, but we couldn't show it," says Summit. "I was afraid they might find a way to take my [adopted] daughter away from me."

In addition to the federal government, at least one local bank was unnerved by the Gay Dollars Campaign. Claiming that gays were defacing currency, Lake View Bank on Diversey Parkway set employees to work on further defacement by blotting out the word "Gay" with black magic marker on any stamped bills they came across. As a result, Summit and Kellas ceremoniously presented the bank's president with a large purple pig trophy as the "Pig Bank of the Year Award."

The campaign lasted for close to a year, ending when the gay-rights bill was passed. According to Summit, a gay man who worked in the federal government told them in confidence that the government estimated more than 17 million dollars had been stamped during the campaign. Because of their work on the Gay Dollars Campaign, Summit and Kellas won both Gay Chicago Magazine's award for Organizers of the Year and the Independent Voters of Illinois–Independent Precinct Organization's Glynn Sudbery Award for Community Service in 1987.

Summit is proud of the impact of the Gay Dollars Campaign but is also bitter about its personal toll, and believes she suffered harassment afterward for her activism. "It cost me my business," she says. "The feds and the city found ways to get back at us, and when I lost my bar, the gay press did nothing to help me." Kellas died in 2003. ▼

THING

FALL 92

NUMBER 7 • $3

WIGSTOCK '92
first photos!

Servin' It!

Larry Tee

Marlon Riggs

Michael Musto

Joan Jett Blakk

Sterling Houston

Lyle Ashton Harris

Reviews
The tee for fall!

The fall 1992 issue of Thing. Right: Earnest Hite (left) with Robert Ford at the June 1994 Chicago tribute to the late African-American gay filmmaker Marlon Riggs. Ford died soon after. Hite, a prominent AIDS activist and writer who lived for two decades with HIV, died in a car accident Jan. 14, 2008, at age 53. Photo by Tracy Baim.

ROBERT FORD: 'SHE KNOWS WHO SHE IS'

by OWEN KEEHNEN

CHICAGO WRITER AND PUBLISHER ROBERT FORD WROTE pieces for various publications such as Planet Roc, Jazzgram, and Babble, but his first venture into publishing was Think Ink, which he described as "very Black, not very gay, but queer-friendly." He considered it a great learning experience. Soon after, Ford hit his stride in the 'zine world with the legendary Thing, the "she knows who she is" publication.

Thing began in 1989 when three friends (Ford, Trent Adkins and Lawrence Warren) decided to start a 'zine that would chronicle, celebrate and recognize the underground world of African-American gay men. He also joked that Thing was a way to "do something with his Macintosh [computer]." It started with a couple of hundred copies.

The 'zine struck a chord. The third issue was sent to the printer for a run of 1,000. Sales continued to climb. The style and layout became graphically slicker, but the content remained hip, urban and sassy. The sixth issue had a print run of 2,000, and eventually rose to 3,000. Those numbers may be relatively small in the magazine world, but for a 'zine (which Ford defined as "any magazine not put out by a corporate entity"), it is huge.

In August 1993, Robert Ford, the publisher, editor, co-art director and primary driving force behind Thing, announced that newly released issue No. 10 would be the final one. Thing had come to an end, but it consistently displayed a quality and style that was nothing short of superb and helped set the standard for underground 'zines. It is often seen as among the format's greatest success stories.

There were several reasons for the end of Thing. Publishing it was dominating Ford's life and taking a toll on his health. "It was too small to generate a lot of funding and too large to run without a staff," he told this writer in an August 1993 interview.

The demands of Thing were also causing him to turn down other projects. After the final issue, Ford was able to devote more time and energy to his weekly music column in Babble and his groundbreaking bimonthly African-American–focused AIDS column in Plus magazine, among other projects. In 1993 Ford was inducted into the Chicago Gay and Lesbian Hall of Fame. He died in 1994 at the age of 32.

Adkins, the co-founder of Thing, was born in 1958 and died of AIDS complications in April 2007. His sister Barbara Walters wrote that he had many passions, including literature, fashion, the arts, music, dancing and much more. ▼

HOT WIRE: DOCUMENTING WOMEN'S CULTURE *by JORJET HARPER*

AS "WOMEN'S MUSIC" BEGAN DEFINING itself in the early 1970s, publications on the subject also began to emerge. Musica, a small newsletter from Oregon edited by Indy Allen, appeared in 1974, and the same year, Paid My Dues, a more ambitious effort edited by Dorothy Dean, started in Milwaukee. In 1977, six Chicago women, including Toni Armstrong, Jr., took over publication of Paid My Dues and kept it going until 1980. In November 1984, a new national publication originated in Chicago, called HOT WIRE: The Journal of Women's Music and Culture. Started by Armstrong, Michele Gautreaux, Anne Morris and Yvonne Zipter, it quickly became the national voice of the burgeoning women's music movement and a wide-ranging chronicle of lesbian feminist culture. After its first year, Armstrong took the helm as publisher and managing editor, with a large crew of dedicated lesbian volunteers. A total of 30 issues of HOT WIRE were published, three times yearly, from 1984 to 1994.

One of HOT WIRE's primary missions was to document and celebrate woman-identified music, writing and performing arts, as well as creative political actions that were of interest to lesbian and feminist readers. Hand-stapled into each issue was a soundsheet—a flexi-disc containing from four to six songs that could be played on a record player—so subscribers could hear the music of performers who were written about in that issue. The magazine garnered subscribers all over the United States, and some in Canada, Mexico, Japan, Australia, Europe and Africa.

HOT WIRE featured cover interviews with women who were well known on the women's music circuit—including Alix Dobkin, Ronnie Gilbert, Linda Tillery, and Melissa Etheridge—as well as interviews with more mainstream figures, like Alice Walker and Kathy Najimy. Centering its reporting on the performers and events at women's festivals, including the National Women's Music Festival, the Michigan Womyn's Music Festival and the East Coast Lesbians' Festival, HOT WIRE also featured women who were prominent in other arts, such as the writer and poet Audre Lorde, the cartoonist Alison Bechdel of Dykes to Watch Out For fame, and the comedians Kate Clinton, Karen Williams, and Suzanne Westenhoefer. All the artists featured were

Two editions of HOT WIRE, including the last (left). Courtesy Jorjet Harper Archives.

women; most were lesbian; and many of them were "stars" in women's music but unknown to the mainstream. The magazine also included straight feminist artists who were gay-friendly.

"We wanted to print a lot of photos. We wanted to cover festivals. We wanted to have feminist writers' input as well—not just in writing articles that are journalistic, but also talking about feminist writing, feminist theater, all of these things, trying to pull together artists who would appreciate each other's work," says Armstrong. "We never covered anything that had men in it. It was all put together by women, every single thing, including the mailing, putting on the stamps, all the writing, everything."

Positioning itself at the intersection of the lesbian movement and the feminist movement, HOT WIRE described, documented and defined an explosive era of lesbian feminist activity. It was a publication that believed in the creative force of liberated women and proud lesbians whom it reported about and spoke to. In the publication's final issue, Armstrong commented that she had been "in the enviable position of interviewing, photographing, and schmoozing with many of the most interesting, talented women of our generation." ▼

FROM OPEN/PAC TO IMPACT: 1980s POLITICS   *by TRACY BAIM*

THE 1980s STARTED ON AN OMINOUS NOTE: Ronald Reagan became president and the world was about to witness the start of a major plague. In Chicago, after the reign of Richard J. Daley, hope was beginning to shine under Mayors Jane Byrne and Harold Washington, and finally a gay-rights bill was passed under Mayor Eugene Sawyer at the end of the decade.

The changes in Chicago between 1980 and 1989 were seismic and may represent the period of greatest political movement for the community. While Chicago still did not see its first gay candidate elected to a major office until the 1990s, there were significant changes that laid the foundation for that to happen.

As the decade began, organizations such as OPEN/PAC (a political action committee), the Chicago Area Republican Gay Organization (CARGO) and the Prairie State Democratic Club had an important impact on electoral politics and served as a training ground for future candidates. CARGO was criticized in 1984 for its endorsement of Reagan, but its members insisted they needed to work from the inside for change. Meanwhile, Democrats strove to further open up their party platform to gays. In the early 1970s, gays had pressured Gov. Daniel Walker on gay rights, and by the 1980s they were pressuring Gov. James R. Thompson to not sign regressive AIDS bills. They marched on Thompson's Chicago home, staging a 24-hour sit-in while other gays met with Thompson or his aides in his office.

In 1987, two gays ran for Cook County commissioner. In that era, County Board seats were filled by citywide elections (rather than by district votes). Openly gay bar owner Jim Flint came in close to the top 10 who would win, and closeted lesbian Lilia Delgado was just a few thousand votes shy of a win, in 11th place. Delgado, who is now out, had served

on the city's Cable Commission for eight years. As part of a blue-ribbon study committee, she pushed for 5 percent set-asides for women-owned businesses, and when Mayor Washington took office he cemented that set-aside for all city contracts—the

Dr. Ron Sable speaks at an IMPACT gala circa 1990. Photo by Lisa Howe-Ebright. Sable ran for alderman twice, and lost; he later died of AIDS.

first time in the nation that such a policy had been enacted.

Tom Hartman, who had been a founding member of Gay and Lesbian Town Meeting, unsuccessfully ran for 48th Ward Democratic committeeman in 1988, and lesbian Jessie Fields ran as a Solidarity Party candidate for the 9th District Congress post that year.

When Ron Sable, an openly gay physician at

Cook County Hospital, ran for 44th Ward alderman against incumbent Bernard Hansen in 1987, AIDS activism was at its peak, and the entire community was becoming more educated and sophisticated about politics. Some gays backed Hansen, but most of the community rallied behind Sable, who came within a few dozen votes of winning. His campaign inspired the creation of the Lesbian and Gay Progressive Democratic Organization, and many of its volunteers went on to help push for Chicago participation in the 1987 March on Washington, the NAMES Project display in Chicago in 1988, and eventually the founding of IMPACT, Chicago's second gay political action committee. IMPACT thrived for many years, with Sable, Laurie Dittman, Nan Schaffer, Robert J. Adams, Nancy J. Katz, Suzanne Kraus, Tom Tunney and many others playing key roles. IMPACT donated money to a wide range of candidates and hosted black-tie galas featuring top local and national leaders, a role inherited in the 1990s by Equality Illinois.

Lesbian and Gay Voter Impact was inspired by IMPACT, and key people including Norm Sloan and Carole Powell spearheaded an effort to register thousands of new voters in 1988.

Sable ran another time for alderman in 1991 but lost by a wider margin. Hansen felt the heat and became stronger on gay issues—so even when gay candidates lost, they inspired the community and caused non-gay politicians to improve. Sable died of AIDS in 1993, but his legacy is still felt more than 15 years later. Crossroads Fund, a progressive funding group close to Sable's heart, honors him each year with an award given in his memory. In 2008, that award was given to Cathy J. Cohen, the well-known Black lesbian professor of political science at the University of Chicago. ▼

Above: Mayor Sawyer and gay activists and allies, from left: Al Wardell, Vince Samar, Steve Jones, Linda Henderson, Larry Rolla, Rick Garcia, Jon-Henri Damski, Art Johnston, Laurie Dittman, Vern Huls, Gerda Muri from PFLAG, Chris Cothran, and Sawyer. Outlines file photo.

Left: Hundreds of people swarmed the Daley Center Plaza on July 27, 1986, to push for a vote on the city's gay bill. From left: Jon Simmons, Achy Obejas, Dewey Herrington, Kit Duffy, Chris Cothran, the Rev. Ninure Saunders and Jim Flint. See pages 166–167 for more details on the rally. Photo by Tracy Baim, Outlines.

Below left: Flier for gays and lesbians backing candidate Washington over Byrne for Chicago mayor. M. Kuda Archives, Oak Park, Ill. Below middle: The race between Jane Byrne and Washington (to his left is Sen. Paul Simon) bitterly divided the gay community. Outlines file photo. Below right: Norm Sloan is honored by IMPACT for his voter registration work. Photo by Lisa Howe-Ebright.

'YES, PROUDLY,' GAY RIGHTS FOR CHICAGO *by TRACY BAIM*

SOUTH SIDE ALD. ANNA LANGFORD WAS A champion for gay rights, and when she had the chance in December 1988 to vote for the bill during the City Council roll call, she proclaimed, "Yes, proudly." After years of failed attempts, of backdoor maneuvering and street-level protests, emotions were high and the relief measurable: Chicago was about to get a gay-rights law.

Seventeen years earlier, in 1971, the first testimony for gay rights was heard in the Chicago City Council under Mayor Richard J. Daley. The remarks by John Abney, president of the Chicago Gay Alliance, were actually not on a gay bill but on two proposed women's-rights bills. On Dec. 7, 1971, Abney issued a statement to the council's Judiciary Committee, supporting the abolition of discrimination on the basis of sex but urging the inclusion of "sexual orientation" as well, because of the unique bias faced by homosexuals. When the effort failed, the group wrote a letter to council members thanking them for allowing the testimony: "For the first time the Chicago City Council was apprised of discrimination against a significant segment of the city's population. … The support we get will be remembered in the voting booths!"

Ald. Clifford P. Kelley, like Langford an African-American, South Side elected official, was a true pioneer for Chicago gay rights. In 1973, he worked with activists from Illinois Gays for Legislative Action (IGLA) to propose the first Chicago bill that would ban bias against gays in jobs, housing and public accommodations. A companion bill would have repealed the law against wearing clothes perceived as those for the opposite sex "with intent to conceal" one's sex. Joining as co-sponsors of Kelley's gay-rights bill were nine aldermen (five were African-American): Eugene Sawyer (future mayor), Robert S. Wilinski, William Cousins Jr. (who later became a Cook County Circuit Court and then a state Appellate Court judge), Anna R. Langford, William H. Shannon, Jimmy S. Washington, Seymour Simon (who later became a state Appellate Court judge and then a state Supreme Court jus-

tice), William S. Singer, and Marilou M. Hedlund. A 10th, Ald. Leon Despres, co-sponsored the trans law repeal but not the gay bill because he objected to the term "sexual orientation."

Kelley's proposals did receive a Judiciary Committee hearing but died when the council session ended. In 1975, with IGLA and a new group, the Task Force on Gay Rights of the Alliance to End Repression, a predominantly straight group, Kelley began work on a new proposal. (That task force eventually became the Illinois Gay and Lesbian Task Force and operated into the late 1980s.) On Feb. 4, 1976, Kelley introduced a new gay-rights bill.

Kelley's new proposals spent several years languishing in committee. The mainstream and gay media covered efforts to reintroduce the legislation, and in 1979 a Chicago Sun-Times series provided an important framework for Chicagoans to understand the gay community better. The series featured interviews with a wide range of gay Chicagoans. Unlike a lot of previous media, this series featured the full names and photos of activists and pointed out that in August, gays had testified for the gay-rights bill at City Hall and that on Sept. 12, 1979, it would face a full City Council vote.

That attempt failed. The anti-gay Plymouth Foundation placed last-minute ads in the mainstream press denouncing the gay bill, warning about gays as police, firefighters and teachers. The right-wing mobilization against the bill would continue until it finally passed nine years later. More opposition came from the Roman Catholic Church and the Rev. Hiram Crawford, a South Side African-American minister. On the eve of a July 1986 full City Council vote, Cardinal Joseph Bernardin, the Catholic archbishop of Chicago, issued a statement opposing the measure and made sure that all 50 City Council members received the statement before the vote. Bernardin said the ordinance could be seen as accepting or approving homosexual activity and that it would infringe on the church's "right to present and practice its moral teaching." Many Catholic

aldermen felt they could not go against their church, and the measure was derailed.

The gay community was outraged, and this time it took to the streets. A massive rally was organized by Mary Mack with support from more than 150 individuals, organizations and gay bars. Hundreds of people swarmed the Daley Center Plaza on July 27 1986 to push for a vote. It was among the most important demonstrations in Chicago's gay history, showing that gays would fight back. Jim Flint was the event's emcee, Art Johnston helped arrange buses from the gay bars, Gary Chichester was stage manager, and Diana Thorpe was the sign-language interpreter. The pumped-up nighttime crowd heard more than a dozen speakers (including Dr. Ron Sable, Achy Obejas, Sister Donna Quinn, Dr. Adrienne Smith, and Ald. Bernard Hansen), and entertainment included Paula Walowitz, the Artemis Singers, the Windy City Gay Chorus and the Chicago Gay Men's Chorus.

The rally worked: There was a vote. The gay-rights bill lost 18–30, but it was considered a victory—gays would know who was for them, and who was against them, when the next aldermanic elections took place. The entire City Council was in chaos those years, with Mayor Harold Washington facing a defiant majority opposition during the "Council Wars." Washington backed gay rights, but he could barely get his own measures through the council. When he died in office in 1987, Ald. Sawyer became his temporary compromise replacement.

After much negotiation with the gay community, in part involving members of the city's gay advisory council as well as representatives of Gay and Lesbian Town Meeting, Sawyer eventually agreed to back a vote on the gay-rights bill in 1988. Town Meeting had formed after the 1986 vote as a coalition organization to act as a clearinghouse for gay bill efforts. It had added structure and officers by 1987, and eventually four people emerged as the primary voice pushing for the 1988 bill. Known as the "Gang of Four," Art Johnston, Jon-Henri Damski,

Laurie Dittman and Rick Garcia spearheaded the efforts, joined by hundreds of activists and dozens of organizations offering support. Though initially resisted by some, a bill that could placate the religious opposition by proposing a coverage exemption for religious activities was drafted, so such opposition was not as strong by the time of the next vote.

There were continued delays into the summer and fall, and on Sept. 14, 1988, the bill was again defeated, 21–26. Activists and City Council allies were defiant, saying it would come up again and again until it won. With a February mayoral election looming, those politicians running citywide wanted to make sure they had the gay vote. Then-State's Attorney Richard M. Daley reportedly lobbied behind the scenes, while his competitors in the mayoral race, Sawyer and Ald. Timothy C. Evans, lobbied for the gay bill in the City Council.

Finally, on Dec. 21, 1988, after 17 years of lobbying by so many diverse groups, the Human Rights Ordinance (as it was unofficially called) passed 28–17 amid loud cheers from supporters. It banned discrimination in employment, housing and public accommodations (and covered other categories such as disability, age and sex). Meanwhile, the city's cross-dressing law had been ruled unconstitutional by Cook County Circuit Judge Jack Sperling in 1973 and was eventually repealed by the City Council on Jan. 27, 1978—"to bring it in compliance with recent decisions of the United States Supreme Court," according to the accompanying council explanation.

The community had arrived, thanks to those initial efforts of Ald. Cliff Kelley and so many others. An entire book could be written on the people and drama behind the eventual passage of gay rights in Chicago and how gays played a role in the mainstream politics of the day. The power and passion of those protests and those City Council votes may never be duplicated. After the 1986 loss, the crowd in the council chamber arose singing "We Shall Overcome." The community did just that, winning full protection two years later. ▼

Mayor Eugene Sawyer (second from left) with his liaison to the gay community, Jon Simmons, and Ald. Anna Langford and Ald. Cliff Kelley, celebrating the gay bill's victory. Simmons was murdered in Los Angeles several years later. Both Sawyer and Langford have also passed away. Photo from Outlines archives.

The Gang of Four + One, in 1988: The informal naming of Art Johnston (from left), Laurie Dittman, Rick Garcia and Jon-Henri Damski as the "Gang of Four" was to note their work on the gay-rights bill's passage. At right is Jon Simmons, who was Mayor Eugene Sawyer's liaison to the gay community. Photo by Lisa Howe-Ebright.

REELING: CHICAGO'S GAY AND LESBIAN FILM FEST *by JORJET HARPER*

REELING: THE CHICAGO LESBIAN & GAY International Film Festival is the second-oldest film festival of its kind in the United States and prides itself on showcasing the best LGBT films and videos annually. It is sponsored every year by Chicago Filmmakers, a nonprofit independent film organization that exemplifies how organizations that are not gay-focused can nevertheless work successfully with the gay community for their mutual benefit.

Executive Director Brenda Webb, who began at Filmmakers in 1978, created the first festival in April 1981. "A lot of the pioneer filmmakers in American avant garde cinema were gay or lesbian people, so it occurred to me to take some of the films that we were showing already and introduce these films to a specific LGBT audience, making those community connections," she recalls.

The first festival was held at Filmmakers' screening room—which was at the time on West Hubbard Street, a space with folding chairs and a maximum capacity of 90—and included mostly experimental films. "The response was so dramatic that it became clear that the festival was fulfilling a need," says Webb. "It took on a life of its own and became an entity that really connected with an audience, using the work as an opportunity to tell the stories of that community. It meant something important and profound—empowering—which was the reason to continue it."

From that beginning, the festival quickly took off. Kenneth Anger appeared in person at the second festival, with Tennessee Williams in the audi-

ence. Through the years, as the festival expanded, films have been screened not only at Filmmakers, but also at a number of other Chicago venues, including the Music Box Theatre, Landmark's Century Centre Cinema, and most recently, the Chicago History Museum. It has introduced the

Promotional photo for the 10th Reeling film fest, with Brenda Webb at left.

work of emerging artists, as for example the first feature film of Gregg Araki and early films of Gus Van Sant.

Chicago Filmmakers was the only gay film festival to screen the film Apartment Zero; it sold out at

the festival, and then returned to the Music Box to set that venue's all-time attendance record. The film did horribly in the overall market, but it did very well in Chicago because the festival had found the audience for it.

The day that Vito Russo, author of The Celluloid Closet, was scheduled to appear at the festival, "the airline he was flying on went bankrupt," recalls Webb. "He was bringing his reels of film with him, and had to scramble to find another flight. It wasn't clear that he was going to make it. He showed up at the door of the Music Box with his film just a few minutes before his show began, saving the day."

The official name of the festival has changed several times over the years, finally settling on Reeling. It has grown from a total of eight screenings for a total audience of 800, to an event that runs over 10 days with about 70 screenings (including short films, 125) and a total attendance of 15,000, with showings at up to six venues around the city plus various parties and other special events. "The festival has obviously changed a lot over the years," says Webb. "Now experimental film is a small part of it. It has more narrative films, documentaries, and a lot of short films, and is much more mainstream than it began, but we do still carve out a space for experimental film."

From award-winning international feature films to social documentaries to experimental shorts, Reeling presents a range of genres that demonstrate the rich diversity of work being produced by, for, and about the LGBT community. ▼

QUEER AUDIENCES, QUEER FILMS *by RICHARD KNIGHT, JR.*

CHICAGO HASN'T BEEN A BIG PLAYER IN the filmmaking industry since Charlie Chaplin stopped making comedies at Essanay Studios in 1916, but the Windy City has been the site of a number of major location shoots. Although very few gay- and lesbian-themed movies have been among them, Chicago's GLBT community has been involved in many historical filmmaking events and trends since the rise of gay liberation in the late 1960s.

Chicago has the unusual distinction of being the home of the Bijou Theater, which advertises itself as "the oldest theatre in the U.S. showing the very finest in gay films since 1969." The Bijou actually opened in 1968 with a program of avant garde and underground films but quickly converted to showing gay porn 24 hours a day.

In 1971, two years after Stonewall, director Colleen Monahan and Elaine Jacobs made Lavender, a 15-minute documentary in which they interviewed a seminary student and her partner. It played around Chicago and the United States and may have been the first lesbian documentary. Queer filmmakers found acceptance for their short documentaries and experimental movies in the underground cinema that flourished at the beginning of the 1970s. The Facets Cinémathèque, opened in 1975, was one of Chicago's first outlets for such movie fare.

The midnight-movie trend created another avenue for films by gay filmmakers. The most prominent were the movies of gay writer-director John Waters, the self-described "Pope of Trash." The bisexual musical The Rocky Horror Picture Show, which kicked off its Chicago run in 1978 at North Lincoln Avenue's legendary Biograph Theater (where gangster John Dillinger was gunned down by authorities in the alley down the street), was the city's most popular Midnight Movie attraction and ran for more than two years.

The GLBT community in Chicago also joined national protests over Hollywood studio films that were considered to have portrayed gays and lesbians in highly prejudicial ways; most prominent among these were 1980's Cruising, 1991's The Silence of the Lambs, 1992's Basic Instinct and 1995's Braveheart.

Portions of the groundbreaking 1984 documentary Before Stonewall were filmed in the city and later shown at Reeling film festival.

The queer movie genre began with a number of landmark films in the early 1990s that helped

Former Chicagoans Guin Turner and Rose Troche during the making of Go Fish. Photo by Tracy Baim.

change outmoded stereotypes. Rose Troche and Guinevere Turner's Go Fish (1994), the wild Judy Tenuta comedy Butch Camp (1996) and the illuminating documentary about gay-bashing, Green on Thursdays (1993), were shot in Chicago as part of the first wave of this movement.

Chicago's diverse gay population has been represented in a number of films and documentaries, including Kevin's Room, a series beginning in 2001 about HIV and STDs produced by Lora Branch in conjunction with the city's Department of Public Health; The Undergrad, Michele Mahoney's hilarious short parody of The Graduate, with all the parts being played by women or drag kings; and On the Downlow, a 2004 film by Tadeo Garcia about closeted Latino street-gang members. Activist Mary Morten and Natalie Hutchison made a short film about African-American lesbians, The Nia Project, in 1993. Ronit Bezalel has made innovative films and her Dyke Diva Web site is a popular destination. Queerborn & Perversion, Ron Pajak's lengthy historical documentary about Chicago's gay community, premiered at Reeling's 2007 festival to wide acclaim.

Another important Chicago filmmaker is Yvonne Welbon, who has been honored for a variety of projects, including Living with Pride: Ruth Ellis at 100, a documentary about an African-American lesbian from Detroit who died in 2000 at age 101. Wendy Jo Carlton is an exciting filmmaker who is relatively new to Chicago. In 2008, a new Chicago-based resource site launched Tello Films, which promotes work by lesbian filmmakers, and Beyond Media does innovative film work.

There have also been a few mainstream films with GLBT themes shot in Chicago. The one with the highest profile is P.J. Hogan's 2002 comedy Unconditional Love, starring gay actor Rupert Everett and Kathy Bates.

A host of gay and gay-friendly film-related personalities were either born and raised in Chicago or spent enough time here to call the Windy City home. Among them: director Vincente Minnelli (father of Liza, one-time husband of Judy Garland), comedic actor and caustic wit Paul Lynde, Oscar scribe and gay icon Bruce Vilanch (who got his start writing at the Chicago Tribune and met his muse, Bette Midler, while she was performing at Mr. Kelly's nightclub), actress Jennifer Beals (Flashdance and The L Word, with fellow Chicagoan Marlee Matlin), and actress Joan Cusack (Oscar-nominated for the queer comedy In & Out). Megan Mullally and Sean Hayes of Will & Grace both have Chicago ties, as do Rent's Anthony Rapp and "D-lister" Kathy Griffin. ▼

THE QUEERING OF CHICAGO CAMPUSES   *by PATRICK K. FINNESSY, Ph.D.*

THE COLLEGE CAMPUS SERVED AS A CLOSET exit for many—students, faculty and staff—during the 20th century. Following World War II, Chicago's campuses became a refuge for gay graduate and undergraduate students who came to the city to attend universities and used college life and the urban environment as part of their coming-out process. Subsequently, professors followed suit, learning from student activism, finding ways to research and discuss gay topics, designing curricula and gradually institutionalizing gay identities into the fabric of the academy.

An emerging public debate about homosexuality crystallized in the 1960s, with students and college professors gradually engaging in the discourse. Although her campus had no visible LGBT presence from students or faculty, Esther Newton, a graduate student at the University of Chicago, wrote a dissertation on drag queens, studying the culture and experiences of primarily gay-identified men who dressed and performed as women to entertain or simply to express their sexual identity. When published, Newton's student work became the first significant anthropological study of a gay community in the United States.

Following Stonewall in 1969, more students initiated lesbian and gay discussion in academic centers throughout the United States, and faculty responded. A new, visible gay presence emerged on Chicago campuses.

One individual at the University of Chicago particularly embodied campus gay visibility. Henry Wiemhoff, a former UC student inspired by Stonewall, organized the University of Chicago Gay Liberation Front. This group hosted a campus dance in February 1970 that was followed by an April 1970 Chicago-area dance at the Coliseum Annex for 2,000 women and men. Not long after these dances, the university group merged with the newly founded Chicago Gay Liberation (CGL), and people from these early groups branched out to form several Chicago LGBT organizations such as the Chicago Gay Alliance, Gay Horizons, and Howard Brown Memorial Clinic (later Health Center).

A few years after Stonewall, students began to use college resources for gay activism. Renee C. Hanover had the assistance of law students when she challenged Section 192-8 of the Chicago Municipal Code, known as the "zipper law," under which, according to police, anyone wearing three items of clothing not commonly worn by the person's own gender was subject to arrest. Law students Kate Dawes, Jo Ann Piontkowski and Marie Kuda, along with William B. Kelley, did the research for a brief in support of a motion to dismiss charges. Subsequently, Kuda has become a prominent activist, researcher and archivist for gay and lesbian culture in Chicago.

In 1973, the Gay Academic Union (GAU) was founded in New York City by an informal group of academics, including eventual University of Illinois at Chicago gay scholar John D'Emilio. The purpose of the GAU was to begin institutionalizing LGBT studies and activism at colleges and universities throughout the United States. A chapter of the GAU opened in Chicago, with Gregory A. Sprague involved in its leadership. The GAU supported early feminist activism, created a gay and lesbian network, and sponsored speakers on topics related to gay studies. A conference for Midwestern gay academics was sponsored by the GAU's Midwest Caucus and held in Ann Arbor, Mich., in 1975. The conference was designed to create solutions for university-related gay problems and develop strategies for gay studies, supporting gay students, group organizing, and legal rights, according to The Chicago Gay Crusader's spring 1975 issue.

In addition to activities with the GAU, Sprague

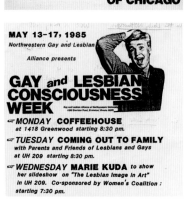

Lavender University's 1978 program, and a flier for 1985 events at Northwestern University. Courtesy M. Kuda Archives, Oak Park.

also taught gay and lesbian history courses at Gay Horizons and Chicago's Lavender University (based on a model on the West Coast). Lavender University was operated by a coordinating committee and assisted by an advisory committee that provided opportunities for lesbians and gay men to share their skills, interests and knowledge in supportive settings. Enrollment was open to everyone regardless of educational background and was co-educational unless same-sex-designated.

During the 1980s, Lavender University became obsolete, as college campuses began to see the slow emergence of gay studies. Chicago's universities also continued to host conferences related to gay issues, topics and concerns, while students rallied against HIV/AIDS.

Also in the 1980s, there was some backlash on campuses as right-wing activists promoted hatred against openly gay students and their allies. At UC, an anti-gay group called "Great White Brotherhood of the Iron Fist" was formed. The Brotherhood published newspapers naming and attacking gays, and threatened them through the mail. Activists, including Irwin Keller, Jonathan Katz, Michèle Bonnarens, Stephanie Bacon and others convinced the administration to act. Keller and Katz became activists on the Chicago gay rights bill before graduating and moving out of town. (Today, Keller is a formerly practicing San Francisco lawyer who is part of the Kinsey Sicks, a male vocal group that performs politically topical humorous material in drag and a cappella at venues nationwide.)

The 1990s saw the institutionalization of gayness in the university setting. Institutions hosted conferences on intersections of race, class, gender and sexuality, and queer studies courses were developed and offered at DePaul University, Northwestern University, the University of Chicago, and the University of

Illinois at Chicago. Other schools such as Northeastern Illinois University, Loyola University, and the Illinois Institute of Technology now had active gay student groups. Several campuses opened offices designed to address lesbian, gay, bisexual and transgender concerns, with paid staff; UIC was the first.

As the century turned, gay activists and scholars were more integrated and assimilated into the fabric of university life. Students were identifying as queer, but their sexuality became less of a primary marker. It is now acceptable to be publicly out without doing gay research or teaching queer studies, as typified by openly gay Roosevelt University President Charles Middleton, or African-American and gay scholar Dwight McBride, who served as UIC's openly gay dean of the College of Liberal Arts and Sciences. Other key professors in the Chicago area who are openly lesbian include Cathy Cohen, Beth Ritchie, Ann Russo, Andrew Suozzo, Jacqueline Taylor, Victoria Shannon, Achy Obejas, and Tonda Hughes. For several years gay historian George Chauncey was based at UC. Jane Saks is doing exciting work as the head of Columbia College's Institute for the Study of Women and Gender in the Arts and Media. The early part of the 21st century also saw collaboration on resources and scholarship through the Chicago Collegiate Pride Fest, a partnership between the city of Chicago and eight universities and colleges, which included debates, roundtables and breakouts on queerness in the new millennium.

By 2008, private, public, secular and religiously affiliated colleges and universities offered queer courses on their Chicago campuses. Today, only 40 years after Esther Newton's dissertation, the queer organizational scene and curriculum are thriving, and there are high-profile queer faculty. Virtually all of the Chicago area's colleges and universities have funded gay student groups, are doing outreach to gay-straight alliances in high schools and are indicating that queerness at the collegiate level has come out of the closet in full force and with no apology. ▼

John D'Emilio, Mark Sherkow and Elizabeth Thomson assisted in the preparation of this article.

Top, from left: Jane Saks of Columbia College, Charles Middleton of Roosevelt University. Bottom, from left: Dwight McBride and John D'Emilio of University of Illinois at Chicago. All photos taken in 2007 by Hal Baim.

A 'CHEERS' FOR CHICAGO: HIS 'N HERS

by JORJET HARPER

Marge Summit (right) with singer Pudgy, who died in 2007. Photo courtesy Gay Chicago Magazine.

Below: Diana Straight-as-an-Arrow lyrics.

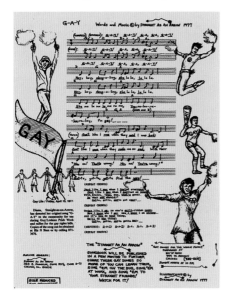

AT A TIME WHEN THE GLBT COMMUNITY was still very fragmented and clannish, His 'n Hers was a lesbian-owned bar that went out of its way to make even straight people feel comfortable. "When I opened His 'n Hers, some gay men thought it was a lesbian bar and lesbians thought it was a men's bar, because usually bars favored one or the other," says Marge Summit. "But I grew up on the South Side in the 1950s, where we had bars where we mixed. Most of my friends were gay men. I call myself a gay woman. So everyone was welcomed at my bar, even straights, as long as you treated everybody with respect."

His 'n Hers first opened on Lincoln Avenue in 1974 and started featuring a small open mike. Diana Straight-as-an-Arrow was a special favorite and a regular open-mike performer in the early years. She wrote songs with gay lyrics, preserved on her album, Diana Straight-as-an-Arrow. She fell ill and died at age 39 and is still remembered fondly by many. Her theme song "G-A-Y" was used at the kickoff of the Chicago Gay and Lesbian Pride March after her death.

In 1976, His 'n Hers moved to a building near Wrigley Field on Addison Street, and in 1979 the groundbreaking record album Gay and Straight Together was recorded there. This collaborative album was the brainchild of Summit and the late singer/songwriter Ginni Clemmens. "We talked to Rich Warren of WFMT. He did the recording for free. He and Ray Nordstrand of WFMT and Chicago magazine loved our open mike and came quite often," says Summit, who was inducted into the Chicago Gay and Lesbian Hall of Fame in 1993. Among selections on the album was a song by Jeff Jones, a straight singer who was initially afraid to perform at a "queer" bar and describes his change of heart in his "Song for His 'n Hers."

As a result of Gay and Straight Together, which was eventually distributed by Folkways Records, His 'n Hers gained some international attention. Gays and lesbians from Europe who had heard the record would stop by the bar when they visited Chicago, just to see the place where it was made. The His 'n Hers open mike became a popular, welcoming community of performers and friends and a fun show for bar patrons. Fledgling musicians were able to gain confidence at the open mikes, and seasoned Chicago performers such as Big Ed and Pudgy were able to try out new material there.

"The open mike really took off after we moved to Addison," recalls Summit. In its heyday during the 1980s, the Sunday-evening open mikes were usually hosted by Dev Singh or the team of Tricia Alexander and Lori Noelle. Many Chicago performers at one point or another graced His 'n Hers' open-mike stage, including Aaron Freeman, Diana Laffey, Paula Walowitz, Toni Armstrong Jr., Frank Tedesso, Sandy Andina, Steve Rich, Alpha Stewart Jr., Doug Lofstrom, and more. His 'n Hers was the only bar in the city where you could regularly see a mix of straight and LGBT performers on the same stage. Over the years, the bar also hosted fundraisers for a variety of causes, including Chicago House and other organizations.

His 'n Hers on Addison closed its doors in 1987, when the building was bought by the Chicago Transit Authority and demolished as part of the renovation and expansion of the Addison el stop. "It was a magic room, thanks to all the entertainers, customers, and employees. We all loved what we did." says Summit. Several of the regular His 'n Hers bartenders went on to establish their own places. Teddy Hoerl opened Opal Station on Clark Street, which featured live music for several years. Michelle Fire went on to open the popular, still-thriving bar Big Chicks. ▼

ART JOHNSTON: FIGHTING FOR EQUALITY IN ILLINOIS
by OWEN KEEHNEN

COMMUNITY LEADER ARTHUR L. JOHNSTON was born in 1943 in North Tonawanda, N.Y. He moved to Chicago to attend Northwestern University, and there he met his partner, Jose "Pepin" Peña. The couple have been together since Oct. 4, 1973.

In 1982 Johnston started working as a weekend bartender at Sidetrack. When the original owner, Rocco Dinverno, died that year, Peña (who compiled the bar's initial video library for Dinverno) and Johnston decided to buy Sidetrack as co-owners. Since that time they have expanded the original space several times, going from 800 square feet to more than 11,000 square feet. Over the past 25-plus years, Johnston and Peña, along with co-owner Chuck Hyde, have revolutionized the video bar concept.

Johnston was an early leader of the Metropolitan Sports Association, serving on its board from 1978 to 1991, and was a board member of the North American Gay Amateur Athletic Alliance. He has served on boards of the Northalsted Area Merchants Association, IMPACT, and the Harvey Milk Fund. He was a founder of the Coalition Against Media/Marketing Prejudice (CAMMP).

As a member of the "Gang of Four" (along with Jon-Henri Damski, Rick Garcia, and Laurie Dittman), Johnston engaged in lobbying efforts that helped persuade the Chicago City Council to pass a human rights ordinance in 1988 banning discrimination on the basis of sexual orientation in housing, employment, public accommodations and credit transactions.

After this groundbreaking success, the group decided to formalize their partnership and, along with Lana Hostetler and Kit Duffy, formed the Illinois Federation for Human Rights in 1992. The organization has since become Equality Illinois (EI). Despite the name change, the mission has remained the same—to "secure, protect, and defend the basic civil rights of gay, lesbian, bi, and transgender Illinoisans." As president of the EI board, Johnston has been a primary driving force of the organization. In 1993, EI helped to extend the basic thrust of the city human rights ordinance victory beyond Chicago borders with passage of the Cook County Human Rights Ordinance. And in 2005, EI was crucial in the inclusion of sexual orientation in the Illinois Human Rights Act. In 16 years, EI has become one of the most powerful civil rights organizations in the Midwest, and the organization was inducted into the Gay and Lesbian Hall of Fame in 2005.

Johnston's generous financial support of numerous gay organizations, his political contributions, his pressuring of corporations to donate to gay causes, and his personal donations to various social groups are too numerous to mention. Sidetrack and its owners have held thousands of benefits for almost every major cause in Chicago, including especially those related to AIDS.

"It would take pages to try to even touch on the

Sidetrack owners Chuck Hyde, Art Johnston and Jose Peña at the bar's 14th anniversary in July 1986. Outlines archives.

devastating personal loss of loved ones and the community loss of a generation and more," Johnston said in 2007. "As a result we all fight harder, work harder, love harder—because we must. The gaping black hole is always there." ▼

SIDETRACK STRIKES GOLD

Sidetrack celebrated its 25th anniversary in 2007 and remains a fixture in Chicago's Lake View neighborhood at 3349 N. Halsted St.

Sidetrack was inspired by the Midnight Sun, a gay bar in San Francisco, and opened April 22, 1982, after its owners spent about two years developing a video library. The club's current owners are Peña, Johnston and Chuck Hyde.

"We always thought the bar would do well and last a long time. We just had no idea it would be as successful as it's been," Johnston said. Sidetrack has 65 employees. The bar sponsors teams in almost every local sport. Sidetrack is one of the strongest supporters of the LGBT community and does not offer any product—beer or liquor—that does not also donate to the community. Sidetrack has raised more than $1 million in sponsorship for a wide range of gay and AIDS organizations. It has also hosted many celebrities and is among the most successful gay bars in the United States, based on volume of sales. **— Ross Forman**

Clockwise from far left: Tim Cain and Boys' Entrance, Chicago's first queer boy rock band. Susan Kahn (left) and Linda Shear in Family of Woman, the first open lesbian rock band in the U.S.; photo by Don Brown in The Paper, 1972. Alexandra Billings before she transitioned to female and lesbian, performing at Club Victoria, mid-1980s. Lesbian singer Vanessa Davis at Taste of Chicago, 1980s, photo by Vern Hester. And Honey West, photographed in 2008 by Amy Braswell. Windy City Times and M. Kuda Archives, Oak Park, Ill.

Linda Shear
A Lesbian Portrait

LESBIAN MUSIC FOR LESBIANS ONLY
Send $6.00 (includes postage & handling) to
OLD LADY BLUE JEANS
Box 515, Dept. MG
Northampton, Ma. 01060

THE ENTERTAINERS: FROM BARS TO BROADWAY *by TRACY BAIM*

EARLIER CHAPTERS COVERED THE DJS and entertainers on the club scene in Chicago. Also important has been the cabaret scene, with gay and non-gay professionals performing at Gentry and other venues. Top names have included Alexandra Billings (also a former Baton girl), Honey West, Karen Mason, Beckie Menzie, Tom Michael, Nan Mason, Rudy de la Mor, Amy Armstrong and Freddy Allen, Daryl Nitz, Stephen Rader, Ginger Tam, Denise Tomasello, Gino DeLuca, Russ Long, Audrey Morris, Suzy Petri, Khris Francis, Michael James, Mama the Last of Song, Debbie Matt, Brad Newquist, Cissy Conner, Shayne Taylor, Paul Marinaro, Steve Wallum and more.

The music at the clubs has also included punk, rock, "homocore" and jazz. Chicago has a long history of alternative music, and the scene has changed over the years, expanding to include a true diversity of music and styles. His 'n Hers and Opal Station catered to a range of gay and lesbian folk performers, while promoters booked queer bands into a variety of straight clubs. Homocore Chicago kept it edgy, booking such acts as Vaginal Creme Davis. Tim Cain started Boys' Entrance, Chicago's first queer boy rock band, in 1991. The nation's first openly lesbian band, Family of Woman, had started in Chicago in the early 1970s, featuring Linda Shear. In the 1980s and 1990s, better-known rockers and

musicians performed outside the closet, including Vanessa Davis, Ellen Rosner, Patty Elvis, Cathy Richardson, Patricia Barber, Ripley Caine, Dylan Rice, Jinx Titanic, Flesh Hungry Dog, Stewed Tomatoes and so many more.

Outlines newspaper (now Windy City Times) produced a benefit CD, High Risk, for the Lesbian Community Cancer Project in the late 1990s, featuring many of Chicago's women's music legends, from rock to folk and punk. Besides some already listed, contributors to the CD included Ginni Clemmens, Diane Laffey, Paula Walowitz, Jorjet Harper, Surrender Dorothy, Laurie Lee Moses, Paula Berg, Betsy Godwin, Pulsation, Kimi Hayes, Anne-Marie

Akin, Michal Brody, Minna Bromberg, Lynne Mandarino, Evil Beaver, Valerie James, Joanne Swanson, Debe Welch, Angie Mead, Linda Smith, Mollycoddle, Godiva!, Three Dollar Bill and Artemis Singers.

LadyFest and, later, Estrojam met the needs of a rocking lesbian younger generation, with dozens of major shows across multiple entertainment platforms. Scott Free's AltQ/Queer Is Folk brings together local and national names to celebrate the queer folk tradition in the 2000s. Homolatte presents alternative music every month for Chicagoans. In addition, Windy City Times sponsors an annual Windy City Gay Idol contest that features some of the top up-and-coming singers of all backgrounds.

Straight women and lesbians teamed for Big Goddess Pow Wows in the 1980s and 1990s, including Marcia Wilkie, Paula Killen and Lisa Buscani. Lesbian comics created their own out routines, including Jessica Halem, Sapna Kumar and Marlene Moore.

A long-running Chicago circuit party has attracted top DJs. It was sponsored annually by the Hearts Foundation, to benefit AIDS charities, but the event imploded under allegations of high expenses for little return.

The Sissy Butch Brothers have brought back burlesque to Chicago, and now that scene is exploding in the 2000s. Also popular are lesbian parties that travel the city to different clubs, with Chix Mix and Dyke Diva among the top promoters. Chicago Kings drag shows were also a big part of the early 2000s scene. Circuit Mom (Matthew Harvat) is an important contributor to benefits and events, bringing style to often-drab black-tie events. Angelique Munro is another top-name local entertainer who can be seen helping to host benefits.

In the 2000s, the entertainment and club scene in Chicago, which had been devastated by AIDS, has seen a resurgence, with entertainers, some of them HIV-positive, refusing to be swallowed into the mainstream. They are doing their thing, whether that is female impersonation or hard rock, club dancing or cabaret singing. From Jackhammer and Mary's Attic to Gentry and newer clubs, performers are finding a way to sing to their own beats. ▼

A Snapshot: Bars 1987

A bar list from Outlines newspaper, July 16, 1987:

ANNEX 3, 3160 N. Clark St., Chicago

AUGIE'S/CK'S, 3726 N. Broadway, Chicago

BATON SHOW LOUNGE, 436 N. Clark St., Chicago

BERLIN, 954 W. Belmont Ave., Chicago

BIG RED'S, 3729 N. Halsted St., Chicago

BLUE PUB, 3059 W. Irving Park Rd., Chicago

BUCK'S SALOON, 3439 N. Halsted St., Chicago

BULLDOG ROAD, 2916 N. Broadway, Chicago

CAROL'S SPEAKEASY, 1355 N. Wells St., Chicago

CHARLIE'S ANGELS, 8710 Golf Rd., Des Plaines

CHEEKS, 2730 N. Clark St., Chicago

CHRISTOPHER STREET, 3458 N. Halsted St., Chicago

THE CLOSET, 3325 N. Broadway, Chicago

CLUB LA RAY, 3150 N. Halsted St., Chicago

COCONUTS, 5246 N. Broadway, Chicago

COMPANY, 2683 N. Halsted St., Chicago

DANDY'S, 2632 N. Halsted St., Chicago

DIFFERENT STROKES, 4923 N. Clark St., Chicago

DOLORES & EDDIE'S, 3700 N. Broadway, Chicago

DOUBLE RR LOUNGE, 200 State St., Calumet City

THE FACTORY, 3474 N. Clark St., Chicago

GENTRY, 712 N. Rush St., Chicago

GLORY HOLE, 1343 N. Wells St., Chicago

GOLD COAST, 5025 N. Clark St., Chicago

HIDEAWAY II, 7301 W. Roosevelt Rd., Forest Park

HIS 'N HERS, 5820 N. Broadway, Chicago

HUNTERS, 1932 E. Higgins Rd., Elk Grove Village

INNBETWEEN, 6301 S. Harlem Ave., Chicago

INNER CIRCLE, 2546 N. Clark St., Chicago

IRENE'S DIAMONDS, 3169 N. Halsted St., Chicago

JEFFERY PUB, 7041 S. Jeffery Blvd., Chicago

JJ'S, 6406 N. Clark St., Chicago

KELLEY'S OUR WAY II,
    648 State Line Rd., Calumet City

L.A. CONNECTION, 3700 N. Halsted St., Chicago

LITTLE JIM'S, 3501 N. Halsted St., Chicago

LOADING DOCK, 3702 N. Halsted St., Chicago

MANEUVERS, 118 E. Jefferson St., Joliet

MANHANDLER, 1948 N. Halsted St., Chicago

MARIA'S LOUNGE, 3037 N. Halsted St., Chicago

MARTIN'S DEN, 5550 S. State St., Chicago

MEDUSA'S, 3257 N. Sheffield Ave., Chicago

MEN'S ROOM, 3359 N. Halsted St., Chicago

MIKE'S TERRACE LOUNGE,
    1137 W. Granville Ave., Chicago

MINESHAFT, 8437 Ogden Ave., Lyons

MR. B'S, 606 State Line Rd., Calumet City

905 CLUB, 905 W. Belmont Ave., Chicago

NORMANDY, 3400 N. Clark St., Chicago

NORTH END, 3733 N. Halsted St., Chicago

NUTBUSH CITY LIMITS, 301 Harlem Ave., Forest Park

131 CLUB, 13126 S. Western Ave., Blue Island

OASIS/MY BROTHER'S PLACE,
    111 W. Hubbard St., Chicago

OFF BROADWAY, 1004 W. Belmont Ave., Chicago

ORBIT ROOM, 3708 N. Broadway, Chicago

PARIS DANCE, 1122 W. Montrose Ave., Chicago

THE PATCH, 201 155th St., Calumet City

THE PELICAN, 6341 N. Clark St., Chicago

PEPPER'S, 1502 W. Jarvis Ave., Chicago

PIGGEN'S PUB, 674 W. Diversey Pkwy, Chicago

POUR HOUSE, 103 155th Pl., Calumet City

RAZMATAZ, 4174 N. Elston Ave., Chicago

RIALTO, 14 W. Van Buren St., Chicago

RICK'S RETREAT, 3445 N. Halsted St., Chicago

RIVERSEDGE, 3548 N. River Rd., Franklin Park

ROCKS, 3320 N. Halsted St., Chicago

ROSCOE'S, 3354-56 N. Halsted St., Chicago

2ND STORY BAR, 157 E. Ohio St., Chicago

SIDETRACK, 3349 N. Halsted St., Chicago

SCOOTERS, 1177 N. Elston Ave., Chicago

SMART BAR, 3730 N. Clark St., Chicago

STOP 65, 65 W. Illinois St., Chicago

21 CLUB, 3042 W. Irving Park Rd., Chicago

TAKE ONE, 2570 N. Clark St., Chicago

TJ'S ON OAK, 46 E. Oak St., Chicago

TOUCHÉ, 2825 N. Lincoln Ave., Chicago

WINDY CITY, 3127 N. Clark St., 2nd Floor, Chicago

FIGHTING BACK WITH CAMMP *by TRACY BAIM*

GAYS STARTED USING THEIR CONSUMER and business clout against corporations in full force in the 1970s, through methods such as protests against the media for anti-gay coverage—by the news divisions and by columnists such as Mike Royko and, as perceived by many in those days, Ann Landers (Landers' later columns were much more balanced on gay issues). There were also pick-

action. Homophobic and AIDS-phobic media and advertising also caused a backlash against corporations. Just as the Gay and Lesbian Alliance Against Defamation (GLAAD) was becoming better-known nationally, Chicago activists took charge of anti-gay slights in our own backyard.

The Coalition Against Media/Marketing Prejudice (CAMMP) announced in January 1988 that it was

CAMMP's Art Johnston, co-owner of Sidetrack bar, wrote a letter to the company in February 1988 asking for an apology and a marketing push to the gay community. As a result, the company took action, and no boycott was necessary.

CAMMP's next action soon followed: a protest against the Kellogg Co. in Battle Creek, Mich., for its TV commercial promoting Nut & Honey cereal,

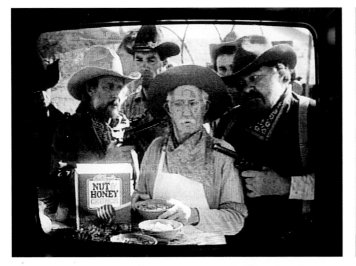

1989
Something NEW for Nuttin' Honey.

which featured an Old West trail cook threatened with bodily harm when the men for whom he cooks mistakenly believe he has called one of them "honey." Kellogg did not respond as quickly as the Stroh company, and Chicago activists spent over a year calling for action. Kellogg cut off communication with CAMMP after the company asserted that the ad did not promote violence. CAMMP's Rick Garcia disrupted a 1988 shareholders meeting where shareholders voted 88 percent to 5 percent against pulling their company out of South Africa because of its apartheid laws. "Of course this company doesn't want to pull out of South Africa," Garcia told Outlines newspaper in May 1988. "It fits perfectly with their attitude toward CAMMP."

At the April 28, 1989, Kellogg shareholders meeting, Joseph Norton, 70, stood up, said he was a relative of the original Kellogg family, came out as a gay man and criticized the anti-gay ad. CEO Bill LaMothe said the company does not believe in violence and did not agree with the interpretation of the ad. However, the company unveiled a new ad that was more benign. Still the pressure continued.

The highly visible work of CAMMP undoubtedly had an impact beyond just those two campaigns—it likely prevented other anti-gay messages in marketing. In the 2000s, more companies than ever are creating gay-specific images for marketing to the community. Today, only a few ads homophobically depict gays as a joke, rather than targeting them as serious consumers. ▼

Top: Nut & Honey ads.
Right: Art Johnston, Linda Henderson, Laurie Dittman and Rick Garcia of CAMMP. Outlines archives.

ets against gay bars for refusing to allow dancing and for racially motivated ID-carding. Groups that were focused on proving the strength of the gay dollar included the Tavern Guild of Chicago and the Metropolitan Business Association.

By the mid-1980s, the AIDS crisis sparked activism against corporate greed and against slow government

taking on the Stroh Brewery Co. for remarks made in The Wall Street Journal by the ad agency handling Stroh beers. Michael Lesser of Lowe Marschalk had said: "I'm surprised beer companies [such as Anheuser-Busch] would think seriously of advertising in gay media. Beer imagery is so delicate that getting associated with homosexuals could be detrimental."

Left: Chicago's sign for the 1987 March on Washington. Right: The front line of the March featured celebrities, movement leaders, and people with AIDS. Photos by Toni Armstrong Jr. and M.J. Murphy for Outlines newspaper.

MARCHING ON WASHINGTON *by TRACY BAIM*

THERE HAVE BEEN FOUR GAY MARCHES ON Washington, but the first two sparked the most grassroots activism back in the marchers' home states. The National March on Washington for Lesbian and Gay Rights, held Oct. 14, 1979, marked the 10th-anniversary year for New York's Stonewall riots and came soon after Dan White's lenient sentence for killing gay San Francisco Supervisor Harvey Milk. More than 100,000 people marched, and many Chicagoans returned home inspired to create political, cultural, sports and other groups.

Eight years later, AIDS had wrapped its tentacles around the gay movement, and it was a very different Second National March on Washington for Lesbian and Gay Rights, held Oct. 11, 1987, with an estimated 500,000 to 650,000 people. The mood was somber at the front of the line, as celebri-

ties such as Whoopi Goldberg were joined by many people with AIDS, in wheelchairs. The NAMES Project's AIDS Memorial Quilt was on display during the weekend, and on Oct. 13 the Supreme Court saw its largest protest since the Vietnam War (more than 800 were arrested, including many future ACT UP Chicagoans and attorney Renee Hanover).

Chicagoans were out in force for the 1987 march, and thousands returned home full of energy and anger, ready to act up and fight back, both in the streets and in the corridors of power. Co-chairs Victor Salvo and Julie Valoni were joined by hundreds of volunteers in the Chicago March on Washington Committee. In subsequent years, Oct. 11 has been marked as National Coming Out Day.

There was also a March on Washington for Les-

bian, Gay and Bi Equal Rights and Liberation that took place in 1993, after Bill Clinton was elected president, so a big focus was on the betrayal of servicemembers under the compromise "don't ask, don't tell" measure. The Millennium March on Washington for Equality, billed as "a national march for gay, lesbian, bisexual, and transgender civil rights," held in 2000, was a more celebrity-filled, corporate-backed event. It was directed by a national board and plagued by controversy because of how it was managed and because funds were reported stolen.

Another important and heavily attended event to which many Chicagoans traveled was the 1994 New York celebration of the 25th anniversary of Stonewall, which coincided with the Gay Games in that city. ▼

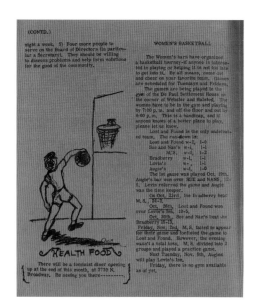

An early 1970s Chicago Lesbian Liberation newsletter promotes a women's basketball league. Before the official gay leagues began, many lesbian and gay bars sponsored teams in various sports. Courtesy M. Kuda Archives, Oak Park, Ill. Former Chicagoan Dave Kopay, a pro football player, came out in the 1970s. He's pictured center in a March 18, 1977, GayLife interview. Right: Diane Gomez has led lesbian pool leagues for decades. Photo by Hal Baim.

Peg Grey was an instrumental leader of the gay sports scene in Chicago, and was the first female co-president of the Federation of Gay Games internationally. She helped start numerous sports leagues and events, including Chicago Metropolitan Sports Association, Women's Sports Association, and the Proud to Run Race. Top left, she played volleyball at Gay Games VII in Chicago in 2006. Bottom left: At the Proud to Run. Right: On the Lost & Found softball team, 1984 (front, fourth from left; Tracy Baim is second from left). Grey died in 2007 at age 61 of cancer. Photos by Bonnie Tunick, Tracy Baim and Outlines.

THE GAY AND LESBIAN SPORTING LIFE *by TRACY BAIM*

FOR THOUSANDS OF GAYS AND LESBIANS, THEIR FIRST STEP INTO THE "GAY WORLD" of Chicago has been onto a softball diamond, a bowling lane, a volleyball court or along the lakefront running paths. The relative safety of the gay-identified sports leagues has fostered the growth of generations of community activists, some of whom eventually became more tied to the community via volunteer work or by becoming leaders and elected officials.

One example is Judge Tom Chiola, an avid athlete since the 1980s on the playing fields of gay sports groups. Competing in a triathlon or a Proud to Run, our city's first openly gay elected official has been intimately connected to the sports scene. Chiola and many like him have become leaders in our community and have also fought the stereotypes of gay men as not being "jocks."

While gay men fight against their often-tortured adolescent experiences of being "last picked," lesbians often have to fight the opposite stereotype. Not all lesbians are jocks, and not all female jocks are lesbians.

In the 1960s and 1970s, lesbians and gays were competing in straight leagues, especially bowling, basketball and softball; they just may not have been "out" while doing it. But by the mid-to-late 1970s, gay and lesbian bars were bolder in their sponsorship of teams. Jan Berger played softball for the Ladybug bar team in a Chicago park, where two-thirds of the teams were made up of lesbians.

Berger, Peg Grey and Jackie Fabri decided to start a league in the late 1970s. The men already had a gay 16-inch softball league that was founded in 1978 as the Gay Athletic Association. By 1983, women's softball was part of GAA. Women's volleyball started that fall (the Swan Club had had a team in the Park District leagues), and women's flag football began in 1988. The league later became the Metropolitan Sports Association and is now known as the Chicago Metropolitan Sports Association (CMSA). More than 30 years later, CMSA is among the largest gay sports organizations in the world, with thousands of members and dozens of sports leagues.

Parallel to CMSA's founding was the creation of a more social group, the Lincoln Park Lagooners (LPL), incorporated in 1977. LPL, which continues to operate in 2008, held massive community events like Cruisin' the Nile in the 1970s, and it hosts social and recreational sports, primarily for men.

Other organizations that started in the 1980s and early 1990s include the Windy City Athletic Association (WCAA), featuring softball, basketball and other sports, and the Women's Sports Association (WSA), founded by Peg Grey and others to create additional opportunities for women across all skill levels. WSA operated from 1993 to 2008, but another group, Women Playing Sports Association, is now taking its place. The competition between the leagues, especially for standing within national sports events, has at times been fierce.

Chicago's lesbian softball was among a handful of women's teams present at the first North American Gay Amateur Athletic Alliance (NAGAAA) women's tournaments, sending CMSA's Irene's Diamonds. Chicago has continued to be well-represented in NAGAAA with teams such as the WCAA Synergy women, among the winningest teams in history. CMSA's Sidetrack and WCAA's Annex men's teams have also had long winning records. The Nubians, an all–African-American women's team in CMSA, has garnered strong attention locally and nationally for its performance and spirit. Several Chicagoans are in the NAGAAA Hall of Fame.

CMSA's strength has been its long-term commitment to fielding a wide range of sports. At its core are softball, flag football, bowling and volleyball, but it has also been strong in other sports and most recently has added soccer and badminton. When it first incorporated as GAA on Dec. 31, 1979, Sam Molinaro was board president, joined by fellow board members Alex Bell, Dan DiLeo, Karen Dillion, Gail Parzygnat, Angelo Rios, Joyce Rzeppa, Kerry Sabinske and Tyrone Sinclair. Art Johnston was also a key early member, and Marcia Hill, 2008 board president, has served the organization for many years as player, official and board member. Dick Uyvari has also been a critical part of CMSA, organizing bowling and being part of national and local bowling tournaments (including the 1983 hosting of the International Gay Bowlers Organization tournament and bowling events at the 2006 Gay Games). CMSA founded and hosted the first annual Chicago Pride Week Invitational bowling tournament.

In 2007, CMSA hosted its first Hall of Fame induction. Those honored were Peg Grey (who had just died of cancer at age 61), Dick Uyvari, Sam Molinaro, Jimmy McKinzey and Marcia Hill. As of 2008, CMSA had 3,100 members. Both CMSA and WCAA have hosted national tournaments in Chicago for softball, volleyball and basketball, and they have sent teams to tournaments around the country.

The Chicago area's longtime sports groups also include the 9 to 12 League for bowlers in the northwest suburbs and the Frontrunners/Frontwalkers (FR/FW) running chapter. While individuals initially started the Proud to Run annual race for charity as part of the CMSA, eventually the race and walk came under the Frontrunners umbrella. The group is well-known for its award-winning refreshment stop along the annual Chicago Marathon route. FR/FW officially started in July 1982 after the success of that first pride run. Peg Grey, Rob Williams and Jim White established the Frontrunners club out of that race. It is part of an international network of Frontrunners clubs; the name comes from the gay track novel The Front Runner by Patricia Nell Warren.

Other recreational groups have thrived in Chicago—some involve sweat; some, brains; and some, both. A long-running bridge club provides a great social outlet. Two exciting additions to the scene in recent years are cheer and performance groups: the Chicago Spirit Brigade and the Righteously Outrageous Twirling Corps (R.O.T.C.). Both have performed all over the city and country and were featured in the Gay Games in Chicago. There have been square dancing groups and the popular drag Chi-Town She-Devils in beards and hoop skirts. The Illinois Gay Rodeo Association also hosts a popular annual gay rodeo event in the Chicago suburbs.

Besides Proud to Run, Chicago athletes have stepped up for other charitable events, especially those focused on AIDS in the 1980s and 1990s. These include the Strike Against AIDS annual bowling benefits at Marigold Bowl, aerobathons, AIDS Walks, AIDS Rides, roller-skating parties at Rainbo Roller Rink, golf benefits and more. CMSA established Athletes Against AIDS in 1987, which helped pay dues for members with AIDS.

CMSA and other sports leagues have been volunteer-run for decades, relying on hundreds of people to pull off complicated and time-consuming tasks. The leagues have survived because of the generosity of their team sponsors, which have been mostly gay and lesbian bars (especially in the early years).

Well before Chicago thought of bidding to host Gay Games VII in 2006, Chicagoans were part of the international Gay Games movement. Peg Grey was the first female co-president of the Federation of Gay Games, and Team Chicago has been a strong local partner for the Federation. Grey, Uyvari and Dave Irvin were early Team Chicago leaders helping to put Chicago on the sports map. In recent years, Team Chicago has pulled existing sports and cultural events under the umbrella of the Midwest GLBT Sports and Cultural Festival.

Openly gay teams, including those playing soccer, men's and women's rugby, and men's ice hockey, peacefully coexist with straight teams in mainstream leagues. Meanwhile, the gay teams are promoted as "gay" but also sometimes include straight players.

Eventually, Chicago's sports infrastructure was strong enough to host Gay Games VII in 2006. Thousands of the city's athletes volunteered to help during the Gay Games, while others competed in events. Many in the cultural community also joined in, singing with choirs, playing with the bands or performing at other events.

Chicago is a sports town, and many gay Chicagoans are also avid spectators. For women there are the Chicago Force pro football team and the Sky pro basketball team. There is pro softball in the suburbs, and possibly there will be a return of pro soccer for women to match the Fire men's team. Many great college teams are in the region. Some of these pro teams, including the Cubs, Sox, Fire, Force and Sky, openly welcome gay fans and have hosted gay events. The Cubs donated Wrigley Field for the Gay Games, and Soldier Field, where the Bears play the macho sport of football, was rented out for the Opening Ceremony.

Sports have come a long way for gay men and women. Pushed ahead by Title IX, women have taken a huge leap forward in the past three decades. Gay men, meanwhile, have fought against stereotypes and achieved great honors. Two former Chicagoans have helped play a role in all of this: pro football player Dave Kopay, who came out in the 1970s, and tennis legend Billie Jean King, who came out strong in the 1980s. Kopay was back for the Gay Games, proud of his home town. King was honorary co-chair for establishing the Center on Halsted.

Athletes are not just jocks. In the gay and lesbian community, they have helped change the world. ▼

MARCIA HILL

Marcia Hill has been a fixture on the Chicago gay sports scene for 25 years. She has been both a participant and an official, and started her second term as president of the Chicago Metropolitan Sports Association in mid-2006, replacing Peter Meyer.

Hill oversees the largest nonprofit, all-volunteer gay and lesbian sports organization in the Midwest, with about 3,000 members—100 of whom are straight.

Originally from Maple Park, Ill., Hill now lives in Chicago. Her favorite sport is softball, and she has played on the same team for 15 years. She was the head referee for men's flag football at the 2005 Gay Super Bowl in San Diego, Calif., and she also officiated the gold-medal game in women's flag football at the 2006 Gay Games VII in Chicago. — *Ross Forman*

Far left: AIDS Ride 1999. Above: The Nubians women's softball team competed in Gay Games VII (photo by Ron Favors) and have represented Chicago at numerous tournaments. Left: Ann Sather's men's basketball from the 1980s. Below, center: CMSA President Lora Kirk and Frontrunners President Bill Greaves (future mayor's liaison) in a promotional photo for the 1993 Proud to Run. CMSA later turned over the event to Frontrunners Chicago. Outlines photos.

The annual Strike Against AIDS bowling tournaments raised funds for numerous local charities. Dick Uyvari (right) has been a key Chicago gay bowling organizer (including for Gay Games VII in Chicago) for three decades. Left: Sponsors, organizers and recipients of funds from a Strike Against AIDS benefit in the late 1980s. Courtesy Gay Chicago Magazine.

LEAPING LESBIAN:
TONI ARMSTRONG JR.

TONI ARMSTRONG JR., A LIFELONG SOCIAL-JUSTICE ORGANIZER who began her activism in high school, first became involved in LGBT issues in 1972 and was a special education teacher and advocate for disability rights for more than 30 years.

She has long been committed to lesbian-feminist women's music and culture, including publishing and editing HOT WIRE: The Journal of Women's Music and Culture, We Shall Go Forth Directory, and Paid My Dues magazine. She was a staff member of the Windy City Times and Outlines newspapers; a concert producer with Chicago's Mountain Moving Coffeehouse; a musician with lesbian bands Surrender Dorothy, Lavender Jane, and others; and a photographer for HOT WIRE as well as women's festivals.

Armstrong advanced LGBT visibility and equality in the K-12 schools, including leading a successful campaign to establish Gay-Straight Alliances in Chicago-area schools and establishing (with Miguel Ayala and the Gay, Lesbian and Straight Education Network [GLSEN]) the national networking alliance of GSAs in the U.S.

Toni Armstrong Jr., in 2007. Photo by Hal Baim.

She has helped launch organizations such as GLSEN Chicago, Color Triangle LGBT anti-racism coalition, Leaping Lesbians Skydiving Club, and the first openly lesbian Red Hat Society chapter (Amazon Lesbian Red Hat Sisterhood).

Armstrong also organized a special daylong program on how lesbian-feminist music changed the course of American history for the Chicago Historical Society; it was the first time any mainstream historical society had acknowledged women's music.

Her achievements have included receiving awards from various women's festivals; playing with Alix Dobkin and Kay Gardner at Carnegie Hall as part of the Stonewall 25 festivities; being named one of the 2006 Gay Games 100 Champions; and being inducted into the Chicago Gay and Lesbian Hall of Fame.

Armstrong moved away from Chicago in 2006, but she maintains contacts in the city and is starting to organize lesbians where she now lives, in Florida. ▼

Mona Noriega (left) and Evette Cardona in 2007. Photo by Hal Baim.

POWER COUPLE

IF EVER THERE WAS A POWER COUPLE IN CHICAGO'S GAY community, it is Mona Noriega and Evette Cardona. They are both active in numerous groups, both within the gay community and in the greater society.

Noriega most recently served as the regional director of the Midwest office of Lambda Legal Defense, which advances civil rights of lesbians, gay men, bisexuals, transgendered, and people living with HIV or AIDS throughout the Midwest. Noriega helped open the Midwest office in Chicago in 1993.

Noriega was founding co-chair and senior bid consultant for Chicago 2006, Inc, where she developed diverse community support for the bid to host the Gay Games. Prior to that, she served as assistant publisher for Windy City Times. Also, Noriega served for eight years on the steering committee of Amigas Latinas.

Cardona is a senior program officer at the Polk Bros. Foundation, the chair of the national organization Funders for Lesbian and Gay Issues and a member of the executive committee of Chicago Latinos in Philanthropy. Cardona is also very active in Chicago's LGBTQ community. She is co-founder of Amigas Latinas and Womyn of All Colors & Cultures Together, a former board member of the Lesbian Community Cancer Project, a current board member of Chicago's first LGBT community center, Center on Halsted, and also a member of Chicago Foundation for Women's Lesbian Leadership Council.

For her work with Amigas Latinas, Cardona was recognized with the Association of Latino Men for Action award for community leadership in 1997; in 2004 she received the María "Maruca" award from Mujeres Latinas en Acción and a Women with Vision award from the Women's Bar Association of Illinois. Seasoned community activists Noriega and Cardona were both inducted into the Gay and Lesbian Hall of Fame. ▼

OUTRAGEOUS POL

by OWEN KEEHNEN

JOAN JETT BLAKK, BORN TERENCE SMITH, HAS BEEN DOING DRAG onstage since Halloween 1974. Blakk first took the spotlight at a 1990 ACT UP demonstration in Chicago when she stepped up and announced, "It's about time Chicago had a queen!" Soon after, Joan Jett Blakk filed to run for mayor of Chicago against Richard M. Daley. She campaigned down Michigan Avenue—going into stores, shaking hands, and even riding in the St. Patrick's Day Parade. The campaign was the subject of the 1991 video *Drag in for Votes*.

Undaunted by the mayoral loss, in 1992 Blakk became the first drag queen to toss her wig into the presidential race. Smuggled into the 1992 Democratic National Convention, she applied her makeup in the bathroom and emerged in a spangled red-white-and-blue outfit onto the floor at Madison Square Garden to announce her candidacy, saying, "If a bad actor can be president, why not a good drag queen?" (It was the first time a candidate has announced an intention to run from the convention floor.)

Running on the Queer Nation Party ticket with the slogan "Lick Bush in '92," Blakk camped it up in her speeches: "I plan to paint the White House lavender and make the Supreme Court more fun by making it the Supremes Court. For national security we will have Dykes on Bikes patrolling the borders, and I plan to fire everyone currently in office." The intention behind her candidacy was to garner as much media attention as possible, bringing visibility to queer people and issues. The gay and lesbian press responded, as did some mainstream media. Blakk even landed a feature piece in the *National Examiner* tabloid.

Following the election, Blakk relocated to San Francisco, where she joined the gay African-American performance group Pomo Afro Homos. In 1996 Blakk once again became a presidential candidate on the Blakk Pantsuit Party ticket, even claiming victory in the Iowa primary. Blakk encouraged voters to vote for her by not voting. The tactic was queerly successful in the Iowa primary, where she received over 440,000 nonvotes. (Former U.S. Sen. Robert J. Dole, the ultimate Republican nominee, received only 25,000 votes.) In 1999 Blakk hit the campaign trail yet again, running for mayor of San Francisco against then-incumbent Willie Brown.

Since then, Blakk has kept very busy on the San Francisco scene, continuing her work as a performance artist, writer and celebrated hostess at club venues and special events. She has appeared in various documentaries such as *Pride Divide* (1997) and *Gendernauts* (2000).

She also remains a visible activist within the community and works with the crystal meth harm-reduction organization, tweaker.org. She is the original hostess at Tina's Cafe and moderates the Gay Men's Community Initiative health forum. She even began the hip live talk show *Late Nite With Joan Jett Blakk*, which celebrates the best in queer art, music, and performance. ▼

Above: Joan Jett Blakk rides in the 1991 Pride Parade as Queer Nation's candidate for U.S. president. Photo by Genyphyr Novak.

Left: Blakk's campaign poster. Outlines photos.

TAKING CHARGE

Gay Men and Lesbians Take Office; People of Color Create Spaces of Their Own

AS THE DECADE DAWNED, AIDS CONTINUED ITS DEADLY GRIP ON Chicago and the world. AIDS activism and institutions changed shape and became more sophisticated, and there was more hope as the administration of Bill Clinton took over the White House in 1992.

Queer Nation's short but inspirational reign also was beginning locally and nationally, as activists sought to reclaim the word "queer," turning it from a slur into a call to arms. They expanded on the media-savvy tactics of ACT UP, fighting against a wide range of enemies.

In 1990, lesbians were also starting to feel the impact of cancer, seeing some of their sisters dying without proper care and resources. The Lesbian Community Cancer Project was formed that year out of a meeting at The Womyn's Gym to fill a critical role for support and visibility, eventually renaming itself as the Lesbian Community Care Project and merging in 2007 with Howard Brown Health Center.

People-of-color organizations were thriving in the 1990s, including Chicago Black Lesbians and Gays, Affinity, Khuli Zaban, Amigas Latinas, Association of Latin Men in Action and Yahimba. As a response to racism within some businesses and organizations, a group called The Color Triangle was formed, bringing together people of color with whites to discuss the hard issues of changing institutions and people. While it lasted just a few years, The Color Triangle brought together some of the community's best leaders to listen and learn.

As a response to increasing violence against the gay community, former Mr. Windy City Alyn Toler formed the Pink Angels in Chicago, a street patrol group modeled after the Guardian Angels. They patrolled heavily gay areas, empowering gay people to take control of the streets. Formal lobbying also took on the need for hate-crimes protections,

Steve Wakefield marches in the 1993 Bud Billiken Parade. Photo by Tracy Baim.

Opposite: Anti-gay Rev. Fred Phelps was confronted by hundreds of gays and their allies when he tried to protest outside the Rev. Greg Dell's Broadway United Methodist Church Nov. 22, 1998. Photo by Tracy Baim.

Supporters surrounded the Rev. Greg Dell's Broadway United Methodist Church in 1998 to protect it from Fred Phelps' protest. Photos by Tracy Baim.

Judge Thomas Chiola.

and the attacks and violent deaths of numerous gay, lesbian and transgender people in the 1990s, including Matthew Shepard in 1998, gave rise to more anti-violence marches and laws. Trans groups in particular focused on the disturbingly high rate of attacks on their community, and community groups educated the public about same-sex domestic violence and police harassment.

The 1990s also saw great progress in the courts locally, including custody and adoption rulings, and support for gays marching in the South Side's Bud Billiken Parade. Chicago attorneys also played roles in critical Midwest and U.S. legal battles, and the opening of a Chicago office of the Lambda Legal Defense & Education Fund provided an important tool for local legal efforts. In addition to work by the American Civil Liberties Union (ACLU) of Illinois, Lambda Legal has been both a visible and supportive partner to individuals and groups in Chicago on AIDS and general gay issues.

The community's groundwork in the 1970s and 1980s, including the races of openly gay candidates, laid a solid foundation for the successful 1990s campaigns of Thomas R. Chiola and Sebastian T. Patti, and created the open atmosphere to allow for later appointments and elections of openly gay and lesbian judges. Larry McKeon also broke new ground when he became the first openly gay person to be an Illinois state representative, and Joanne Trapani crashed the mayoral ceiling, becoming village president of suburban Oak Park. Gays used their clout to

defeat anti-gay pols, like Penny Pullen, and a Black drag queen (Joan Jett Blakk) even ran for mayor and then president.

The Illinois Federation for Human Rights (now Equality Illinois) tried valiantly to pass a state gay-rights bill, but with the state mostly under Republican control, it took years for the bill to get the votes needed to send it to the governor. Cook County made progress on gay rights.

In Chicago, Mayor Richard M. Daley's first term in office was rocky, especially as it related to AIDS issues. He was protested against and screamed at by activists like Danny Sotomayor for not backing more AIDS funding. Eventually, Daley appointed gays to administration posts and overcame his earlier gaps, supporting the Center on Halsted and events such as the Gay Games. Daley backed the rainbow pylon streetscape program along North Halsted Street, supported his gay advisory council's creation of a Gay and Lesbian Hall of Fame, and hosts an annual Pride reception for hundreds of people in the community. He has come a long way on gay issues, in part because of his close friendships with some gay and lesbian people.

The media landscape continued to change in the 1990s. Windy City Times, Outlines, BLACKlines, En La Vida, Gay Chicago Magazine, LesBiGay Radio, Chicago Free Press and the Internet impacted how the community heard about the news. The mainstream media, helped along by newly out gay and lesbian reporters and editors (after much internal debate

about objectivity), took a dramatically different perspective on covering the gay community.

On the youth front, a powerful new group came into play as the Chicago chapter of the Gay, Lesbian and Straight Education Network (GLSEN) helped teachers come out, helped students form gay groups in their high schools, and held a groundbreaking annual scholarship program to honor the next generation of leaders.

One of the most powerful events of the 1990s occurred in 1998. The Rev. Greg Dell of Broadway United Methodist Church was suspended from his duties because he had dared to perform a union ceremony for two gay men. Dell and his wife Jade suffered through tough times, and on Nov. 22, 1998, the anti-gay Rev. Fred Phelps decided to picket the church, located in the heart of Chicago's significantly gay Lake View neighborhood. The gay and non-gay secular and religious community took this as a huge affront and made a major call for people to surround the church that day. Similar to the encirclement of Medinah Temple in 1977 against Anita Bryant's appearance there, more than 1,500 people created a safe zone around Dell and his church. Tears streamed down the cold cheeks of hundreds of people holding hands, making a chain of support.

But unlike in 1977, this 1998 action showed that the non-gay community, more than ever, was willing and able to come to the assistance of its gay friends and neighbors, its family members and colleagues. The world was changing, and with each "coming out," new allies were born. ▼ — Tracy Baim

Far left: Amigas Latinas host a picnic in the 1990s. Top: ALMA marches in the July 1996 Puerto Rican Day Parade. Left: Julio Rodriguez of ALMA. Photos courtesy Hal Baim and Outlines archives.

GAY AND LESBIAN LATINOS REACH OUT *by TRACY BAIM*

THE SIZE AND DIVERSITY OF CHICAGO'S Latino/a communities have often made it difficult to coalesce under a single organization. The differing needs of those born in the United States and immigrants, of those who speak Spanish and those who speak only English, and of those who are geographically and economically diverse have challenged organizers. As with the African-American community, gay, lesbian, bisexual and transgender Latinos have worked within predominantly white gay groups, have worked within predominantly straight Latino organizations as out gay people, and have created stand-alone Latin LGBT organizations.

In the 1980s, as AIDS was beginning to hit Chicago, some agencies started to deal with Latino AIDS issues, including Vida/Sida and Project Vida. Individual activists worked on political and cultural Latina issues, including Mona Noriega, Carmen Abrego, Diane Gomez, Lillian Anguiano, and Amparo Jimenez, who started Latinas Lesbianas en Nuestro Ambiente (LLENA) in the 1980s.

By the mid-1990s, two strong Latin organizations emerged that have played critical roles into the 2000s. Amigas Latinas, co-founded by Evette Cardona, Noriega, Mary Torres and Lydia Vega, has provided hundreds of women with support and networking over the years. It has sponsored community events and scholarships and has provided a safe place for those just coming out. The Association of Latino Men for Action (ALMA) has similarly provided an important safe space for Latino gay men.

The two groups, Amigas and ALMA, are a good example of companion organizations working together and with mainstream gay groups for the betterment of the entire Chicago gay community. Mona Noriega, who served for eight years on the Amigas steering committee, was also a key founding staff member of Lambda Legal's Midwest Regional Office in Chicago. Javier Barajas, Julio Rodriguez, David Munar, Robert Castillo and many others have helped lead ALMA. ALMA and Amigas members played an important role when the na-

tional LLEGÓ gay Latino conference was held in Chicago in October 1998.

An organization started in the 2000s is Orgullo en Acción, a co-gender group working on Latino/a issues co-founded by writer Carlos Mock, activists Nicole Perez and Nilsa Irizarry, and others. On the media front, En La Vida, a sister publication to BLACKlines and Outlines (which is now Windy City Times), ran for 10 years, eventually merging with BLACKlines to become the online magazine Identity. The National Museum of Mexican Art hosts Radio Arte (WRTE, 90.5 FM), which includes the first U.S. radio show hosted by and for Latino GLBT youth, Homofrecuencia, founded by Jorge Valdivia.

As with all of the Chicago lesbian, gay, bi and trans community, summarizing the work of hundreds of Latino activists is not possible in a few short paragraphs here. The Web site www.ChicagoGayHistory.org goes into greater detail, including interviews with key activists. ▼

SOUTH SIDE PRIDE: GAYS IN BILLIKEN PARADE *by TRACY BAIM*

JANICE LAYNE HAD AN IDEA: WHY NOT MARCH AS GAY PEOPLE IN our own communities? Layne wanted an openly gay contingent in the South Side's annual Bud Billiken Parade, the largest African-American parade in the United States. The parade began in 1929 and was based on a character created by gay Chicago novelist Willard Motley. Layne brought her idea to Chicago Black Lesbians and Gays (CBLG), but even some within CBLG felt it would be too risky. So Layne, some CBLG members, and others formed the Ad Hoc Committee of Proud Black Lesbians and Gays (APBLG) to march in the 1993 parade.

The group submitted two applications, one using the word gay, the other turned in later and badly written but with no mention of being a gay group. The second application was accepted. The Chicago Defender newspaper's charity arm, which in the 1940s took over operation of the parade, turned down the gay group, and the legal action started. Assisted by the newly forming Chicago office of the Lambda Legal Defense & Education Fund, APBLG fought back

against Defender Charities. It filed a complaint with the Chicago Commission on Human Relations. APBLG and Lambda convinced the Defender to settle out of court, and its members marched near the front of the parade.

In August 1993 and in two subsequent years, the gay contingent received an almost universally warm acceptance from the crowd. Besides Layne, key people involved were Stephanie Betts, Julianna Cole, Karen Hutt, Saundra Johnson, Karen Long, Lisa Marie Pickens, Stephanie Stephens, Valeria Lopez, Robert T. Ford, Michael O'Connor, Michael Harrington, Michael Norman Haynes, Max Smith and Shelton Watson. Otis Richardson videotaped the marches.

The bold move to be out where you live, or with your ethnic community, inspired the Association of Latin Men in Action, Amigas Latinas and others to march in parades such as those for Mexicans, Puerto Ricans, and even St. Patrick's Day. In 2007, the Parents and Friends of Lesbians and Gays suburban group marched openly in the Crystal Lake Independence Day Parade—their determination reminiscent of that 1993 Bud Billiken Parade. ▼

THE FIGHT WITHIN AND BEYOND THE GAY COMMUNITY

by TRACY BAIM

CHICAGO'S GAY COMMUNITY IS A REFLECTION OF THE GREATER divisions within the city, which is among the nation's most racially segregated. Many generations grew up in homogeneous neighborhoods with stereotypes that were played up in the media and by politicians. The violent 1960s demonstrations on the city's West Side showed that a northern city like Chicago could seem just as racist as those in the nation's South.

The Black Panther Party of the 1960s and 1970s provided a training ground for Black and white gay activists. Many of Chicago's gay activists grew up in that era, and some of the white ones learned important lessons about diversity, while others remained isolationist, treating people of color as tokens or, worse, trying to keep them out of gay bars and neighborhoods.

The Chicago Gay Alliance of the early 1970s had a Black caucus, but it soon broke away to become Third World Gay Revolutionaries. The fight for identity for African-Americans took many forms: political, cultural, social, athletic and spiritual. Sons of Sappho had been a longtime Black lesbian group, going back to the 1940s: Earnestine Medley and Yvonne Hudson were two of the club's early pioneers.

Some African-American gays worked within predominantly white organizations. Others formed independent Black gay groups, and others worked as out gay people within mainstream groups, such as Operation PUSH. When lesbian bars were carding Blacks more aggressively than whites, Pat McCombs initiated a fight for the right to enter and also helped create safe spaces for African-American lesbians with business partner Vera Washington. Their Ex-

ecutive Sweet organization remains important nearly three decades later.

Because of AIDS, the out African-American gay community became larger and more organized in the 1980s, starting organizations such as Kupona Network and Image PLUS (co-founded by Earnest E. Hite Jr., who died in 2008). Men and women of all colors came together in AIDS organizations to provide services and to ACT UP. The Rev. Jesse Jackson's 1980 presidential campaign and the support of gay issues by the Rev. Willie Barrow, an Operation PUSH leader whose son died of AIDS, helped to cement strong ties between non-gay and gay African-Americans. While some Black churches shunned their gay members, others opened their arms. Black politicians in Chicago were overwhelmingly supportive of gay rights, with a few exceptions.

But by the 1990s it was clear that Black gays needed their own institutions to wage a battle on two fronts—the mainstream and the gay community—for visibility, power and access to resources. Key leaders emerged through Chicago Black Lesbians and Gays, a critical unifying agency that brought together individuals and representatives from other organizations. CBLG hosted national Unity conferences, an annual Martin Luther King Jr. breakfast and other events.

Church of the Open Door provided religious services. Yahimba held important conferences in the 1990s for Black lesbians, and Literary Exchange still provides support for Black women writers. The annual Bayard Rustin Awards by Derrick Hicks' Greater Chicago Committee were an important community event in the early 1990s. Affinity Community Services for South Side African-American lesbians is among the city's most important agencies in the 2000s. Adodi,

Left: The 1994 Black gay and lesbian contingent for the Bud Billiken parade. Above: The August 1993 report in Outlines newspaper that the group's request to march was initially rejected. Photo by Tracy Baim.

for African-American gay men, has been a longtime core of the community, with members including Max Smith and Alden Bell keeping it networked with the national movement.

Talents of Chicago has provided social outlets for Black gays, as have DJ Sheron Denise Webb and the late Chef Tania Callaway. Onyx created a safe space for Black leathermen. A Real Read in the 1990s and early 2000s introduced Chicago to a new generation of performers, some of them still active in the 2000s in the POW WOW poetry slam group. Lorraine Sade Baskerville and her Transgenesis group mounted an important interracial trans effort, and Baskerville was a frequent speaker at gay events until she moved away. Art "Chat Daddy" Sims is a party host and columnist working to build bridges between many communities.

Richard Gray created a photo exhibit showing the faces of African-American gays and lesbians. New generations of Black gays are creating spaces for youth, and "houses" take the place of parents who have kicked out their gay teens. The Chicago Black Gay Men's Caucus, including the Rev. Kevin Tindell, is continuing the battle for HIV education.

In the media, Robert Ford's Thing 'zine was around for just a few years but had a huge impact. It was followed for 10 years by BLACK-lines, which merged with En La Vida to become Identity, an online-only publication. Vernita Gray, Max Smith, Donna Weems, Earnest Hite, Lynnell Stephani Long, and others have contributed to BLACKlines and other Windy City Media Group publications. Kevin's Room, a wonderful three-part film series about Black

Renae Ogletree in 2007.
Photo by Hal Baim.

gays and AIDS, has had a national impact, thanks to the work of Lora Branch.

The Rev. Deborah Lake has started Sankofa Way in the 2000s, and some mainstream Black churches are trying to embrace their gay members.

The battles in the 2000s will continue to be against the disproportionate impact of AIDS on the Black gay community and for making sure that Black gay youth and seniors receive the services they need. There are also divisions within the Black gay community, including competing Black Pride events, which show that the community is struggling with unity but is large enough to support multiple projects.

Many longtime activists from the African-American gay community have played integral roles in the wider community's gay and lesbian activism, including Mary Morten, Lora Branch, Vernita Gray, Jackie Anderson, Richard Gray, Israel Wright, Steve Wakefield, Chris Smith, Max Smith, Renae Ogletree, Natalie Hutchison, Lloyd Kelly, the Rev. Juan Reed, Ronald Wadley, Sherri Jackson, Sanford Gaylord, Byron Stewart, C.C. Carter, Gladys Croom, Melba Poole, Vada Vernee, Ted Dobbins, Barb Smith, Michael Harrington, Michael O'Connor and hundreds more. Many more have died, such as E. Kitch Childs, Ortez Alderson, Earnest Hite, Charles Clifton, Thom Ford, Troy Ford, Derrick Hicks and Chris Cothran. Many have worked to dismantle individual and institutional racism at a high personal cost in an effort to change both the gay community's and mainstream society's stereotypes of what it means to be (to paraphrase lesbian playwright Lorraine Hansberry) "young, gifted, Black—and gay." ▼

API GAYS AND LESBIANS CREATE SAFE SPACES *by LOLA LAI JONG*

THE FIRST SECTION OF THIS ARTICLE LISTS pan-Asian groups that shared common goals—most importantly, creating a safe space for gay and lesbian Asian Pacific Islanders (APIs), many of whom were not "out" in the Western sense, to leave their isolation and gather for mutual support and education. API lesbian women were also active in multicultural groups, including The Color Triangle and Womyn of All Colors & Cultures Together (WACT).

1985—Chicago Asian Lesbians Moving (CALM). Co-founders: Patricia Kimura, Mutiara Timor, Lola Lai Jong. Published CALM Voices, the first Midwestern API lesbian newsletter.

1988—Asian Pacific Lesbian Network (APLN). A national organization formed by 31 Asian Pacific lesbians. Made herstory by organizing the first APLN Retreat in the world. APL Network '89: Coming Together, Moving Forward took place Sept. 1–4, 1989, in California. Midwest representatives: 1988, Lola Lai Jong; 1989, Fong Hermes; mid-1990s, Neena Hemmady.

1989—Midwest Asian Dykes (MAD). From Chicago and Madison, Wis. Held fundraisers to support and publicize the first national APLN Retreat.

1989—PALs Networking–Chicago: Pacifica Asian Lesbians. Co-founders: Judy Chen, Mars, Lola Lai Jong. Lesbian, bisexual and questioning women, through 1999.

1990—Asian American AIDS Foundation (AAAF). Provided support through visibility, fundraising and bridging gay and non-gay APIs.

1995—Gay Asian Pacific Islanders of Chicago (GAPIC). Founders: Paul Hagland (now Pauline Park), I Li Hsiao, Lance Chen-Hayes, Sam Chiu. For API gay men, through 1998.

1996—Asian Pacific Islander and South Asian Coalition (APISAC). Included: Chingusai, GAPIC, Khuli Zaban, KoALA, PALs Networking–Chicago, SANGAT/Chicago. May—First API/LGBT presence in Chicago Asian American Parade. June—Marched together in Chicago's Pride Parade, followed by AAAF and AFC.

2005—Invisible to Invincible (i2i): Asian & Pacific Islander Pride of Chicago. Initiated by David Amarathithada and Karl Kimpo. Playwright Dwight Okita also active with i2i. API/LGBTQ group. On the Web at www.chicagoi2i.org.

While sharing the above common goals, the organizations below primarily focused on their respective ethnicities.

1986—SANGAT/Chicago (from the Sanskrit for "togetherness"). Founder: Ifti Nasim. For South Asians and Americans. Also raised AIDS awareness among gay and non-gay South Asians. On the Web at members.aol.com/youngal/sangat.html.

1995—Khuli Zaban (Urdu for "open tongue"; "symbolizes the end of silence that women in our cultures have been forced into"). Founders: Ameel, Aneen. For South and West Asian lesbian, bisexual and questioning women. For more information, contact nhemmady@hotmail.com.

1996–97—Korean American Lesbi Advocate (KoALA). Founders: Jesook Song, Sunyoo Kim. To educate and foster LGBT acceptance among non-gay Korean Americans.

1996–97—Chingusai-Chicago (Korean American Bisexual, Gay, Lesbian and Transgendered Advocate). Founder: Gil Guag.

1996—Korean American (LGBT) Helpline. Sponsors: Chingusai and KoALA. A medium for Korean American LGBT contact.

1997—Lavender Phoenix. Formed by five women tongzhi (comrades), now called Lala in U.S. For lesbian and bisexual women living in or who originally came from China. Hosted several gatherings and remain connected online. On the Web at www.chicagoi2i.org.

Finally, the longest continually operating:

1984—Asians and Friends–Chicago (AFC). Bringing together Asian and non-Asian gay people (historically, nearly all of them male) interested in understanding Asian cultures and in developing friendships through social, cultural and educational activities. AFC was co-founded by Samson Chan when he was just 23 years old. Chan returned to his native Hong Kong in 1991, where he died of AIDS complications in 1995. See www.afchicago.org. ▼

Gays and lesbians march in the 1997 Asian American Parade. Photo courtesy Lola Lai Jong. Right: Longtime Asian lesbian activist Lola Lai Jong is a poet who was part of the LOC (Lesbians on the Couch, or, alternatively, Lesbians of Color) performance group in the 1980s. Photo in 2007 by Hal Baim.

WACT (left) and MACT, mid-1990s. Photos by Tracy Baim, Outlines.

COLOR TRIANGLE: CONFRONTING RACISM *by TRACY BAIM*

CHICAGO'S LONG LEGACY OF GEOGRAPHIC segregation based on race and class has been reflected back through the lens of the gay community. Ongoing instances of racial bias (whether in bars or organizations), along with cross-cultural socializing and political collaboration, have inspired many groups to find better ways to work together.

As the community has grown, so, too, has the number of organizations serving it. As a result, there has been some self-segregation, as some women and men, transfolk, and people of color have created safe spaces to be with their own kind, rather than always being the "tokens" in a group, trying to educate others about sexism, racism, transphobia, etc. But from time to time there have been opportunities to work together on these issues.

In the 1980s, a prominent organization was Black and White Men Together (BWMT), later known as Men of All Colors Together (MACT). Many within BWMT joined primarily for the social interaction and dating opportunities, but the mere existence of BWMT—which was part of a national movement—helped transform opinions. Similarly, Chicago's primarily social Asians and Friends group,

which is still in existence in the 2000s and inspired the formation of similarly named groups elsewhere, has political implications by bringing Asian and non-Asian men together.

Womyn of All Colors and Cultures Together (WACT) was founded in the 1990s based on the MACT model, and into the 2000s it has provided a monthly social opportunity for women of all backgrounds to come together. A truly diverse group, it has nurtured dialogue between many women. "It was because of WACT that groups like Amigas Latinas, Khuli Zaban, and even Affinity were able to begin or expand and strengthen," says WACT cofounder Evette Cardona.

While not an official organization, the International Women's Day Dance also brought diverse women together for many years, starting in the 1980s and moving into the 2000s. Several women's groups started the annual event at a union hall, and later it was held at downtown hotels, attracting more than 1,000 women, straight and gay and across all color lines, to celebrate diversity. The host groups changed over the years, but they included Chicago Women in Trades, Literary Exchange, Mountain Moving

Coffeehouse for Womyn and Children, Affinity, Amigas Latinas and more.

The Color Triangle—probably the most purposefully political of the groups—operated from 1997 until the early 2000s. Founded in part by LesBiGay Radio's Mary F. Morten and Alan Amberg as a way to bring diverse parts of the community together, The Color Triangle was specifically designed to be a coalition of LGBT community leaders committed to ending racism in the LGBT community.

The group held events and forums with titles such as "Confronting Hatred Across Communities," and facilitated organizations' coming together to host dances and cooperate on innovative new multicultural projects (such as the GLSEN Youth Scholarships). It was successful due to the involvement of key leaders such as Morten, Cardona, Toni Armstrong Jr., Renae Ogletree, Chris Smith, Neena Hemmady, Sharmili Majmudar, Mona Noriega, Casey Reese, Javier Barajas, RoiAnn Phillips and many more, most of whom were officers in prominent LGBT organizations. The impact of the Color Triangle group is still felt in Chicago. ▼

Left: An Aug. 24, 1991, Queer Nation anti-violence protest in Lake View.
Above: Robert Castillo and John Pennycuff are partners in life, and in community activism, through Queer Nation, marriage and many other issues.
Below: A Dec. 8, 1991, Queer Nation protest against Cracker Barrel Old Country Stores for their firing of gay people. This protest in Hobart, Ind., was part of a nationwide boycott.

QUEERING THE NATION *by TRACY BAIM*

AS THE ACT UP YEARS WERE COMING TO A close—partly because so many leaders had died and those who survived had fought beyond the point of burnout—Queer Nation rose up. Gays reclaimed the word "queer" in an effort to diminish its power and also because it was seen as a better, all-inclusive name for the community of gay, lesbian, bi, trans, queer/questioning, intersex and allies (GLBTQIA).

New York ACT UP members were outraged at anti-gay violence, so in 1990 they started Queer Nation as a response. Soon, the movement spread across the United States and to a strong Chicago chapter. "We're here, we're queer. Get used to it," shouted members outside a Cracker Barrel restaurant in southern Cook County to protest that company's anti-gay policies. They fought against media bias, closeted politicians and other homophobic obstacles. While QN-Chicago existed only in the early-to-mid-1990s, QN activists including Robert Castillo and John Pennycuff carry on the tradition today, still protesting in the streets with other groups such as Coalition Against Bashing Network in the late 1990s and its renamed continuation, Gay Liberation Network, in the 2000s.

Another queer group that operated in the mid-to-late-1990s was Chicago's Queer to the Left (QTL). "Many queers were dismayed by what they saw as the mainstream gay community's move to-wards assimilation and inattention to issues of economic and political disenfranchisement," said QTL's Yasmin Nair. "QTL used many of the insurgent tactics of ACT UP but worked on distinctly local campaigns—like low-cost housing, in collaboration with COURAJ [Community of Uptown Residents for Affordability and Justice]. QTL also took on the death penalty, arguing that homophobic juries and judges were more likely to sentence queers to the death penalty. QTL began as a crucial voice in Chicago radical organizing. Its membership fell in later years and it became racially and economically homogeneous. Finally, gay marriage divided members (on which direction to take on the issue)." ▼

WITNESS AGAINST BIGOTRY: REV. GREG DELL   *by WILLIAM BURKS*

BROADWAY UNITED METHODIST CHURCH, AT THE corner of West Buckingham Place and North Broadway in Lake View, was at the forefront of lesbian and gay acceptance in a mainstream Protestant denomination. In a 2007 interview, the Rev. Gregory Dell said he estimated the congregation's gay membership at as much as 40 percent when he became its pastor in 1995.

Dell, whose ministry had long involved social issues, including travel to Tehran in 1980 as part of a delegation hoping to resolve the Iran hostage crisis, became more involved in gay and lesbian Christian issues at Broadway Methodist, and celebrated more than 30 commitment ceremonies for same-sex partners. One in 1998, intended to be private, was reported in Windy City Times.

When his defiance of church rules on same-sex marriage was brought to the attention of his bishop, Dell was indicted, tried and convicted in an ecclesiastical court. Stunned, his supporters urged him to appeal the decision, but the result was a one-year suspension of his ministry in the United Methodist Church.

Publicity over his case led the Rev. Fred Phelps of Westboro Baptist Church in Topeka, Kan., to announce that his congregation would picket Broadway Methodist Church on Nov. 22, 1998. Phelps, a rabid homophobe, had picketed the funeral of slain Wyoming youth Matthew Shepard just weeks earlier. In modern times, Phelps' actions have included picketing the funerals of servicemen and women from the Iraq war, blaming their deaths on American acceptance of homosexuality.

Dell's supporters from the Lakeview Action Coalition and dozens of religious organizations surrounded the church with a "Circle of Care" estimated to number at least 2,000, to confront the eight picketers consisting of Phelps and his family members across the street. Contrasting signs—"Fags Die. God Laughs." on Phelps' side and "Sharing God's Love for All People" on the church building itself—distinguished the sentiments of the two groups.

Dell noted at the time that Phelps' actions show that "the power of evil is real," and he remarked on the difference between using the Bible as "an instrument of injury" and "a source of healing." Church member Brian Savage called that Sunday "the most overwhelming day of my life."

Dell served his one-year suspension and then returned to the church. He retired for health reasons in 2007. ▼

Top: Police escort Phelps and his followers from the 1998 protest. Left: Anti-gay Phelps. Right: The Rev. Greg Dell in 2007. Photos by Tracy Baim and Hal Baim.

LESBIANS ORGANIZE TO FIGHT CANCER *by TRACY BAIM*

IN OCTOBER 1990, A SMALL GROUP OF WO-men met to create a new organization for lesbians impacted by cancer. They deliberately wanted to use "lesbian" in the title, and focus on cancer, because it was hitting so many lesbians. The founding meeting was hosted by Nancy Lanoue, who herself had survived cancer, and whose partner, Jeanette Pappas, died of the disease in 1989. It was held at Lanoue's business, Women's Seido Karate (first opened as The Womyn's Gym and now known as Thousand Waves Martial Arts and Self-Defense).

The Lesbian Community Cancer Project (LCCP) thus started small, but eventually had a major impact on Chicago. While the staff itself never grew beyond more than four or five at a time, a lesbian organization that actually used that "L" word meant lesbians were more likely to have a seat at the table for major community debates and discussions. Executive directors including Norma Seledon, Vicki DiProva and Jessica Halem became spokespersons for more than just cancer issues—they were also lesbian leaders on a variety of platforms.

Part of LCCP's mission was visibility. The annual Coming Out Against Cancer balls grew from a few hundred people to 2,000 in a few short years, placing it among the biggest lesbian benefits in the Midwest.

LCCP moved into the Howard Brown Health Center's space in 2004, forming a strong partnership that enabled both organizations to better serve the lesbian, bisexual and transgender community. In 2007, the merger became official, and LCCP is now known as the Lesbian Community Care Program, a part of Howard Brown Health Center.

While many lesbians wanted LCCP to remain independent, funding realities presented a harsh landscape for a stand-alone organization. In addition, in 2007 two LCCP leaders, acting Executive Director Lisa Tonna and former Board President Mary York, were both battling cancer. In early 2008, they lost their lives to the disease, joining a string of cancer-related diagnoses and losses faced by LCCP founders and supporters. ▼

Nancy Lanoue in 2007. Photo by Hal Baim.

Above: Tracy Baim. Photo by Hal Baim. Below: Kevin Boyer. Photo by Gary Ward.

BUSINESS MATTERS

Gay and lesbian business owners have gathered together in various alliances through the years. In the 1970s and 1980s, the Tavern Guild was a network of bar employees and owners. The Gay and Lesbian Coalition of the 1970s included bars. The Metropolitan Business Association (MBA), which I covered in the 1980s, served as a networking and professional group for many types of businesses. But by the 1990s, there was no citywide gay business group—just gay businesses active within their own mainstream chambers of commerce.

In 1995, with one year to go before Chicago would host the Democratic National Convention (DNC), Chicago business owners Art Johnston (Sidetrack), Carrie Barnett (People Like Us Books) and Tom Tunney (Ann Sather) met to see how the gay community could sponsor events that would coincide with the DNC and promote gay businesses. I had been thinking about starting a business group, especially since MBA had closed down several years before. So I brought the idea of a Chicago Area Gay and Lesbian Chamber of Commerce to the three of them. They liked it, and decided a gay business map should be among the new organization's first projects, since it was something tangible that could be handed out during the DNC.

I asked Kevin Boyer, who had served as board president of Gerber/Hart Library, to join me as co-chair of the group, and together we started gathering information to form an official organization. By the summer of 2006, we had elections, and Boyer and I would serve for four years as co-chairs before we stepped down to concentrate our efforts on the bid to host the Gay Games in Chicago. The chamber has grown to hundreds of members, and it hosts professional and social events year-round.

While there have been many gay business groups in the United States, Chicago's is believed to be the first to use the word "Chamber" in its name, a decision that achieved its goal of getting large-scale publicity for the clout of the gay business community. There is now also a nationwide gay business group, and it, too, uses the word "Chamber"—the National Gay and Lesbian Chamber of Commerce. **— *Tracy Baim***

Left: 1996 and 1997 Dyke Marches in Chicago.
Below: The 2005 Dyke March, as participants marched from
Andersonville along Bryn Mawr Avenue to the lakefront.
Photos by Tracy Baim, Outlines newspaper.

DYKE MARCH, CHICAGO STYLE *by AMY WOOTEN*

THE FIRST DYKE MARCH, CREATED BY THE DIRECT-ACTION GROUP
Lesbian Avengers, took place in New York City in 1992 as a response to the predominantly white, gay-male-dominated Pride Parade. In 1993, the group put on a well-attended national Dyke March in Washington, D.C. Soon after, other cities across the United States adopted the grassroots event, which typically takes place the day before a city's Pride Parade.

A Chicago troupe of the Lesbian Avengers brought Dyke March to the Windy City in 1996 as a response to what they considered the city's male-dominated, corporate Pride Parade. Every Saturday before the annual Pride Parade, participants march through the streets of Andersonville and Edgewater, ending at Hollywood Beach (officially Kathy Osterman Beach, renamed in honor of the late pro-LGBT city alderwoman) to enjoy a rally and live en-

tertainment. (The first march took place in Lake View at night.)

The Chicago volunteer-led, non-corporate grassroots event has evolved over the years. In the beginning, primarily all-white organizers put the event together. Eventually, a number of organizations, such as Amigas Latinas and Affinity, became involved in the process out of concern that the annual event lacked diversity.

Around the year 2000, Chicago's Dyke March became much more diverse and inclusive, with individuals from a variety of organizations participating. The Chicago Dyke March continues to emphasize the importance of bridging gaps within the LGBT community.

Although more than a decade later the Dyke March remains a direct-action event at its core, it has also evolved into a networking event for the diverse Chicago lesbian community. ▼

CHICAGO AND ILLINOIS: MAKING IT LEGAL   *by TRACY BAIM*

"CLOUT" IS A WORD OFTEN HEARD IN CHI- cago, particularly in reference to Richard J. and Richard M. Daley. But in the 1980s, the gay community started to show its own clout, starting with the administration of Mayor Jane Byrne. When law enforcement officers raided gay bars during Byrne's tenure, bar owners and activists pressured her, and she came down on the side of the community.

When Mayor Harold Washington took office in

time community liaison in 1987, but her term was affected by Washington's death on Nov. 25, 1987. Baker continued as liaison for another year, but Mayor Eugene Sawyer eventually replaced her with Jon Simmons in 1989. Sawyer lost an election campaign to Mayor Richard M. Daley on April 4, 1989, but Simmons stayed on for some time during Daley's troubled early years, serving until June 23, 1991, as Daley gained his footing with a com-

gressive tone at the start of the meeting; others said that attorney and activist Larry Rolla was wrong to attack the administration's honesty and integrity during his own speech; and others blamed ACT UP members who heckled the mayor.

The next day, about 200 activists turned out for a protest at City Hall, with 14 staging a sit-in, and several people were arrested, including ACT UP's Danny Sotomayor. This period of time was tense, as the community was testing the new mayor on his commitment to AIDS and gay issues. Daley subsequently met with gay leaders and the gay media.

Despite those early bumpy years, Daley became an extremely popular mayor among most of the Chicago gay community.

In 1991, COGLI became the Advisory Council on Gay and Lesbian Issues (now called the Advisory Council on Lesbian, Gay, Bisexual and Transgender Issues) and was attached to the reorganized city Human Relations Commission, along with other similar councils. Lawrence J. "Larry" McKeon served as the gay and lesbian advisory council's director and community liaison from January 1992 to January 1996, and Mary F. Morten served from August 1997 to March 2000. William W. "Bill"

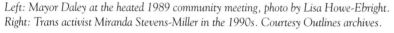

Left: Mayor Daley at the heated 1989 community meeting, photo by Lisa Howe-Ebright.
Right: Trans activist Miranda Stevens-Miller in the 1990s. Courtesy Outlines archives.

1983, he did so in part with support from a diverse coalition, including gays and lesbians. He soon appointed a part-time liaison to the Illinois Gay and Lesbian Task Force, Kenneth E. Glover, a straight, African-American man. When Glover left Chicago, Kit Duffy—a straight woman—took his place in April 1985 and expanded the role of liaison to a more comprehensive one that served the entire gay and lesbian community. Duffy was well liked in her role and, though her term was short, she made a significant impact. While Duffy was liaison, Washington appointed a mayoral Committee on Gay and Lesbian Issues (COGLI) in 1985.

Lesbian activist Peggy Baker became the full-

munity ravaged by AIDS and also distrustful of authority.

In that period, Daley reorganized the city's advisory bodies, so he was criticized for a long delay on appointments. Daley appointed lesbian activist Nancy Reiff to a post of special assistant to the mayor within the mayor's office itself. Some felt having dueling liaisons caused strife. Reiff served from June 28, 1989, to January 1992. During a November 1989 gay community meeting at the Ann Sather restaurant on West Belmont Avenue, Daley and Reiff were booed by many of the more than 100 attendees, and the meeting deteriorated. Daley eventually walked out, saying "Adios." Some blamed the mayor for his ag-

Greaves has been director and community liaison since December 2000. He has served longer in this position than any other person.

The advisory council, along with external advocates, fought a long battle to have the city's human rights ordinance include explicit protections against discrimination based on gender identity. The campaign finally succeeded, and the ordinance was amended on Nov. 6, 2002. Among those advocating for this change were Robert Castillo, John Pennycuff, Catherine Sikora, Morten and Greaves from the advisory council, and Miranda Stevens-Miller from It's Time, Illinois, which is now called Illinois Gender Advocates. ▼

A SEAT AT THE TABLE *by TRACY BAIM*

THE 1990s STARTED WITH A SENSE OF INEVITABILITY FOR POLITICAL activists: Someday there would be a gay or lesbian person elected to a major office in Illinois. Dr. Ron Sable failed in his second attempt for alderman in 1991, and it would be another decade before the City Council had an openly gay man. But there was hope for change.

The 1990s did start out with a big victory for the community. Openly gay Terry P. Cosgrove and Personal PAC, a pro-choice group, were among those spearheading the effort to oust incumbent Republican state Rep. Penny Pullen from her post because of anti-gay and AIDS-phobic efforts. Pullen had been appointed to President Ronald Reagan's President's Commission on the HIV Epidemic despite her horrible record on the issue. An editorial in Outlines newspaper in July 1987 called the appointment an "assassination attempt" by Reagan because he was stacking his panel with ignorant people who would cause the deaths of even more people with AIDS. Republican Rosemary Mulligan won a very close primary race over Pullen in 1992, was elected, and serves still in 2008 as a pro-gay, pro-choice advocate.

That same year, the gay and lesbian community stood solidly behind the race of pro-gay Carol Moseley Braun, who became the first African-American woman ever elected to the U.S. Senate. Gays played a critical role in her election, including appearances at huge gay rallies for her, and she did not disappoint while in office, appointing a gay liaison and opposing the "don't ask, don't tell" military gay ban.

Thomas R. Chiola broke the pink ceiling for good in 1994 when he won a Cook County Circuit Court judgeship. He ran a tough race throughout the 8th Subcircuit and against the Democratic machine. By 2008, there were more than a dozen openly gay and lesbian judges: Sebastian T. Patti, Nancy J. Katz (the first appointed open lesbian judge), Cheryl Cesario, Sophia Hall, Stuart P. Katz, Patricia M. Logue, Noreen V. Love, Michael B. McHale, Sherry Pethers (the first open lesbian to win her judgeship by election), Mary Colleen Roberts, Colleen F. Sheehan, James E. Snyder and Lori M. Wolfson. An effort to unseat anti-gay Judge Susan J. McDunn, who ruled against a same-sex adoption, was unsuccessful but still showed that gays were gaining clout even in races far down on the ballot. The judicial victories were assisted greatly by the work of the Lesbian and Gay Bar Association of Chicago (LAGBAC).

Even today, gays who become judges are faced with a difficult dilemma: rules that keep them silent on our issues. The real need was for a wider range of officials. In 1996, Lawrence J. McKeon met that need, becoming the first openly

Larry McKeon, the state's first openly gay legislator, during his years as a state representative. Courtesy Outlines newspaper archives.

gay person elected to the state legislature, from the North Side's 34th House District. Larry McKeon had been Mayor Richard M. Daley's gay liaison, and he served as state representative until resigning for health reasons in 2006. McKeon was also the first openly HIV-positive Illinois officeholder, so when he stepped down, the politicians appointing a replacement tapped an openly gay, HIV-positive activist and aldermanic aide, Gregory S. Harris. Greg Harris easily won election to a full term in 2007.

In near west suburban Oak Park, Joanne Trapani, a former New Yorker who had been a leader of the Illinois Gay and Lesbian Task Force, was making her own history. She won a seat on the Oak Park village board in 1997, and in 2001 she was elected village president, thus becoming the first openly lesbian mayor in Illinois. Ray Johnson, a gay man, was elected to the Oak Park board in 2001.

IMPACT, a gay political action committee started in the late 1980s, was gone by the mid-1990s, in part because some people felt it was too aligned with the Democratic Party; they wanted a more bipartisan political action committee. By the early 1990s, a new organization was lobbying and fundraising: the Illinois Federation for Human Rights. It eventually became Equality Illinois, which in 2008 still lobbies on statewide issues, besides supporting gay and pro-gay candidates.

The 1988 race for governor was a perfect example of the need for a bipartisan group: The Democratic candidate supported by the party was Glenn Poshard, widely perceived as anti-gay. Some gays were tired of Democrats taking them for granted, so they voted instead for George Ryan, who eventually won (and backed the state gay bill when in office). State Rep. Larry McKeon was among those Democratic elected officials who bucked their party because of Poshard's record. Some Dems, including Tom Tunney (who would become a Chicago alderman in 2003), formed Progressives in Politics to support Ryan and some pro-gay Democrats.

Other important political groups for Chicago included the national Gay and Lesbian Victory Fund, which raises money for gay candidates around the United States, and the Human Rights Campaign (HRC), an organization that lobbies for federal laws and funding. HRC sponsors an annual Chicago black-tie gala and numerous community events, and several Chicagoans have served in prominent positions on its national leadership boards. In recent years, HRC has taken heat for its flip-flopping on trans issues, first winning kudos for its work on inclusion, and then in 2007 upsetting trans people and their allies for supporting a federal job protection bill that eliminated explicit gender-identity coverage. ▼

SOME KEY DATES IN CHICAGO AND ILLINOIS:

Elimination of the state's ban on consensual sodomy, 1961.

Passage of Chicago's human rights ordinance, Dec. 21, 1988.

Passage of a gay amendment to the Illinois hate crimes law on Sept. 11, 1990, with an effective date of Jan. 1, 1991.

Establishment of the Chicago Gay and Lesbian Hall of Fame, June 1991.

Approval of city government employees' bereavement leave for domestic partners, 1993.

Passage of an ordinance granting fringe benefits to same-sex domestic partners of city government employees, March 19, 1997.

Designation of North Halsted Street—between West Belmont and West Waveland avenues—to mark an officially recognized gay neighborhood in 1997, and dedication of the North Halsted Streetscape on Nov. 14, 1998.

Passage of a gender-identity ordinance, which added "gender identity" as a protected class under Chicago human rights legislation, Nov. 6, 2002.

Passage of a Cook County domestic partnership registry ordinance in June 2003; the registry opened Oct. 1, 2003, with Castillo and Pennycuff first in line.

Establishment of the city's annual "Salute to LGBT Veterans," the only one of its kind in the United States, June 22, 2004.

Addition of "sexual orientation" (which, by express definition, includes "gender identity") as a protected class under the Illinois Human Rights Act; the amendment passed both houses, January 2005; was signed by Gov. Rod Blagojevich, Jan. 21, 2005; and became effective Jan. 1, 2006.

On the bad side:

The Illinois Defense of Marriage Act was passed May 24, 1996, and became effective immediately.

—Tracy Baim, with research contributions by William W. Greaves.

Lambda Legal in the 1995 Chicago Pride Parade. Photo by Tracy Baim.

CHANGING THE COURTS   *by TRACY BAIM*

CHICAGO IS HOME TO KEY GAY LEGAL AD-vocates, including individual attorneys, small firms, large international partnerships and legal advocacy groups. The American Civil Liberties Union (ACLU) of Illinois has worked on gay and AIDS cases since the 1980s, and Chicago was fortunate, thanks to a bequest from the late Bon Foster, to open the Midwest office of Lambda Legal Defense & Education Fund here in the early 1990s. Attorney Patricia M. Logue (now a judge) and activist Mona Noriega (who later returned to head the Midwest office) opened that office and set a strong pace for future victories in Illinois and surrounding states.

Both Lambda and ACLU have fought for gays and people with AIDS on a number of fronts, including precedent-setting cases on employment, public accommodations, housing and much more. They have worked on adoption and custody issues, against anti-gay policies by the Boy Scouts and schools, on transgender rights, and on nationally significant cases. Logue has been active in U.S. Supreme Court cases and was inducted in 2003 into the Chicago Gay and Lesbian Hall of Fame. Noriega is in the Hall of Fame for her legal work and community activism.

Individual firms such as Mulryan and York—attorneys Rosemary Mulryan and Mary York (who died of cancer in 2008)—have teamed with others to fight for custody and adoption rights. Professors such as Mark Wojcik and legal activists such as Susana Darwin have kept legal and judicial-election issues in the spotlight, including their work through the Lesbian and Gay Bar Association of Chicago.

Legal progress of LGBT issues in Illinois has been remarkable since the 1970s, due in large part to the hundreds of attorneys, law firms and activists helping to shape the legal landscape. Although the first openly gay judge was not elected until the 1990s, now there are more than a dozen, and still more will be joining those already on the bench. ▼

OUT OF THE CLASSROOM CLOSET   *by TRACY BAIM*

IN 1969, MARGARET "SKEETER" WILSON started what may have been the first national group for gay teachers, the National Gay Teachers Association. She spoke at Chicago Pride rallies and advocated for more open policies for both teachers and students. During early Pride parades, teachers could not march openly without fear of losing their jobs. Some even marched with their faces covered.

But in the mid-1990s, Chicago's teachers and students began to burst out of the closets. The Chicago chapter of the Gay, Lesbian and Straight Teachers Network (GLSTN) (later renamed GLSEN, the Gay, Lesbian and Straight Education Network) was founded by teacher Matt Stuczynski in 1994 and ran strong for several years. Leaders included Betty Lark Ross, Richard Rhykus, Daniel Bender, Peg Grey, Alice Cozad and dozens of others.

While college and university gay campus groups had existed since the 1970s, high schools were another matter entirely. The Chicago area was among the early places that established Gay-Straight Alliance (GSA) clubs in city and suburban high schools. Whitney M. Young Magnet High School started the first high-school–based GSA in Chicago, co-founded by Miguel Ayala and Tiffani St. Cloud in 1996. Soon thereafter, Ayala joined with GLSTN

Youth Leadership Development coordinator Toni Armstrong Jr. to start Student Pride Chicago, the networking alliance of gay student clubs; this program was adopted and further developed by the national GLSEN organization.

Armstrong was a key motivator and mentor for many youth and helped to foster interschool networking through regional Youth Leadership Summits, helping to train the next generation of GLBT leaders. Several of those individuals, including dozens acknowledged through the annual GLSEN youth scholarships, went on to key positions within the Chicago gay community today, including Joe Hollendoner, Tony Alvarado Rivera, and Casey Schwartz. Miguel Ayala moved to Washington, D.C., and became communications director of the Congressional Hispanic Caucus. GLSEN's annual scholarships awards ceremony was among the top events of the year, featuring a panel of the best and brightest queer youth speaking about their experiences of homophobia and activism.

GLSEN also helped teachers. For example, Patricia Tomaso worked tirelessly to get sexual orientation added to the fair practices section of the Chicago Teachers Union contract, among other progress at CTU. GLSEN raised funds and spear-

headed a major campaign to work with Mayor Richard M. Daley's liaison Mary F. Morten to buy hundreds of copies of the documentary It's Elementary: Talking About Gay Issues in School and to distribute them free to the Chicago schools, a groundbreaking effort to provide a well-rounded educational video about respecting and protecting all youth. The women's sports pioneer Billie Jean King was an early major financial supporter of the project.

While the Illinois Gay and Lesbian Task Force and other 1970s and 1980s groups had done considerable outreach to school counselors and educators, the impact of GLSEN has been profound. The Chicago chapter folded in the 2000s, but the work that was done will be invaluable for many years to come.

There are several resources for teachers and youth today, among them the Illinois Safe Schools Alliance, Center on Halsted's youth program, Howard Brown Health Center's Broadway Youth Center, Du Page QYC, About Face Youth Theatre, the South Side Youth Pride Center, Affinity Community Services' youth outreach, and dozens of support groups in high schools and on college campuses. Windy City Times newspaper also honors youth, with its 30 Under 30 annual awards. ▼

GLSEN in Chicago Pride, 1990s. Photo courtesy Toni Armstrong Jr. (in blue shirt, holding banner). Right, Margaret "Skeeter" Wilson in 2007. Photo by Hal Baim.

TRIBUTES: CHICAGO'S GAY AND LESBIAN HALL OF FAME *by JORJET HARPER*

THE CHICAGO GAY AND LESBIAN HALL Of Fame is the first municipal institution of its kind in the United States, and possibly in the world. It was established in June 1991 with the support of the city Commission on Human Relations' Advisory Council on Gay and Lesbian Issues (now called the Advisory Council on Lesbian, Gay, Bisexual and Transgender Issues [ACLGBTI]) to honor the many contributions of Chicago's gay, lesbian, bisexual and transgender people, organizations and "friends" of the community, and is a unique tribute to dedicated individuals and organizations whose services have improved the quality of life for all of Chicago's citizens.

The Hall of Fame recognizes both volunteer and professional achievements within the GLBT community and the contributions of community members to the wider city of Chicago. Nominations to the Hall of Fame are open to anyone who has made a long-term contribution that has had significant, far-reaching effects on the quality of life of the community or the city. Nominees are selected in three categories: Individuals, Organizations, and "Friends of the Community." Those in the Hall of Fame include organizations such as ACT UP/Chicago,

American Veterans for Equal Rights and the Gay, Lesbian and Straight Education Network as well as many individuals.

The first Hall of Fame induction ceremony took place during Gay and Lesbian Pride Week at City Hall and was hosted by Mayor Richard M. Daley. The mayor has continued to attend the annual ceremonies, and was himself honored with induction in 2006 as a Friend of the Community. Each year's Hall of Fame event is a celebration that brings together activists, politicians, and community members from many fields.

The Hall of Fame is privately funded through donations from individuals, businesses and organizations. Staff support is provided by the city Commission on Human Relations, members of ACLGBTI, and volunteers. Since its inception, the Hall of Fame's mission has continued to expand. In addition to selecting each year's new inductees, a large portion of the organization's time is devoted to being custodian of records for the inductees that have been honored: "As time passes, it is our goal to see that the achievements of our predecessors are not lost or forgotten." The Hall of Fame's Web site is located at www.glhalloffame.org. ▼

Left: Alice Cozad and Mary Morten promote the distribution of 2,000 copies of the film It's Elementary to Chicago Public Schools in the late 1990s. Right: Morten in 2007. Photos by Hal Baim and Tracy Baim.

MORTEN SHINES

Mary F. Morten is a shining example of a member of the Chicago Gay and Lesbian Hall of Fame—she has had an impact not just on Chicago's gay and lesbian community, but also on the women's community and the overall city of Chicago. She has had a significant impact on gay rights nationally through her involvement with the National Gay and Lesbian Task Force and media projects such as It's Elementary.

In the 1980s, Morten was the first African-American president of Chicago's National Organization for Women chapter, and she has gone on to be involved in numerous organizations. She is a producer of videos, including The Nia Project documentary, and she was a co-host for LesBiGay Radio.

Morten was Mayor Richard M. Daley's liaison to the gay community and director of the city Advisory Council on Lesbian and Gay Issues from 1997 to 2000. She has been a leader in the Women's Self-Employment Project and the Chicago Abortion Fund, and in 2008 she serves as interim executive director of the Chicago Foundation for Women. Morten crosses boundaries across many communities. ▼

VIEW LOOKING NORTH FROM THE ROSCOE STREET INTERSECTION

VIEW LOOKING SOUTH FROM THE GRACE STREET INTERSECTION

Left: In 1997, the city revealed this poster at a public hearing about the Halsted Street renovations. Right: A rainbow pylon in 2007 in front of the new Center on Halsted. Photos by Tracy Baim, Outlines newspaper.

HALSTED GETS OFFICIAL *by TRACY BAIM*

CHICAGO MAYOR RICHARD M. DALEY MADE HISTORY NOV. 14, 1998, when he dedicated the first-known gay neighborhood designation in the world: North Halsted Street between approximately West Belmont and West Waveland avenues. Daley was just making it part of his general neighborhood beautification plans around the city, but for gays, this was unique.

It was not all smooth sailing, with controversy on a number of fronts, starting when the project was first announced in the summer of 1997: Straight people said they felt it would alienate them and hurt property values; gay people felt it was not needed because gays were everywhere; gay people felt it was like putting a target on their backs for attackers; many did not like the "phallic" rainbow designs; Halsted had never been home to many lesbians or lesbian businesses; and businesses were worried about losing parking spaces and truck parking access. In fact, by 1998, many gay residents and businesses had moved on to other areas of town, and no one neighborhood had ever contained all queer people. But not least because Daley is so pow-

erful, the project went through, with completion announced Jan. 4, 1999.

The rainbow pylons work in a sense, because the Northalsted Area Merchants Association (NAMA, founded in 1980) is a strong business association, and two major community events are in the district each year: the Pride Parade and Northalsted Market Days, a NAMA-sponsored festival that grew from a few thousand to hundreds of thousands of attendees in just two decades. In years past, gay people were forced out of areas when the rents got too high; the situation is different along Halsted because many gays there own real estate, and they have become integral leaders in the area's development.

With Center on Halsted opening in 2007, with a rainbow pylon right out front, the area has literally cemented its future as a gay district for many years to come, for residents and tourists alike. It will never be the only one, with Andersonville rivaling it in terms of sheer numbers of gay men and by far more lesbians, but the community is now larger and more sophisticated—and it has been validated with permanent government structures. ▼

A MODEL COMMUNITY: OAK PARK PIONEERS DIVERSITY *by MEL WILSON*

OAK PARK IS A COMMUNITY OF 51,000 PEO- ple located eight miles west of Chicago's Loop. The village is famous worldwide as the childhood home of Ernest Hemingway and for its historic homes—most notably, a large concentration of structures designed by Frank Lloyd Wright. In the last 40 years, the village has become recognized for its early adoption of open housing laws and efforts at managed integration. Today, the village is nationally recognized for its diversity. Oak Park was one of the first communities in Illinois to ban discrimination on the basis of sexual orientation.

Pluralism has not always been a characteristic of this once exclusively white, Protestant, middle-class community. However, an aggressive citizen movement in the mid-1950s led to adoption of home rule and a village-manager type of government, which opened the way for deliberate transformation of Oak Park to a racially integrated community, according to lesbian writer Carole Goodwin in her 1979 book The Oak Park Strategy: Community Control of Racial Change (University of Chicago Press). The

success of these actions made Oak Park a leader in integration efforts nationwide and provided a model for a later village LGBTQ rights movement.

Throughout the 1970s and '80s, Oak Park's LGBTQ residents remained mostly hidden, although known meeting places existed, including Val's Halla record store (owned by Val Camilletti, now located at 239 Harrison St.) and the now-closed Left Bank Bookstall, a focus for feminist activities (co-owned by partners Goodwin and the late Carol Zientek, who died in a car crash). Local low-profile gay and lesbian organizations developed, including Lavender Bouquet, a women's social group, and Parents and Friends of Lesbians and Gays (PFLAG), which met in local churches.

Although many Oak Parkers were active in LGBTQ organizations in Chicago, it was not until the late 1980s that they joined together to address civil rights and open inclusion in their own community. They first came forward in churches, leading several churches to adopt inclusionary policies.

The advent of HIV/AIDS brought a small group

of concerned health workers and residents together in 1988 to form the Oak Park AIDS Network. In early 1989, the first west suburban AIDS support organization, Community Response, was established, and began lobbying for local government and community support.

In the spring of 1989, three Community Response board members initiated a campaign for civil rights protections for LGBTQ residents of the village (including the late Bryan Findlay, Nathan Linsk and Mel Wilson, the author of this article). They drew together a small group of gay and lesbian advocates who quickly coalesced into an organization: the Oak Park Area Lesbian and Gay Association (OPALGA). In June 1989, amid loud public opposition, the Oak Park village board unanimously amended the village human rights law to include "sexual orientation" among classes protected in matters of public accommodations and employment.

Within weeks, the board of the Oak Park–River Forest High School proposed amendment of its own human-dignity policy to include gay and lesbian students and faculty among those cited for protection. Following a six-month firestorm of controversy, an exhausted school board adopted the revised policy—the first such policy in any public school in Illinois. A few years later, District 97 (Oak Park elementary and junior high schools) adopted similar protections.

By January 1990, OPALGA membership had grown to more than 100, and it had become the recognized voice of the gay and lesbian community of Oak Park. It was asked to provide representation to village commissions and many community groups and to conduct in-service sensitivity training for the Oak Park police.

In addition to advocacy, OPALGA developed as a social organization holding regular events in both public and private venues. It participated in the village festival, Day in Our Village, and within a year OPALGA held its own concert and Cultural Arts Festival. The festival became an annual event with wide village support from 1991 to 1996. Other events have included cabarets, drag shows, poetry readings and an annual gala banquet fundraiser. Ricky Sain and Jim Boushay created popular potlucks that attracted a wide diversity of Oak Parkers.

In 1992, OPALGA opened a youth drop-in center, Prism, for sexually questioning youth between the ages of 14 and 18, which attracted participants from Chicago as well as several western suburbs. PRISM founders were Nancy Johnson, Curt Hicks and Rebekah Levin. In 1997, OPALGA hired a part-time social worker, Susan Abbott, who extended outreach and advocacy for sexually questioning youth to high schools throughout the western suburbs. The drop-in center drew support from Oak Park's village government, its park district, the Cook County Public Health Department and several local churches. In recent years, the center has added a group led by the late Rob Ward, Spectrum, for young adults.

In 1994, Oak Park's village board enacted a domestic-partnership ordinance providing equitable benefits for municipal employees in same-sex partnerships. Three years later, the board established the first domestic-partnership registry in Illinois. The registry provided no tangible benefits but was hotly contested by conservative Oak Parkers, who quickly mounted a referendum aimed at repeal of the ordinance. The repeal effort was defeated by a coalition of Oak Parkers and organizations led by Alan Amato

(who for a time operated the gay bookstore Pride Agenda in Oak Park). Defeat of the repeal effort marked the first time a same-sex partnership registry had ever been supported on an election ballot.

In recent years, LGBTQ people have come to be a part of Oak Park community life. Joanne Trapani's election to the village board in 1997 made her the first open lesbian elected official in Illinois. Four years later, she was elected village president, and Ray Johnson, a former co-chair of OPALGA, was elected to the village board. In 2000, local Parent Teacher Organization members successfully forced expulsion of the anti-gay Boy Scouts from Oak Park's public schools. In 1994, a congregation of the Metropolitan Community Churches, now the New Spirit MCC, was established in Oak Park under the leadership of the Rev. Bradley Michelson. The congregation has since purchased a church building on Scoville Avenue.

By 2004, OPALGA had established a storefront community center hosting youth and young adult programs, a women's group and a Latino support group—Amigos Latinos Apoyando Siempre. In 2006, OPALGA joined together with the Oak Park Visitors Bureau, Oak Park–River Forest High School and the Oak Park Park District to provide sites for Gay Games VII sports and culture events, welcoming thousands of people from around the world. ▼

Opposite page: Joanne Trapani with AIDS activist Danny Sotomayor at the famous 1989 community confrontation with Mayor Richard M. Daley (see previous chapters). Photo by Lisa Howe-Ebright. This page: Carole Goodwin (left) and Val Camilletti. Photos by Hal Baim.

OUT ON THE AIR

Radio has come a long way in recent decades, and just like other media, it feels the impact of the Internet. The Feb. 18, 1977, issue of GayLife announced what it said was the first gay radio program in Chicago, Midnight at Harlow's, hosted by veteran radio and TV personality Bob Sanders on WVVX, 103.1 FM, Monday through Friday, from 10 p.m. to midnight. The show was broadcast live from Harlow's bar.

In 1988, radio consultant Barry Wick wrote a column in Outlines urging a gay businessperson to start a gay radio show or network in Chicago as a valuable opportunity. By June 1994, Alan Amberg launched LesBiGay Radio as a Sunday-morning show on WCBR. It then moved to WNDZ for a daily morning-drive slot (the first daily drivetime gay show in the U.S.), and then moved to WSBC and WCFJ for the evening drive slot. At its peak it was producing 260 shows a year, an average of 10 to 15 hours a week.

Amberg, as owner, was a featured host, but he was joined over the years by Carrie Kaufman, Mary Morten, Honey West, Alexandra Billings, Trish Cook, Amy Matheny and many more. Dozens of volunteers kept the show running. LesBiGay was involved in sponsoring and hosting many community events, and it inspired formation of such groups as the Color Triangle. But by 2001, the show's expenses were too much to maintain, and Amberg sold it to Tracy Baim of Windy City Media Group. Baim decided to focus on a one-hour show delivered by a strong FM signal, so it moved to Sunday nights on WCKG. Amy Matheny has been the driving force for what became Windy City Radio in 2001, continuing to host the show with contributions by others. The show moved from its FM brokered time slot in 2006 to the Internet as a twice-weekly podcast at www.windycityradio.com.

Another important radio program in Chicago is hosted by the National Museum of Mexican Art. The Radio Arte station (WRTE, 90.5 FM) includes the first show by and for Latino GLBT youth, Homofrecuencia.

LITERARY MATTERS: WRITING FOR OUR LIVES   *by TRACY BAIM*

THE GAY OR LESBIAN WRITERS WHO AT ONE time called Chicago their home are too numerous to mention. In previous chapters we profiled some of the literary pioneers, including Henry Blake Fuller, Nella Larsen, Willard Motley, Jeannette Foster, Valerie Taylor, Sam Steward, Lorraine Hansberry, Jon-Henri Damski, Robert Ford, Scott McPherson, the women of The Little Review and other authors, journalists and playwrights. We can only do a brief overview in this book, but the www.chicagogayhistory.org Web site will have more details about writers with a Chicago connection.

The American Library Association's Task Force on Gay Liberation (later known as the Gay, Lesbian and Bisexual Task Force) held the first gay book awards ceremony in the United States in 1971, and the event was held in Chicago many times—including 1995 for the 25th anniversary of the awards program, with Quentin Crisp as the keynote speaker. The Lambda Literary Awards were also presented several times in Chicago, coinciding with American Booksellers Association conventions. Marie J. Kuda was very active in the ALA Task Force, and she did a bibliography of lesbian books that is recognized as a key work in the early documentation of the community. Barbara Gittings, who dropped out of Northwestern University to find herself as a lesbian, was a frequent return visitor to Chicago because of her involvement in the ALA Task Force awards and other activism.

On the academic side, we have been fortunate to have eminent professors based here working on important projects. Educators including George Chauncey, John D'Emilio, Sarah Hoagland, Cathy Cohen, Beth Ritchie, Dwight McBride, Deirdre McCloskey, and E. Patrick Johnson have contributed key texts.

A brief look at other important writers from Chicago, or with an impact here, must include

Langston Hughes, who at one time wrote a column for the Chicago Defender. Studs Terkel, while not gay himself, is among the most important writers of the last century, and his book and radio interviews included stories of gay pioneers, including George Buse, Henry Wiemhoff, Valerie Taylor, and Jim Bradford (pseudonym of James B. Osgood). Prominent national writers with a Chicago connection include

Achy Obejas in 2007. Photo by Tracy Baim.

Ann Bannon, born Ann Weldy in Joliet, Ill., in 1932; Judy Grahn, born in Chicago in 1940; Ned Rorem, born in Richmond, Ind., in 1923, who attended the University of Chicago Laboratory Schools and Northwestern University; Lanford Wilson, born in Lebanon, Mo., in 1937, who attended the University of Chicago; and Bonnie Zimmerman,

born in Chicago in 1947.

Kathleen Thompson was an important 1970s feminist activist-turned-author. She was a co-founder of Chicago Women Against Rape and co-author, with Andra Medea, of the book Against Rape (Farrar, Straus and Giroux, 1974). More recently, she co-wrote A Shining Thread of Hope (Broadway Books, 1998), the first narrative history of Black women, with Darlene Clark Hine, and co-edited three visual histories with Hilary Mac Austin. She also served on the board of senior editors for the Oxford University Press revision of the encyclopedia Black Women in America (OUP, 2005).

Former Chicagoan Jean Hardisty, the founder and president emerita of Political Research Associates, a Boston-based research center (founded in Chicago) that analyzes right-wing, authoritarian and anti-democratic trends and publishes educational materials for the general public, wrote a critical book published by Beacon Press in 1999, Mobilizing Resentment: Conservative Resurgence from the John Birch Society to the Promise Keepers. Her analysis of the right wing, and her role in starting several 1970s Chicago feminist projects, contributed to her induction into the city's Gay and Lesbian Hall of Fame.

Former Chicagoan Arny Christine Straayer wrote Hurtin & Healin & Talkin It Over (Metis Press, 1980) and Deviant Eyes, Deviant Bodies: Sexual Re-orientations in Film and Video (Columbia University Press, 1996). She is associate professor of cinema studies at New York University.

Dwight Okita is an openly gay Japanese American writer in Chicago. Okita's first novel, The Prospect of My Arrival, was among the top three 2008 finalists in the Amazon Breakthrough Novel Award contest. His published works include his poetry book, Crossing With the Light (Tia Chucha Press, 1992), and his stage play, The Rainy Season,

From top: Yvonne Zipter, Mark Zubro and Ifti Nasim, all in 2007. Photos by Hal Baim.

printed in Asian American Drama (Applause Theatre Book Publishers, 1997).

Self-published chapbooks in the 1970s and 1980s were the only way for some to be heard. There was a strong women-of-color poetry scene, including Vernita Gray, Lola Lai Jong, Donna Weems, Carmen Abrego and Diane Gomez. The local and national Women in Print movement and the Lesbian Writers' Conferences both contributed to expanding the availability of publishing to more women. Chicagoans have been well represented in numerous anthologies, from the academic to the erotic.

Third Side Press was an important Chicago press for several years. Among others, they published the plays of Claudia Allen. Gay author E. Lynn Harris once lived in Chicago, and some of his books are about Chicago characters dealing with being Black and gay. He worked hard to gain an audience and eventually became a national sensation for books such as Just as I Am (Doubleday, 1994). University of Chicago alumnus Darrell Yates Rist made it big in New York with Heartlands: A Gay Man's Odyssey Across America (Dutton, 1992). He died of AIDS complications in 1993 at age 45.

Iftikhar "Ifti" Nasim is probably among Chicago's most distinctive gay writers. Openly gay and Pakistani, he has written books in his native Urdu language and has been widely published on gay and Pakistani issues. He also helped start a gay South Asian men's support group, Sangat/Chicago. Among his books is Myrmecophile: Selected Poems, 1980–2000 (Xlibris Corp., 2000). His efforts caused his family to reject him, and he did not return to his native country for 14 years because a fatwa had been issued against him.

Roger Sutton produced a groundbreaking book for young adults, the nonfiction Hearing Us Out: Voices from the Gay and Lesbian Community (Little, Brown & Co., 1994). He profiled prominent gay and lesbian Chicagoans, with photos by Lisa Howe-Ebright. Sukie de la Croix, a Chicago transplant from England, has worked documenting Chicago gay history for many years, including work on a forthcoming book.

Former Chicagoan Michal Brody contributed a book about lesbian media in Chicago: Are We There Yet? A Continuing History of Lavender Woman, a Chicago Lesbian Newspaper, 1971–1976 (Aunt Lute Book Co., 1985). Judith Markowitz published The Gay Detective Novel: Lesbian and Gay Main Characters and Themes in Mystery Fiction (McFarland & Co., 2004). Darlene R. Stille has written dozens of books over the last three decades on a wide range of mainstream topics. Mary Becker, partner of former Oak Park village President Joanne Trapani, has written books, including Cases and Materials on Feminist Jurisprudence: Taking Women Seriously, with two co-authors (West Publishing Co., 1993 and subsequent editions). Suburban lesbian activist Carole Goodwin's books include The Oak Park Strategy: Community Control of Racial Change (University of Chicago Press, 1979).

Camarin Grae is a pseudonym for a former Chicagoan who produced several well-received lesbian fiction books, including The Winged Dancer (Blazon Books, 1983, and later Naiad Press, 1991). Chicagoan Nikki Baker's mystery fiction for Naiad Press includes In the Game, The Lavender House Murder and Long Goodbyes. Elizabeth Ward, a Chicago police officer, self-published her first novel, City Boots, through IUniverse Inc. in 2003. More recent books by Chicago lesbians include Jacqueline Taylor's Waiting for the Call: From Preacher's Daughter to Lesbian Mom (University of Michigan Press, 2007) and Jennifer Parello's Dateland (McKenna Publishing Group, 2007).

Jorjet Harper, a collaborator on Out and Proud, is a prominent journalist and writer in Chicago. She has written several books, including the humor collection Lesbomania (New Victoria Publishers, 1994). Kathie Bergquist and Robert McDonald produced A Field Guide to Gay & Lesbian Chicago (Lake Claremont Press, 2006), in time for visitors to the Gay Games in Chicago.

Carlos Mock hit the literary ground running after retiring from practicing medicine. His books have taken an in-depth, fictional look at gay and Puerto

Left: Dwight Okita in 2007. Photo by Hal Baim. Center: Hearty Boys Dan Smith and Steve McDonagh with son Nate in 2007. Photo by Hal Baim. Right: Art Smith. Photo by Bruno Eris.

Rican issues, including Borrowing Time: A Latino Sexual Odyssey (Floricanto Press, 2003). POW WOW poet C.C. Carter's Body Language (Kings Crossing Publishing, 2002), collected some of her most sensual poems into a stylish book.

Robert Rodi is among the better-known writers of gay fiction in Chicago. His witty books, including Fag Hag (Dutton Books, 1992), have been successful across the United States. David Trinidad's work includes Answer Song (Serpent's Tail/High Risk Books, 1994), a poetry and prose book about life and love as a gay man. Owen Keehnen's Starz (Star-Books, 2004) is a book for the porn fan within—interviews with more than 60 of the top performers in the men's porn business. Former Chicago author Rick Reed is best-known for twisted horror stories.

Achy Obejas has been a critical figure in Chicago's activist and literary scenes for three decades, in part because of her political columns for Windy City Times. Her writing is passionate, very openly lesbian, and frequently about her dual identities—Cuban and lesbian. Her books include Days of Awe (Ballantine Books, 2002) and We Came All the Way from Cuba So You Could Dress Like This? (Cleis Press, 1994). Obejas has received local and national honors for her work.

More mainstream authors, including Ana Castillo, Lisa Alvarado and Sara Paretsky, are well loved within the lesbian community for their strong characters, including gays and lesbians. Chicago native April Sinclair, raised on the South Side, has used the city as setting for all three of her novels to date. Coffee Will Make You Black (Hyperion, 1994)

is set in the turbulent 1960s, beginning at a time "before black was beautiful." Coffee is a coming-of-age novel in which a teenage woman's sexuality is awakened more by a white nurse than by her Black boyfriend. Despite its many awards, some schools tried to ban the book.

Carol Anshaw is an adjunct professor in the Master of Fine Arts in Writing program at the School of the Art Institute of Chicago. She first moved to Chicago in 1968 after earning her bachelor's degree at Michigan State University and has made Chicago her home ever since. Anshaw came out as a lesbian in her early 30s, and it had a tremendous impact on her writing. She is the author of the much-honored novels Aquamarine (1992), Seven Moves (1996), and Lucky in the Corner (2002), all published by Houghton Mifflin Co. Among Chicago critic Andrew Patner's works is I.F. Stone: A Portrait (Pantheon Books, 1988).

Yvonne Zipter is a poet, columnist and humorist who has had a tremendous impact on Chicago's LGBT community. She was born in Wisconsin and came out of the closet when she lived in California, but she didn't find her voice as a writer until she became part of Chicago's lesbian and gay community. She has written columns for Chicago's LGBT newspapers (GayLife, Outlines, and Windy City Times) for more than 20 years. Zipter's passion is poetry: The Patience of Metal (Hutchinson House, 1990) was a Chicago Book Clinic Honor Book and a finalist for Lambda and Melville Cane (Poetry Society of America) awards. She has written two nonfiction books.

Diamonds Are a Dyke's Best Friend (Firebrand Books, 1988), which is still in print, examines the love that lesbians have for softball, and Ransacking the Closet (Spinsters Ink, 1995) is a collection of Zipter's newspaper columns.

R.D. Zimmerman is best-known in the Chicago gay community for his award-winning mystery series about Todd Mills, a gay TV journalist. His historical novels about Russia (written under the pen name Robert Alexander) have become national bestsellers.

Fred Hunter (1954–2006) was a lifelong Chicagoan. Gay Chicagoans know him best for his comedic mystery series starring a trio of amateur detectives: Alex Reynolds, Alex's life partner Peter Livesay, and Alex's mother Jean Reynolds.

Possibly one of our town's most prolific writers is Frank M. Robinson, but he moved to San Francisco in the 1970s to become a speechwriter for Harvey Milk. He started two gay newspapers in Chicago and co-wrote The Glass Inferno (Doubleday, 1974), which became the film The Towering Inferno. He wrote numerous other books and is an important part of Chicago activist and literary tradition.

Mark Richard Zubro is another of Chicago's prolific gay activists and writers. Zubro's legacy is in both quality and quantity: "In Chicago, I am ... the most published openly gay author, using openly gay characters, being published by a mainstream house in New York." St. Martin's Press has published all of Zubro's books, including Why Isn't Becky Twitchell Dead? (1990) and Everyone's Dead but Us (2006).

In the 2000s, some celebrity gay Chicagoans have

also published books. Chef Art Smith, an Oprah favorite, has published books including Back to the Family: Food Tastes Better Shared With Ones You Love (Thomas Nelson Inc., 2007). Smith is also teaching young people about food at his Common Threads kitchen at Center on Halsted. The Hearty Boys, the first openly gay couple with a TV show on the Food Network, also give back extensively to the community. In 2007 the couple, Dan Smith and Steve McDonagh, published Talk With Your Mouth Full: The Hearty Boys Cookbook (Stewart, Tabori & Chang). Former Chicagoan Ted Allen, one of the Queer Eye for the Straight Guy stars, has written his own books and co-written others.

On the sports front, gay runner Andrew Suozzo wrote a comprehensive book on Chicago's top running event, The Chicago Marathon (University of Illinois Press, 2006). Karen Lee Osborne co-edited Reclaiming the Heartland: Lesbian and Gay Voices from the Midwest (University of Minnesota Press, 1996), among other literary contributions.

African-American and gay activist Max Smith, a fixture in Chicago's gay movement through numerous actions for more than 30 years, has written about Black gay men and safer sex in newspaper columns and books (including Staying Power! The Unoffical Guide to Maintaining Positive African American Male Relationships, Chicago Moon Publishing, 2004). Former Chicagoan Phill Wilson, an internationally recognized AIDS activist, has written about Blacks and AIDS in several books. Chicago lesbian health-care provider Lise Alschuler released a book in 2007, Alternative Medicine Magazine's Definitive Guide to Cancer, with her co-writer Karolyn A. Gazella (Celestial Arts), a comprehensive look at cancer prevention, treatment and healing. Also in 2007, Chicagoan Kevin G. Barnhurst edited a book, Media Q: Media/Queered: Visibility and its Discontents (Peter Lang Publishing), with several Chicago media people among its contributors.

There have been important organizations promoting gay, lesbian and feminist work, including the long-running New Town Writers Guild, the Feminist Writers Guild, TallGrass Writers Guild, and Literary Exchange, an African-American organization that, along with Affinity Community Services, has hosted literary events and conferences. ▼

With contributions by Judith Markowitz.

TAKING IT TO THE STREETS: PINK ANGELS

Chicago's activist tradition helped build the gay movement in the 1970s and 1980s, including the women's Take Back the Night anti-violence marches. At the end of the 1980s, gays started to march against hate crimes because of an increase in attacks from simple assaults to murders, locally and nationally. Transgender people were especially vulnerable.

Annual anti-violence marches were organized and sponsored by individuals and groups, including Chicago Anti-Bashing Network; It's Time, Illinois (now Illinois Gender Advocates); Horizons Community Services (now Center on Halsted); and many other groups. Key anti-violence leaders were Paul Adams (who died of AIDS in 2000), Andy Thayer, and Lisa Tonna, who died in

Alyn Toler with Curtis Sliwa of the Guardian Angels. Outlines newspaper archives.

2008 of cancer. The fight against violence had many targets, not just anti-gay attacks, but also domestic violence and police harassment. The rallies would increase in size when highly visible crimes were documented, including the shootings of Ron Cayot, who was shot while leaving a gay bar on Halsted; Adrian "Pebbles" Perez, who was shot in 1999 by intruders who left her friend Buretta Williams dead and Perez severely injured in a South Side apartment; or the killing of Wyoming college student Matthew Shepard. In the 2000s, the murders continued, including the slaying of Chicagoan Kevin Clewer, a 2004 mystery that remains unsolved, and of young gay and trans youth across the country.

One group that caused a particular spark was the Pink Angels Anti-Violence Project. Started in 1991 by Alyn Toler (like Adams, Toler was a former winner of Gay Chicago Magazine's Mr. Windy City contest), the Pink Angels were modeled on the Guardian Angels, which assisted Toler's group. While it lasted only a few years (Toler died of AIDS complications), Pink Angels took control of the streets and gave confidence to a generation of activists, training them in self-defense and encouraging them to report hate crimes.   — *Tracy Baim*

PROSPECTS FOR THE FUTURE

Building a Center on Halsted, Hosting the World for Gay Games VII, and Looking to the Future

CHICAGO STARTED THE 2000s WITH SOME HOPE ON THE HORIZON. AIDS drugs introduced in the mid-1990s slowed down the impact of the disease, but many people are still dying from it and no cure has been found. Community institutions were stronger than ever, despite the fact that some of the grassroots passion and activism was waning.

Part of the picture was that more people than ever have become "professional" gays—earning pay as elected and appointed officials, as staff members at gay and AIDS organizations, or even as liaisons within major corporations. The community was seeing a new breed of "activist," ones who were not street-level radicals. The theatrical, telegenic days of ACT UP and Queer Nation gave way to more black-tie galas, corporate sponsorships and foundation grants. Donors helped shape the community, making the institutions strong and creating a "gay-industrial complex."

This is a necessary part of a maturing movement. As with the Black, Latino, Asian and women's communities, the survival of a movement depends on securing a more permanent infrastructure. First it was "out of the closets and into the streets." Now it is "out of the streets and into the buildings and boardrooms."

This does not mean there is no longer a need for protests and pickets. When anti-gay forces tried to push Kraft and Walgreens from their sponsorships of the Gay Games in Chicago, pro-gay forces joined together to show their support, and the companies stayed the course. Center on Halsted was built not just with million-dollar donations but also with smaller giving generated at gay bars.

The 2000s still have activists; they just have a wider definition. There are still hate-crime marches, and gays participating in anti-war and pro-choice marches. There are AIDS

Matthew Cusick in rainbow shadow at the Gay Games Opening Ceremony. Photo by Amy Moseley for Chicago 2006, Inc.

Opposite: The Opening Ceremony for Gay Games VII in Chicago, July 15, 2006. Photo by John Faier for Chicago 2006, Inc.

A press conference for the groundbreaking for the Center on Halsted construction project, in June 2005, from left: Denise Foy, Dan Foy, Senate President Emil Jones, then State Treasurer Judy Baar Topinka, Attorney General Lisa Madigan, Patrick Sheahan, Mayor Richard M. Daley, Ald. Helen Shiller and state Sen. John Cullerton. Above, a view from the inside of the Center, 2008. See pages 100–103 and page 214. Photos by Tracy Baim.

protests in front of pharmaceutical companies, and trans protests outside gay benefits. There are also tens of thousands of other gay people doing their form of activism, whether for marriage rights or the right to dance in a straight bar.

The fight for marriage probably best reflects the 2000s for the community—not because it will happen in this decade nationwide, but because it has happened legally in Massachusetts and in other countries, including Canada and South Africa. The attempts of mayors to circumvent anti-gay laws, and even Mayor Daley's support of gay marriage in Illinois, show that the tide is turning. Whether fighting for the right of gays to marry or their right to serve in the military, the issues of this decade have moved beyond the scope of limited rights and into the realm of full equality. Marriage is an endgame, one that widens the net of issues. Not everyone has to back marriage to understand that it will have a cascade-like effect on thousands of other laws. In the fight for marriage rights, what we have gotten is concessions on "lesser" issues like hate crimes and employment rights, issues that are "safer" for our allies to push for.

The Democratic presidential candidates of 2008 more fully "get" gay people than ever before. They back some form of same-sex unions, and myriad other issues that our 1970s counterparts would not have dreamed possible this quickly.

We are also electing our own in greater numbers than ever, whether to judgeships or aldermanic offices, with Tom Tunney in 2002 becoming the city's first openly gay alderman. The clout of Equality Illinois and its allies finally achieved gay rights legislation across the entire state of Illinois, a bill signed into law just in time to help the Gay Games prevent a battle over public accommodations—permitting use of Crystal Lake for rowing.

The decade also saw a new emergence of playful sexuality. Whether in Chicago Takes Off for Test Positive Aware Network, or the Sissy Butch Brothers Gurlesque Burlesque shows, or the poetry slams of POW-WOW, Chicagoans let off steam through entertainment. Great new theater and cinema works were created, and writers and artists continued to put Chicago on the creative map.

What is next for the city? A need for more emphasis on cross-generational programs and support. Making sure the next generation, which is more accepting and diverse than ever before, has a safe place to grow and change. Honoring the next generation through scholarships, and events such as the Windy City Times 30 Under 30 Awards. Making sure transgender and intersex people are fully integrated into the community and feel a safe part of our GLBTQI alphabet world. Racist, sexist, geographic and class boundaries continue to poison the currents of our community. How will we fix this? Now, as the community and individuals within it continue to age, issues affecting senior gays are more at the forefront than ever before. You can judge a community by how it treats its youngest, oldest and most vulnerable. How will history judge us? ▼   — *Tracy Baim*

Equal Marriage Now in the 2004 Chicago Pride Parade. Photo by Tracy Baim.

WAITING AT THE ALTAR: GAY MARRIAGE IN ILLINOIS

by AMY WOOTEN

MARRIAGE BECAME A HOT-BUTTON ISSUE all over North America in 2003 and 2004, and Illinois was no different. No same-sex marriages took place in Illinois, but Massachusetts became the first state to legalize such unions in 2003, and in 2004 mayors in San Francisco and New Paltz, N.Y., tried to end-run around the law to formalize such unions. Meanwhile, Canada had legalized gay marriages countrywide in 2003.

Activists of previous generations will recall that the issue of marriage is not new. A 1972 national political convention held in Chicago addressed the topic. And in 1975, Toby Schneiter and Nancy Davis staged a sit-in at a Cook County marriage license facility, but their protest sparked mostly anger among activists, who believed it was a badly planned and timed action that would hurt efforts to pass a gay-rights bill. There were similar marriage protests staged at the marriage license bureau in the 1990s and 2000s.

Chicagoans (including Robert Castillo and John Pennycuff) were among those traveling to Canada and San Francisco to marry. At least several dozen same-sex Chicago couples are known to be legally married in Canada, something that potentially will challenge Illinois and federal law in years to come as the courts deal with custody, divorce, inheritance and other issues for such marriages.

Although Illinois law prohibits same-sex marriage thanks to a state Defense of Marriage Act passed in 1996, conservative legislators attempted to further ban same-sex unions. Chicago Mayor Richard M. Daley stated his support of same-sex marriage in 2004, but Cook County Clerk David Orr would not follow San Francisco's lead in issuing licenses for such marriages, saying it was a state issue. Future state Rep. Deb Mell was among hundreds of activists, including those from the Gay Liberation Network, challenging Orr to force the issue in 2004 and 2005. Meanwhile, gay allies and activists had to fight three proposed amendments to the state constitution. None of the anti-gay-marriage bills proposed in 2004 made it out of committee, so they never came to the state Senate or House floor for a vote.

The marriage fight continued. The conservative group Protect Marriage Illinois (PMI), an arm of the Illinois Family Institute, tried to place an anti-gay-marriage referendum on the November 2006 ballot. The PMI initiative was similar to marriage bans that successfully passed in multiple states in both 2004 and 2006.

In the summer of 2006, several local organizations (including the state gay lobby group Equality Illinois) united under the rubric of Fair Illinois to counter the referendum push by legally challenging the validity of the signatures gathered. Future Cook County Circuit Judge Jim Snyder chaired the group, which also received donations from politicians. The Illinois State Board of Elections refused to certify the referendum petitions because the signature requirement wasn't satisfied. The 7th U.S. Circuit Court of Appeals in Chicago and then the U.S. Supreme Court rejected efforts by PMI to challenge the state's referendum requirements.

With those battles behind the LGBT community, many have their eye on securing legal recognition of same-sex relationships. In 2007, openly gay state Rep. Greg Harris (D-Chicago) introduced the Illinois Religious Freedom Protection and Civil Unions Act. The bill passed through committee and awaits debate on the state House floor as of early 2008. In February 2008, state Sen. David Koehler (D-Peoria) introduced the Senate version of Harris' civil-union legislation. If passed, Illinois will become the fourth state to authorize same-sex civil unions. Both heterosexual and same-sex couples could enter civil unions that offer the same state-level protections as marriage. Under the legislation, Illinois would also recognize same-sex unions from other states. ▼

GAY RIGHTS SUCCESS IN ILLINOIS   *by AMY WOOTEN and TRACY BAIM*

ALMOST 30 YEARS AFTER GAY RIGHTS LEG-islation was first offered in the Illinois General Assembly, a state gay rights bill was signed into law Jan. 21, 2005, making sexual orientation (including gender identity) a protected class. The debate began in the early 1970s: The first bill was introduced in 1976 by three forward-thinking legislators of that era at the request of gay activists. Urbana, Champaign, Evanston, Oak Park, Chicago and Cook County passed their own gay rights laws before the state finally did.

The 2005 amendment to the Illinois Human Rights Act was signed by Gov. Rod Blagojevich and championed by key politicians such as openly gay state Rep. Larry McKeon, as well as state Sens. Carol Ronen and Emil Jones and Rep. Sara Feigenholtz. The gay rights group Equality Illinois (EI), formed in 1992, was the chief organization lobbying for its passage in the final 13 years of the campaign to enact such legislation. EI's Political Director Rick Garcia, as well as board members including Art Johnston, were aided by a range of progressive and business groups.

The amendment bans discrimination based on sexual orientation and gender identity in housing, jobs, credit and public accommodations. Illinois became the 16th state to pass such a law, and one of only seven states that have expressly included gender identity in the legislation.

The Illinois Human Rights Act is administered by the Department of Human Rights. An openly gay man, Rocco J. Claps, is its director.

The state is continuing to move forward in its effort to further protect LGBT Illinoisans. In 2007, a civil union bill was introduced by openly gay state Rep. Greg Harris, who replaced McKeon. It passed through committee and awaits debate on the House floor. In 2008, similar legislation was introduced in the state Senate. If the bill is passed, Illinois not only would legalize civil unions for same-sex and heterosexual couples—which would provide the same state-level protections within Illinois as marriage—but would also recognize as civil unions any civil unions or same-sex marriages performed in other states and countries.

The first gay-rights bill in Illinois was passed in Urbana in 1975, notes Art Johnston. In 1977, Champaign passed its gay-rights law. Evanston also passed a gay-rights bill before Chicago. All three of these cities later added gender identity to the list of protected groups.

ILLINOIS GAYS FOR LEGISLATIVE ACTION (IGLA) was among groups pushing for state gay-rights protections in the early 1970s. A March 27, 1973, news release noted that gays were pressuring Gov. Dan Walker to protect gays' state-government job rights by issuing an executive order. Gay activists followed Walker around Illinois, asking him at public forums about his stance on gay job rights.

After IGLA dissolved because of internal squabbling, the Alliance to End Repression's Gay Rights Task Force, which eventually became the stand-alone Illinois Gay Rights Task Force (IGRTF) and then the Illinois Gay and Lesbian Task Force (IGLTF), filled the void and worked on the state gay bill into the 1980s. Key members of the Alliance's steering committee were Betty Plank, Mary Powers, and Bobbie and Herb Hazelkorn; John Chester became the steering committee's first openly gay member. At the time, Chicago usually elected both Democratic and Republican members from each district (a total of three members per district), and a more nonpartisan approach was possible. The legislative cutback, a subsequent reduction of the state House's size from three-member to single-member districts, which effectively eliminated minority-party representation from each House district, "really hurt us big-time," said Chester. "It also gave leadership much more control over its members, which has hurt Illinois ever since. Intransigence replaced negotiation."

Chester said the Alliance's executive director, John Hill, was the one who found Rep. Susan Catania, a Republican from Chicago's Near South Side, to sponsor a gay bill.

As early as 1976, gay bills were being introduced by Reps. Robert E. Mann of Chicago's Hyde Park area, Leland H. Rayson of Tinley Park (another liberal Democrat), and Catania as chief sponsors. In

1977, Democrat Mann and Catania were joined by another Chicago Republican, newly elected Rep. Elroy C. Sandquist Jr. (who represented a Mid-North Side lakefront district and had specifically asked to be included), as chief sponsors of four gay-rights bills. GayLife newspaper reported Feb. 18, 1977, that the bills would end bias in jobs, housing and public accommodations. The similar legislation that had been submitted in the House in 1976 was thought by some to be a "joke," GayLife said. Actually, the chief sponsors said at the time that the 1976 filing was meant to be an icebreaker, since they knew that under legislative rules no substantive legislation would be taken up except in odd-numbered years.

The co-sponsors in 1976, 1977 or both were Reps. Boris R. Antonovych (R–Chicago), Woods Bowman (D–Evanston), Lewis A.H. Caldwell (D–Chicago), Alan J. Greiman (D–Skokie, now an Illinois Appellate Court judge), James M. Houlihan (D–Chicago, now the Cook County assessor), Ted E. Leverenz (D–Maywood), Ellis B. Levin (D–Chicago), Jesse H. Madison (D–Chicago), William A. Marovitz (D–Chicago, later a state senator), Peggy Smith Martin (D–Chicago), Daniel P. O'Brien (D–Chicago), Helen F. Satterthwaite (D–Urbana), Arthur A. Telcser (R–Chicago), Harold Washington (D–Chicago, later the city's mayor), Jesse C. White Jr. (D–Chicago, now the Illinois secretary of state), Anne W. Willer (D–Hillside) and Wyvetter H. Younge (D–East St. Louis, still in the House in 2008 at age 77). In all, the 21 sponsors in 1976 and 1977 numbered five women and 16 men, six Black and 15 white. Nineteen were from Chicago-area districts, and four were Republicans.

For many years, activists attended lobby days in Springfield, either as part of IGLTF or eventually as part of the Illinois Federation for Human Rights (which later became Equality Illinois). Individuals and groups from all over the state would attend the events. Especially important were religious groups and Roman Catholic nuns, Parents and Friends of Lesbians and Gays, and gays and lesbians who lived in suburban and downstate districts, whose elected representatives needed to see people from their own areas. Sometimes these lobby days coincided with hearings on the bills, with activists testifying.

A hearing was also held March 6, 1980 at Wellington Avenue United Church of Christ in Chicago; 600 people attended. A subcommittee of the Illinois House's Human Resources Committee convened the event to hear from citizens. GayLife's March 14 issue stated that lesbian activist Marie J. Kuda "brought the house to a standing ovation several times as she detailed specific governing gay rights legislation in other states and municipalities across the nation." GayLife said Max Smith of IGRTF was "another powerful speaker."

In addition to those listed above, other key people in Chicago and downstate—many of whom played roles over the years—include David Boyer, James Bussen, Scott Burgh, Thomas R. Chiola, Terry P. Cosgrove, Robert Michael Doyle, Timothy E. Drake, Martha Fourt, Vernon E. Huls, William B. Kelley, Mildred Leonard, Kathy McCabe, Tom Stabnicki, now-former state Treasurer Judy Baar Topinka, Illinois Attorney General Lisa Madigan, Dorothy Tollifson, Larry Gulian, Barry Friedman, James K. Lively, IGLTF's chairperson Allan Wardell, and professional lobbyist Lana Hostetler. The last five died in the 1990s: Gulian (1994), Friedman (1994) and Wardell (1995) from AIDS, Lively (1998) at age 82, and Hostetler (1999) in a house fire. Tollifson, who along with Powers was supportive as a non-gay ally in the Alliance to End Repression, died in 2004 at age 95.

Much of the 1990s battle was just trying to get the bills onto the full Senate floor for a vote, as Senate President James "Pate" Philip was a constant obstacle. While many Republicans of the 1990s and 2000s were opponents of the measure, eventually even Gov. George Ryan was in favor of it. But it did not pass until Democrats regained control of the House and Senate, and by 2005 a Democrat was leading the state—Blagojevich. After some 30 years of work by successive waves of activists and organizations, gays and transgender people were finally protected in Illinois. ▼

With research contributions by William B. Kelley.

Top: State bill lobbyists in Springfield in the 1980s. Photo by Tracy Baim.

Above: Gov. Rod Blagojevich greeting his sister-in-law Deb Mell, along with other activists and politicians, on the day he signed the state bill into law. Photo by Suzanne Kraus.

Left, at the June 2007 ribbon-cutting for the Center on Halsted, from left: Incoming board President Robert Kohl, outgoing board President Patrick Sheahan, Executive Director Robbin Burr (who handed over the top spot to Modesto "Tico" Valle the next month), and Mayor Richard M. Daley. Below, top: Gay philanthropist Michael Leppen with his aunt Miriam Hoover (left), who donated $1 million to the Center, and his mother, Vi, also a supporter (Vi died at the end of 2007). Below, bottom: Billie Jean King at the dedication of the gym named for her. Photos by Tracy Baim.

IN THE CENTER OF THE COMMUNITY

THE GAY AND LESBIAN CENTER ON HALSTED OPENED ITS DOORS in 2007, after several years of fundraising and construction. The entirely new building, featuring some of the 1920s terra-cotta facade of the previous automobile showroom and garage structure at that location, is at 3656 N. Halsted St., in the heart of the Halsted gay business district.

The grand opening gala featured more than 1,000 people celebrating the historic moment for the community. Honorary co-chairs Billie Jean King and Mayor Richard M. Daley attended various events for the kickoff, including the dedication of spaces in the building named for them: the gym for King,

and the rooftop garden for Mayor Daley.

The very environmentally friendly building, at 55,000 square feet (not counting Whole Foods' space on the ground level at the south side of the building), also features a theater, a seniors space, a youth space, a Cybercenter, offices and a lobby. It was designed by the international architecture firm Gensler and won a silver rating in Leadership in Energy and Environmental Design from the U.S. Green Building Council.

The history of community centers in Chicago is detailed in the 1970s chapter (pages 100–103). ▼

GAY GAMES: WHERE THE WORLD MEETS *by TRACY BAIM*

CHICAGO HOSTED THE WORLD FROM JULY 15 TO 22, 2006, AT GAY Games VII. During a stifling heat wave, 12,000 athletes and cultural participants from nearly 70 countries competed or performed in more than 34 events across the city of Chicago and in suburbs including Oak Park, Evanston and Crystal Lake (after some initial controversy about having a gay event in that town). Chicago had a shortened time frame to put on Gay Games VII, but despite this, the host organization, Chicago 2006, Inc., eventually broke even—the first Gay Games to do so in 20 years.

The path to hosting the Gay Games was unusual. Chicago lost its first Gay Games bid attempt in 2001, when the Federation of Gay Games (FGG) awarded hosting rights to Montreal. But after two years of rancorous negotiations, Montreal walked away from the table and decided to create their own competing event. They waited until late 2003 to do this, hoping FGG would "blink" and change the year of its event. FGG did not see any options to switch from the Olympic-style, four-year cycle, and held firm, rebidding for a new host. Chicago defeated Los Angeles and in March 2004 began planning for the events.

Thousands of volunteers and a few dozen staff members eventually came together for that week, with the Opening Ceremony at Soldier Field and Closing Ceremony at Wrigley Field. I was honored to be co-vice-chair of the board of directors, a board made up of all volunteers (including co-vice-chair Kevin Boyer and co-chairs Sam Coady and Suzi Arnold) who put in tens of thousands of hours to oversee the planning of Gay Games VII.

A key supporter of the Gay Games was Mayor Richard M. Daley. All city departments, from police to emergency services, parks to culture, played key roles in making sure there were no major incidents that week. Daley's moving speech at Soldier Field is still remembered two years later as a pivotal moment in Chicago gay history. Many older Chicago gays, those who could remember the darker years of the 1960s and 1970s, had tears running down their cheeks, seeing more than 30,000 people at the iconic Soldier Field. Daley was so inspired by the Gay Games that he kicked into high gear his own attempts to bring the Olympics to Chicago in 2016. Chicago is the U.S. bid city, and the winning city will be announced in 2009.

Since this book is a summary of Chicago gay history, with a special emphasis on pre-1980 work, we will not go into detail about the Gay Games here. See the companion book, Gay Games VII: Where the World Meets, available at www.lulu.com, for more than 1,000 photos and background details about Gay Games VII. ▼

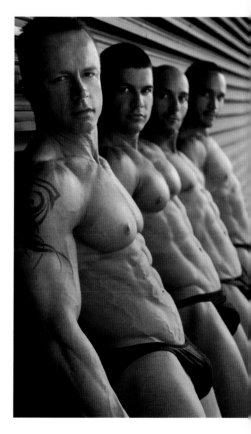

Athletes from track and field (left) and physique (right) compete at the Gay Games in Chicago. Above: Cyndi Lauper sang her "True Colors" at the Closing Ceremony at Wrigley Field. Left and center by Steve Becker, www.beckermedia.com, right by Athen Grey, www.AthenGreyImaging.com. Courtesy Chicago 2006, Inc.

Top left: Greg Harris on the night of his appointment in 2006. Top right: Pat Logue, who became a judge in 2007. Bottom left: Nancy Katz, now a judge, with Bob Adams, the late executive director of IMPACT. Bottom right: Tom Tunney, future alderman, at his Ann Sather restaurant on Belmont, circa 1990. Photos by Outlines newspaper, Tracy Baim and Hal Baim.

MANY 'FIRSTS': POLITICS IN 2000s

by RON DORFMAN and TRACY BAIM

THOMAS M. TUNNEY, ELECTED ALDERMAN OF THE 44TH Ward in 2003, did not have to run an insurgent campaign to become the first openly gay member of the Chicago City Council. The gay community was by that time an established part of the Democratic coalition both nationally and locally, and to the bean-counters of Chicago politics the 44th Ward seat in 2003 was rightfully gay. Retiring incumbent Ald. Bernard Hansen resigned shortly before the election so Mayor Richard M. Daley could appoint Tunney. Grant Ford, publisher of GayLife, had made a run at the same ward's seat in 1979 after Dick Simpson, the last independent to hold the seat, retired; Dr. Ron Sable was a serious contender in 1987 and 1991; but like the rest of the lakefront, the gay 44th was no longer monolithically anti-machine.

"The gay community became an obvious political constituency of importance from Harold Washington's election" in 1983, Simpson observed. Energized by the AIDS crisis, lesbians and gay men organized a host of new service and advocacy groups and aggressively cultivated straight allies. In 1985 Washington appointed the first mayoral liaison to the LGBT community, Kenneth E. Glover, followed by Kit Duffy. In 1988, under Mayor Eugene Sawyer, a human rights ordinance—proposed in its first form by 20th Ward Ald. Clifford P. Kelley in 1973 but defeated every time it was called up—finally was passed, thanks to a masterful job of mobilizing gays and their allies by the Town Meeting "Gang of Four": Jon-Henri Damski, Rick Garcia, Laurie Dittman, and Art Johnston. A similar ordinance was enacted by the Cook County Board in 1993.

In the early 1990s, Gays and Lesbians in Government met with various elected officials including one breakfast with Mayor Daley. The meetings were not just for senior management officials; they were open to all LGBT employees of government agencies, according to Greg Harris, openly gay chief of staff for Ald. Mary Ann Smith at the time.

Thomas R. Chiola subsequently was elected to a judgeship on the Circuit Court of Cook County in 1994, becoming the first openly gay elected official in Illinois, and Laurie Dittman was appointed deputy city treasurer, at the time the highest-ranking openly gay or lesbian city official (although there are and were closeted persons, elected and appointed, who have held higher city posts).

Deputy Cook County Clerk Brandon Neese was the highest openly gay official on the county payroll until his retirement in 2007. Longtime activist William B. Kelley relinquished his 12-year part-time, unpaid tenure as founding chairperson of the county Human Rights Commission in 2003, though he remains a commissioner. Veteran activist and former Oak Park village president Joanne Trapani has filled an LGBT liaison role in county government while a staff member of the Human Rights Commission, where she still works.

Gov. Rod Blagojevich has appointed gay people to top positions as well, including Rocco J. Claps (director of the state Human Rights Department) and Michael T. McRaith (state Insurance Division director). State Rep. Larry McKeon, who had been Mayor Daley's LGBT liaison and director of the city Human Relations Commission's Advisory Council on Gay and Lesbian Issues, was the first out politician elected to the Illinois Legislature, in 1996. McKeon, who was also openly HIV-positive, retired in 2006 after achieving passage of his amendment adding sexual orientation to the protected categories in the Illinois Human Rights Act. He was succeeded by another out gay man, Rep. Greg Harris.

A Metropolitan Water Reclamation District election is not very sexy, but in 2006, lesbian environmental activist Debra Shore helped make it so. She campaigned relentlessly throughout Cook County, and despite the odds, she won the post and is busy safeguarding the county water supply.

In the February 2007 aldermanic primary, while Tom Tunney easily won re-election (his 2003 race featured several opponents, including gay activist Richard Ingram), pro-gay Ald. Helen Shiller faced a gay opponent, James Cappleman, in the 46th Ward. The district is heavily gay, and she had faced a previous gay opponent, Vincent J. Samar, years earlier. She won again in 2007, despite a strong push by Cappleman.

As we move into 2008, another barrier is about to be broken on the gay political landscape. Deborah Mell, the daughter of Ald. Richard Mell (an original opponent of gay rights who eventually changed his vote), decided to run for state representative from the city's 40th District. The incumbent saw the writing on the wall and ran, unsuccessfully, for the state Senate. Mell, a lesbian, faced no opposition in the primary, and in the fall of 2008 she also has no challengers. That means in 2009 the state will have its first open lesbian state legislator.

Gays have also been active in mainstream campaigns for many decades. The 2008 presidential election saw prominent activists and fundraisers playing key roles in the Hillary Clinton and Barack Obama races. Michael Bauer is among the most frequent contributors to both local and national races, as are Fred Eychaner, Nan Schaffer, Art Johnston, Phil Burgess, Phil Palmer, and many more. The community's voting and fundraising clout have clearly had an impact on changing the hearts and minds of candidates in Chicago and across Illinois. ▼

CONFRONTING 'TINA'

In 2004, methamphetamine use became a focus of the national gay movement. The Chicago community, including local law enforcement, politicians, former and current users, public health workers and others, banded together to fight the drug. They were motivated by a few high-profile arrests of gay activists and some notable crime tied to meth use.

Drug use among the gay community has always been a hot topic, whether it was marijuana in the 1960s through today, club drugs such as "poppers" in the 1970s, cocaine throughout the 1980s, or methamphetamine in the present day. Meth, also known by other names such as crystal or Tina, has been around for decades, but an increase in production and use across the United States (particularly the Midwest) brought it into the spotlight.

The drug can easily be made in small, homemade labs using products such as over-the-counter cold medications. Meth causes a euphoric high and puts users at risk for HIV because it encourages many to engage in unprotected sex.

Although meth is not just a gay problem, community studies conducted by organizations like Howard Brown Health Center, Test Positive Aware Network and others found Chicago men who have sex with men engaging in unprotected sex while using the drug.

Illinois police and the Drug Enforcement Administration also saw an increase in meth-related activity on Chicago's North Side, where many LGBT people live and play.

To crack down on meth production, distribution and use, the state Methamphetamine Control and Community Protection Act took effect in 2005. Illinois Attorney General Lisa Madigan was instrumental in making meth a top priority. In 2006, state legislation on cold medications, the Meth Precursor Control Act, took effect.

Public health workers also banded together to combat the drug, focusing largely on the LGBT community. In 2005, the Crystal Meth Task Force was formed by the AIDS Foundation of Chicago and the Chicago Department of Public Health. The task force launched a citywide campaign called "Crystal Breaks" soon after its formation.

Treatments for addicts continue to advance. Organizations such as Howard Brown offer recovery program and outpatient services, and many current and former users participate in Crystal Meth Anonymous groups.

After so much attention on methamphetamine, public health workers want to return to looking at the whole picture. After all, many in the gay community feel an impact from substance abuse, and not just meth. In November 2007, Crystal Meth Task Force changed its name to Chicago Task Force on LGBT Substance Use and Abuse and expanded its mission to include all drugs that affect the gay community. The Task Force is overseeing a five-year meth research initiative, Project Crystal Prevention (Project CRYSP), which will focus on combating meth use and high-risk sex in the LGBT community. It is a collaborative effort between Center on Halsted, Howard Brown, Test Positive Aware Network and AIDS Foundation of Chicago. — *Amy Wooten*

WHAT THE FUTURE HOLDS   *by TRACY BAIM*

THE "GAY" COMMUNITY IS FAST MORPHING INTO A NEW FUTURE, one with great diversity and new leaders who will create their own vision of what gay, lesbian, bisexual, transgender, intersex, queer, questioning and allied people will want and need.

This book examines more than 120 years of our community in Chicago, but it is only the tip of the iceberg. It cannot fully report on the tens of thousands of people, organizations and businesses who have influenced our movement, for good or bad. There are gay serial killers and meth addicts, philanthropists and elected officials. In some ways, there is a gap in progress between those who have wealth and access to power, and those who have always been underserved and plagued by economic or racial bias. But as a community, most boats have been lifted—and there are those who are making sure we include more people under our rainbow flag.

What is clear from working in the community for 24 years, and from interviewing hundreds of people for this project, is that we have had an impact not just on our gay community but on the entire Chicago region. Our gay history IS part of Chicago's history, and we should not allow our history to remain segregated. The Chicago History Museum is trying to remedy this problem by hosting groundbreaking gay programming and making sure to collect archives from our community.

What is next? In 1970, who could have predicted that a few hundred people marching would grow to 400,000 at the Pride Parade less than 30 years later? That our gay rights would be secured at the city, county and state levels? That we would fight back successfully against Anita Bryant, Cardinal Bernardin, Fred Phelps and Hiram Crawford? That we would change the mainstream media forcefully, through protests and by coming out in the newsroom? That our own gay media would change with the times, from newspapers and magazines to the World Wide Web? That we would face a plague like AIDS head-on, act up, fight back, and change society in the process? That we would take to the streets again to combat hate crimes?

If we have accomplished this much in 30 years, imagine what the next 30 years will hold.

A few key issues face our community in the coming years.

New definitions of family: They were once two women together, and now they are female and male: Laura and Logan Grimes after Logan transitioned to male, pictured in 2007 with their daughter. Activists are creating many new definitions of "queer," "male," "female," and "gay." Photo by Tracy Baim.

(1) AIDS is not over, and neither is cancer nor other diseases our community faces on a daily basis. We must fight against apathy and for smarter prevention methods, more research and more support. We must not fight each other for funding, but rather work for a larger overall budget.

(2) The next generation may have different labels for themselves, but they are still experiencing bias from their families and schools. They need our help, and our service providers need to better reflect the demographic shifts of the younger generation—which is ever more diverse. There are some exciting potential projects, including gay foster care, and responsible adults are needed to make such programs work.

(3) There have always been gay and lesbian seniors, but as members of our activist generation age they will not go quietly into that dark nursing home. We must provide a comprehensive plan for our community as it ages—training for existing institutions, creating residential care facilities in Chicago, psychosocial and physical support and more. We can build on what we have learned from the AIDS movement.

(4) Diversity: What does it mean, really? The Color Triangle of the 1990s provided a good base to learn from one another about diversity issues, and we could use a similar organization again. True diversity includes all groups: racial, ethnic, economic, age, disability, and more. Our events should have sign-language interpreters and disability access. Our bars should not try to keep out those who do not fit the mold. We should have safer spaces for gay youth. Co-gender should mean truly equal. People of color should not be tokens. Coalitions should represent the geographic and demographic diversity of our community. We are stronger now because of our diversity, but that progress is tenuous and can slip back because of minor disagreements.

(5) Marriage. I am the first to disagree with the push for marriage rights, based on political issues. But if the government is going to stay in the business of marriage (which I believe it should not), it should treat gays and lesbians equally. As the community ages, we see just how horrible it is when your partner cannot inherit with the same rights as heterosexual married couples, get pension and Social Security benefits, or sue for wrongful death. Many of our seniors are already at an economic disadvantage; the government just piles it on. The military ban on gays must also be overturned and the gay partners of servicemembers must be treated equally.

(6) Philanthropy and support, from individuals, foundations, government and corporations, should better reflect the importance of our community. Our

The 2007 Windy City Times newspaper 30 Under 30 Award honorees: The future is in their hands. Photo by Kat Fitzgerald.

community has been supremely generous in building the Center on Halsted, hosting the Gay Games, and so on. But that burden fell disproportionately on a few individuals; we need to grow a wider base of people willing to stand up and support our causes. On the foundation front, only a few Chicago-based foundations have given substantial money to gay and AIDS causes. We need to hold all foundations accountable, especially because much of their money comes from our community. On the government side, we simply need to ask for more of our share of taxes, for nonprofits working on issues ranging from AIDS to youth to seniors. Corporations have been much better in recent years at giving back to the community through donations and marketing, but there are thousands of companies that just take the money and run, avoiding controversy but also disrespecting their gay customers and employees.

(7) Gender-identity rights are becoming a significant part of our national gay debate. Chicago has been pretty strong in recognizing gender identity legally, and male-to-female and female-to-male trans individuals are pushing hard to make sure they are not left out of our community. We must never forget that mainstream society, including everyone from employers to violent attackers, does not usually distinguish between us; we are all the same queers to them. The transgender are often the most vulnerable (such as from violent crime) because they are the most visible and transgressive.

(8) Finally, we have succeeded as a movement in major part because of our straight allies. We will continue to progress only if we fully embrace our non-gay supporters, and if Chicago continues to recognize the contributions of our community to the successes of the city. Mayor Richard M. Daley acknowledges the importance of gays in our city, as do other leaders. We need to continue to hold them accountable, to keep our seat at the table and to make sure that more parts of our community are fully represented at that same table.

FOR A COMMUNITY AS YOUNG AS OURS, THE FUTURE CAN SEEM full of both excitement and fear. Building new institutions or tapping new leadership is never easy. But if we want our history to be remembered, we must lay those foundations now. Otherwise, that history will be as ephemeral as the histories of many of the pre-1970 activists who could not be featured in this book: They are our lost generations. ▼

BIBLIOGRAPHY

What follows is a bibliography of humanities scholarship that informs Out and Proud in Chicago and the Chicago Gay History Project.

Note: This book was done in journalistic style; therefore, most entries quote directly from sources and do not use footnotes. Below are some of the books consulted for background, and other books that would be useful to those researching gay history. While there are hundreds of related books, those listed here either have a particular interest for Chicago, are national in scope, or are books on other cities that show how their own communities developed. For a more complete bibliography, interviews with many of the people who are mentioned in this book, thousands of photos, an archives list, and stories of hundreds of gay Chicagoans, see www.ChicagoGayHistory.org.

BOOKS

— Are We There Yet? A Continuing History of Lavender Woman, a Chicago Lesbian Newspaper, 1971–1976, by Michal Brody, Aunt Lute Book Co. (1985)

— An Autobiography of Black Chicago, by Dempsey J. Travis, Urban Research Institute (1981)

— Beautiful, Also, Are the Souls of My Black Sisters: A History of the Black Woman in America, Jeanne L. Noble, Prentice-Hall (1978)

— Becoming Visible: An Illustrated History of Lesbian and Gay Life in Twentieth-Century America, by Molly McGarry and Fred Wasserman, Penguin Studio Books (1998)

— Black Boy, by Richard Wright, Harper Perennial Modern Classics (paperback 2007, first published by Harper & Bros. 1945)

— Cherry Grove, Fire Island: Sixty Years in America's First Gay and Lesbian Town, by Esther Newton, Beacon Press (1993)

— The Chicago Marathon, by Andrew Suozzo, University of Illinois Press (2006)

— Chloe Plus Olivia: An Anthology of Lesbian Literature from the Seventeenth Century to the Present, edited by Lillian Faderman, Viking (1994)

— Creating a Place for Ourselves: Lesbian, Gay, and Bisexual Community Histories, edited by Brett Beemyn, Routledge (1997)

— Different Daughters: A History of the Daughters of Bilitis and the Rise of the Lesbian Rights Movement, by Marcia M. Gallo, Seal Press (paperback 2007, first published by Carroll & Graf Publishers 2006)

— Encyclopedia of Lesbian and Gay Histories and Cultures, Vol. 1 on lesbians edited by Bonnie Zimmerman, Vol. 2 on gay men edited by George Haggerty, Garland Publishing (2000)

— Frontline Feminism, 1975–1995: Essays from Sojourner's First 20 Years, edited by Karen Kahn, Aunt Lute Books (1995)

— Gay American History: Lesbians and Gay Men in the U.S.A: A Documentary History, by Jonathan Ned Katz, Meridian Books (revised edition 1992, first published by Thomas Y. Crowell Co. 1976)

— Gay & Lesbian Literature, edited by Sharon Malinowski, Tom Pendergast and Sara Pendergast (2 volumes), St. James Press (1994–98)

— Gay by the Bay: A History of Queer Culture in the San Francisco Bay Area, by Susan Stryker and Jim Van Buskirk, Chronicle Books (1996)

— Gay Games VII: Where the World Meets, by Tracy Baim, www.lulu.com (2007)

— Gay L.A.: A History of Sexual Outlaws, Power Politics, and Lipstick Lesbians, by Lillian Faderman and Stuart Timmons, Basic Books (2006)

— The Gay Liberation Movement, by Jack Onge, Alliance Press (Chicago, 1971)

— The Gay Metropolis: The Landmark History of Gay Life in America, by Charles Kaiser, Grove Press (paperback 2007, first published by Houghton Mifflin Co. 1997)

— Gay New York: Gender, Urban Culture, and the Makings of the Gay Male World, 1890–1940, by George Chauncey, Basic Books (paperback 2003, first published 1994)

— Gay Seattle: Stories of Exile and Belonging, by Gary L. Atkins, University of Washington Press (2003)

— Gentleman Jigger: A Novel, by Richard Bruce Nugent, edited by Thomas H. Wirth, Da Capo Press (2008)

—Great Events from History: Gay, Lesbian, Bisexual, and Transgender Events, 1848–2006 (2 volumes), editorial board includes Lillian Faderman and others, Salem Press (2007)

— Hearing Us Out: Voices from the Gay and Lesbian Community, by Roger Sutton, photographs by Lisa Ebright, Little, Brown & Co. (1994)

— Hidden from History: Reclaiming the Gay and Lesbian Past, edited by Martin Bauml Duberman, Martha Vicinus and George Chauncey, Jr., Meridian Books (1990, first published by New American Library 1989)

— A History of Chicago, by Bessie Louise Pierce (3 volumes), University of Chicago Press (paperback 2007, first published 1937)

— Hollis Sigler's Breast Cancer Journal, by Hollis Sigler, with texts by Susan M. Love and James Yood, Hudson Hills Press (1999)

— Homosexuality: A History, by Colin Spencer, Fourth Estate (1995, reissued in U.S. as Homosexuality in History, Harcourt Brace & Co. 1995)

— If Christ Came to Chicago! A Plea for the Union of All Who Love in the Service of All Who Suffer, by William T. Stead, Chicago Historical Bookworks (1990, first published by Laird & Lee 1894)

— Improper Bostonians: Lesbian and Gay History from the Puritans to Playland, compiled by The History Project, Beacon Press (paperback 1999, first published 1998)

— In the City of Men: Another Story of Chicago, by Kenny J. Williams, Townsend Press (1974)

— International Mr. Leather: 25 Years of Champions, edited and written by Joseph W. Bean, Nazca Plains Corp. (2004)

— James Baldwin, by Randall Kenan, Chelsea House Publishers (2005, first published 1994)

— The Lavender Screen: The Gay and Lesbian Films: Their Stars, Makers, Characters, and Critics, by Boze Hadleigh, Citadel Press (2001, first published by Carol Publishing Group 1993)

— The Lesbian Almanac, compiled by the National Museum & Archive of Lesbian and Gay History, Berkley Books (1996)

— Lesbian Culture, An Anthology: The Lives, Work, Ideas, Art and Visions of Lesbians Past and Present, edited by Julia Penelope and Susan J. Wolfe, Crossing Press (1993)

— Living for the Revolution: Black Feminist Organizations, 1968–1980, by Kimberly Springer, Duke University Press (2005)

— Lost Prophet: The Life and Times of Bayard Rustin, by John D'Emilio, University of Chicago Press (2004, first published by Free Press 2003)

— Making Gay History: The Half-Century Fight for Lesbian and Gay Equal Rights, by Eric Marcus, Harper Perennial (revised paperback edition 2002, first published as Making History: The Struggle for Gay and Lesbian Equal Rights, 1945–1990: An Oral History, HarperCollins Publishers 1992)

— The Mayor of Castro Street: The Life and Times of Harvey Milk, by Randy Shilts, St. Martin's Press (paperback 1988, first published 1982)

— Media Q: Media/Queered: Visibility and Its Discontents, edited by Kevin G. Barnhurst, Peter Lang Publishers (2007)

— Moving the Mountain: The Women's Movement in America Since 1960, by Flora Davis, University of Illinois Press (paperback 1999, first published by Simon & Schuster 1991)

— Odd Girls and Twilight Lovers: A History of Lesbian Life in Twentieth-Century America, by Lillian Faderman, Penguin Books (paperback 1992, first published by Columbia University Press 1991)

— The Other Side of Silence: Men's Lives and Gay Identities: A Twentieth Century History, by John Loughery, Henry Holt & Co. (paperback 1999, first published 1998)

— Out for Good: The Struggle to Build a Gay Rights Movement in America, by Dudley Clendinen and Adam Nagourney, Simon & Schuster (paperback 2001, first published 1999)

— Out in All Directions: The Almanac of Gay and Lesbian America, edited by Lynn Witt, Sherry Thomas and Eric Marcus, Warner Books (paperback 1997, first published 1995)

— Out of the Past: Gay and Lesbian History from 1869 to the Present, by Neil Miller, Alyson Publications (revised edition 2006, first published by Vintage Books 1995)

— A Raisin in the Sun, by Lorraine Hansberry, Random House (2002, first published 1958)

— Reports from the Holocaust: The Story of an AIDS Activist, by Larry Kramer, St. Martin's Press (revised edition 1994, first published 1989)

— Sexual Politics, Sexual Communities: The Making of a Homosexual Minority in the United States, 1940–1970, by John D'Emilio, University of Chicago Press (2nd edition 1998, first published 1983)

— Sex Variant Woman: The Life of Jeannette Howard Foster, by Joanne Passet, Da Capo Press (2008)

— Shattered Applause: The Eva Le Gallienne Story, by Robert A. Schanke, Barricade Books (1995, first published as Shattered Applause: The Lives of Eva Le Gallienne, Southern Illinois University Press 1992)

— Tales of the Lavender Menace: A Memoir of Liberation, by Karla Jay, Basic Books (1999)

— Tallulah! The Life and Times of a Leading Lady, by Joel Lobenthal, Regan Books (2004)

— They Fought Like Demons: Women Soldiers in the American Civil War, by DeAnne Blanton, Louisiana State University Press (2002)

— To Be Young, Gifted and Black: Lorraine Hansberry in Her Own Words, adapted by Robert Nemiroff, Vintage Books (1995, first published by New American Library 1969)

— To Believe in Women: What Lesbians Have Done for America—A History, by Lillian Faderman, Houghton Mifflin Co. (paperback 2000, first published 1999)

— Virtual Equality: The Mainstreaming of Gay and Lesbian Liberation, by Urvashi Vaid, Anchor Books (paperback 1996, first published 1995)

— We Can Always Call Them Bulgarians: The Emergence of Lesbians and Gay Men on the American Stage, by Kaier Curtin, Alyson Publications (1987)

— Who's Who in Gay and Lesbian History: From Antiquity to World War II, edited by Robert Aldrich and Garry Wotherspoon, Routledge (2002)

— Women Building Chicago 1790–1990: A Biographical Dictionary, edited by Rima Lunin Schultz and Adele Hast, Indiana University Press (2001)

ONLINE RESOURCES

Chicago Gay History Project:
  www.ChicagoGayHistory.org

Chicago Gay and Lesbian Hall of Fame:
  www.GLHallofFame.org

Chicago Theological Seminary LGBT Religious
  Archives Network: www.lgbtran.org

Chicago Women's Liberation Union (1969–1977)
  history project: www.cwluherstory.com

CHICAGO PUBLICATIONS CONSULTED FOR RESEARCH:

— The Chicago Gay Crusader

— HOT WIRE

— Lavender Woman newspaper

— The Original Lavender Woman newspaper

— GayLife newspaper

— Gay Chicago Magazine

— Windy City Times newspaper

— Outlines newspaper

— Nightlines/Nightspots magazine

— BLACKlines newspaper

— En La Vida newspaper

LIBRARIES AND ARCHIVES :

— Chicago History Museum

— Leather Archives & Museum

— The Newberry Library

— The University of Chicago Library

— Lesbian Herstory Archives

— Chicago 2006, Inc., Gay Games VII

— Mountain Moving Coffeehouse Archives

ARCHIVES OF INDIVIDUALS AND BUSINESSES:

— Marie J. Kuda

— Tracy Baim

— Caryn Berman

— Nancy Katz

— Julie Zolot

— Otis Richardson

— Lisa Howe-Ebright

— Genyphyr Novak

— Rex Wockner

— Chuck Renslow

— Lori Cannon

— Jorjet Harper

— Hannah Frisch

— Judith Markowitz and Susan Franz

— Mary Patten ▼

TRACY BAIM is a native Chicagoan who began her journalism career at GayLife newspaper at age 21, in 1984. She co-founded Windy City Times in 1985. She is the publisher and executive editor of Windy City Media Group (Windy City Times, Nightspots, Windy City Queercast and www.windycity mediagroup.com). Baim was founding co-chair of the Chicago Area Gay and Lesbian Chamber of Commerce, was recognized as one of Crain's Chicago Business 40-Under-40 leaders and is an inductee to the Chicago Gay and Lesbian Hall of Fame. Baim served as co-vice-chair of Gay Games VII. Her books include Where the World Meets: Gay Games VII and Half Life, a novel adapted for stage. She received a Studs Terkel Community Media Award in 2005, among other honors. She started www.ChicagoGayHistory.org in 2007.

JONATHAN ABARBANEL is an award-winning Chicago critic, arts journalist and dramaturge. He is theater editor of Windy City Times, theater critic for Chicago Public Radio and senior writer for the trade paper PerformInk and the program magazine Footlights. His articles have appeared in American Theatre, Back Stage, Show Music and Variety, among other publications.

JEFF BERRY was DJ at Bistro, Paradise, Bistro Too and other clubs beginning in 1981 and spanning several decades. He has been with Test Positive Aware Network for 15 years and serves as editor of Positively Aware magazine.

WILLIAM BURKS was involved in the startup days of Windy City Times, having served as a writer, photographer and assistant editor, in addition to building a darkroom and serving as the paper's photo lab, before moving into corporate public relations. He was for four years an Anglican Benedictine monk; his interests include religion, spirituality, gay/lesbian issues, books, music and travel.

JOHN CEPEK is active in Parents, Friends and Families of Lesbians and Gays in suburban Chicago and nationally.

RICHARD COOKE is a longtime activist and journalist in the gay community, having written for GayLife, Gay Chicago, and later Babble magazine. He initially wrote about the music, but his column expanded to other issues of interest.

ANDREW DAVIS is managing editor of Windy City Times newspaper, a publication he has worked for, as a freelancer and then senior reporter, for more than a decade.

JOHN D'EMILIO is a pioneer in the field of gay history and studies. He was the author or editor of half a dozen books, including the prize-winning Sexual Politics, Sexual Communities: The Making of a Homosexual Minority in the United States, 1940–1970; Lost Prophet: The Life and Times of Bayard Rustin, which was a National Book Award finalist; and, with Estelle Freedman, Intimate Matters: A History of Sexuality in America. He was a founder of the Gay Academic Union in 1973; co-chaired the board of the National Gay and Lesbian Task Force; and was the founding director of NGLTF's Policy Institute. He teaches gay and lesbian studies courses and history at the University of Illinois at Chicago.

SUZANNE DEVENEY is the chief communication officer for Howard Brown Health Center.

RON DORFMAN was a founder and editor of the pioneering Chicago Journalism Review (1968–75) and later served as articles editor of Chicago magazine; editor of The Quill, the national magazine of the Society of Professional Journalists; and director of publications at the Field Museum. He is the editor of Harold! Photographs from the Harold Washington Years, among other important illustrated books.

RON EHEMANN was a volunteer at Beckman House and for the Gay Helpline (929-HELP) in the 1970s. He was associate editor of Gay Chicago Magazine. After becoming an attorney, Ehemann continued to write a weekly legal and political column for several years, eventually moving it to GayLife newspaper.

PATRICK K. FINNESSY, PH.D., is the director of the Office of GLBT Concerns at the University of Illinois at Chicago. Finnessy teaches ethics and identity within the UIC Honors College and has an appointment with the Gender and Women's Studies program. He created and published a curriculum guide for the New Press anthology Growing Up Gay/Growing Up Lesbian.

LUCINDA FLEESON's journalism has appeared in The Philadelphia Inquirer, The Washington Post, Mother Jones, American Journalism Review, The Boston Globe and Ms. Magazine. Her nonfiction memoir about her two years working in a botanical garden in Hawaii includes the story of Robert Allerton, the heir of a Chicago meatpacking fortune who built one of the most beautiful gardens in Hawaii. For decades Allerton and his companion, John Gregg, lived as father and son. The book will be published in 2009 by Algonquin Books of Chapel Hill. She teaches in the Philip Merrill College of Journalism at the University of Maryland.

ROSS FORMAN has written about Chicago's gay sports scene for more than five years, including articles for Windy City Times. Forman also writes for the Chicago Tribune and other mainstream publications.

WILLIAM GREAVES holds a doctorate in inorganic chemistry. In 1995 he was appointed to the City of Chicago Commission on Human Relations' Advisory Council on Lesbian, Gay, Bisexual and Transgender Issues and, in 2000, was appointed the council's director.

JORJET HARPER is a writer, editor and photographer. She is the author of two books of lesbian humor, Tales from the Dyke Side and Lesbomania. Her journalism and cultural commentaries have appeared in Blazing Star, GayLife, Windy City Times, HOT WIRE and Outlines—where she was also arts and entertainment editor—and in many other publications, including several cover stories for the groundbreaking national gay newsweekly OutWeek.

CHAD HEAP is associate professor of American studies at The George Washington University in Washington, D.C. He received his doctorate in history from the University of Chicago, where he curated an exhibition and wrote an exhibition catalog titled Homosexuality in the City: A Century of Research at the University of Chicago. He is also the author of Slumming: Sexual and Racial Encounters in American

Nightlife, 1885–1940, which will be published by the University of Chicago Press in 2008.

LISA HOWE-EBRIGHT is a Chicago-area photographer who documented many of Chicago's most important gay and AIDS protests of the 1980s and 1990s. See www.LHEphoto.com.

JONATHAN NED KATZ is among the top historians of gay, lesbian, bi and trans American history. His books include Gay American History: Lesbians and Gay Men in the U.S.A.: A Documentary History; Gay/Lesbian Almanac: A New Documentary; The Invention of Heterosexuality; and Love Stories: Sex Between Men Before Homosexuality.

OWEN KEEHNEN's 200-plus interviews have appeared in gay and lesbian papers nationwide. His poetry, stories, erotica and reviews have appeared in dozens of publications, including Penthouse Forum, Christopher Street, The New York Native, Best Gay Erotica of 1996, Thing and others. He has published three books of interviews with gay male XXX stars: Starz, More Starz and Ultimate Starz.

WILLIAM B. KELLEY is in his fifth decade as a gay activist and has also been a journalist, editor and lawyer. He is profiled on pages 74–75 of this book.

RICHARD KNIGHT, JR., is the cinema writer for Windy City Times and his own Web site, www.knightatthemovies.com. Two collections of his film reviews and celebrity interviews have been published. He has written for the Chicago Tribune, the Chicago Reader and other publications.

MARIE J. KUDA is a Chicago native. She says she is a "storyteller, pack rat, and midwife. Born 1939, will die soon."

LOLA LAI JONG is a proudly womonloving, butchy-femme lesbian, Seung-jee/Tofu fah, Chicago-born Chinese, wordsmith, Taoist, Asian Pacific Islander queer activist, involved with i2i (Invisible to Invincible: API Pride of Chicago). She collectively produced Lesbians of Color programs in Chicago and the Midwest, co-founded Pacifica Asian Lesbians–Chicago, co-facilitated the Womyn of Colors Tent at the Michigan Women's Music Festival

and co-founded Asian American Literary and Arts Society. Her name means Strong Beautiful Dignity.

DR. JUDITH MARKOWITZ is internationally recognized as a "thought leader" in the high-tech field of speech processing. She has published more than 200 articles and two books. Since coming out in the 1970s, she has contributed to the LGBT community as a Lavender University instructor; musician; reviewer for Lambda Book Report; and lecturer at Gerber/Hart Library. She wrote The Gay Detective Novel and is secretary of the board of the Lambda Literary Foundation.

GENYPHYR NOVAK earned a living as a freelance journalist and photographer in Chicago in the late 1980s through the late 1990s. She was active in ACT UP, Queer Nation and Women's Action Coalition. Her work has been published in Windy City Times, Bay Area Reporter, Chicago magazine and other publications, including several books. She has resided in the French Alps since 2001: www.flickr.com/photos/genyphyr.

RICHARD PFEIFFER has been coordinator of the Chicago Annual Pride Parade since the early 1970s. Other volunteer involvement has included being a writer for The Chicago Gay Crusader and GayLife; president of the Chicago Gay Alliance and Gay Horizons (now the Center on Halsted); founder and coordinator of the Gay Speakers Bureau; a member of the Mayor's Advisory Council on Gay and Lesbian Issues; a Lavender University participant; and more.

JOHN D. POLING earned a Master of Science degree in history from Illinois State University. He is the author of Mattachine Midwest: Examining Chicago's Gay Rights Movement Before Stonewall (2002). He also wrote "Chicago" in the Encyclopedia of Lesbian, Gay, Bisexual, and Transgender History in America (2004) and "Standing Up for Gay Rights" in Chicago History magazine (2005). Poling's area of interest is mid-20th-century gay political history. He is a history instructor at Parkland College in Champaign, Ill.

OTIS RICHARDSON has devoted much of his artistic talent to the gay community. His work as a

filmmaker has screened in numerous gay and lesbian film festivals. His artwork has appeared in publications including BLACKlines, Windy City Times, The Advocate, Thing and Blackfire.

JOHN "JACK" RYAN created and executive-produced The 10% Show, a monthly program covering the social, political, cultural and entertainment activities of Chicago's LGBT community, from 1989 to 1992.

TIM SAMUELSON is the city of Chicago's cultural historian, a position he has held since 2002. Working with the Chicago Department of Cultural Affairs, he has developed numerous exhibitions and programs portraying diverse and often little-known aspects of the city's history. He is the author of several books and articles on Chicago history and architecture and is a frequent contributor to television documentaries and public radio programming.

CATHY SEABAUGH, a former newspaper and magazine journalist, is founder of A Sister's Hope, an international organization dedicated to raising money for breast cancer research (www.ASistersHope.org). Seabaugh continues writing about topics that touch her heart, including the Gay History Project story on Hollis Sigler. To be published in 2008, Seabaugh's lesbian novel addresses the challenges of love and living that face women in midlife.

MEL WILSON is a longtime Oak Park activist and writer.

AMY WOOTEN is senior news reporter at Windy City Times.

YVONNE ZIPTER is the author of the critically acclaimed poetry collections Like Some Bookie God and The Patience of Metal, the nonfiction books Ransacking the Closet and Diamonds Are a Dyke's Best Friend, and, formerly, the nationally syndicated column "Inside Out." Her poems, essays and features have appeared in numerous periodicals and anthologies. Several short stories have also appeared in print. ▼

— Chicago writer Henry Blake Fuller publishes the first gay play in U.S., At Saint Judas's, in The Puppet-Booth: Twelve Plays (1896).

— In 1880s and early 1890s, Dr. James G. Kiernan of Chicago is the first researcher to study and document lesbianism in the U.S. as a frequent contributor of articles to medical journals on "passing" women who marry other women, tribadism, and sexual "perversion" in women. Many of his cases are included in Havelock Ellis' seminal work, Studies in the Psychology of Sex.

— Bisexual Ellen Van Volkenburg (with husband Maurice Browne) co-founds Little Theatre at Chicago's Fine Arts Building in 1912, accepted as the beginning of the "little theater" or art theater movement in the U.S. She wrote, produced, directed and acted in her own plays in Chicago, on Broadway, and abroad. She separated from Browne in 1919 and divorced in 1926. She had a 15-year intimate relationship with a woman.

— In response to a speech by Edith Lees (lesbian wife of Havelock Ellis) in Orchestra Hall Feb. 4, 1915, Margaret Anderson publishes earliest known defense of homosexuality by a lesbian in the U.S., in March 1915 issue of The Little Review. "It constituted an individual act of lesbian resistance," said historian Jonathan Ned Katz.

— Ma Rainey records "Prove It on Me Blues" in Chicago, 1920s. This is believed to be the first recorded lesbian song, and it was recorded by a bisexual Black blues artist.

— Mark Turbyfill is principal dancer with Adolph Bolm's Allied Arts, the first U.S. "ballet theater" company, founded in Chicago, 1924.

— Illinois grants the first charter for homosexual emancipation organization in the U.S. when Henry Gerber and six other men incorporate the Society for Human Rights, Oct. 10, 1924.

— Life partners Frances Hamill and Margery Barker open their first bookstore in Chicago's Towertown area in 1928. Among the earliest rare book dealers in the U.S., they were the first to promote Virgina Woolf and the (très gay) Bloomsbury group to collectors.

— Scholar, librarian, and Oak Park native, Dr. Jeannette Howard Foster publishes Sex Variant Women in Literature: A Historical and Quantitative Survey (1956), her pioneer study.

— Attorney Pearl M. Hart is the first lesbian to practice before U.S. Supreme Court (1957).

— In 1958, Chuck Renslow and Dom Orejudos open the first gay leather bar in the U.S., the Gold Coast, 501 N. Clark St.

— Chicagoan Lorraine Hansberry becomes the first lesbian, and first Black woman, to receive the New York Drama Critics' Circle Award, for her (Chicago) play, A Raisin in the Sun (1959).

— In 1961, Illinois becomes first state to decriminalize certain sexual acts between consenting same-sex adults in private.

— NACHO (North American Conference of Homophile Organizations) delegates from 26 organizations meet in Chicago Aug. 12–17, 1968, and pass a five-point "Homosexual Bill of Rights." Delegate Franklin Kameny's "Gay Is Good" is voted as slogan for the movement.

— In February 1970, Mattachine Midwest Newsletter editor David Stienecker becomes the first "official of a homophile organization … arrested for writing an article" when Sgt. John Manley charges him with "criminal defamation" for alerting readers to Manley's arrest methods.

— In 1970, a Mattachine Midwest Newsletter writer suggests having a day when every gay person would "come out." In 1988, the now HRC-sponsored "National Coming Out Day" started.

— The first nationwide conference to set gay political strategy is held Feb. 11–13, 1972, in Chicago. A 17-point "Gay Rights Platform in the United States" was approved by delegates, representing more than 80 national organizations.

— Colleen Monahan and Elaine Jacobs' film Lavender (1972), about a Chicago seminary student and her partner, is the first lesbian documentary to be nationally distributed.

— New Alexandria Library for Lesbian Wimmin, housed in Lesbian Feminist Center, becomes the first circulating library for lesbians in the U.S. (1973). Later, founder JR Roberts (also known as Barbara Henry) was compiler of the first Black lesbian bibliography (1981).

— The first annotated bibliography of lesbian literature, Women Loving Women, edited by Marie J. Kuda, is published in Chicago (1974).

— The first national Lesbian Writers' Conferences are held in Chicago from 1974 to 1978.

— Chicago-based American Medical Association passes a resolution urging repeal of all state laws against consensual sex between adults (1975).

— Frankie Knuckles invents "house" music in Chicago in the 1970s. The name "house" comes from a gay bar, the Warehouse, 206 S. Jefferson St., owned by Robert Williams.

— In 1977, Chicagoan William B. Kelley is one of 14 activists in Washington participating in the first White House conference on gay rights.

— The first "Gay Film Festival" showing lesbian and gay documentary films is held June 25–28, 1978, in Chicago at the American Library Association's Annual Conference, as part of programs by the ALA Social Responsibility Round Table's Task Force on Gay Liberation.

— The first International Mr. Leather Contest is held in 1979.

— In 1983, Rick Paul's Lionheart gay theater company in Chicago presents the world's first play about AIDS, One, by Jeff Hagedorn.

— Chicago Mayor Richard M. Daley inaugurates first municipally-backed Gay and Lesbian Hall of Fame in the U.S. (1991).

— The City of Chicago establishes North Halsted Streetscape, the first official gay neighborhood designation in the U.S., in 1997.

— The City of Chicago establishes an annual municipal Salute to Gay Veterans (2004), the first in the world. ▼